Resourcing the Christian Seasons

BOOK 1

Compiled by

NICK FAWCETT

kevin
mayhew

First published in 2003 by
KEVIN MAYHEW LTD
Buxhall, Stowmarket, Suffolk IP14 3BW
E-mail: info@kevinmayhewltd.com

For a list of sources from which this book was compiled
see page 535.

9 8 7 6 5 4 3 2 1 0

ISBN 1 84417 008 X
Catalogue No. 1500561

Cover design by Angela Selfe
Typeset by Richard Weaver

Printed and bound in Great Britain

Contents

HOLY WEEK

EASTER

ASCENSION

Foreword

It's been another busy week, and once again Sunday looms large on the horizon, yet you've barely had time to think about the services you're due to lead, let alone to prepare an address, family talk, prayers and so forth. Worse still, you've somehow found time, only to find your mind a blank, the wellspring of inspiration having run dry. Anyone who has been involved in the ministry or the leading of public worship will empathise with such scenarios all too well. Such moments of crisis can strike at any time, but perhaps most commonly during the great festivals and seasons of the Christian Year. Christmas, Holy Week and Easter, in particular, can be frenetic times with a host of extra events and services to organise, yet, as the years pass we can find it increasingly difficult to find new ways of approaching passages and stories from Scripture that we have already explored countless times before.

This miscellany of material has been put together as a tool for all those entrusted with the responsibility of leading worship. Drawing from such writers as Susan Sayers, Michael Forster, Katie Thompson, Peter Dainty, Pete Townsend and Gerald O'Mahony, among many others and from my own books, it offers a resource book covering the principal Christian seasons. It includes a variety of prayers, all-age-talk suggestions, service outlines, poems, meditations, sketches and other reflective material, together with introductory comments concerning key festivals and practical suggestions as to how these might be celebrated.

Most of the material can be used as it stands, though some – the all-age-talk material in particular – will require further thought and preparation. Nobody can provide a complete off-the-shelf package, and of course we would not want that, for we need to make worship our own, prayerfully seeking God's guidance as we weave diverse threads into a single tapestry. My hope, though, is that this book will help provide some of these threads, and so serve as a tool to all given the responsibility and privilege of leading the worship of God's people.

NICK FAWCETT

Advent

The Second Coming

Be ready to meet Christ

A reading from the Gospel of Mark (13:33-37)

Jesus said:

> Stay awake and be alert, because you have no idea when the Son of
> Man will come. Think of the man who leaves his servants in charge
> while he travels abroad. He warns them to watch for his return, when-
> ever that might be, so he doesn't find them sleeping when he returns
> unexpectedly. So to all of you I say, stay awake and keep yourselves
> ready!

KATIE THOMPSON

Introductory material

The 'coming season'

In the Church's season of 'the coming', we find not just one meeting of 'Love'
and 'Time' prepared for and celebrated, but three. The liturgy of Advent speaks
of the three 'comings' of Jesus. This can be a little confusing, unless clearly spelt
out and thought about:

1. The coming of 'Love' as a baby – the first coming of Jesus as a member of a
   human family.
2. The coming of 'Love' as the Word of God – the second coming of Jesus at the
   age of 30 as a preacher.
3. The coming of 'Love' as the judge – the final coming of Christ at the end of
   time as our judge.

In the four weeks of Advent these three 'comings' of Jesus are recalled. It is a
time to consider their importance for us.

In family life so much is learned in a cumulative way by the constant repetition
of advice or a good habit or practice. That is the way children learn how to
behave. It is the same in the family of the Church. The Church's year, like
Nature's seasons, comes round again and again. We do not need to be anxious
about doing and learning everything at once. The repetition has an effect and the
influence builds up over the years. How then can we best use the time of Advent
to grow in knowledge and love of God? Here are two practical suggestions:

Advent resolutions

A new year, a new beginning and an ideal opportunity to make a fresh start or at least a special effort.

If giving time to our children is a mark of our love for them, so too giving time to God is an expression of love. For centuries Christians have used Advent and Lent to make a renewed effort at building a closer relationship with Christ. Simply, not-too-difficult-to-fulfil resolutions help to keep the family on course for a more satisfying celebration of Our Lord's birthday and all that it implies for us. If prayer has been neglected in the family, now is the chance to make a new start; if some of the following ideas seem attractive and feasible, now is the opportunity to introduce a few of them (more can be added next time Advent comes round!).

But beware! During the season of Advent the commercial world is trying hard to 'sell' Christmas to the shopper. Their interest in Christmas starts long before Advent begins and closes with the shops on Christmas Eve. For us, that is when Advent ends and we *begin* to celebrate Christmas, a celebration that runs on until 6 January and the feast of the Epiphany. In some traditions it continues until Candlemas, the Presentation of the Lord, on 2 February.

The Jesse Tree

The Jesse Tree has a longer and more Christian history than the 'traditional' Christmas tree. The ordinary family Christmas tree can be dressed up as a Jesse Tree (until Christmas Eve when it can be decorated in traditional fashion). The children may copy and then decorate cut-out pictures of symbols representing people or events that prepare the way, through the Old Testament, for the coming of Jesus. Those who use this method to make their Christmas tree fulfil a religious role in the run-up to Christmas use symbols from throughout the Old Testament and not just from King David's time onwards. For example, creation can be represented by a cut-out sun and moon; the fall of Adam and Eve by an apple. A cardboard outline of an Ark can be used for Noah and his family; a bundle of sticks for Isaac; a ladder for Jacob, a harp for King David and so on. It is certainly an excellent way for the children to become familiar with the people of the Old Testament. Bible colouring books, which can be purchased in Christian book shops around the country, can be invaluable as a basis for the decoration and the colouring.

If a family prefers not to use the Christmas tree, a small branch of a tree can be used instead. The size of the branch will depend upon whether the Jesse Tree is going to be a table decoration or stand on the floor on its own. Stripped of its bark and painted with silver paint, it can stand in a pot or suitable receptacle, awaiting the addition of the symbols, either daily from the beginning of Advent or each day of the last week.

TONY CASTLE

Prayers

Praise and confession

Loving God,
    we praise you again for this season of Advent,
        this time of preparation, thanksgiving, challenge and reflection.
    Open our hearts to all you would say now,
        and help us to listen.

    We praise you that in fulfilment of your eternal purpose
        you came to our world in Christ,
        revealing the extent of your love,
        showing us the way to life,
        allowing us to know you for ourselves.
    Open our hearts to all you would say now,
        and help us to listen.

    We praise you that you came again in Christ
        to his disciples after his resurrection,
        bringing joy where there had been sorrow,
        hope where there had been despair,
        and faith where there had been doubt.
    Open our hearts to all you would say now,
        and help us to listen.

    We praise you that through your Holy Spirit
        you make Christ real to us each day,
        filling us with his power,
        his peace,
        and his love.
    Open our hearts to all you would say now,
        and help us to listen.

    And we praise you for the promise that Christ will come again
        to establish his kingdom,
        to begin a new era,
        to bring us and all your people life everlasting.
    Open our hearts to all you would say now,
        and help us to listen.

Loving God,
    forgive us that so easily we lose sight of that message of Advent,
        allowing its wonder to be swamped
        by our busy preparations for Christmas,
        by concerns which are so often unimportant,
        by our carelessness and disobedience in discipleship.
    Open our hearts to all you would say now,
        and help us to listen.

Forgive us that we forget your promises,
    we frustrate your Spirit,
    we lose sight of your love.
Open our hearts to all you would say now,
    and help us to listen.

Meet with us, we pray, through this time of worship,
    through your living Word,
    through the fellowship we share,
    and through the risen Christ.
Open our hearts to all you would say now,
    and help us to listen.

So may we truly celebrate the Advent of your Son,
    and be equipped to serve him better,
    to the glory of your name.
    Amen.   NICK FAWCETT

Advent waiting *(based on Habakkuk 2)*

Eternal God,
    Ruler over space and time,
        Lord of history,
        before all, in all, and beyond all,
        we worship and acknowledge you,
        recognising afresh that your ways are not our ways,
        nor your thoughts our thoughts.
    Lord, in your mercy,
        hear our prayer.

Forgive us for sometimes losing sight of that fact,
    presuming we know better than you,
    even expecting you to do our bidding
    rather than we do yours.
Lord, in your mercy,
    hear our prayer.

Teach us that you are beyond our greatest imagining,
    higher than our loftiest dreams;
    and that you do things in your own way and time,
    expecting us to wait patiently,
    trusting in your wisdom and purpose.
Lord, in your mercy,
    hear our prayer.

When our prayers do not seem to be answered,
   our ambitions remain unfulfilled,
   and our faith appears to be in vain,
   save us from premature judgements.
Lord, in your mercy,
   hear our prayer.

Teach us that it is often at such times as these –
   especially at such times as these –
   that we need to believe in you and your timing.
Give us grace to accept our part in your scheme of things,
   and leave the rest to you.
Lord, in your mercy,
   hear our prayer,
   through Jesus Christ our Lord.
   Amen.
NICK FAWCETT

Intercession

We need to prepare ourselves right away so that we shall be ready and receptive when Christ comes again in glory at the end of time. The great hope of Israel has already been fulfilled in the first coming of Jesus, born as a baby. We look back to that with wonder. The enormous love it shows, highlights the supreme goodness and compassion of the God whose second coming we await.

My brothers and sisters in Christ,
as we watch together for his coming
let us pray together for the Church and for the world.

Lord, strengthen and guide your Church in its mission to the world;
that sinners may be alerted to repentance and many may be brought
to the joy of living in your love.
Silence for prayer
Lord, come to us:
live in us now.

Lord, we pray for the whole created world and its peoples;
that no evil may thwart your will, but that rather your kingdom
may be established and your will done.
Silence for prayer
Lord, come to us:
live in us now.

Lord, bless this parish and all who serve our community;
that we may strive each day to align our lives
with the life of Christ who saves us from sin.

Silence for prayer

Lord, come to us:
live in us now.

Lord, we pray for all who suffer – mentally, physically and spiritually;
for those who see no further than immediate, material comforts,
and do not realise their spiritual poverty.

Silence for prayer

Lord, come to us:
live in us now.

We commend to your love
all who have completed their life on earth,
that they may rest in your peace and share in your risen life.

Silence for prayer

Lord, come to us:
live in us now.

Thank you, Lord, for the richness of your companionship;
for the joy and peace your constant presence gives.

Silence for prayer

Merciful father,
**accept these prayers
for the sake of your Son,
our Saviour Jesus Christ.
Amen.**

SUSAN SAYERS

A short prayer

Lord Jesus Christ,
   we have come to worship you
   in this glad season of Advent –
   a season of expectation,
   of celebration,
   and above all of preparation.
We come now, because we want to be ready –
   ready to give thanks for your coming,
   ready for all the ways you come to us now,
   ready to welcome you when you come again.
Open our hearts as we worship you,
   so that all we share during this service
   may give us a deeper understanding of this season
   and a fuller experience of your love.
Amen.

NICK FAWCETT

All-age-talk material

Keywords for Advent

Aim

To emphasise the serious message of Advent.

Preparation

Print the following in large letters on strips of card and stick them to a board:

> ???? YOU WERE HERE
> ???? DANCING
> DON'T ???? UP
> GREAT ????????????
> ?????, STEADY, COOK!
> THE ?????? OF SHERLOCK HOLMES
> TALES OF THE ??????????
> ????????, SURPRISE
> ?????DOG
> ????? WITH MOTHER

Print off the words in bold under **Talk** below, and retain these for use as required.

Talk

Display the board and invite the congregation to suggest the missing words. You will need participation from older members of the congregation, since many of the answers won't mean much to the children. Insert the missing words over the question marks using a piece of Blu-Tack, as follows:

> **WISH** YOU WERE HERE
> **COME** DANCING
> DON'T **WAIT** UP
> GREAT **EXPECTATIONS**
> **READY**, STEADY, COOK!
> THE **RETURN** OF SHERLOCK HOLMES
> TALES OF THE **UNEXPECTED**
> **SURPRISE**, SURPRISE
> **WATCH**DOG
> **WATCH** WITH MOTHER

The names of films, books or television programmes provide us with keywords for Advent, each reminding us what this season is all about.

From early in their history, the Jewish nation held on to the WISH that the promised Messiah would COME. Across the centuries they learned to WAIT patiently for his coming, although sometimes they found it hard to curb their EXPECTATIONS. Yet when Jesus finally came they were not READY to receive him.

Advent warns us against doing the same. It calls us to be ready for the RETURN of Christ whenever that might be.

So Matthew tells us:

You must be ready because the Son of Man will COME at an UNEXPECTED hour . . . *(Matthew 24:44)*

Or as Paul's first letter to the Thessalonians puts it:

This day should not SURPRISE you! *(1 Thessalonians 5:4)*

Again we read, this time from the Gospel of Mark:

What I say to you I say to everyone: 'WATCH!' *(Mark 13:37)*

And finally, from the Gospel of Matthew:

Keep WATCH, because you do not know the day or the hour . . . *(Matthew 25:13)*

Advent is a special time which looks forward to Christmas. But it is also a time with a message of its own – a message we cannot afford to ignore.

NICK FAWCETT

Mr Wolf

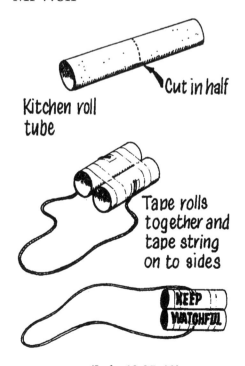

Kitchen roll tube

Cut in half

Tape rolls together and tape string on to sides

KEEP WATCHFUL

(Luke 12:35-48)

AIM: To help the children recognise that sin creeps up on us if we aren't watchful.

Give the children large labels to wear round their necks, or headbands which have on them such things as: being greedy, being mean, being unkind, being thoughtless, being rude, being lazy, etc.

Play the Mr Wolf game with a difference, with all the evil creeping upon Mr Wolf while he isn't looking. Mr Wolf can only stop the evil getting at him by catching sight of someone moving. Point out that the more watchful he is, the less chance there is of them getting him. Now read the passage from Luke 12 to them, and help them make a pair of cardboard binoculars to remind themselves to keep watchful.

SUSAN SAYERS

Keep ready!

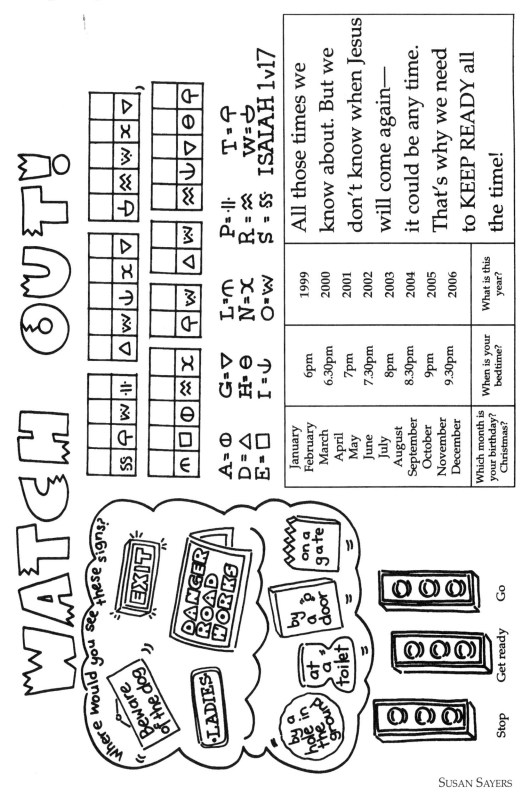

A = θ	G = ▽	L = m	P = -		-	T = ?
D = △	H = θ	N = x	R = ⋈	W = ↩
E = □	I = ↵	O = ω	S = ss	

ISAIAH 1v17

Which month is your birthday? Christmas?	When is your bedtime?	What is this year?
January		1999
February		2000
March	6pm	2001
April	6.30pm	2002
May	7pm	2003
June	7.30pm	2004
July	8pm	2005
August	8.30pm	2006
September	9pm	
October	9.30pm	
November		
December		

All those times we know about. But we don't know when Jesus will come again— it could be any time. That's why we need to KEEP READY all the time!

Where would you see these signs?

Beware of the dog

EXIT

LADIES

DANGER ROAD WORKS

by "a" a door

at "a" a toilet

on a gate

by a hole in the ground

Stop   Get ready   Go

SUSAN SAYERS

Jesus will come back

JESUS WILL COME BACK! ARE YOU READY FOR HIM?

Matthew 24:6-8

CHRIST will come again

WORD SEARCH

```
J ! A F P T V B
E B O O ? E R A
S D M R N Q U C
U L C K I W Y K
S ? R E A D Y !
Y E M J S R X A
F O G ! H I M ?
C H U Z W I L L
```

Jesus told us there would be ☐☐☐ in the ☐☐, and ☐☐☐☐,there would be ☐☐ and ☐☐☐☐☐ before he comes again.

wars
sun
moon
earthquakes
signs

Did you know that one day (we don't know which day) Jesus will come back again, and on that day everyone in the whole world will see him?

Draw what happens next

Colour the picture very carefully

What does this sign mean?

Waiting in hope

Beforehand get a kitchen timer, and one of those automatic timers which you fix on a lamp.

Begin by explaining how you are going to set the timer for X minutes, at which time the talk should be finishing. You are also setting the light to come on half-way through the talk. (Do this.)

Talk about the way things seem to take ages coming, because we want them so much – like birthdays, Christmas, holidays, pension day or tea time. Other things seem to come too fast – like telephone bills, exams or dentist appointments – because we aren't looking forward to them at all.

The early Christians were really looking forward to Jesus coming back in glory, and it seemed to be taking for ever. People who expected it to happen before they were 16, grew to 75 and died, and still Jesus hadn't come. It has been about 2000 years now, and he still hasn't come.

Now as soon as we start measuring the time for something, it seems to make us impatient. 'A watched pot never boils', they say. Because you know this talk will end when the ringer goes, you are probably all waiting for it to ring at any moment, especially as the light will remind you that it's all being timed. Peter told the people not to think God was slow in coming; he was just patiently waiting for the right time, and that might be any time. That's still true – Jesus could come again at any moment, on any day. All we know for certain is that he is definitely going to return in glory, and we can't give an exact time and date to it. Meanwhile, we can live our lives to the full, living the life of love that God shows us, and keeping in close contact with him through prayer and worship, so that we are ready when he does appear.

SUSAN SAYERS

Watch for Jesus

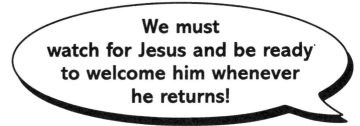

KATIE THOMPSON

Don't fall asleep

KATIE THOMPSON

Stay awake!

Follow the instructions below to find the warnings given in Mark 13:33, 35

1. **Cross out the 'sleepy' letters**
   B Z Z E Z O Z Z N Z

2. **Cross out the letters that sound like a snake**
   S S G S U S S A R S S D S

3. **Cross out the following letters – G F D L J**
   G F S D T J A G Y L D A F W G A J K F E D

Fill in the blanks with the remaining letters

1. __ __   __ __

2. __ __ __ __ __

3. __ __ __ __   __ __ __ __ __

KATIE THOMPSON

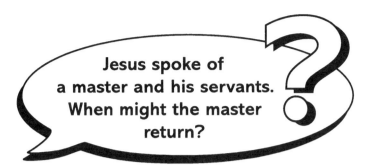

Jesus spoke of a master and his servants. When might the master return?

Solve the clues to find the missing letters

A cupboard for clothes

<u>14</u> <u>15</u> <u>13</u> <u>7</u> <u>13</u> <u>11</u> <u>16</u> <u>1</u>

Opposite of woman

<u>6</u> <u>15</u> <u>3</u>

False hair

<u>14</u> <u>4</u> <u>5</u>

Ruler who wears a crown

<u>12</u> <u>4</u> <u>3</u> <u>5</u>

Used for talking or singing

<u>2</u> <u>11</u> <u>4</u> <u>10</u> <u>1</u>

Clothing worn on your head

<u>8</u> <u>15</u> <u>9</u>

<u>1</u> <u>2</u> <u>1</u> <u>3</u> <u>4</u> <u>3</u> <u>5</u> ,

<u>6</u> <u>4</u> <u>7</u> <u>3</u> <u>4</u> <u>5</u> <u>8</u> <u>9</u> ,

<u>10</u> <u>11</u> <u>10</u> <u>12</u> <u>10</u> <u>13</u> <u>11</u> <u>14</u> OR

<u>7</u> <u>15</u> <u>14</u> <u>3</u> **!**

Mark 13:35

KATIE THOMPSON

Things to come (Mark 13:24-37)

Jesus was sitting on the Mount of Olives talking to the disciples about things to come. Some of the disciples were concerned about the things Jesus was saying regarding his death and his return. They wanted to know how they would recognise the things he was talking about (see verses 24-27). Jesus told them to 'learn a lesson from the fig tree'. In Palestine the fig tree loses its leaves in winter. When the leaves begin to reappear, it is a sign that summer is on its way. At the time that Jesus spoke (the Passover time), the leaves of the fig trees were just beginning to sprout. Jesus was encouraging his disciples to keep their eyes open and be ready for anything at any time!

   The challenge that Jesus was giving to his disciples, and all of his followers, was not to sit and wait for things to happen or constantly to be guessing when he would return, but to live in the 'here and now'. As followers of Jesus, the idea of his return should encourage us to live as he would have us live, a life actively involved with the people around us, and try to avoid the 'if only I'd . . .' or 'I wish I had . . .' or even 'If only I hadn't . . .'.

PETE TOWNSEND

Reflective material
(sketches, meditations and poems)

Meditation of a Zealot

The Messiah – not coming?
Don't make me laugh!
He's coming, all right,
    and it won't be much longer, you take it from me,
    any day now, I shouldn't be surprised.
How do I know?
Well, it's obvious, isn't it?
Just look around you at the world we're living in –
    the state of our society,
    the corruption,
    greed,
    self-interest;
    so much contrary to God's will –
    do you really think he's going to sit back
    and let that carry on for ever?
I can't see it, somehow.
No, he may be taking his time,
    and the delay may be hard to understand,

but sooner rather than later
the day of the Lord will be here,
and what a day it will be,
what a moment for us all!
At last we'll be free,
a light rather than laughing stock to the nations,
a sovereign people instead of subject state,
for surely when he *does* come
the call to arms won't be far behind,
the sound of trumpets summoning us into battle
and onwards to victory.
That's what God's promised us, isn't it? –
a new kingdom,
a fresh start,
deliverance from slavery –
and I can hardly wait for it to begin.
Just imagine the scene if you can,
Jesus and Pilate head to head,
Roman governor versus King of the Jews –
that should be worth watching!
I could almost feel sorry for Pilate if I didn't hate him so much,
for he won't know what's hit him,
the might of his army powerless against the Lord's hand.
What will he do?
Oh, no doubt he'll wriggle and squirm a bit,
even wash his hands of all responsibility,
pretending it was all in the line of duty,
but there'll be no escape,
no way of avoiding final judgement,
for, remember, it's God's anointed we're talking about here,
the one who will come to establish justice and righteousness,
to drive out evil,
and finally, when the enemy is defeated, to bring us peace.
I know it's not been easy this time of waiting,
hoping against hope for some sign of the Messiah,
but God has promised that deliverance will come,
and what he says we know he will do.
So don't tell me he's not coming.
It's just a matter of time, nothing more,
the dawn of his kingdom round the corner,
here before you know it.
I only hope I'm still around when it arrives, able to see it for myself,
for it will have been worth waiting for, no doubt about that –
quite simply, out of this world!

NICK FAWCETT

Meditation (of Matthew, one of the twelve disciples)

The time is coming, they tell me:
   the day of the Lord's return,
   when we shall stand before him
   and he will separate the sheep from the goats,
   the wicked from the righteous.
So forget about the present,
   think instead of the future,
   for that's what matters –
   our final destiny,
   the life to come –
   nothing else.
Well, I'm sorry, but have I missed something?
For that's not the way I heard it,
   not what I thought Jesus was saying at all.
Keep alert, he warned, certainly,
   for the day will dawn as God has promised,
   but when that will be we've no idea;
   today, tomorrow or far beyond, who can say?
It's not the 'when' of his coming that should concern us,
   but the fact that he will,
   and the difference that makes, not to the future
   but to the here and now,
   to the way we live every moment of every day.
We've a job to be doing,
   a broken world out there needing to hear his word
   and know his love;
   and that's what will concern him when he comes,
   not whether we've been looking forward eagerly to his kingdom
   but whether we're doing something to make it happen,
   to help build heaven on earth.
So what will he find in you?
A life dedicated to his service,
   continuing his ministry where he left off,
   or an obsession about the future so strong
   that you've forgotten about the present?
A life lived for others,
   committed to bringing light where there is darkness,
   joy where there is sorrow,
   or a preoccupation with yourself,
   with securing your own salvation?
Don't think I doubt his promise.
The time is coming, just as they say,
   a day when we will be called to account,
   made to answer for the way we've lived our lives.

But if I were you I wouldn't dwell on that too long:
    I'd get down to the business of discipleship,
    to walking the way of the cross,
    or otherwise you may find, when the moment comes
    and judgement is pronounced,
    that the verdict is very different from the one you had in mind.

NICK FAWCETT

Advent

Shall we gaze into the sky,
    waiting for the coming of the Christ
    who never left us?
Do we look to the heavens
    for the one who lives in our hearts?
Has he left the stage
    of the world's drama
    in order to return in triumph
    and save us all
    just in time?

Or will the flash of his appearing
    strike upon our vision
    not from the clouds above,
    but from the depths of faith and love
    in those who already see him?

PETER DAINTY

Be prepared

Written with the season of Advent in mind, this sketch asks us to question our whole notion of being prepared. In Advent we are to prepare, not only for the coming of Jesus at Christmas, but also for his second coming.

As Christians, we are always tempted to believe that we are the ones who are ready, whilst those outside are passing by at an incredible speed, unaware of what it is all really about.

During his ministry on earth, Jesus often mocked, spurned, chastised, and even ignored those who believed they were spiritually and religiously ready, turning instead to those considered unfit and unready.

In the following sketch it is the one who appears to be more prepared, the one who has all the answers, who misses the train. Perhaps we need to take time out to look more closely at our own lives so we do not make the same mistake.

The Passenger and Scout are standing on a platform waiting for a train. The Passenger, dressed in ordinary clothes, carries a large suitcase. The Scout is in full uniform, with a rucksack and sleeping bag and various items tied to his belt.

Passenger   I hope the train isn't going to be late.

Scout   It doesn't matter if it is, I've got my flask and my sandwiches, I'm prepared. That's the Scouts' motto, you know, 'Be Prepared'.

Passenger   It's a bit draughty on this platform.

Scout   Never mind, I've got my scarf. *(Takes out scarf; wraps it round his neck)*

Passenger   My feet are killing me! Why aren't there any seats on this flipping station to sit on?

Scout   *(Takes out shooting stick and unfolds seat)* Always be prepared, that's my motto. *(He sits)*

Passenger   The train must be late now. I wish I had remembered to put my watch on. I can see it now, lying on the table at home.

Scout   That's no problem for a Scout. If you hold your arm up straight to the sun *(He puts his arm up in the air)* and you look at the angle you can tell it is now ten past two.

Passenger   But there isn't any sun in here. You can't possibly tell the time like that. You're just making it up.

Scout   No I'm not! If there was some sun I could tell the time easily, but anyway, it is ten past two.

Passenger   How do you know that then?

Scout   It says so, over there, on the station clock.

Passenger   Oh very droll. I would eat this orange *(Takes out orange)* if only I had remembered to bring a knife to peel it with.

Scout   No problem. Give it here. *(Takes orange and gets knife from his belt)* This super Scout knife can perform a multitude of tasks. Peeling an orange is no problem. *(Begins to peel orange)* Do you know, there is even a thing for taking a stone out of a horse's hoof?

Passenger   Do you come across many horses with stones in their hooves, then?

Scout   No, but I meet a lot of unprepared people who need their oranges peeled.

Passenger   What if the train is cancelled? It's the only one today you know. We'll have to spend the night here on this platform. They don't even have a waiting room here. It's going to be very cold and uncomfortable.

Scout   Not for a Scout, it's not. I've got my sleeping bag. You see, we're always prepared for everything.

Passenger   My case is so heavy, it will be all I can do to lift it onto the train. How do you manage to carry so much?

Scout   You just have to be prepared. A good rucksack is essential, and we learn all kinds of knots so I can carry everything I need. Do you know, we have a knot for every occasion?

Passenger   Wow! That is impressive! I think perhaps I would have been wise to have been a Scout.

Scout   Absolutely! They teach us everything and, what's more, we are prepared for every situation. Nothing can ever faze a Scout.

Passenger   Here comes the train.

                Three or four people enter each behind the other. They use their arms like pistons and make a train sound.

Passenger   *(Reaches into his pocket)* Must check I've got my ticket. I'm always afraid I'll forget it. No, here it is. *(Shows ticket)*

                The train stops and Passenger gets on behind the others. They begin to move away slowly, using their arms as pistons and making a train noise.

Scout   Ticket! Oh no, I forgot to get a ticket!

Passenger   *(As train leaves)* Bye! Isn't it good to be prepared? *Exit train.*

Scout   Missed it again! Oh well, I guess I'll have to be prepared . . . to walk. *Exit Scout.*

                                                                       DAVID WALKER

De'ath meets . . . Dr Putitov

Characters   De'ath, chat-show host and Dr Putitov.

Scene   De'ath is dressed in suit with very loud tie. Dr Putitov is wearing a baggy jumper, ragged trousers and has a number of pencils sticking in his hair.

Props   small coffee table
water jug and two drinking glasses
two comfy chairs

De'ath   Hello, and good evening. Welcome to my humble accommodation. I trust that you've eaten and that I won't be disturbed by strange gurgling sounds emanating from the back row!

Now, to the purpose of our little gathering. As you may, or may not know, I like to keep up to date with things, such as the cost of coffee, beer consumption and the number of estate agents going broke. However, more importantly, I like to keep an eye on what I call my little 'protégés'. I like to make sure that they are on the right track, as it were, and to offer any help or guidance to encourage them on their way.

Some people might call me an interfering old fool. Still – I like to think of myself as someone who cares enough to make sure that his little 'protégés' fulfil their potential, that they avoid the pitfalls that might keep them on the straight and narrow!

Now, you've heard enough of me. Let me introduce you to my guest for the evening. Throughout his career, my guest has led the way in the study of tomorrow. He has been hailed as a pioneer of idleness, a champion of couch potatoes and is the distinguished author of the best-selling book *Maybe*. Ladies and gentlemen, I give you Dr Putitov!

Putitov   Thank you, thank you, you're too kind. Such flattery is almost embarrassing, almost but not quite!

De'ath   Dr Putitov, you have become a leading expert on the subject of 'tomorrow'. It could be said that you have made 'leave it until tomorrow' an art-form! What is your philosophy?

Putitov   Well, many people have wondered what the secret of life is. How do we live to a grand old age? How do we keep our own teeth? What's the price of parsnips? Well, it's relatively simple! You have to learn to avoid doing anything today which could be left until tomorrow, or even the day after.

De'ath   Ah, yes. This concept of tomorrow. Now, correct me if I'm wrong, but are we not told that tomorrow never comes?

Putitov   Exactly! This is a myth told to us by parents who want the bedroom tidied today when it could be done just as easily tomorrow – maybe.

De'ath   So what you're saying is, tomorrow is a concept that has been threatened with extinction, like the dinosaur?

Putitov   Precisely. It's under threat from people who want something done today which could just as easily be done tomorrow.

De'ath   Have you an example?

Putitov   (*Sits back and rubs eyes*) Example? Er, let me see. Could we discuss this some other time? Maybe tomorrow?

De'ath   (*Leans forward and replies with anger*) Well, it would be nice if you could give us one or two examples now . . . Oh! I see, that was an example. Very good. You had me going for a moment. What do you put your success down to?

Putitov   You only have to take a look around you to see how useless you all are!

De'ath   (*Again leans forward with anger*) How dare you imply that I'm useless. What on earth do you mean? After all that I've done for you!

Putitov   Again I rest my case. Just look at yourself, all flustered and hot under your neatly washed and ironed collar. What a waste of effort. Why didn't you wait until tomorrow to become angry?

De'ath   Well, you wouldn't have been here and I would have looked rather daft getting angry at an empty chair! People would talk!

Putitov   Exactly what I'm trying to get at. Deal with things later, leave them until tomorrow. That way nobody gets flustered and nothing gets done!

De'ath   But nothing gets sorted out either!

Putitov   Who wants to get things sorted out?

De'ath   Surely we can't put everything off until tomorrow. It would become a very busy day.

Putitov   Then you put into practice my principle of 'maybe'.

De'ath   Which is?

Putitov   'Maybe' it will be done tomorrow or 'maybe' it won't!

De'ath   So what you're saying is 'leave everything until tomorrow' or 'maybe' leave it!

Putitov   Maybe!

De'ath   Ha, ha, very good. But aren't you a little concerned that using your 'maybe' principle, people will think of you as someone who doesn't get anything done or someone who doesn't sort things out?

Putitov   Saves a lot of energy that way!

De'ath   But what about all those situations which need a decision or need dealing with before they turn into major hassles or mega problems? What do you say to the beautiful woman who asks you out for a date? Maybe?

Putitov   What's with the decisions all of a sudden? Leave it, put it off until tomorrow. Tell people 'maybe'! Always leave people wanting more.

De'ath   More what? More blood? Because that's certainly what they'd want if you put everybody off until tomorrow!

Putitov   That's their problem, not mine. Why should I go out of my way to sort out other people's hang-ups? I'm OK. Let them sort out their own lives.

De'ath   Good, good. That's nice and selfish, isn't it?

Putitov   I certainly hope so. I didn't get where I am today by wearing myself out dealing with other people's problems!

De'ath   So your advice is 'maybe put it off' or 'leave it until tomorrow'?

Putitov   Couldn't have put it better myself. You learn quickly. Just one final thing.

De'ath   And what might that be?

Putitov   When do I get paid for this interview?

De'ath   Tomorrow . . . maybe!   PETE TOWNSEND

Order of service

The Bidding

We are a chosen people,
a people belonging to God,
who has called us out of darkness
into his wonderful light.
In his name we come together
to celebrate once again
the coming of God's kingdom among us,
and to wonder afresh
at the mystery of his loving purposes for us.

Let us confess our sins and failings to God
in penitence and faith:
words spoken without sensitivity;
actions lacking in compassion;
attitudes rooted in selfishness.
May we seek his pardon
for our divisions and disunity,
our failure to live in his light,
and receive with joy his forgiveness and peace.

Silence

Let us listen with open ears and minds
to the good news of God's kingdom
and receive it into our hearts and lives.
May we gladly celebrate
the birth of our Saviour,
and willingly respond to the message
of peace on earth
and goodwill to all people.

Silence

Let us commit ourselves anew
to serving God faithfully
as we pray for those in need –
the vulnerable and exploited,
the anxious and fearful,
the unloved and lonely,
the grieving and hopeless.
May we demonstrate in our lives
the reality of God's love
as seen in Jesus Christ,
and reflect the justice and peace
of his kingdom.

Silence

> Let us express the Christian hope
> of eternal life in our praise and worship,
> as we remember those
> who have gone before us
> in the faith of Christ;
> as we serve him day by day
> in the power of his Spirit;
> as we look forward with confidence
> to that day when we will see him
> face to face.

Silence

> Lord, guide us in the ways of peace,
> lead us in your righteousness,
> and set our hearts on fire with love for you,
> now and for ever.
> **Amen. Come, Lord Jesus.**

The sharing of the light

> Jesus said,
> 'I am the light of the world.
> Whoever follows me
> will not walk in darkness,
> but have the light of life.'

As each person passes the light to another:
The light of Christ
As each person receives the light from another:
Thanks be to God.

During this, a Taizé chant could be sung softly;
'The Lord is my light' (HON* 486) is especially suitable.

Hymn

Make way, make way (HON 329) or
Thou, whose almighty Word (HON 514)

Confession and absolution

> We bring all our sins to Christ,
> the Light of the World,
> confessing them openly and honestly.
>
> **Lord Jesus,**
> **you call us to be good stewards**
> **but often we fail you.**

*HON refers to Hymns Old and New (Kevin Mayhew)

**You call us to use your gifts
for the wellbeing of others,
but we stockpile them for our own comfort.
You call us to show compassion
to the stranger and the prisoner,
but we think only of our own interests.
You call us to be merciful to others
as you are merciful to us,
but we harbour resentment and jealousy in our hearts.
We repent of our sins and wrongdoing
and ask you to forgive us.
Strengthen us to serve and obey you,
and prepare our hearts
for the day of your coming in glory.
Amen.**

May God in his mercy
pardon and cleanse us,
keep us faithful in his service,
and make us ready to stand before him
and hear him say 'Well done',
through Jesus Christ our Lord.
Amen.

Hymn

O come, O come, Emmanuel (HON 358)

The following readings are associated with each of the commonly sung verses of this hymn, and could be read in between them:
Isaiah 11:1-4 ('O come, thou Rod of Jesse . . .')
Numbers 24:15b-17 ('O come, thou Dayspring . . .')
Isaiah 22:21-23 ('O come, thou Key of David . . .')
Exodus 3:1-6 ('O come, O come, thou Lord of Might . . .')

The Promise of His Glory[*] *also contains a short prayer after each of these, to which the congregation responds*: **Amen. Lord, have mercy.**

Old Testament reading

Isaiah 52:7-10

Hymn

How lovely on the mountains (HON 219)

[*] Published by Church House Publishing. Also available on CD: *Visual Liturgy.*

New Testament reading

Romans 13:11-14

Anthem

There is probably as much music for church choirs to sing at Advent and Christmas as there is for the rest of the year! Choice of material will depend largely on the standard of the singers and the amount of time available for rehearsal, though the anthems beloved of Anglican choirs won't always sit easily in a multi-denominational setting. One of the following choral pieces would be effective as part of an Advent Sunday act of worship with a choir drawn from the participating churches:

4-part anthems:
'O thou the central orb' (Wood)*
Favourite Anthem Book 1
'How beauteous are their feet' (Stanford)
Favourite Anthem Book 4
'Light of the world' (Elgar)
Favourite Anthem Book 8
'The shepherd' (Mawby)
Twelve Sweet Months
'Great Father of light' (Mawby)
Fourteen New Anthems

* Also available in 3-part settings in *Favourite Anthem Book 3.*

New Testament reading

Matthew 25:31-46

Hymn

Heaven shall not wait (HON 207)

Address or meditation

Song

You are the King of Glory (HON 570)

Intercessions

Creator God,
you made this world out of nothing
and saw that all of it was good.
How it must grieve you
to see how we have abused and spoiled
its riches and beauty!

We pray for those who work to look after it
and ensure its resources
are distributed more fairly among all people.

Father in heaven,
Hear our prayer.

Emmanuel, God with us,
you came to share our human life
that we might share your eternal life.
How you must weep
over the bitterness and hatred,
the selfishness and lack of care
which afflict our society.
We pray for those
on the margins of the community:
the lonely and unloved,
the homeless and helpless,
the abused and vulnerable,
the anxious and depressed.

Father in heaven,
Hear our prayer.

Holy Spirit, Comforter and Enabler,
you are the presence of God within us,
our conscience, encourager and guide.
How you long for us to be more open
to your teaching and leading!
We pray for your Church throughout the world,
and especially here in . . . ,
that we may be united in worship and witness,
and dedicate ourselves
to bringing the light of Christ
to all whom we meet.

Father in heaven,
Hear our prayer.

Holy and loving God,
fill us with joy and hope
as we work for the coming of your kingdom
and look forward to that day
when we will see you face to face,
through Jesus Christ our Lord.
Amen.

Our Father . . .

Hymn

Hills of the north, rejoice (HON 209) or
We will cross every border (*The Source* 560)

Final prayer

**Come among us
and dwell with us, Lord Jesus.
Come and bring light
to dispel our darkness.
Come and bring hope
to drive out our fear.
Come and bring joy
to banish our sorrow.
Come and bring love
to fill our longing hearts,
that through us the whole world
 may come into your light.
Amen.**

Blessing

May God our Father,
the Creator and Sustainer of all,
give us a fresh vision of his kingdom.
Amen.

May Christ his Son,
the Saviour and Redeemer of all,
cleanse us from all sin
and open up for us
the way of eternal life.
Amen.

May his Holy Spirit
fill us with divine love,
empower us to live for his glory,
and make us ready
for the day of his coming.
Amen.

Hymn

Lo, he comes with clouds descending (HON 307) *or*
Lord, the light of your love (HON 317)

STUART THOMAS

John the Baptist

A voice in the wilderness

A reading from the Gospel of Mark (1:1-8)

This is the beginning of the Gospel written about Jesus Christ, the Son of God. The prophet Isaiah had written long ago:

> See, I will send my messenger before you
> to prepare your way;
> a single voice calling out in the desert,
> 'Get ready for the Lord who is coming.
> Make a straight path for him!'

So it was that John the Baptist began preaching in the desert, calling the people to make amends for their sins and to be baptised. From as far as Jerusalem and all over Judea, people came to confess their sins and to be baptised in the River Jordan as a sign of their repentance. John wore a simple camel-hair coat, fastened around the middle with a leather belt, and locusts and wild honey were his food.

As he was preaching one day, he said to the crowd, 'There is someone coming who is much greater than I am, and I am unworthy even to kneel at his feet and undo his sandals. I have baptised you with water, but he will baptise you with the Holy Spirit.'

This is the Gospel of the Lord
Praise to you, Lord Jesus Christ   KATIE THOMPSON

Introductory material

As well as introducing the figure of the Baptist, the Gospel is a call to prepare for the One who is to come. John proclaims that it is through a baptism of 'repentance' – a turning away from the anxieties of our minds to the unseen Christ – that gradually, imperceptibly, the roughness and crookedness which bedevil us may be healed so that we may *see*, that is, be open to the mysterious presence of God.

Let the meanings you discover today connect with meanings and understandings from your experience.   PATRICK WOODHOUSE

Prayers

Praise – the assurance of the Advent

Loving God,
   we rejoice in this season of good news and good will,
      we celebrate once more the birth of your Son,
      our Saviour Jesus Christ,
      the Prince of Peace
      the Lord of lords,
      the Word made flesh,
      and we praise you for the assurance of his final triumph.
   As you came through him,
      so you shall come again.

For coming among us through Jesus,
   for bearing our flesh and blood,
   for living our life and sharing our humanity,
   for entering our world,
   loving God, we praise you!
As you came through him,
   so you shall come again.

For suffering and dying among us,
   for your victory over death,
   your triumph over evil,
   and your promise that the kingdom will come,
   loving God, we praise you!
As you came through him,
   so you shall come again.

For the wonder of this season,
   for its message of love and forgiveness,
   its promise of peace and justice,
   and the gift of life everlasting of which it speaks,
   loving God, we praise you!
As you came through him,
   so you shall come again.

Loving God,
   we rejoice again in this season of good news and good will,
      and we look forward to that day
      when the Jesus of Bethlehem will be the Lord of all.
   As you came through him,
      so you shall come again.

In Christ's name we praise you!
Amen.   NICK FAWCETT

Thanksgiving – a voice in the wilderness

Living God,
   we thank you today for those who have the courage
      to stand up and speak out against evil and injustice;
      those who are ready, if necessary,
      to stand alone for their convictions,
      enduring mockery and rejection,
      sacrificing status and security,
      willing to risk everything for what they believe to be right.
   We thank you for their vision,
      their determination,
      their willingness to be a voice in the wilderness.
   May your glory be revealed,
      and all people see it together.

Living God,
   we thank you for those who have the compassion
      and concern for others to reach out and bring help –
      ministering to the sick,
      comforting the bereaved,
      visiting the lonely,
      providing for the poor,
      giving hope to the oppressed,
      bringing laughter to the sorrowful.
   We thank you for their dedication,
      their understanding,
      their goodness,
      their willingness to speak your word in the wilderness.
   May your glory be revealed,
      and all people see it together.

Living God,
   you call us to reach out to your broken world –
      to those walking in darkness,
      wrestling with despair,
      craving affection,
      thirsting to find purpose in their lives.
   Give us faith, wisdom, tenderness,
      and love to meet that challenge.
   Help us to venture into the wilderness ourselves,
      and there, gently but confidently,
      to speak your word of life.
   May your glory be revealed,
      and all people see it together,
      in the name of Christ.
Amen.   Nick Fawcett

Intercession

Father, we think of the difficulties facing the Church;
and pray for all who minister your love.

Silence for prayer

We believe and proclaim:
Jesus is Lord in every situation.

Father, we think of the way our world
is torn apart by war and lack of love.

Silence for prayer

We believe and proclaim:
Jesus is Lord in every situation.

Father, we think of those
whose lives are hard and twisted.

Silence for prayer

We believe and proclaim:
Jesus is Lord in every situation.

Father, we think of the great pressures
on this generation to abandon your ways,
and of all those who feel lost
and without real value.

Silence for prayer

We believe and proclaim:
Jesus is Lord in every situation.

Father, we think of those we find it hard to relate to,
and of those who sometimes find us
difficult to get on with.

Silence for prayer

We believe and proclaim:
Jesus is Lord in every situation.

Father, we think of all
who fill our days with love and friendship.

Silence for prayer

Merciful father,
accept these prayers
for the sake of your Son,
our Saviour Jesus Christ.
Amen.

SUSAN SAYERS

Intercession

As we recall Christ's first coming
and prepare for his return,
let us turn to God our loving Father
who sent his only Son to be our Saviour,
as we pray:

For all who hunger;
that we will feed their hunger for food and love
in our world today.

Silence

Lord, hear our prayer:
may we make you welcome.

For all who thirst;
that we will quench their thirst
for justice and equal rights
in our world today.

Silence

Lord, hear our prayer:
may we make you welcome.

For all who are alone;
that we will welcome them
and make them feel that they belong
in our world today.

Silence

Lord, hear our prayer:
may we make you welcome.

For all who are poor and naked;
that we clothe them with our love
and show them that we care.

Silence

Lord, hear our prayer:
may we make you welcome.

Father,
in the hustle and bustle
of Christmas excitement and preparations,
may we make time to welcome you
in the ordinariness of the everyday people
whom we meet in our everyday lives,

so that we will be ready to greet you
when you return in glory.
We ask this through Christ our Lord.
Amen.

KATIE THOMPSON

A short prayer

Gracious God,
   your word was in the beginning
   and shall continue until the end of time.
It brought life itself into existence,
   and controls the destiny
   of everything you have created.
What you have decreed shall be,
   for no word of yours returns to you empty.
Help us, then, to listen to what you would say to us
   today and throughout this season of Advent.
Open our ears,
   open our hearts,
   open our minds,
   so that we may hear your voice
   and respond in joyful service;
   through Jesus Christ our Lord.
Amen.

NICK FAWCETT

All-age-talk material

PREPARE THE WAY OF THE LORD

John the Baptist prepared people for Jesus. Colour this road as you like:

- saying sorry=BLUE
- forgiving=GREEN
- stop cheating=RED
- stop swearing=YELLOW

You can't tell from the outside what someone is like, but God knows us inside and out. Which of these people is **mean**?   Who is **kind**?   Who is **selfish**?

Workmen prepare a new road. Colour the picture carefully:

Today I will be kind by...

Draw yourself doing two kind, thoughtful things.

SUSAN SAYERS

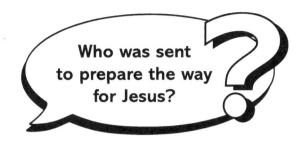

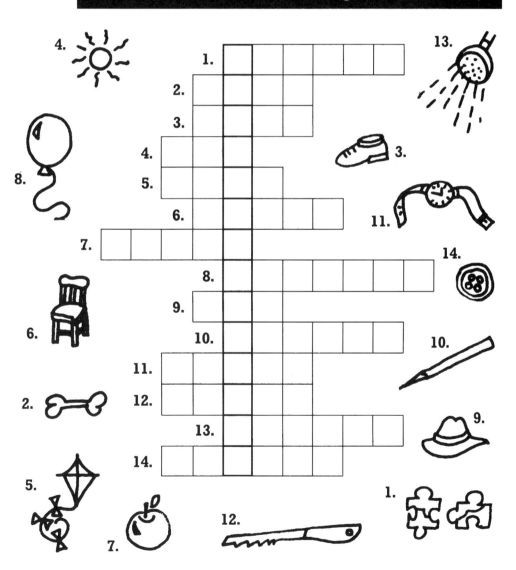

A time to prepare

Aim

To bring home the fact that Advent is a time of preparation, not just for Christmas but for the final return of Jesus Christ.

Preparation

Print in large, bold type the letters in the following wordsearch:

	1	2	3	4	5	6	7	8	9	10	11	12	13	14
1	A	L	O	C	U	S	T	S	D	N	H	O	J	R
2	S	S	E	N	E	V	I	G	R	O	F	V	L	E
3	H	E	I	S	A	I	A	H	N	Y	A	W	L	P
4	O	R	E	T	A	W	T	B	B	E	L	T	I	E
5	L	T	H	O	N	E	Y	A	Y	O	J	A	H	N
6	Y	R	T	D	R	O	L	P	S	N	I	S	E	T
7	S	E	H	A	I	R	I	T	M	E	E	L	L	A
8	P	S	T	N	O	S	O	I	J	C	E	E	I	N
9	I	E	P	W	I	N	E	S	E	I	V	V	J	C
10	R	D	N	R	U	T	R	E	S	O	O	E	A	E
11	I	E	Y	D	A	E	R	D	U	V	D	L	H	P
12	T	J	O	R	D	A	N	A	S	R	L	O	W	E

Attach magnetic tape to the back of each letter and arrange them on a magnetic board exactly as above. (You may find it helpful to draw in the lines of the grid using a washable marker pen.)

Talk

Explain that you have prepared a quiz based on Isaiah 40:1-5; Mark 1:1-13; Luke 1:8-7:2, together with a wordsearch on which can be found the answer to each of the questions. Ask the following questions one by one, and see if anybody can spot the appropriate word or words on the wordsearch. Remove them letter by letter from the board. The answer and its location in the wordsearch are given after each question.

1. Who were the two New Testament readings about?
   JOHN (top row, reversed)

2. What two things are we told John ate?
   LOCUSTS (top row, across) and HONEY (row 5, across)

3. What were John's clothes made from?
   HAIR (row 7, across)

4. What did John wear around his waist?
   BELT (row 4, across)

5. What didn't John drink?
   WINE (row 9, across)

6. Where did John preach?
   DESERT (column 2, up)

7. What was Zechariah told John's birth would bring to him?
   JOY (row 5, reversed)

8. Which prophet foretold John's coming?
   ISAIAH (row 3, across)

9. What was God's messenger sent to prepare?
   WAY (row 3, reversed)

10. What did Isaiah say the rough ground would become?
    LEVEL (column 12, up or down!)

11. What would every mountain be made?
    LOW (bottom row, across)

12. What every other thing would be made low?
    HILL (column 13, up)

13. What did Isaiah say would be heard in the desert?
    VOICE (column 10, up)

14. Whose glory did Isaiah say would be revealed? The glory of the . . .
    LORD (row 6, reversed)

15. In whose spirit and power did John come?
    ELIJAH (column 13, down)

16. What did John do to Jesus and the people?
    BAPTISED (column 8, down)

17. In which river did John baptise?
    JORDAN (bottom row, across)

18. What did John baptise with?
    WATER (row 4, reversed)

19. What did he say Jesus would baptise with?
    HOLY SPIRIT (column 1, down)

20. What did people have to show before being baptised?
    REPENTANCE (last column, down)

21. What does repentance mean?
    TURN (row 10, reversed)

22. What did this repentance lead to?
    FORGIVENESS (row 2, reversed) of SINS (row 6, reversed)

23. What descended on Jesus after John baptised him?
    DOVE (column 11, up)

24. What did God call Jesus after his Baptism?
    SON (row 8, reversed)

25. What was John send to make the people?
    READY (row 11, reversed)

26. For whom did John make the people ready?
    JESUS (column 9, down)

The display board should now read as follows:

A							D			
									V	
	E						N			
					T					
									A	
		T								
					I		M	E		
		T			O					
		P								
					R					
	E									P
						A	R			E

The remaining letters spell out a message: Advent – a time to prepare.

This one phrase summarises all the words we have picked out from the wordsearch, for Advent is, above all, a time for preparing, for ensuring we are ready to celebrate the coming of Christ and to welcome him when he finally comes again. It is the need to prepare for the coming of the Messiah which Isaiah was talking about, which John the Baptist preached about, and which this season is all about.

Isaiah spoke of God's messenger who would prepare the way for the promised Messiah. John came to prepare that way, making it clear what people needed to do if they were to be ready for his coming, and today challenges us in turn to ask whether we are ready for his return.

Advent is not simply a countdown to Christmas; it is a God-given time to prepare ourselves to receive Christ, to receive the forgiveness and new life he brings, and to commit ourselves afresh to his service. Have we made time to prepare?

NICK FAWCETT

Use clues in this picture to help you unscramble the words that are jumbled

John lived in the _____ .
SERDET

He wore _____ skin, and lived on _____
MACLE   COLUSTS

and _____ .
NOHYE

Mark 1:4, 6

KATIE THOMPSON

A book of books

Aim

To show that the Bible is not one book written about 'religion' at a certain place and time, but a collection of living stories, written over thousands of years, and reflecting the needs and situations of countless people – a book which is challenging to read, but rewarding for those who persevere.

Preparation

Print off the following on strips of card:

DOMESDAY
LIBRARY
HYMN
NOTE
TEXT
HAND
GUIDE
PRAYER
EXERCISE

Attach these to a board and display at the front of the church.

Talk

Show the congregation the words above, and ask what single word could be placed after each of them. The answer, of course, is BOOK. Explain that these are just some of the many books they might read or use during the course of an average week. Invite them to guess from the clues below the names of other types of book they might read.

1. A special sort of book published once each year.
    (Annual)

2. A book used for checking the meaning or spelling of words.
    (Dictionary)

3. A book for listing items, or for mail order.
    (Catalogue)

4. A book you may need if you want to ring somebody.
    (Telephone directory)

5. A book for looking up information.
    (Encyclopedia)

6. A book full of maps covering the whole world.
    (Atlas)

7. A book used for planning ahead, or for recording past, present and future events.
    (Diary)

8. A book for storing things like photos, stamps and cards.
   (Album)

9. An instruction book.
   (Manual)

10. A book used for looking up Bible verses.
    (Concordance)

11. A book you might use to find words of the same or a similar meaning.
    (Thesaurus)

12. The name sometimes given to a personal organiser.
    (Filofax)

13. A book used to write down music.
    (Score)

14. The book through which we believe God speaks to us.
    (Bible)

These are examples of all kinds of books written for all kinds of purposes by all kinds of people. And in a sense that is exactly what we find in the Bible, for it is not just one book but a whole collection. Some are about history, others hymns and songs; some are full of proverbs, others of words spoken by the prophets; some are letters, others stories about Jesus; some are about the future, others about the past. Though we call it *the* Bible, it is not *one* book but *sixty-six*, each of them different, reflecting different situations, different needs, different times! That is why there is always something more to learn and something new to discover within its pages, and that is why this collection of books speaks to so many people in so many ways.

But there is one thing that binds all the books of the Bible together, and we can see what that is in Paul's second letter to Timothy:

> As for you, continue in what you have learned and firmly believed, knowing from whom you learned it, and how from childhood you have known the sacred writings that are able to instruct you for salvation through faith in Christ Jesus. All Scripture is inspired by God and is useful for teaching, for reproof, for correction and for training in righteousness, so that everyone who belongs to God may be proficient, equipped for every good work.
> *(2 Timothy 3:14-17)*

The Bible is not always an easy book to read. We need help and guidance to understand it. But if we make time to study what it has to say, we will discover words which give meaning to all of life!

NICK FAWCETT

Read Mark 1:1-8

The Gospel of Mark is written in a journalistic style giving us short 'news' stories relating to Jesus. John the Baptist began to declare the coming of the 'Good News' against a background of political and civil unrest. The Romans had been in control of Judea since approximately 63 BC. Roman rule was often directed through local kings as a way of trying to put an acceptable 'face' on the Roman occupation. The most famous of these local rulers was Herod the Great, who was king when Jesus was born.

Under Roman rule trade prospered within a single market that stretched from France to Egypt and North Africa. Within this trade area there was relative peace, enforced by harsh penalties for those who 'broke' Roman law. For most Jews there was another negative aspect of the Roman occupation, that of taxation. It is thought that the Jewish public paid out almost half of their income in taxes. Every Jewish male had to pay a tax for the maintenance of the Temple and to keep the priests in food and clothes. To make matters worse, the Romans imposed taxes which included a poll tax, a land tax and a sales tax. It wasn't surprising that several groups who opposed Roman domination were waiting for an opportunity to get rid of the Romans.

In the reading from Mark, we are introduced to John the Baptist who, quoting from the Old Testament, declared 'Clear a path in the desert! Make a straight road for the Lord our God' (Isaiah 40:3). John the Baptist was the 'advertising campaign' for Jesus. He was calling people back to God and everywhere John went crowds gathered to hear what he had to say. The heart of John's message was about Jesus. His, John's, role was to prepare the way and get the attention of the people, to prepare them heart and mind for the 'Good News'.

Some advertising campaigns use catchy slogans while others use visual images to 'get the message across'. John the Baptist was an extremely effective 'advert' for Jesus: in his actions and in what he said. Ask the group to separate into twos or threes and write a one-sentence headline which John the Baptist might have used to announce the coming of the 'Good News'.

PETE TOWNSEND

Equipment

Cards, or sheets of paper with parts of headlines written in large letters
paper and pens

Distribute the cards to each member of the group. (Some members may have more than one card.) Divide the group into twos or threes. Ask each group to try and make 'headlines' using the words on their cards. Can anyone make up a story to match the headline?

Headline words:

One man	Purple shoes	for
Toffee ice-cream	Mild explosion	and
Escaped budgie	in	today
Last night	Runs around	with

Toothless monkey	yesterday	next
Hours	Rubber bucket	of
Attempts to fly	in	the
an	a	

Ask the group to think quickly of one or two current TV adverts. Can they remember the catch line or 'hook' for the adverts? It is important to market a product or service as effectively as possible. Unfortunately some companies didn't get it quite right:

• Scandinavian vacuum manufacturer Electrolux used the following advert in America: 'Nothing sucks like an Electrolux!'

• In Taiwan, the translation of the Pepsi slogan 'Come alive with Pepsi' came out as 'Pepsi will bring your ancestors back from the dead!'

• In China, the Kentucky Fried Chicken slogan: 'finger-lickin' good' was translated as 'eat your fingers off!'

• In Italy, a campaign for Schweppes Tonic Water translated the name into 'Schweppes Toilet Water!'

Getting the right message across is important.

PETE TOWNSEND

Reflective material
(sketches/meditations/poems)

Wild John

Isn't it time for someone
   to shout in the desert
   like wild John;
   to come out from hiding
   in those stone cold cathedrals
   and mahogany chapels,
   to climb down
   from those polished pulpits,
   and leave those pre-conditioned
   packaged congregations?

Isn't it time for someone
   to go out and shout in the desert
   like wild John;
   someone not dressed up

in man-made fibres,
or driving a limousine,
living on super-bread,
or sleeping on Slumberland,
or receiving ecclesiastical commission;
but someone like wild John,
with a wilderness diet,
and dressed for the desert;
apart from it all,
where he can see it straight?

Isn't it time for someone
to shout loud in the desert
like wild John;
washing the dust off our civilisation,
before the fire comes
and burns up the chaff;
cleansing the dirt
from a sordid generation
in a river of hope,
and bathing the wounds
of the violent centuries,
ready for healing?

Isn't it time for someone
to shout in the desert
like wild John:
'Level off the unjust hills;
fill in the oppressed valleys;
straighten the crooked ways
and make a smooth road
for the Lord to enter his kingdom'?

PETER DAINTY

The Bible

(The reader should hold a large black Bible.)

I do not love this book because it is
black enough to please Puritans,
holy enough to scare demons,
thick enough to stop bullets,
heavy enough to squash flies;
but because sometimes when I read it
I am moved
deeper than tears.

I do not love this book because
    they say it is the very words of God,
    and polish every dot and comma,
    like golden ornaments
    in an idolatrous temple;
    but because sometimes when I read it
    God speaks in a strange tongue
    deeper than words.

I do not love this book because
    the passionate preacher
    beats the truth out of it
    with his blunt fist
    and sharp ideas,
    (for some use the book
    to support their opinions,
    as others might use it
    to support their tables).
But I do love this book
    because sometimes when I read it
    I am disturbed by a truth
    deeper than thought.

And when I read of Jesus,
    then I know,
    that *he* is the Truth
    that moves my soul –
    the living Word of God.

PETER DAINTY

Here's one I read earlier!

The message
To introduce the Bible and its message.

Characters
1 = librarian
2 = customer

Setting the scene
A man wandering up and down obviously looking for something. He stops to look carefully then continues with his search. Standing behind a desk piled with books, is the librarian. She is clutching a book in one hand holding it in front of her to read. Aware of the person pacing about she keeps glancing up to take a look.

Script

1   Can I help you, please?

2   I'm looking for a book.

(Librarian raises her eyebrows)

1   Really?

2   Yes.

1   Any one in particular?

2   Yes . . . but I'm not sure which one. Can you help me?

1   Um . . . That depends. In our library we have . . . *(Stops to look at some infor-mation on desk)* . . . 25,321 books at present. Which one in particular would you like?

2   That's the problem. I'm not sure. I know I want a particular book but I'm not sure which one.

1   Perhaps if you narrowed it down to a category? You know. History, art, science, education, law, biography, fact, fiction, adventure, thriller, romance. Category?

2   I see what you mean. Perhaps . . .

(Librarian leans forward)

1   Yes?

2   Perhaps . . . history.

1   Ah, history. A favourite of mine. Now which period? Victorian, Elizabethan, Tudor, Dark Ages, World War One, World War Two, twentieth century, medieval?

2   They all sound very interesting but I wanted a book that told me the history of mankind from when we began to how we will finish.

(Librarian looks perplexed)

1   I don't know if we have such a book.

2   Oh, well, perhaps a book on the law.

1   Ah, yes, we have many fine volumes from the Magna Carta to the concise book of bye-laws on how to treat the countryside. *(Looks very pleased)*

2   Um . . . none of those books. It's a book on the kind of laws which we all have to live by. Moral laws as well as civic ones. How the two are perfectly combined together so we live healthily in our own life as well as with our fellow man.

1   I don't think I have such a book.

2   Oh, well, perhaps adventure.

1   Adventure books, one of my favourites. We have Alistair MacLean, Tom Clancy, John Grisham, Enid Blyton, C. S. Lewis, you name it, we've got it.

(Librarian looks very satisfied)

2   The kind of adventure I was looking for was one which affected the whole of mankind in the most dramatic and amazing way.

1   I don't think we stock such a book.

2   A book that tells about the fall of man and his redemption, his eternal destiny.

1   I'm very sorry.

2   I could give you the author's name and the title, will that help?

(Librarian brightens up)

1   Yes, that would be perfect.

2   The author's name is God. The book is the Bible. Do you have one?

(Freeze)

Application

The Bible is a unique book in the whole world of literature as it declares that this book is the Word of God. It is the world's best seller because it is a real life-changer, God's living word.

Discussion starters

- What makes the Bible unique?
- How should we read the Bible?
- How does the Bible change us?

Bible verses

- Hebrews 4:12
- 2 Timothy 3:16

TONY BOWER

John the Baptist

Witnessing to the light

A reading from the Gospel of John (1:6-8, 19-28)

God sent a man whose name was John. He came as a messenger, to tell the people about the light, so that through him they would believe in that light. He himself was not the light, but simply a messenger sent on behalf of the light.

The Jews sent some priests to John the Baptist to ask him, 'Who are you?'

'I am not the promised one,' he answered.

'Are you Elijah or a prophet?' they asked.

'No, I am neither of these,' he replied.

'Well, who are you then, and why are you baptising these people?'

John answered using the words of the prophet Isaiah, 'I am a voice crying out in the desert, "Prepare a way for the Lord!" I baptise you with water, but there is one you do not yet know, who stands among you – one who is coming after me. I am not fit even to undo his sandals.'

All this occurred at a place called Bethany, where John had been baptising people in the River Jordan.

This is the Gospel of the Lord
Praise to you, Lord Jesus Christ   KATIE THOMPSON

Prayers

Praise: Advent promise

Lord Jesus Christ,
> we rejoice today that you came in fulfilment of age-old prophecy,
>> vindicating at last the long-held expectations of your people.
> After so many years of frustrated hopes,
>> so many false dawns and disappointments,
>> you dwelt among us,
>> the Prince of Peace,
>> the promised Messiah,
>> Son of David,

Son of man,
Son of God.
You have shown us that what God promises shall be accomplished:
we praise you for that assurance.

We rejoice that we are heirs to those promises of old,
for you came not only to your own people
but to the whole human race,
born to set us free from everything that enslaves us
and to open the way to eternal life
to anyone willing to follow you.
You have shown us that what God promises shall be accomplished:
we praise you for that assurance.

We rejoice that your purpose for the world continues,
and that the time will come
when your kingdom shall be established
and your victory be complete.
We thank you that, as you came once, so you will come again;
as you departed into heaven, so you will return in glory,
to establish justice throughout the earth,
and to reconcile all creation through your love.
So we look forward in confidence
to that day when there will be no more sorrow or suffering,
hatred or evil,
darkness or death;
that day when you will be all in all.
You have shown us that what God promises shall be accomplished:
we praise you for that assurance.

Lord Jesus Christ,
we rejoice in this season, so full of promise;
this time which reminds us of all that has been
and all that is yet to be.
May the words we hear today,
the worship we offer
and the events we remember
teach us to trust you completely,
knowing that, whatever else may happen,
your saving purpose will be fulfilled.
You have shown us that what God promises shall be accomplished:
we praise you for that assurance.

In your name we pray.
Amen.

NICK FAWCETT

Intercession

Through his messengers God prepares the way for salvation.

Father, into every situation of doubt and despondency
among your followers,
breathe your faithfulness.

Silence for prayer

Prepare us, O Lord:
to walk in your ways.

Father, into our strongholds of ambition
and defensiveness,
breathe your humility.

Silence for prayer

Prepare us, O Lord:
to walk in your ways.

Father, into the prisons of guilt and revenge,
breathe the grace of forgiveness.

Silence for prayer

Prepare us, O Lord:
to walk in your ways.

Father, into the darkness of pain and fear,
breathe your reassurance.

Silence for prayer

Prepare us, O Lord:
to walk in your ways.

Father, into the flabbiness of complacency,
breathe your zeal.

Silence for prayer

Prepare us, O Lord:
to walk in your ways.

Father, into our homes and places of work,
breathe your fellowship and love.

Silence for prayer

Prepare us, O Lord:
to walk in your ways.

Father, into the whole of your creation,
breathe your joy and peace.

Silence for prayer

Merciful Father,
accept these prayers
for the sake of your Son,
our Saviour Jesus Christ, Amen.

SUSAN SAYERS

A short prayer

Loving God, we praise you
   for fulfilling your age-long purpose
   through the birth of Jesus.
We thank you that your promises are not simply empty words
   like so many of ours,
   but pledges we can rely on,
   knowing they will always be honoured.
Teach us, then, to read the Scriptures as Matthew read them,
   hearing your word revealed in Christ
   and trusting in the promise of new life
   you have given us through him.
Amen.

NICK FAWCETT

The third Sunday of Advent

Lord, it is easy to think that it gets dark too quickly, that clouds obscure the sun.
When it's night someone, somewhere else, is enjoying the light.
Our darkness can often seem to last longer than everyone else's.
Help us to see.
Help us to open up the dark areas for your light to shine.
Help us to trust you when dark clouds gather on the horizon.
Be with us as the shadows give way to the brightness of your Son.
Amen.

PETE TOWNSEND

All-age-talk material

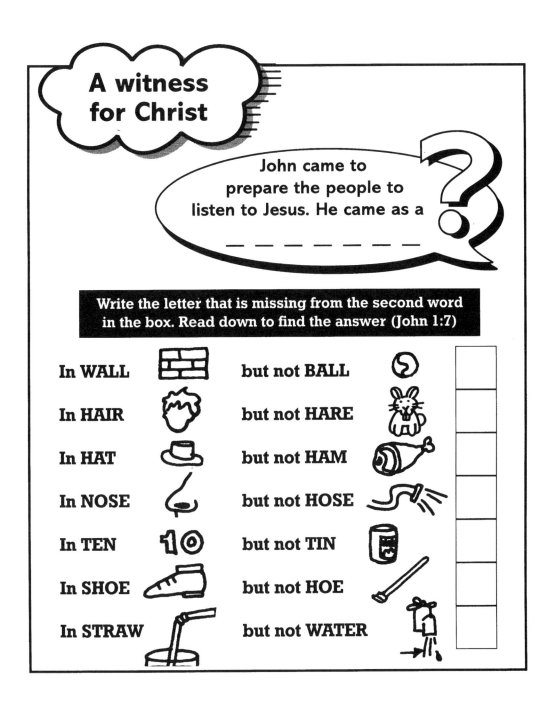

A witness for Christ

John came to prepare the people to listen to Jesus. He came as a

_ _ _ _ _ _ _

Write the letter that is missing from the second word in the box. Read down to find the answer (John 1:7)

In WALL   but not BALL

In HAIR   but not HARE

In HAT   but not HAM

In NOSE   but not HOSE

In TEN   but not TIN

In SHOE   but not HOE

In STRAW   but not WATER

KATIE THOMPSON

The people wondered if John was the Messiah promised by God. What did he tell them?

Cross out every second letter. Copy the remaining letters in order on to the spaces below

Start → I X̸A J M P N L O R T B T E H S E C C J H R R K I M S J T

'___ ___ ___ ___ ___ ___

___ ___ ___

___ ___ ___ ___ ___ ___,'

John 1:20

KATIE THOMPSON

The forerunner

First talk with the children about how their town or country prepares its streets for important visitors such as royalty, a winning football team or a film star. There may be flags hung up, streamers waving, a red carpet rolled out on the pavement and flowers planted round all the lamp posts, for instance. If you have any photographs of such events, or a local carnival, show them around.

Now read John 1:19-28 where John the Baptist uses the prophecy to explain his own job. Unroll a length of white material, about a yard wide and four yards long. (A double sheet split down the middle and joined end to end makes the right size: it is important that it looks big.)

The children are going to turn this strip of boring material into a highway for Jesus. At Christmas time it can be laid down in church so that when the Christ child is brought to the manger he is carried along the children's highway.

Have ready plenty of colourful oddments of material, a really efficient fabric glue, scissors, pens and templates. Discuss ways in which we can prepare ourselves for Jesus, and write these at intervals along the highway with coloured pens. On flower shapes they can write thank-you messages.

SUSAN SAYERS

Jesus fulfils the prophets

Prepare this crossword puzzle on the OHP or a large sheet of card.

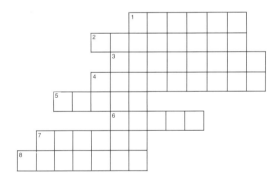

Give out each clue in turn; I have suggested [in parenthesis] who to allow to answer each one but do of course change this to suit the group. Make sure that everyone present has a chance to answer at least one clue.

Across:
1 (For uniformed people only)
   The plural of person.
2 (For those with long hair only)
   To say what will happen in the future.
3 (For those with short hair only)
   Truthfully.

4 (For those wearing green)
  Special and significant.

5 (For those with brown eyes)
  The real facts about something.

6 (For those without brown eyes)
  The name of Mary and Joseph's son.

7 (For those who like pizza)
  Christmas without the last three letters.

8 (For those who can / could skip)
  Fills with meaning; manages to accomplish something.

Down:

1 (Everybody)
  The hidden word in this puzzle, the solution to 1 down: PROPHETS

Now ask everyone to help you with your sermon notes by calling out the words as you point to them. Read the message so that everyone joins in at the right places, like this:

PROPHETS are PEOPLE. False PROPHETS FORETELL what PEOPLE are wanting to hear, but good PROPHETS FORETELL HONESTLY IMPORTANT TRUTH from God. To FORETELL doesn't just mean to FORETELL the future, it can also mean to speak out God's TRUTH even when PEOPLE don't want to hear it. JESUS CHRIST FULFILS the IMPORTANT TRUTH about God which the good PROPHETS were able to FORETELL HONESTLY. In everything JESUS does, both during his time on earth and ever since through PEOPLE who believe in him, JESUS shows the IMPORTANT TRUTH about God's love for PEOPLE. So who are PROPHETS? PROPHETS are PEOPLE who FORETELL HONESTLY IMPORTANT TRUTH from God, and JESUS CHRIST FULFILS it.

SUSAN SAYERS

Read John 1:6-8

Announce to the group that, like John the Baptist, you are going to tell them the truth about the 'light'. Read the following to the group:

Light, or electromagnetic radiation, is the agency by which objects are rendered visible. Newton, in 1666, was the first to discover that sunlight is composed of a mixture of light of all different colours in certain proportions and that it could be separated into its components by dispersion. The speed of light in a vacuum is approximately 300 million metres per second or 186,000 miles per second.

Ask the group if that has made things a little clearer! The reaction may not be too positive! Ask the group for their definition of 'light'. What is it? How does it work?

The writer of the Gospel, John, was anxious that everyone should 'find their way' to Christ (John 20:30-31). So, by referring to Christ as the light of the world he was declaring that this 'true' light would illuminate the way for 'all people' to be reunited with God. This 'true' or 'genuine' light was not a flicker of light in the darkness which would eventually fade and disappear, but a light which would remain constant, the only light which would show everyone the way to God.

Again the writer of the Gospel wanted to make it clear that the light would show the way to God for *all* people regardless of race, wealth, colour or class. Christ was the true light with no shadows (race, wealth, colour or class).

Now read John 1:19-28. John the Baptist was quizzed by the priests who wanted to know who he was. They knew that John's father had been a priest and, as being a priest was hereditary, John was also a priest. But they didn't know who John was claiming to be. John the Baptist made it very clear that he wasn't the Christ or the prophet of Elijah. (It was a Jewish belief that the prophet Elijah would return to prepare the way for the arrival of the Messiah.) John the Baptist told the priests that he was nothing more than a voice encouraging people to prepare themselves for the arrival of the Lord. The idea behind John's reply was that most of the roads in that part of the world were little more than dirt tracks. When a king was about to visit an area, all the roads would be smoothed and straightened out in preparation for the arrival of the king. John the Baptist wanted the people to understand that although he wasn't the light he was a pointer to the light.

PETE TOWNSEND

Reflective material
(sketches, meditations and poems)

Morning star of God

Leader   Morning star of God
rising in beauty from
the ashes of our night,
encourage us your servants
who walk in darkness
and need the loving
touch of your light
to lift us into joy.

All   Be gracious to us
for without your light
we are left in our
darkness for ever.

Leader   Morning star of God,
              clothed in unattainable glory,
              enfold us in your
              robes of light,
              that we may stand
              in gladness before you
              in the beauty
              of your presence.

All   Be gracious to us
              for without your light
              we are left in our
              darkness for ever.

Leader   Morning star of God,
              our joy and our desiring,
              come to us we beseech you,
              shine upon us once again
              for life is cold without you.
          Our bodies, minds and spirits
              ache with longing for
              the glory of your light.

All   Be gracious to us
              for without your light
              we are left in our
              darkness for ever.

MARY HATHAWAY

Light in darkness

Leader   Beautiful is the moonrise
              in a circle of perfection,
              her face is pale gold
              and the light she spreads
              is silver.

All   But more beautiful
              is the mind of our God
              who brought light
              out of darkness
              before time began.

Leader   Lovely are the stars
              as they sprinkle
              the heavens
              with gladness

All   But more lovely
                is the joy of our God
                for his laughter
                fills the universe.

Leader   Deep are the shadows
                of the moonlight lying
                in pools of blackness.

All   But deeper are the ways
                of our God and his thoughts
                beyond our knowing.

Leader   How lovely is light
                when it shines
                in darkness!

All   But how terrible is night
                without moonlight
                and how lonely the sky
                without stars!   Mary Hathaway

Order of service

Service of Holy Communion

Theme: A witness to the Light

Directions: A small, unlit tea light candle should be placed on every seat or pew, enough for all who will attend. A large unlit candle should be placed on a table visibly at the front of church.

Welcome and notices

Warm and inviting. Visitors and newcomers should be made particularly welcome.

Short pause

Introduction to the theme

Stand

Acclamation

Restore us, Lord God of hosts:
show us the light of your face, turned towards us.

Will you not give us life again:
that your people may rejoice in you?

Show us your mercy, O Lord:
and grant us your salvation.

Blessed is the King who comes in the name of the Lord!
Peace in heaven and glory in the highest.

Move directly into praise and worship

Sung Praise and Worship

Hymn Lift up your hearts! *(Complete Anglican Hymns Old and New)*

Song Great is the darkness *(The Source)*

Play soft instrumental music in background. Open to the Holy Spirit. The congregation may be encouraged to reflect, pray quietly or out loud. It is important for the worship leader to direct sensitively at this point.

Open worship

(Open to God, open prayer or praise, reflecting, sharing gifts)

Sit if not already doing so. Soft instrumental music continues in background.

Preparation and confession

Let us pray together:

Almighty God,
to whom all hearts are open,
all desires known,
and from whom no secrets are hidden:
cleanse the thoughts of our hearts
by the inspiration of your Holy Spirit,
that we may perfectly love you,
and worthily magnify your holy name;
through Christ our Lord.
Amen.

When the Lord comes,
he will bring to light things now hidden in darkness,
and will disclose the purposes of the heart.
Therefore in the light of Christ let us confess our sins.

Most merciful God,
Father of our Lord Jesus Christ,
we confess that we have sinned
in thought, word and deed.
We have not loved you with our whole heart.
We have not loved our neighbours as ourselves.
In your mercy
forgive what we have been,

help us to amend what we are,
and direct what we shall be;
that we may do justly,
love mercy, and walk humbly with you, our God.
Amen.

May the God of all healing and forgiveness
draw us to himself,
that we may behold the glory of his Son,
the Word made flesh,
and be cleansed from all our sins through Jesus Christ our Lord.
Amen.

Towards the conclusion of the Absolution an extended introduction to the chorus of the song should be played.

Song   Great is the darkness (chorus only)

Chorus should be sung more slowly and quietly to conclude time of Preparation and Confession.

Collect
O Lord Jesus Christ,
who at your first coming sent your messenger
to prepare your way before you:
grant that the ministers and stewards of your mysteries
may likewise so prepare and make ready your way
by turning the hearts of the disobedient
to the wisdom of the just,
that at your second coming to judge the world
we may be found an acceptable people in your sight;
for you are alive and reign with the Father
in the unity of the Holy Spirit,
one God, now and for ever.

Short pause

The Liturgy of the Word
Atmospheric music plays in background during the readings. Photograph slide of 'Daybreak' or 'sprouting plant' projected onto screen.

Reading 1
Short time of silence

Reading 2
Short time of silence

After the second reading a member of the congregation comes forward to light a large candle. (Photograph off. Candle remains lit.)

Sermon

Sermon linked to theme. Challenging and affirming, giving practical help for discipleship.

Silence

For reflection on Sermon. Background music plays softly during intro to Response and builds into the singing of the song. Lights are dimmed. Invite the congregation to answer the call to be a witness to the light – Jesus – to commit themselves to sharing the good news in word and action.

Response – A call to be a witness to the light.

Song   The Spirit of the Lord *(The Source 2)* sung during time of response.

Informal Peace (optional)

People can respond privately in their hearts or can bring out their candle, light it from the large candle and leave it on the table. This will show a personal and collective response by joining each light together. Candles then remain lit as visual focus. The Peace could be shared informally during this time of Response, ideally with people around the table of candles or with nearby people in the pews.

Stand (Instrumental music continues softly)

Affirmation of Faith

Do you believe and trust in God the Father,
who made all things?
We believe and trust in him.

Do you believe and trust in his Son Jesus Christ,
who redeemed the world?
We believe and trust in him.

Do you believe and trust in his Holy Spirit,
who gives life to the people of God?
We believe and trust in him.

This is the faith of the Church.
This is our faith.
We believe and trust in one God,
Father, Son and Holy Spirit. Amen.

Affirmation of Commitment

Will you continue in the apostles' teaching and fellowship,
in the breaking of bread, and in the prayers?
With the help of God, I will.

Will you persevere in resisting evil, and, whenever you fall into sin,
repent and return to the Lord?
With the help of God, I will.

Will you proclaim by word and example the good news of God in Christ?
With the help of God, I will.

Will you seek and serve Christ in all people,
loving your neighbour as yourself?
With the help of God, I will.

Will you acknowledge Christ's authority over human society,
by prayer for the world and its leaders, by defending the weak,
and by seeking peace and justice?
With the help of God, I will.

Music ends. Prayers continue unannounced.

Prayers

Let us sit or kneel to pray together:

Come, Lord.
Be our glorious King, enthroned on the praises of your people.
Establish your kingdom in the hearts of your church and make us one in you.
Send us out in the power of your Spirit
to live for your praise and glory,
taking your light wherever we go.

Silence

We pray:
come, Lord Jesus.

Come, Lord.
Be our King of kings.
Before you all creation will sing your name,
every knee will bow and every tongue confess that you are Lord.
May your Lordship be known through all the earth
and may your power be displayed.
We pray for our rulers and governments
and long that they too will acknowledge your authority
over every decision, issue and event.

Silence

We pray:
come, Lord Jesus.

Come, Lord.
Be our servant King.
Just as you sacrificed everything,
may we too give you our all.
Grant us your servant heart
so that we may give of ourselves freely.
Help us to love as you love us
and to reach out to those who do not know you.

Silence

We pray:
come, Lord Jesus.

Come Lord.
Be our victorious King.
You have defeated sin and death
and shown your power over sickness and suffering.
In faith we lift to you those who are suffering
through sickness, tragedy or bereavement.
Bring healing where there is none,
hope where there is despair
and life where there is death.

Silence

We pray:
come, Lord Jesus.

Come, Lord.
Be our one true King.
You have shown that there is only one path to walk, one journey to make
and one direction in which to travel – towards you.
Help all Christian people who profess your Gospel
to unite under your gracious power
and join with all the saints to cry . . .
come, Lord Jesus.
Amen.

Stand

(The Peace) (If not shared already)
In the tender compassion of our God
the dawn from on high shall break upon us,
to shine on those who dwell in darkness
and the shadow of death,
and to guide our feet into the way of peace:
The peace of the Lord be always with you . . .
and also with you.
Let us offer one another a sign of peace.

All may exchange a sign of peace.
After the Peace or prayers the hymn is announced.

Offertory Hymn: O for a thousand tongues to sing *(The Source)*

The Eucharistic Prayer (E)

The Lord is here.
His Spirit is with us.

Lift up your hearts.
We lift them to the Lord.

Let us give thanks to the Lord our God.
It is right to give thanks and praise.

It is indeed right and good to give you thanks and praise,
almighty God and everlasting Father,
through Jesus Christ your Son.
For when he humbled himself
to come among us in human flesh,
he fulfilled the plan you formed
before the foundation of the world
to open for us the way of salvation.
Confident that your promise will be fulfilled,
we now watch for the day
when Christ our Lord will come again in glory.
And so we join our voices with angels and archangels
and with all the company of heaven
to proclaim your glory,
forever praising you and saying:

Holy, holy, holy Lord
God of power and might,
heaven and earth are full of your glory.
Hosanna in the highest.

We praise and bless you, loving Father,
through Jesus Christ, our Lord;
and as we obey his command,
send your Holy Spirit,
that broken bread and wine outpoured
may be for us the body and blood of your dear Son.

On the night before he died he had supper with his friends
and, taking bread, he praised you.
He broke the bread, gave it to them and said:

Take, eat; this is my body which is given for you;
do this in remembrance of me.

When supper was ended he took the cup of wine.
Again he praised you, gave it to them and said:
Drink this, all of you;
this is my blood of the new covenant,
which is shed for you and for many
for the forgiveness of sins.
Do this, as often as you drink it, in remembrance of me.
So, Father, we remember all that Jesus did,
in him we plead with confidence
his sacrifice made once for all upon the cross.

Bringing before you the bread of life and cup of salvation,
we proclaim his death and resurrection
until he comes in glory.

Praise to you, Lord Jesus:
Dying you destroyed our death,
rising you restored our life;
Lord Jesus, come in glory.

On the words 'come in glory' instrumental introduction to 'Great is the darkness' begins.

Lord of all life,
help us to work together for that day
when your kingdom comes
and justice and mercy will be seen in all the earth.

Look with favour on your people,
gather us in your loving arms
and bring us with (*N and*) all the saints
to feast at your table in heaven.

Through Christ, and with Christ, and in Christ,
in the unity of the Holy Spirit,
all honour and glory are yours, O loving Father,
for ever and ever.
Amen.

Song Great is the darkness (chorus only)
Sing softly to conclude the Eucharistic Prayer.

Music ends.

The Lord's Prayer
Let us sit or kneel as we pray for the coming of God's kingdom in the words
our Saviour taught us:

Our Father in heaven,
hallowed be your name,
your kingdom come,
your will be done,
on earth as in heaven.
Give us today our daily bread.
Forgive us our sins as we forgive those who sin against us.
Lead us not into temptation
but deliver us from evil.
For the kingdom, the power,
and the glory are yours
now and for ever.
Amen.

Breaking of the Bread

The president breaks the consecrated bread.

Every time we eat this bread and drink this cup:
We proclaim the Lord's death until he comes.

Giving of Communion

Draw near with faith.
Receive the body of our Lord Jesus Christ
which he gave for you,
and his blood which he shed for you.
Eat and drink in remembrance that he died for you,
and feed on him in your hearts
by faith with thanksgiving.

The president and people receive Communion.
Authorised words of distribution are used.

Songs How deep the Father's love for us *(The Source)*
Such love *(The Source)*
Thank you for saving me *(The Source)*

Prayer after Communion

We give you thanks, O Lord, for these heavenly gifts;
kindle in us the fire of your Spirit
that when your Christ comes again
we may shine as lights before his face;
who is alive and reigns now and for ever.
Amen.

Almighty God,
we thank you for feeding us
with the body and blood of your Son Jesus Christ.

**Through him we offer you
our souls and bodies
to be a living sacrifice.
Send us out in the power of your Spirit
to live and work to your praise and glory.
Amen.**

Stand

Intro to the song begins immediately after the prayer.

Song   We'll walk the land *(The Source)* or
Men of faith *(The Source)*

All move outside on to the street for the conclusion of the worship. Torches, lanterns or candles are taken if done at night.

The Blessing and Dismissal

Christ the Sun of Righteousness shine upon you,
scatter the darkness from before your path,
and make you ready to meet with him when he comes in glory;
and the blessing of God almighty,
the Father, the Son and the Holy Spirit,
be among you and remain with you always.

Go in peace to love and serve the Lord.
**In the name of Christ.
Amen.**

TIM LOMAX

Mary Receives Gabriel's Message

God's promised kingdom dawns

A reading from the Gospel of Luke (1:26-38)

God sent the angel Gabriel to a town in Galilee called Nazareth, to a young woman there called Mary. She was engaged to marry a carpenter called Joseph, a descendant of King David's family.

The angel greeted Mary with the words, 'Be glad, Mary, for God is with you and has given you great blessings.'

Mary was troubled and wondered what the angel's words meant.

'There is nothing to fear,' Gabriel assured her. 'You will have a son and name him Jesus. He will be called Son of the Most High, whose reign will never end.'

'How can this happen,' asked Mary, 'when I am not married?'

'The Holy Spirit will come to you,' said Gabriel. 'Therefore this child will be holy and be known as the Son of God. Nothing is impossible for God. Your cousin Elizabeth who was childless, is herself expecting a baby.'

Then Mary said, 'I am God's servant, and will do whatever he asks. Let everything happen just as you have said.'

Then the angel left her.

This is the Gospel of the Lord
Praise to you, Lord Jesus Christ

KATIE THOMPSON

Introductory material

'Let us go in heart and mind even unto Bethlehem' – the beautiful words of the bidding prayer used in the traditional service of nine lessons and carols. And those are words which sum up what this service today is designed to help us do. Through slides, music, readings and meditations we shall attempt to step back in time and hear what Mary, Joseph, the shepherds, the innkeeper, the magi, and those living in Bethlehem might have said about the astonishing events they were part of. But we do not simply ask what they might have said. We ask also, and far more importantly, what God is saying to us now.

NICK FAWCETT

Prayers

God who uses the small things of this world

Eternal God,
  you came to our world not in a blaze of publicity,
    surrounded by pomp and show,
    nor to the frenzied acclaim of crowds
    gathered to greet your coming,
    but quietly,
    unassumingly,
    almost unnoticed,
    in the quiet of the night in the little town of Bethlehem –
    born in a manger,
    to the Virgin Mary,
    your coming first witnessed by shepherds
    out working in the fields.
As the heavens are higher than the earth,
  so our ways are not your ways,
  nor our thoughts your thoughts.

Time and again you have chosen the small,
  the humble,
  the insignificant,
  and worked out your purposes through them.
You have shown your strength in what the world counts weakness,
  you have made the last first, and the least the greatest.
As the heavens are higher than the earth,
  so our ways are not your ways,
  nor our thoughts your thoughts.

Teach us what that means today –
  that you can use us beyond our imagining,
  that you can take what seems unimportant
  and turn it into something wonderful,
  that you can work among us in ways
  that exceed our wildest expectations.
Teach us to see life not merely from our own perspective
  but from yours,
  and so may your strength be made perfect in our weakness.
As the heavens are higher than the earth,
  so our ways are not your ways,
  nor our thoughts your thoughts.
Thanks be to God, through Jesus Christ our Lord.
Amen.

NICK FAWCETT

Carol service – remembering and reliving

Almighty and loving God,
  we come together on this day
    to celebrate the birth of your Son,
    the child laid in a manger,
    our Lord and Saviour Jesus Christ.
  You have done great things for us,
    and we are glad.

We come recalling that first Christmas centuries ago;
    the message proclaimed by the angels –
    news of great joy!
  You have done great things for us,
    and we are glad.

We come remembering the faith of Mary,
    the thanksgiving of the shepherds,
    and the worship of the wise men.
  You have done great things for us,
    and we are glad.

We come reminding ourselves of your great love
    shown to us and all people
    through your coming and sharing our humanity,
    through your living and dying amongst us.
  You have done great things for us,
    and we are glad.

Loving God,
  we thank you for this time of year –
    its mood of joy and celebration,
    its spirit of goodwill and desire to work for peace,
    the renewing of old friendships
    and the coming together of families,
    the lessons and carols which we know and love so well.
  You have done great things for us,
    and we are glad.

Save us, O Lord, from becoming over-familiar with this season,
    from ever imagining we know all there is to know about it,
    or presuming we have understood all there is to understand.
  You have done great things for us,
    and we are glad.

Teach us to listen for your voice and look for your presence,
    to hear your call and respond to your guidance.
  You have done great things for us,
    and we are glad.

May we, like Mary, have the faith to believe
   that with you nothing is impossible;
   like the shepherds to go in heart and mind even to Bethlehem
   to see what you have done;
   like the wise men to offer you our worship
   and present to you our gifts;
   like the great company of angels
   to sing glad and joyful songs of praise.
You have done great things for us,
   and we are glad.

And so may we, when the festivities are over and Christmas is past,
   return to our daily lives glorifying and praising you
   for all we have seen and heard,
   the wonder of your love revealed in Christ!
You have done great things for us,
   and we are glad.
Praise be to you, now and for ever!
Amen.   NICK FAWCETT

Intercession

Mary was chosen by God to be the mother of Jesus, our Saviour. God's great sign of love is that he is carried through a human pregnancy and born into a human family which is descended from David. In this way the prophecies are fulfilled and God's glory revealed to the whole world.

Fellow travellers of Christ's Way,
as we walk together through life,
let us pray together in his Spirit.

Father, we bring to your love
all who serve Christ in his church;
that they may not flinch
from responding to their calling,
but rather abandon themselves
to your guidance and protection.

Silence for prayer

Heavenly Father:
let your will be done.

Guide all who are in authority
throughout the world;
that they may be strengthened
to stand firm in what is right even if it is unpopular.

Silence for prayer

Heavenly Father:
let your will be done.

Father, in your love we remember our own mothers,
all parents and foster parents,
all women in labour at this moment
and all who are pregnant;
that they may be blessed and supported.

Silence for prayer

Heavenly Father:
let your will be done.

Father we commend to your love
those who have been rejected or abandoned
by their families or by society;
those who are constantly
ridiculed, criticised or badly treated;
may your love break down prejudice,
disperse hatred and build bridges of reconciliation.

Silence for prayer

Heavenly Father:
let your will be done.

Father, into your hands we commend
all who have died and those who mourn.

Silence for prayer

Heavenly Father:
let your will be done.

Father, our lives are so rich with all your blessings,
and we thank you for all your love.

Silence for prayer

Merciful Father,
accept these prayers
for the sake of your Son,
our Saviour Jesus Christ, Amen.

SUSAN SAYERS

A short prayer

Lord Jesus Christ,
    we are here just a short time away from Christmas –
    that great festival which we know and love so well –
    which perhaps we know and love too well!
We have heard the stories and sung the hymns so many times
    that there is a danger of the medium
    becoming more important than the message.

We come today wanting to avoid that,
    eager instead to reflect on the meaning of your coming –
    for yesterday, for today, for tomorrow.
So now,
    we come to worship you.
Speak to us, we pray,
    so that this season of Advent
    may not simply be a part
    of our build-up to Christmas,
    but a time in its own right
    which deepens our faith
    and strengthens our commitment.
Lord Jesus Christ,
    meet with us now,
    and speak your word.
Amen.

NICK FAWCETT

All-age-talk material

THE ANGEL VISITS MARY

The angel told Mary:-

Jesus To Going Name His Are A You Have Will Baby Be

Mary was

She said

YES NO

Colour the picture carefully.

What was the name of the angel?

SUSAN SAYERS

Think and Look Ahead

Now four candles are lit on the Advent wreath! What are we ready to celebrate?

See what answer the gift tags spell out!

KATIE THOMPSON

Mary's child would be called the 'Son of God'. What name was Mary told to give him?

Cross ✗ out the letters with a ✡ and see what name appears!

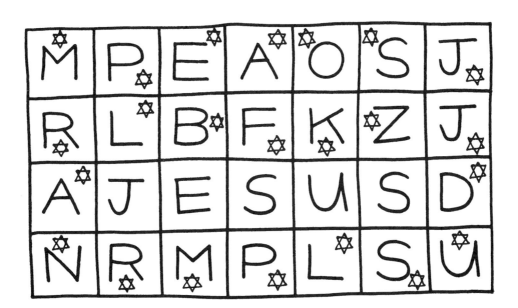

God's messenger!

The angel Gabriel was sent by God to visit Mary. Where did Mary live?

Follow the line and see where it leads!

Cana

Bethlehem

Nazareth

A startling piece of news!

Read the following news stories. After each one ask the group if they think it is true or false. Don't tell them if they are right or wrong. When you have read the last story tell them that every story was in fact true!

1. A policeman responded to a report of a robbery at a local school. When he arrived three teenagers started to run away. The policeman, knowing he couldn't catch them, shouted, 'Stop or I'll set my dog on to you' (even though he didn't have a dog). The teenagers kept on running. So, the policeman took the idea one stage further and began barking. Immediately the three teenagers stopped running and gave themselves up!

2. A man in New Mexico got drunk and started to shoot at giant cacti. One fell on him!

3. A man walked into a newsagent's shop and put a twenty pound note on the counter and asked for it to be changed. When the newsagent opened the cash register the man pulled out a gun and demanded the contents of the cash register. He took the cash and ran out of the shop, leaving the twenty pound note on the counter. He escaped with fifteen pounds!

The group may have guessed that the stories were all true. They may even know of stranger stories! We are used to hearing all sorts of weird and wonderful stories. It's quite possible that Mary had heard a few wacky stories as well. But nothing could have prepared her for the visit of the Angel Gabriel.

Read Luke 1:26-38

The Angel Gabriel greets Mary and says, 'You are truly blessed! The Lord is with you.' There are two things to note here. First, meeting with an angel was not an everyday occurrence! So this would have put Mary in a bit of a spin. Second, the Angel Gabriel told Mary that the Lord had blessed her! She somehow had found favour with God! She was confused and must have wondered what on earth was going on. The angel notes that Mary is a bit confused and tells her not to worry: 'Don't be afraid.' This is not a gentle pat on the hand or 'Shall we have a cup of tea and talk this over?' No! The Angel Gabriel launches straight in with, 'The Lord is pleased with you and you're going to have a baby. He will be called the Son of God the Most High!' Well, of course this happens to every young woman! Doesn't it? At this point Mary is really feeling the heat. First, she is greeted by an angel. Second, she is told that she is blessed by God and then told she's going to have a baby who will rule the people of Israel! And this is before she is even married!

Mary was engaged to Joseph. The normal engagement lasted about a year and was as legally binding as being married. The engagement could only be broken off through a divorce. Mary listened to the Angel Gabriel's message and answered, 'I am the Lord's servant! Let it happen as you have said.' Mary didn't want to argue with God. She recognised that God had chosen her to do something special for him. She didn't know the full story or have a complete picture of what was going to happen. She didn't know how Joseph would react to the news. She didn't even know why God had chosen her for this task. Mary placed her trust in God.

PETE TOWNSEND

Reflective material
(sketches, meditations and poems)

Mary – unexpected mother
Thinking about it

What's the point?

God is the true source of life. However much we people – and especially men, even today – may think that we are in charge of things, the real source of everything good is God. And Mary – ordinary, humble Mary – was as surprised as her cousin Elizabeth to find that God had chosen to work a miracle in her life.

Doing it

Prayer

Loving God,
thank you for valuing all of us,
whether we *seem* important or not.
Help us learn to value one another
through the things that we do together.
Amen.

From the known to the unknown

Have the children ever had wonderful surprises – maybe a present, or an outing? God often works in unexpected ways, and sometimes the people he gets to help him in his work would never have expected it.

Tell the story: Luke 1:26-38

An angel with an angle

Mary was having one of those days – you know, when nothing goes quite the way you expect. She got up that morning, full of good intentions. 'Right,' she thought, making a mental list in her head, 'I've got to mend the goat, milk the cat and take the gate to the vet's – where shall I start? Just a minute, that doesn't sound quite right to me.'

'Oh, dear,' she thought, 'that's what happens when your body wakes up before your brain does. Anyway, I'll make a start with that gate – Dad's never going to get round to it. Now, where did I put the hammer?'

'Is this what you're looking for?'

Mary turned to see a very strange-looking man standing behind the broken gate and leaning on it. She could see he was wearing a pair of blue jeans (something Mary had never seen before and probably never would again) and a T-shirt with something she couldn't make out written on it, and his hair was short and stood straight up in spikes. Altogether, he seemed a very strange sight to Mary. He smiled at her, mischievously. 'You wanted a hammer, I believe?' He snapped his fingers and a hammer appeared in his hand.

'Neat trick,' said Mary, 'and I suppose you've got some nails handy, too?'

The man looked offended. 'Oh, don't be so mundane,' he said with mock severity. 'Here you are with the Archangel Gabriel right in front of you, and the most exciting thing you can ask for is a box of nails!'

Mary stared. 'Archangel Gabriel? You don't look much like an angel to me.'

'That's what they all say,' said Gabriel, 'but I can't go around in wings and a halo all the time – it's just *so* not cool. I don't want people thinking I'm some sort of poser, now do I?' So saying, he pushed himself off and floated gently up over the gate and back down to the ground, smiling smugly as if to say, 'Look, no wings!'

As he landed he held up a hand modestly. 'No applause, please, this is a solemn moment. Now, I've got to get the next bit right because it'll probably get into the papers or something.' He straightened up, put on a long face that didn't suit him at all, and said, 'Greetings, O favoured one – the Lord is with you.'

Mary stifled a giggle, pulling an exaggeratedly solemn face in the process. 'Don't be afraid, Mary,' Gabriel tried to reassure her. 'God's really pleased with you – like, totally ecstatic, know what I mean? Now, you're going to have a baby – there, how about that, then! He's going to be great – I mean, really mega – and you're to call him Jesus. He'll reign over God's people for – oh, at least – well, for ever, really – probably more with a bit of Providence. And there'll be no end to his kingdom. Good, eh?'

'Terrific,' Mary agreed, 'except that my mum told me it takes two to make a baby, and there's only me.'

'Oh, no prob,' Gabriel said, airily. 'God can do anything he likes – and he's got it all sorted. I mean – oh, do I have to spell it out? – it's going to be God's Son. Look, you know your cousin Elizabeth? The one everyone said couldn't have a baby short of a miracle? Well, she's having one.'

'Baby,' Mary asked, 'or miracle?'

'Well, both, as it goes,' Gabriel answered. 'She's been pregnant for the past six months, now – see what I mean – this is God we're talking about, and the only thing that's impossible for him is nothing.'

Mary was amazed. 'Well!' she exclaimed. 'What can I say?'

'"OK" would be a start,' Gabriel said. 'Or you could be really tedious and demand to see my ID card or something.'

'No need for that,' said Mary. 'I know you're an angel, all right – no one as off-the-wall as you could possibly be mortal.' She took a deep breath. She didn't know what she'd be letting herself in for – or how she was ever going to explain it to her parents – but one thing she did know was that God was doing something pretty cosmic and she had the chance of being right at the heart of it.

'OK, then,' she said. 'You just tell God that I'm up for it. Whatever he wants, he's the boss and I'll do it. Can I go now, please? I've got to go and find Elizabeth so that we can celebrate together. The gate can wait – boy, are we going to party!'

MICHAEL FORSTER

Drama: An angel with an angle

Narrator Mary was having one of those days – you know, when nothing goes quite the way you expect. She got up that morning, full of good intentions.

Mary Right, I've got to mend the goat, milk the cat and take the gate to the vet's – where shall I start? Just a minute, that doesn't sound quite right to me. Oh, dear, that's what happens when your body wakes up before your brain does. Anyway, I'll make a start with that gate – Dad's never going to get round to it. Now, where did I put the hammer?

Gabriel Is this what you're looking for?

Narrator Mary turned to see a very strange-looking man standing behind the broken gate and leaning on it. She could see he was wearing a pair of blue jeans (something Mary had never seen before and probably never would again) and a T-shirt with something she couldn't make out written on it, and his hair was short and stood straight up in spikes. Altogether, he seemed a very strange sight to Mary. He smiled at her, mischievously.

Gabriel You wanted a hammer, I believe?

Narrator He snapped his fingers and a hammer appeared in his hand.

Mary Neat trick, and I suppose you've got some nails handy, too?

Gabriel (*Looking offended*) Oh, don't be so mundane! Here you are with the Archangel Gabriel right in front of you, and the most exciting thing you can ask for is a box of nails!

Mary Archangel Gabriel? You don't look much like an angel to me.

Gabriel That's what they all say, but I can't go around in wings and a halo all the time – it's just *so* not cool. I don't want people thinking I'm some sort of poser, now do I?

Narrator So saying, he pushed himself off and floated gently up, over the gate and back down to the ground, smiling smugly as if to say, 'Look, no wings!' As he landed he held up a hand modestly.

Gabriel No applause, please, this is a solemn moment. Now, I've got to get the next bit right because it'll probably get into the papers or something.

Narrator He straightened up, and put on a long face that didn't suit him at all.

Gabriel Greetings, O favoured one – the Lord is with you.

Narrator Mary stifled a giggle, pulling an exaggeratedly solemn face in the process.

Gabriel Don't be afraid, Mary, God's really pleased with you – like, totally ecstatic, know what I mean? Now, you're going to have a baby – there, how about that, then! He's going to be great – I mean, really mega – and you're to call him Jesus. He'll reign over God's people for – oh, at least – well, for ever, really – probably more with a bit of Providence. And there'll be no end to his kingdom. Good, eh?

Mary Terrific, except that my mum told me it takes two to make a baby, and there's only me.

Gabriel Oh, no prob, God can do anything he likes – and he's got it all sorted. I mean – oh, do I have to spell it out? – it's going to be God's Son. Look, you know your cousin Elizabeth? The one everyone said couldn't have a baby short of a miracle? Well, she's having one.

Mary Baby, or miracle?

Gabriel Well, both, as it goes. She's been pregnant for the past six months, now – see what I mean – this is God we're talking about, and the only thing that's impossible for him is nothing.

Mary (*Amazed*) Well! What can I say?

Gabriel 'OK' would be a start. Or you could be really tedious and demand to see my ID card or something.

Mary No need for that, I know you're an angel, all right – no one as off-the-wall as you could possibly be mortal.

Narrator Mary took a deep breath. She didn't know what she'd be letting herself in for – or how she was ever going to explain it to her parents – but one thing she did know was that God was doing something pretty cosmic and she had the chance of being right at the heart of it.

Mary OK, then, you just tell God that I'm up for it. Whatever he wants, he's the boss and I'll do it. Can I go now, please? I've got to go and find Elizabeth so that we can celebrate together. The gate can wait – boy, are we going to party!

MICHAEL FORSTER

Meditation of Mary, mother of Jesus

Was it all a dream,
　　a figment of my imagination?
It feels like it now, I have to say,
　　but at the time it was all too real –
　　wonderful, exhilarating,
　　yet at the same time terrifying.
'Blessed are you, Mary, for you have found favour with God.'
My heart leapt when I heard that –
　　me, Mary, singled out for special blessing,
　　chosen by God himself.
But then the angel spoke again,
　　'You will conceive, and bear a son, and call him Jesus.'
Well, that took some getting used to, believe me,
　　the last thing I was expecting!
And yet, strangely, I didn't put up much resistance –
　　just the one token query: 'How can this be?' –
　　and then meek, docile submission.
I marvel now, looking back,
　　yet at the time it seemed perfectly natural,
　　as though no other response would do.
Why?
Well, to be honest, I suppose I never really believed it anyway.
I wondered, of course I did,
　　and half accepted,
　　yet if you'd pressed me hard enough
　　there was always a little doubt at the back of my mind,
　　the questions I couldn't dismiss –
　　had I misread the signs,
　　imagined the whole thing,
　　or simply been listening to too many old wives' tales?
But that wasn't the whole reason,
　　for to tell the truth, despite everything,
　　I wanted to believe it more than you'll ever know.
Wouldn't you have with a promise like I was given? –
　　'He will be great, and will be called the Son of the Most High,
　　and the Lord God will give to him
　　the throne of his ancestor David.
　　He will reign over the house of Jacob for ever,
　　and of his kingdom there will be no end.'
Need I say more?
If a child was unexpected, *that* was mind-boggling –
　　a ruler over Israel,
　　God's promised deliverer,
　　born of my womb,
　　flesh of my flesh.

It was too much,
   beyond anything I could bring myself to imagine,
   and yet too wonderful to dismiss altogether.
Was it all a dream?
Well, *you* might still think so,
   but *I* don't,
   not any more,
   for as I speak these words I am sitting in a stable,
   looking down into a manger,
   and there gazing up at me is my little boy,
   Jesus.
It happened, you see,
   exactly as I was promised,
   just as the angel said it would,
   and if God was right in that,
   then why not the rest too?
How can I not believe?

NICK FAWCETT

Meditation of Mary, mother of Jesus

'You've got it wrong,' I told him.
'You can't mean me,
   no way!
Someone else perhaps,
   more worthy,
   more important,
   but not me!'
Honestly, what did I have to commend me?
No connections or special qualities,
   nothing –
   just an ordinary girl from Nazareth,
   so what could God see in me?
But it was academic anyway, for I wasn't even married yet,
   and there was no way I'd sleep with Joseph until I was.
So I came out with it straight,
   'Sorry, but you're wrong!'
Only he wouldn't take no for an answer.
Just stood there smiling,
   unruffled;
   and before I knew it he was off again –
   the message even more fantastic than before:
   God's power overshadowing me,
   a child born of the Holy Spirit,
   the Son of God!

It was way over the top,
    and I should have turned him out there and then,
    but I was flummoxed,
    too amazed to reply.
Even when I found my tongue it wasn't much use to me –
    my mind so befuddled with questions
    that I ended up saying, of all things,
    'Here am I, the servant of the Lord,
    let it be with me according to your word.'
Oh, it sounded good, granted –
    the epitome of humility –
    but if you only knew what I was thinking,
    you'd have a different picture then.
So what got into me, you ask?
How could I be so meek and accepting?
Well, what choice did I have, let's be honest,
    for as the angel said, 'With God, nothing will be impossible.'
How could I argue with that?
There was no way out, was there?
But it's one thing to accept that in principle,
    another when it turns your life upside down.
Do I believe it?
Well, I didn't at the time,
    but I do now,
    for I've just discovered I'm pregnant,
    and I say this perfectly reverently, God knows how!
It's astonishing and terrifying,
    exciting yet mystifying,
    my mind in turmoil, not quite sure what to think any more.
But one thing is plain now,
    beyond all question –
    with God, quite clearly, *nothing* is impossible!

NICK FAWCETT

Christmas

Christmas Day

The good news

A reading from the Gospel of Luke (2:1-14)

Caesar Augustus, the Roman Emperor, ordered a census to be taken, and everyone returned to the town of their family origin to be registered. So it was that Joseph and Mary left Nazareth in Galilee and returned to Bethlehem in Judea, King David's childhood home. This was because Joseph was a descendant of David's royal line.

While they were there, the time came for Mary to have her baby, and she wrapped him in strips of cloth and laid him in a manger, because there was no room at the inn.

On a hillside near the town, some shepherds were watching over their sheep. Suddenly, an angel appeared and the sky was filled with God's glory. The shepherds were terrified, but the angel said, 'Do not be afraid, for I have great news for you. Today a baby has been born in Bethlehem. He is Christ the Lord, and you will find him lying in a manger.'

The sky was filled with the sound of angels singing, 'Glory to God in the highest, and peace to all people on earth!'

This is the Gospel of the Lord
Praise to you, Lord Jesus Christ   KATIE THOMPSON

Introductory material

Christingle

Jesus is part of everything

Christingle services occur in many churches and are part of the annual fund-raising programme for the Children's Society.

Reading

Christingle services usually take place around Advent or Christmas, and therefore a Christmas reading is appropriate.

Story and talk

This story and talk is combined, and is in three parts. Each should be based and told from a different area of the church. You will need the phrase CHRIST IN written up on a large sheet of paper and displayed, and the G, L and E on pieces of paper to put with it.

1. Christ in G. Stand near the crib or tree if you have one in place. Ask a child to hold up the letter G. Explain that G is for gifts. Jesus was a gift which we remember at Christmas, as God send Jesus as the best present we could ever have. But we all have gifts to use too that come from Jesus. We can share, love, care, etc.

    Key message: Christ is a gift from God, and gives us gifts.

2. Stand near a candle. Ask a child to hold up the letter L. Explain that L is for light. Jesus brought light to the world. When he had grown up he went from town to town and village to village speaking to people, healing and helping them. He also explained who he was, on one occasion saying 'I am the light of the world'. He brings light to the darkness and sad times in our lives.

    Key message: Jesus is the light, and brings light to our dark times.

3. Stand amongst the congregation. Ask a child to hold up the letter E. Explain that E is for Everyone. Because Jesus was the best gift, and because he brings light to all the world, we can all have Jesus with us. Another name for Jesus is Immanuel, which means 'God is with us'. Jesus wants to be with everyone, including all of us here.

    Key message: Jesus wants to be with everyone, but do we want Jesus?

Many churches find the Christingle symbolism helpful; leaflets providing an outline of Christingle, using the traditional orange (as the world) and candle (as the light of Christ) can be obtained from The Children's Society, Old Town Hall, Kennington Road, London SE11 4QD.

It is important that children feel part of the family worship at the festival. Perhaps they would have practised a special carol which they can sing during the service, or they may present a nativity play or tableau during or just after the Gospel.

Elderly residents in nursing homes love to hear children singing, too. If cards are made and distributed at the same time, the children will be providing a most valuable ministry.

SUSAN SAYERS

Good news

'I am bringing you good news of great joy for all the people: to you is born this day in the city of David a Saviour, who is the Messiah, the Lord' – words announcing to the shepherds the glad tidings of the birth of Jesus Christ. But they are words not only to the shepherds, nor simply confined to that day long ago, but words for us today, spoken to you, to me, to everyone – 'good news of great joy for all the people'. That is the wonder of Christmas; the one thing behind all the trivia with which we have surrounded this festival that gives it meaning – the dawn of God's kingdom through the birth of his son, the coming of the Word made flesh; his sharing our humanity so that we may share his eternity. Come then and hear again the familiar story, for to *you* has been born in the city of David a Saviour, who is the Messiah, the Lord!

NICK FAWCETT

Prayers

Praise

Gracious God,
  this is a time which means so much to us
    and which says so much in so many different ways,
    but if there is one thing which stands out above all others,
    it is the joy you brought through the birth of Jesus.
  A child is born for us,
    a son is given –
    with joy we greet him!

  When Mary learned that she was to be the mother of the Saviour
    she sang out her praises,
    and when Elizabeth greeted her,
    the baby in *her* womb leapt for joy.
  When the multitude of angels appeared to the shepherds,
    they proclaimed news of great joy for all people,
    and when both shepherds and wise men
    had seen the Lord for themselves,
    they were overwhelmed by the wonder of it all,
    going on their way rejoicing.
  Time and again it was the same story of spontaneous celebration.
  A child is born for us,
    a son is given –
    with joy we greet him!

Gracious God,
  in all the hustle and bustle of Christmas,
    the ceremony and tradition with which we surround it,
    we can lose sight, sometimes, of the joy at its heart.
  We can put so much energy into having a good time,
    that we forget what it is we are meant to be celebrating,
    only, when it is over, to be left with a sense of emptiness,
    a feeling that it hasn't been like Christmas at all.

Help us to enjoy all the fun and festivity,
    the love and laughter,
    the giving and receiving,
    but help us also to keep in mind
    the reality at the heart of this season,
    the message which it is finally all about.
A child is born for us,
    a son is given –
    with joy we greet him!

May the glad tidings of the angels,
    the news of great joy for all people,
    stir afresh our imagination,
    so that we may experience and understand for ourselves
    the great truth of Christmas –
    that a Saviour is born who is Christ the Lord.
A child is born for us,
    a son is given –
    with joy we greet him!

Gracious God,
    this is a time for rejoicing,
    for celebration,
    for exulting in your goodness.
We praise and thank you for the wonder of your love
    and for the supreme demonstration of that love
    in Jesus Christ.
A child is born for us,
    a son is given –
    with joy we greet him!
Amen.

NICK FAWCETT

Penitential reflection

Son of God made man:
Lord, forgive us.
Lord, forgive us.

Friend of the friendless, and Saviour of all:
Christ, forgive us.
Christ, forgive us.

Light of the world and Prince of peace:
Lord, forgive us.
Lord, forgive us.

(Carefully and slowly, light a candle on either side of the place where God's
Word is to be proclaimed.)

KATIE THOMPSON

Thanksgiving – a time of promise

Loving God,
> we remember today the birth of Jesus Christ –
>> your gift to humankind,
>> your coming among us as flesh and blood,
>> your honouring of age-old promises
>> spoken through the prophets.
> The Word became flesh and dwelt among us,
>> full of grace and truth:
>> **thanks be to God!**

> We do not remember those promises alone,
>> but so many others associated with this time –
>> your promise to Mary that she would bear a son,
>> to Simeon that he would not taste death
>> before seeing the Messiah,
>> and, above all, your promise
>> to anyone who receives Christ and believes in his name
>> that they will become your children,
>> born not of human will,
>> but through your gracious purpose
>> sharing in your eternal life.
> The Word became flesh and dwelt among us,
>> full of grace and truth:
>> **thanks be to God!**

Loving God,
> we praise you that all you promised to do
>> was wonderfully fulfilled in Christ,
>> that through him your faithfulness
>> was most marvellously demonstrated;
>> the ultimate proof of your love and mercy.
> We praise you for the reminder this Christmas season brings
>> that you are a God we can always depend on,
>> one in whom we can put our trust, though all else fails.
> The Word became flesh and dwelt among us,
>> full of grace and truth:
>> **thanks be to God!**
> So now we look forward in confidence
>> to the ultimate fulfilment of your word,
>> that day when Christ will be acclaimed
>> as King of kings and Lord of lords.
> Until then, we will trust in you,
>> secure in your love,
>> confident in your eternal purpose,
>> assured that, in the fullness of time, your will shall be done.

The Word became flesh and dwelt among us,
  full of grace and truth:
    thanks be to God!
Amen.

NICK FAWCETT

Petition – a time of new beginnings

Lord Jesus Christ,
  we celebrate today your birth in Bethlehem –
    a birth that changed the course of history for ever.
  We rejoice that the future of the world
    was shaped by your coming,
    irreversibly transformed
    by your life, death and resurrection.
  A new chapter had begun:
    help us, in turn, to start again.

  We remember how you brought a new beginning to so many –
    not just to Mary and Joseph on the night of your birth,
    but to countless others throughout your ministry
    and to innumerable generations since,
    offering the opportunity to put their mistakes behind them,
    to let go of the past and embrace the future,
    secure in your forgiveness,
    transformed by your grace.
  A new chapter had begun:
    help us, in turn, to start again.

  So we come now, this Christmas-time,
    acknowledging our faults and repeated disobedience.
  We come recognising our need for help
    and our dependence on your mercy.
  We come to hear the good news of your birth,
    the glad tidings of the dawn of your kingdom,
    and, in the light of that message,
    to seek your renewing touch upon our lives.
  A new chapter had begun:
    help us, in turn, to start again.

Lord Jesus Christ,
  we have no claim on your love,
    no reason to expect your goodness,
    for we fail you day after day, week after week.

Yet we celebrate today the glorious truth
　　that you came into our world,
　　you lived among us,
　　you died our death,
　　and you rose again, victorious over sin and death!
A new chapter had begun:
　　help us, in turn, to start again.

In your name we ask it.
Amen.

NICK FAWCETT

Intercession

Jesus Christ is God's good news in language humankind can understand.

We pray for all the groups of Christians
who are celebrating your birth today.
Silence for prayer
O God, we thank you:
for loving us so much.

We pray for all babies,
that they may be given love and care.
Silence for prayer
O God, we thank you:
for loving us so much.

We pray for all who are missing their loved ones,
and all who find Christmas difficult.
Silence for prayer
O God, we thank you:
for loving us so much.

We pray for all those in pain
and those with debilitating illness.
Silence for prayer
O God, we thank you:
for loving us so much.

We pray for those in prison
and for their families.
Silence for prayer
O God, we thank you:
for loving us so much.

We pray for the homeless,
and all refugees.
Silence for prayer

O God, we thank you:
for loving us so much.

We thank you for the joy of Christmas
and welcome you in our homes.
Silence for prayer

Merciful Father,
accept these prayers
for the sake of your Son,
our Saviour Jesus Christ, Amen.   SUSAN SAYERS

Short prayers

Gracious God,
    we thank you for the good news of Jesus Christ
    which we celebrate today,
    the message which brought joy
    to Mary and Joseph,
    to shepherds and wise men,
    and to so many others in the years following his birth.
We thank you that this message has continued
    to be good news for successive generations,
    bringing joy, hope and meaning to untold lives.
Speak to us now and give us ears to hear.
Meet with us now and give us hearts to respond.
So may Christ be born in us today,
    to the glory of your name.
Amen.   NICK FAWCETT

Lord Jesus Christ,
    you came to our world, to your people,
    yet among so many you found no welcome.
From the very beginning the majority shut you out,
    and of those who did accept you
    many did so only half-heartedly.
Forgive us that sometimes we do the same.
Help us to make room for you,
    and to give you not just a token place,
    but to put you at the very centre of our lives.
Amen.   NICK FAWCETT

All-age-talk material

God with us!

Aim

To show that Christmas is as much about us today as those who were present in Bethlehem on the night Jesus was born.

Preparation

Cut out pictures from old Christmas cards, books and magazines to illustrate the following: Bethlehem, angel, manger, night-time, three kings, inn, shepherds, angels, stable. Avoid any picture which specifically shows Jesus as a baby or child. Place the pictures in prominent positions around the church.

Write or print the following on strips of card in large capital letters:

> O LITTLE TOWN OF BETHLEHEM
> THE ANGEL GABRIEL FROM HEAVEN CAME
> AWAY IN A MANGER
> BORN IN THE NIGHT
> WE THREE KINGS FROM ORIENT ARE
> NO ROOM FOR THE SAVIOUR IN BETHLEHEM'S INN
> WHILE SHEPHERDS WATCHED
> ANGELS FROM THE REALMS OF GLORY
> CHRIST IS BORN WITHIN A STABLE
> UNTO US A BOY IS BORN

Fix these to a board or the wall at the front of the church.

Talk

Tell the congregation you have prepared a Christmas quiz for them, based on the words of the Christmas carols displayed at the front of the church. Invite volunteers to come forward and match one of the pictures to one of the carols.

At the end of this exercise there should be the first line of one carol left on its own with no picture to match, *Unto us a boy is born*.

We have found pictures which illustrate each of the carols except this last one, and there's a good reason, for Christmas is not only about Bethlehem, the stable, Mary, the wise men and shepherds, but about us! That is what the reading from Matthew tells us:

> The virgin will be with child and will give birth to a son, and they will call him Immanuel – which means, 'God with us'.
> *(Matthew 1:23)*

Today we look back to the very first Christmas, to what God did in Bethlehem nearly two thousand years ago. But we also celebrate *this* Christmas, and what God has done, and is doing, for *us*, here and now!

For to us a child is born, to us a son is given, and the government will be on his shoulders. And he will be called Wonderful Counsellor, Mighty God, Everlasting Father, Prince of Peace.
(Isaiah 9:6)

That is the truth we celebrate today – Jesus has been born for us. So if we want a picture to illustrate this carol, let's stop when we get home and look in the mirror. And, when we do that, let's ask ourselves two more questions: Have we understood what Christmas is all about? And, if so, have we accepted the gift God has given us in Christ?

NICK FAWCETT

Ideas for activities

Play 'pass the parcel', with all the layers in different Christmas wrapping paper. At each layer have a section of a Christmas card illustrating the stable scene, so that by the end the whole picture is made clear.

SUSAN SAYERS

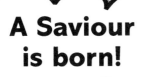

A Saviour is born!

The Emperor Caesar Augustus had ordered a census. Everyone had to return to their home town

**Using the directions below,
follow the route that Joseph and Mary took.**

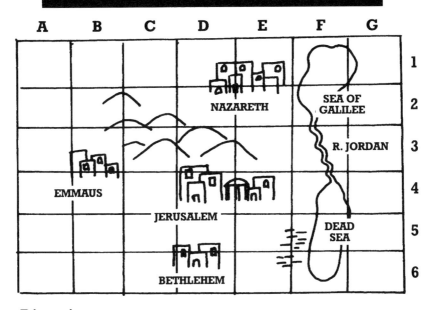

Directions
1E, 1D, 2D, 2E, 3E, 3F, 4F, 4E, 5D, 5C, 6C, 6D

KATIE THOMPSON

The time came for Mary to have her baby, but there was no room at the inn. What did she do?

Use the Christmas code to find out (Luke 2:7)

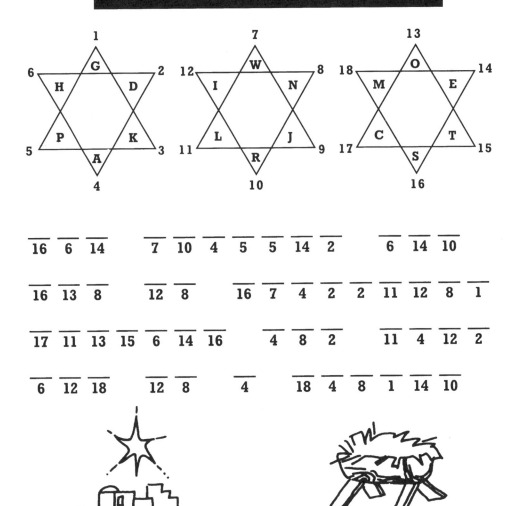

$\overline{16}\ \overline{6}\ \overline{14}$ $\overline{7}\ \overline{10}\ \overline{4}\ \overline{5}\ \overline{5}\ \overline{14}\ \overline{2}$ $\overline{6}\ \overline{14}\ \overline{10}$

$\overline{16}\ \overline{13}\ \overline{8}$ $\overline{12}\ \overline{8}$ $\overline{16}\ \overline{7}\ \overline{4}\ \overline{2}\ \overline{2}\ \overline{11}\ \overline{12}\ \overline{8}\ \overline{1}$

$\overline{17}\ \overline{11}\ \overline{13}\ \overline{15}\ \overline{6}\ \overline{14}\ \overline{16}$ $\overline{4}\ \overline{8}\ \overline{2}$ $\overline{11}\ \overline{4}\ \overline{12}\ \overline{2}$

$\overline{6}\ \overline{12}\ \overline{18}$ $\overline{12}\ \overline{8}$ $\overline{4}$ $\overline{18}\ \overline{4}\ \overline{8}\ \overline{1}\ \overline{14}\ \overline{10}$

KATIE THOMPSON

Mary's child
was almost ready to be
born when she and Joseph had
to make a long journey
to Bethlehem

**Add the numbers together to find how many
kilometres they had to travel**

25 + 13 + 10 + 27 + 15 + 17 + 13   Bethlehem

_____ **kilometres**

KATIE THOMPSON

Everyone had
to return to their home town
to be counted for the
Roman census

Find which road Joseph and Mary took

The message of Christmas

Reading

Luke 2:8-20

Aim

To remind us that, in all the fun and celebration of Christmas, there is the special message of God's coming to us in Christ.

Preparation

Print the following words in large letters on separate strips of card:

```
        PUDDING
       CAROL
          SHOPPING
         CARD
         DAY

       PARTY
         STOCKING

            TREE
     FATHER
          EVE

     PRESENTS
    CRACKER
            WHITE

          BONUS
  DECORATIONS
       FAYRE
       DINNER

       CAKE
     CACTI
   WRAPPING PAPER
        LIGHTS
```

Attach magnetic tape to the back of each piece of card.

Talk

Tell the congregation you have prepared a festive quiz for them. Explain that all the answers have 'Christmas' in them, and all they have to do is supply the missing word from the clues you give them. Read the following clues, and after each correct answer, stick the appropriate piece of card on a magnetic board, ensuring you position each one precisely as shown above:

1. Something we eat after Christmas turkey?
2. Songs we sing at Christmas?

3.   Buying in food and presents for Christmas?

4.   Something we send to our friends?

5.   Comes after Christmas Eve?

6.   A special festive occasion we might enjoy at work, school, or home?

7.   Something we hang up before going to bed on Christmas Eve?

8.   Something we bring into the house and cover in lights and decorations?

9.   Someone who comes down the chimney bringing presents?

10.   Comes before Christmas Day?

11.   Things we give to family and friends?

12.   Something we pull at Christmas?

13.   What we call Christmas when it snows?

14.   Extra pay we may be lucky enough to receive at Christmas?

15.   Things we hang on trees or round rooms and shops?

16.   A fund-raising event we may hold at church?

17.   What we tuck into as part of our celebrations?

18.   Something else we may eat at Christmas?

19.   Plants that flower around Christmas time?

20.   Something we use to cover our presents before we give them?

21.   Something we put on the Christmas tree, or which we might see in a town centre?

All these things together go to make up our celebration of Christmas; all kinds of things which we will be enjoying over this season. And there is no reason why we shouldn't have a good time and enjoy them all.

But are they finally what Christmas is about? The answer, of course, is no, but there is a danger if we focus on them too much that they may hide the true message of Christmas. In fact, they have done just that here. Ask if anyone has spotted the true message of Christmas hidden within the answers – 'Glory to the new-born king'.

These are words we sing in the great carol *Hark, the herald-angels sing*, and words which take us to the heart of Christmas – not presents or turkey or cards or pudding, special though all these may be, but the birth of Jesus Christ, the Son of God, the one who reveals the glory of God and shows his love for the world.

NICK FAWCETT

Reflective material
(sketches, meditations and poems)

Listen to Africa

Many people do not have a deep-rooted home. Even those who have to be away from home, for work or other reasons, are lonely and would welcome friendship. 'At Christmas' was written in London by Janan Saab from Lebanon.

At Christmas

I miss my children,
my home, my country,
I miss the sea
with its waves,
I miss the sunshine
with its shining rays
glittering
on the whitely dressed
mountain landscapes.

I miss my friends,
my relatives,
myself
when I was living among my folks
and felt right.
I miss what was
Christmas for me.
It doesn't seem right
with no family
nearby.

from Sharing Ways and Wisdoms by Barbara Butler

Do not call me 'Stranger'

Rafael Amor, from Zaire

Do not call me 'stranger' because in a mother's love we all receive the same light; in their songs, their kisses, close to their breast, they all dream about us being equal.

Do not call me 'stranger'. Do not think of where I came from. Better to think of our common destiny, and to look at where time is leading us.

Do not call me 'stranger' because your bread and your fire assuage my hunger and cold, and because your roof shelters me.

Do not call me 'stranger'. Your wheat is like mine and your hand like my own! And hunger, never overcome, wanders about everywhere, constantly changing its victims. And you call me 'stranger' because your way drew me and because I was born in another country; because I have known other seas and sailed from other ports. And, for all that, the handkerchiefs that wave to tell us goodbye are all the same, and the same also the eyes moistened by the tears of those we leave behind. The same are the prayers and the love of those who dream of our return.

Do not call me 'stranger'. We all cry with the same voice and share the same fatigue which we carry about since the beginning of time when frontiers had not been invented, well before the arrival of those who divide and kill, of those who sell our dreams and would, one day, invent the word 'stranger'.

Do not call me 'stranger'. It is a sad word, a cold word, evocative of exile.

Do not call me 'stranger'. Watch your son run with mine, hand in hand, until the end of the road.

Do not call me 'stranger' because they understand nothing about language, about frontiers, about flags. See them go up to the heavens: a single dove carries them, united in a single flight.

Do not call me 'stranger'. Look at me straight in the eye, beyond hatred, egotism, and fear and you will see . . . I cannot be a stranger.

from *Sharing Ways and Wisdoms* by BARBARA BUTLER

No room

Most kings warn of their coming
    with planning committees
    and security checks, red carpets
    and well-rehearsed fanfares.
But this king always comes
    unexpectedly, and in the wrong places,
    unheralded, except by unbelievable angels.
So it was no wonder when he came
    that there was no room at the inn.
Incognito, he always surprises us,
    or passes our way unrecognised.
'When did we see you, Lord?' we ask;
    and he answers:
'There was a pregnant woman
    looking for a decent place to have her baby
    and only finding a stable;
    there was an innocent man
    staring down from a cross,
    searching for humanity
    and finding no room in your hearts.'

PETER DAINTY

The Christmas story – according to the angels!

God called a meeting of his angels and archangels. 'I have decided that my Son Jesus will be born tonight as a human child in a stable in Bethlehem,' he announced as he pointed to a carefully marked 'X' on a map of Judea. 'Did he say, "stable"?' asked one of the angels. 'Yes, but I'm sure he meant to say, "palace",' added another. 'Make sure that there is plenty of hay for the manger, and clean strips of cloth handy for Mary his mother to wrap him in,' God continued.

The angels ruffled their feathers in disbelief and were deeply concerned. 'There must be some mistake!' they exclaimed. 'Surely God doesn't mean this very night! There is far too much to arrange beforehand. The angelic choirs will need more time for rehearsals, and there is so much to organise and plan before the whole world can celebrate such a unique and joyful event properly. And as for the idea of setting all this in a smelly old stable!' And great debates about God's low-key plans broke out among the ranks of angels.

To put an end to all this squabbling, the angel Gabriel, who was one of God's favourite messengers, decided to check out God's plan and get some answers from the Boss himself. God smiled and listened patiently as Gabriel carefully explained the angels' concerns that perhaps a palace would be more appropriate for the birth of his beloved Son than a stable with hay and strips of swaddling; and how they would need more time to arrange suitably important visitors to welcome this very special child into the world, because an ox and ass were all that were available at such short notice; and then there was the problem of . . .

But God stopped Gabriel before he could go any further. 'My Son will be born in humility to serve the world in humility,' he said. 'Do not worry, Gabriel, his glory and power will be revealed all in good time and according to my carefully prepared plan.'

Now Gabriel knew that although he seldom understood God's plans for the world and the people he loved above all else, they always seemed to work out just fine. After all, he had made rather a good job of creation! So after further discussion with God, Gabriel returned to the hosts of angels and explained everything the Almighty had told him.

Later that same night, everything came to be, just as God had planned. Christ the Saviour of the world was born in the humble surroundings of a simple stable, and wrapped in swaddling cloths by Mary his loving mother.

God was so touched by the concern of Gabriel and the other angels that he was persuaded to make one final adjustment to his perfect plan. And so it came about that Gabriel and his fellow angels were allowed to announce their news of great joy to an unsuspecting group of shepherds on a hillside – the only available audience at that time of night – and, despite a serious lack of rehearsal time, wow them with their enthusiastic heavenly tunes as together they sang, 'Glory to God in the highest heaven, and peace to all people on earth'.

More than two thousand years have gone by since the Son of God was born in a place called Bethlehem, and laid lovingly in a manger by Mary his mother. Every year, during the season of Advent, we remember and retell the events which led up to the birth of our Saviour, Jesus Christ. We recall that God's love for the world was, and still is, so great that he sent his only beloved Son to show us the way to his love and his kingdom.

And yet, as we are caught up in the busy preparations for the Christmas celebrations, we need to remind ourselves that Jesus isn't simply someone who belongs in the past events of two thousand years ago, or someone who has promised to return at some unknown time in the future. He is here now – God living with us in the present. We bump into him every day in the people we meet all around us. So perhaps as Christmas draws closer, we should ask ourselves, 'Do we welcome Jesus into our lives every day, or do we restrict our welcome to this special time once a year?'

KATIE THOMPSON

There's a baby in my dinner

Why are human beings so obsessed with numbers? They count everything! You wouldn't find self-respecting donkeys like us wasting all our time counting things. Life's too short for that. Humans, though – well! I know a person, not very far away, who has lots of bags full of little bits of gold. I can't see the fascination, personally – when you've seen one bit of gold you've seen them all. But he spends hours every night counting them.

Now let me see, what was I working up to? Oh, yes – the census. That's how we came to be in the silly situation we're in now. Apparently, the government had the bright idea of counting all the people. I mean, can you imagine it? How can you count people when they won't stand still for ten minutes at a time? Well, they decided to tell all the people to go back to the town where they were born and register their names; and my master, Joseph, comes from Bethlehem. Now, make no mistake, Bethlehem is a wonderful place to come from – a lousy place to go to, but wonderful to come from. Trouble was, we had to go to it. And now we're here.

To make matters worse, Joseph's wife Mary was nine months pregnant, and seemed to think that gave her the right to ride on my back everywhere. Now that's all very well, but when did you last see a pregnant donkey being given a piggyback by a human? Never. Precisely. It's species discrimination and I intend to make a complaint about it.

Anyway, that's how we came to be here. We had a terrible journey – not a service area in sight the whole way, and the road's been neglected for years. My feet are killing me – and I've got twice as many as you have! Still, we eventually got here, and I was really looking forward to a warm stable, some soft straw and a good square meal. Well, you'll never guess. All the rooms in the hotels were full – I told Joseph he should book, but would he listen? The first I knew about the problem was when I was just about to lie down on the straw and in came the innkeeper and offered Joseph and Mary my room. I don't know what the world's coming to. Not only that, but when the baby was born they put it to bed in my dinner! No kidding! Slapped it straight into the manger without so much as a 'by your leave'! Human beings really are an underdeveloped species, you know. I mean, we donkeys think nothing of having babies. We just get on with it, without fuss and bother, and when it's born it has to stand on its own feet – literally – straightaway. These humans, though, you never saw such a carry-on.

Still, I must admit there's something very special about human babies – they're sweet little things. So naturally I wanted to have a look. I wandered over to the manger – it was meant to be for me, after all – and had a look inside. As I looked in I caught the smell of the hay, and thought I'd just get a quick nibble while I was there. You'd have thought I was doing something dreadful! Mary screamed, and Joseph got hold of my collar and started to drag me away. I tell you I'd just about had enough. What with the walk, the invasion of my privacy and now not even being allowed to eat a bit of my own food. So maybe I overreacted, I don't know, but I did something that comes very naturally to us donkeys. I dug my hooves into the earth floor and refused to move an inch. Even though my feet were hurting, it was worth it. I didn't realise Joseph even knew some of the words he used! Very soon, the innkeeper and his wife came over to see what the fuss was about and I had a real live audience to play to, but they didn't stay long. The wife disappeared to the house and came back with a bucket of the most delicious-smelling oats you ever saw in your life. 'Well,' I thought. 'Somebody cares about me.' Then she went and put it the other side of the stable . . . I knew what the game was, but I decided I'd made my point. After all, we donkeys are stubborn but we're not stupid. So I walked over to the bucket and had a good feed and pretended not to notice Joseph tying me up.

Anyway, things have improved a bit now. We've got some visitors, and Mary's letting them hold the baby, which gives me a chance for a good look. Mind you, I'm not too happy about the visitors – they've got a distinct smell of sheep about them, and little bits of wool all over their clothes. They *say* they're shepherds, and they're telling some incredible story about angels coming to them and saying that a baby had been born. They say that they were so excited they left their flocks in the fields and came rushing over to see the baby. They certainly look and smell like shepherds, but I know their game. I mean, what shepherd who's any good leaves the sheep in the field at night without protection? Even if they did, they wouldn't admit it to strangers.

No – I've got their number. Oh, I'll admit they're playing the part very well, right down to the grass stains on their clothes and the mud on their sandals, but I've got them rumbled. I know travelling salesmen when I see them. You mark my words, before those people leave, Mary and Joseph will have spent money they can't afford on pretty little bootees and silly cardigans with lambs all over them – now donkeys I could understand.

Still, even though I don't like to admit it, I can see what the fuss is all about. He really does look like a pretty special baby.

(Do you think the donkey's right about the visitors?)

MICHAEL FOSTER / SIMON SMITH

Order of all-age service

A new start in valuing people
(*'A new start for the world's poor'*)

Teaching point
Everybody is a VIP. And God showed that the people we should value most are the ones who normally get left out – not because they're good, but because they have greater need. The traditional, cosy Christmas crib scene should really be turning our whole world upside down by its radical values.

Preparation
Acetates of suitable story illustrations.

Photocopy the badges on page 128 onto card and attach either a piece of stick-on Velcro or a safety pin to the back of each one.

Ask someone to be your 'assistant' for the first activity, and rehearse it carefully together so each of you knows exactly what should be happening.

Prepare people in advance to play the roles of Mary, Joseph, shepherds and wise men. The only thing they actually need to do is give the candles and the verbal charge to the various people; so clear speaking voices, and a willingness to be 'on show' are all that will be required of them. The former is especially important – you want the whole congregation to hear what they say. Write their words on card so they will read them confidently.

For the second activity, prepare eight small candles in suitable holders (simple blocks of wood with holes in them are fine).

Checklist
At the service, you will need:
- an overhead projector
- the story illustration acetates
- eight chairs, facing the congregation, for the VIPs
- the candles, placed under or near each chair (unlit!)
- a wax taper for the child who will light the candles during the service
- matches (in the safe keeping of a responsible adult until they're needed).

Service outline
(Mary, Joseph, Shepherds and Wise Men are waiting in the vestry.)

Welcome and introduction to the theme
Example:

Welcome to this service, and a very happy Christmas to you all. We're going to think about how God's coming into the world challenges and changes our values. But first, we'll sing a hymn.

Hymn or song

Prayer

Loving God, we come to celebrate this Christmas morning. Thank you for all the love you give to the world, and thank you most of all for sending Jesus to show us your love in new ways.

Please forgive us when we say or do things that make you seem unloving to others, and help us to be lights, shining in the world, a sign of your love and your care. Amen.

Activity 1

Excuse yourself for some reason – there's something you've forgotten to do – and ask your 'assistant' to take over and get the VIPs seated. As you leave, your 'assistant' asks for eight volunteers and gives each one a badge, with some verbal explanation, such as, 'You can be a local councillor'. Each of them is shown to a seat (it doesn't really matter on which of the VIP seats any particular person sits) and then the assistant can say something like, 'Well, isn't it good to have so many really important people here for our service?' That's the cue for you to return, with 'Joseph' and 'Mary', and for the 'assistant' to sit down in the congregation.

Something seems to be wrong – Mary's and Joseph's seats have been taken. Joseph is a carpenter – he's a very important member of the community – imagine nobody having any furniture in their houses! And Mary is his wife, and she's going to be a mother, and you don't get much more important than that. So the MP and the Mayor return to the congregation, *keeping their badges of office on*, and Mary and Joseph sit down. Then three 'Shepherds' arrive. What? No room for them? Well, the councillors will just have to be asked to move back to the congregation (if they do so with poor grace it will be even better!) but again, they keep their badges on. The 'Priests' could then be asked how safe they're feeling! By now, no one should be surprised when the 'Three Wise Men' enter. Foreign visitors! Now we really *must* make them welcome. So back go the three 'Priests', keeping their badges on, and the 'Wise Men' take their place.

You can then explain to the rest of the congregation that the clergy and the other VIPs weren't the only ones who were inconvenienced or sidelined on that first Christmas day – and now they're going to hear the story as seen by one of the *really* humble characters. (The new VIPs remain where they are until the end of the second activity.)

Bible-based story

There's a baby in my dinner (Luke 2:1-20) – see page 124.

Talk

Point out that the donkey wasn't the only character to find the world turned upside down by Jesus. Everybody was affected in some way, having to leave

Mayor
MP
Local Councillor
CLERGY
CLERGY
Local Councillor
Local Councillor
CLERGY

home or work, putting up with rather unpleasant conditions, etc. But most of all, the people who thought they were the VIPs had *their* world turned upside down. This was the most important event in God's entire cosmic calendar, and they weren't even there! And this foreshadowed Jesus' whole ministry of putting 'unimportant' people first, which became so threatening to the powerful people that they had to get rid of him. (That's another story of course, but it begins right here at the Nativity!) Jesus changes our values: calls us to a radical reassessment, and offers us a new start in the way we value people – and donkeys (at least he was there!).

Hymn or song

Old Testament reading
Isaiah 9:2-7

Activity 2
Explain that the displacement of the original VIPs doesn't mean they're not important – they're very important indeed. Their role is to keep the light shining – the light of justice, of peace, of compassion, and most of all, of love. They've got power – and with power goes responsibility. And it's the Church's job to ensure that they always remember that responsibility. So they are now going to come forward again. In turn, each of the new VIPs takes the candle near their chair, lets the child with the taper light it, and then hands it to one of the old VIPs with a spoken charge such as, 'Use your position of power to keep the light of God's love alight in the world'. As each is given the candle and the charge, he or she places it safely in some part of the worship area, so that the congregation is surrounded by the light of Christ for the rest of the service.

Offertory and prayer
Loving God, we thank you for sending Christ to be our light. Please take what we offer here and help us to make your light shine into the lives of people in your world. Amen.

Hymn or song
During which the 'VIP' participants join the main congregation.

Notices and family news
To feed into the Intercessions

Prayers of Intercession
Also including, for example:
   World: Dictatorship, and all places where power is misused – that people may learn the true value of one another.

Places of conflict, especially religious conflict, where the desire to be important makes people hate the fellow human beings they should love.

Church: The Church worldwide, especially where it has influence with the powerful – that it may use that to ensure good government in the world.

People: Those who find themselves adversely affected by Christmas: the poor who come under pressure to spend, the lonely who have their loneliness highlighted, etc.

Hymn or song

Blessing

MICHAEL FORSTER / SIMON SMITH

The Weeks
after Christmas

First and Second Weeks After Christmas

---

1. The Shepherds Hurry to Bethleham

A reading from the Gospel of Luke (2:16-21)

The shepherds hurried to Bethlehem and found the place where the baby lay in a manger, watched over by Mary and Joseph. The shepherds told them what they had seen and heard that night, and Mary and Joseph shared their wonder. Mary listened carefully and cherished all these things in her heart.

Then the shepherds went back to their flocks on the hillside, singing God's praises because everything had been as the angel had said.

When the time came for the child to be circumcised on the eighth day, they named him Jesus, just as the angel had told them.

This is the Gospel of the Lord
Praise to you, Lord Jesus Christ   Katie Thompson

2. The Word made Flesh

A reading from the Gospel of John (1:1-18)

At the beginning of time, the Word already existed. The Word was with God; and the Word was God. From the very beginning, all things were created through him. All life came from the Word, and this life was the light for all people. The light shines out from the darkness, and the darkness could never overcome it.

God sent a man called John, to be a witness for the light, so that others would believe because of him, even though he was not the light. The real light was the Word who was coming into the world to give light to everyone.

He was in the world created through him, and yet the world did not know him. He came to his own people and they did not accept him. To those who did receive him he gave the right to become children of God, the offspring of God himself.

The Word became flesh and he lived as a man among us. We saw his glory given by the Father to his only Son, who is full of grace and truth.

John came to be his witness and he said: 'This is the one whom I spoke of when I said, "He who succeeds me, has passed before me, because he already existed." We received God's law through Moses, but it is through Jesus Christ that we receive many gifts and his grace and truth. God has never been seen, but Jesus, his only beloved son, has made God known to us as never before, because he is very close to his Father's heart.'

This is the Gospel of the Lord
Praise to you, Lord Jesus Christ   Katie Thompson

3. Simeon rejoices in the birth of Jesus
Presentation (Luke 2:22-32)

Simeon's Nunc Dimittis *is still part of the Church's evening prayers. Those who have seen Jesus have seen all that God has to give.*

Forty days after Jesus was born
    Mary and Joseph went up to Jerusalem to be churched.
According to the Bible,
    the first boy in a family had to be taken to the temple,
    and the parents had to bring two pigeons to thank God.

An old man called Simeon happened to be in Jerusalem:
    an honest and devout man who longed
    for his people's freedom.
God had assured him he would see the Messiah before he died.
With this hope in his heart, he went up to the temple
    and at the end of the service took the baby in his arms, and said:

'Almighty Lord and Master
    at last you keep your promise,
    and give your faithful servant
    leave to go in peace.
At last I see the Saviour
    whom you have sent to free us,
    to enlighten those in darkness
    and lead us into glory.'

H. J. RICHARDS

Prayers

Thanksgiving – a time of light

Loving God,
    we thank you for the great truth we celebrate at Christmas,
      the fact that, in Christ, your light shines in the darkness
      and that nothing has ever been able to overcome it.
    Despite hostility and rejection,
      the combined forces of hatred and evil,
      still the radiance of your love continues to reach out.
    The people that walked in darkness have seen a great light:
      thanks be to God!

We thank you for the light that dawned
    in the life of Zechariah and Elizabeth,
      that transformed the future for Mary and Joseph,
      and that lit up the sky on the night of the Saviour's birth.
    The people that walked in darkness have seen a great light:
      thanks be to God!

We thank you for the light that flooded into the lives of shepherds,
    that guided wise men on their journey
    to greet the newborn king
    and that answered the prayers of Simeon and Anna.
Always you are with us,
    in life or in death leading us through the shadows.
The people that walked in darkness have seen a great light:
    thanks be to God!

We thank you for the light you brought
    through the life and ministry of Jesus –
    freedom for the captives,
    sight to the blind,
    healing for the sick,
    comfort to the broken-hearted,
    peace after confusion,
    acceptance after condemnation,
    hope after despair,
    joy after sorrow.
The people that walked in darkness have seen a great light:
    thanks be to God!

We thank you for the light that illuminates our lives today
    and which leads us step by step on our journey through life –
    the lamp of your word,
    the beacon of prayer,
    the glow of fellowship,
    the tongues of fire of your Holy Spirit,
    and the living reality of Jesus by our sides,
    the dawn from on high.
The people that walked in darkness have seen a great light:
    thanks be to God!

Loving God,
    you came to our world in Christ, bringing life and light for all.
    Shine now in our hearts
        and may the flame of faith burn brightly within us,
        so that we, in turn, may bring light to others,
        and, in so doing, bring glory to you.
    The people that walked in darkness have seen a great light:
        thanks be to God!
        Amen.

NICK FAWCETT

Petition – a time of acceptance

Gracious God,
>we thank you today for your extraordinary gift of Christ
>>and all that it points to –
>>the wonder of your love,
>>the extent of your love
>>and the constancy of your purpose.
>And we thank you for the most extraordinary thing of all,
>>that you came in Christ not simply to a few but to all –
>>to good and bad, saints and sinners,
>>to ordinary, everyday people like us.
>You reached out and accepted us as we are:
>>**teach us to accept others in turn.**

>We thank you that you chose Mary,
>>representative of the powerless,
>>to be the one to bear your Son;
>>that you chose shepherds,
>>examples of the socially marginalised,
>>to be the first to hear the good news;
>>that you chose Bethlehem,
>>symbol of the least and lowest,
>>to be the place where you were born.
>Through the manner of your coming among us,
>>and through the life you lived in Christ,
>>you repeatedly overturned this world's values and expectations,
>>demonstrating your special care
>>for the poor, the needy, the weak and the humble,
>>all those ready to admit their dependence on you
>>and seek your help.
>You reached out and accepted us as we are:
>>**teach us to accept others in turn.**

>We do not find it easy to accept others –
>>we are biased towards the attractive and the successful,
>>taken in by appearances,
>>blind to the reality beneath the surface.
>Our attitudes are shaped
>>by deep-rooted prejudices and preconceptions
>>which make us wary,
>>suspicious,
>>even hostile towards those
>>who do not conform to our flawed expectations.
>We jump to conclusions which all too often
>>say more about ourselves than anyone.

Though we claim it is wrong to judge,
    in our hearts we not only judge but condemn.
Forgive us, and remind us of the example of Christ
    whom the so-called righteous repeatedly condemned
    for associating with the unacceptable.
You reached out and accepted us as we are:
    teach us to accept others in turn.

Gracious God,
    you have a place in your heart not just for the few but for all,
        not only for the good
        but for the unlovely, the undesirable, the undeserving.
    You look deep into the hearts of all,
        and where we see ugliness, you see someone infinitely precious,
        so valuable that you were willing to endure death on a cross
        to draw them to yourself.
    Help us to recognise that no one,
        no matter who they are,
        is outside the breadth of your love or the scope of your mercy.
    You reached out and accepted us as we are:
        teach us to accept others in turn.

Through Jesus Christ our Lord.
Amen.

NICK FAWCETT

Petition – a time for reflection

Gracious God,
    there are so many lessons we can learn from this season,
        but none more important than that shown to us by Mary.
    After the events leading up to the birth of Jesus –
        the shock,
        the excitement,
        the uncertainty,
        the celebration –
        we read that she 'treasured all these words
        and pondered them in her heart'.
    While shepherds made their way home
        exulting in all they had seen and heard,
        she made time to stop
        and think
        and take stock;
        time to reflect on what it all might mean
        for herself
        and others.

You come still,
  you speak still:
  teach us to make space to listen,
  to understand
  and to respond.

Gracious God,
  teach us this Christmas-time,
    like Mary, to ponder all that you have said and done;
    to listen again to familiar readings and carols,
    to hear again the story we know so well,
    but to consider what it all might mean,
    what you are saying not just to others but also to us.
  In all the celebrations and rejoicing,
    the praise and the worship,
    help us to be still before you,
    so that our lives may be opened to your living Word,
    your renewing love
    and your redeeming power.
  You come still,
    you speak still:
    teach us to make space to listen,
    to understand
    and to respond.

Through Jesus Christ our Lord.
Amen.

NICK FAWCETT

Intercession

First Sunday after Christmas

We can see the great love of God personally in Jesus, the Christ. All the promises and hopes are fulfilled by the birth of this baby in Bethlehem, because he is the one who can set us free from our slavery to all that is evil. His salvation, beginning in Israel, extends outwards to include every created person.

Let us pray to God our Father
because he loves us so dearly.

We pray that the light of the world may shine so
brightly in our lives that other people notice it and are
attracted to you by the way we live and love.

Silence for prayer

Father, live among us:
live through our lives.

We pray that our world may stop
its noise, chatter and arguing
long enough to hear the angels
singing of hope and peace.

Silence for prayer

Father, live among us:
live through our lives.

Father, we pray for our families
and all our friends and neighbours;
may every relationship we have
be filled with your love.

Silence for prayer

Father, live among us:
live through our lives.

We pray for the homeless and all refugees and exiles;
for children from broken homes,
and all who are destitute, malnourished or ill.

Silence for prayer

Father, live among us:
live through our lives.

We pray for all from whom we are separated now
through death;
may they live in your light for ever
and may their loved ones know your comfort.

Silence for prayer

Father, live among us:
live through our lives.

Father, we can never thank you enough
for coming to rescue us,
and we praise you now and in our lives.

Silence for prayer

Merciful Father,
accept these prayers
for the sake of your Son,
our Saviour Jesus Christ, Amen.

SUSAN SAYERS

A short prayer

Loving God,
    we come today to remember with gratitude
    the birth of your Son.
We remember how prophets foretold his coming,
    and how those words were wonderfully fulfilled
    in Bethlehem.
We remember how you needed Mary
    to bring him into the world,
    and how she willingly allowed you
    to work through her.
We remember how shepherds heard the good news,
    and how, having seen the truth of it for themselves,
    they went on their way rejoicing.
We remember how Simeon held you in his arms,
    and with praise in his heart gave thanks to you.
We remember how generations since
    have seen your face revealed in Christ,
    and through him heard you speaking
    in a new way.
Lord Jesus Christ,
    we come to look back
    so that we may discover you in the present,
    and find faith for the future.
Be born in our hearts this day
    that we may be born again to eternal life.
Amen.

NICK FAWCETT

All-age-talk material

When they found Mary, Joseph and the baby what did they say?

Follow the arrow to find out!

L	R	W	H	A	L	H	O	P
P	D	M	T	A	N	E	A	B
S	T	L	E	T	G	D	O	U
B	M	H	O	H	S	I	T	T
Ⓣ	Y	T	G	L	A	D	I	H
E	H	E	S	N	C	L	E	C

Ⓣ

KATIE THOMPSON

The shepherds' visit

When the angels had left them, what did the shepherds say to one another?

Use the code to find out!

Luke 2:15-21

KATIE THOMPSON

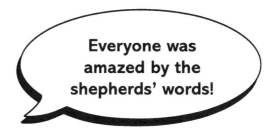

Everyone was amazed by the shepherds' words!

This code will reveal what Mary did

1	K	R	I	L
2	S	C	N	D
3	E	A	M	P
4	T	H	L	G
	✏	▲	✚	◉

2✏ 4▲ 3✏   2▲ 4▲ 3✏ 1▲ 1✚ 2✏ 4▲ 3✏ 2◉

3▲ 4✚ 4✚   4✏ 4▲ 3✏ 2✏ 3✏

4✏ 4▲ 1✚ 2✚ 4◉ 2✏   3▲ 2✚ 2◉

1✏ 3✏ 3◉ 4✏   4✏ 4▲ 3✏ 3✚

1✚ 2✚   4▲ 3✏ 1▲

4▲ 3✏ 3▲ 1▲ 4✏

Luke 2:19

KATIE THOMPSON

Headlines – news travels fast

Take ten cards and write the following headlines:

'Budgie eats tube of Smarties!'

'Sales of coloured tissues drop'

'Two injured in ice-cream fight!'

'Forty witnesses to chocolate bar theft'

'Lorry carrying paint overturns. Multicoloured motorway'

'Police fear local car thief may strike again'

'Government declare national holiday every Monday'

'Island disappears after volcanic eruption'

'United Nations calls for world-wide nuclear testing ban'

'Local man swallows Guinness book of records!'

Show each headline to the group. For each headline ask the group whether it should be reported in the local newspaper or national newspaper; on local radio or national radio; local TV or national TV?

Pete Townsend

Read John 1:1-18

John writes that in the beginning was the 'Word'. The term 'in the beginning' is to remind the reader of Genesis, the first book of the Old Testament. It is a reminder of the creation, the beginning of the world.

John is saying, particularly to those readers with a Jewish background, that Jesus was God's spoken Word which brought about creation. The 'Word', Jesus, gave life and light (verses 3-4) to the world when it was dark and without form. In other words, Jesus is the life-force by which everything exists. John then tells us that this light (verse 5), which lit up creation, can never be put out; it cannot be extinguished!

Now God's Word, Jesus, who had brought light and life to creation, was coming into the world to bring light where there was darkness (sin) and life where there was death (evil). John says that the Word became a human being (verse 14) and lived 'here with us'. That is to say, Jesus knows the problems we have and he wants to bring us light and life. Jesus doesn't want our problems to fester in the darkness or cause us pain. He would rather 'live with us' and help us overcome those problems. This is what the angels were rejoicing about. This is why they were so happy to see the 'Word' of God coming into the world to be light and life for us.

Pete Townsend

Reflective material
(sketches, meditations and poems)

Meditation of Simeon

It was as though a wave of peace engulfed me,
   a great surge of tranquillity flooding my soul
   with a quietness beyond expression –
   for I held him in my arms,
   God's promised Messiah –
   there, in that little wrinkled face,
   that tiny, vulnerable child staring up at me,
   the fulfilment of God's eternal purpose.
I just can't tell you what that meant to me,
   not only the joy but the relief I felt,
   for there had been times when my faith had begun to waver.
No, I don't just mean my conviction
   that I'd see the Messiah's coming,
   though I did question that sometimes, it's true.
It went deeper than that,
   to the very heart of my faith,
   to those words of the prophet
   about us being a light to the Gentiles,
   bringing glory to God through our life and witness.
I'd always believed that implicitly,
   the vision stirring my imagination and firing my faith,
   but over the years the flame had begun to splutter,
   doused by the harsh realities which surrounded me.
The fact is we'd turned inwards rather than outwards,
   our concern more for ourselves than the world beyond,
   and, if anything, our horizons were growing narrower by the day.
It was understandable, of course,
   the oppression we'd suffered across the centuries
   enough to dampen anyone's fervour,
   but that didn't make it any easier to stomach,
   still less offer any grounds for hope.
Could things change, I wondered?
Was there really any chance we might recapture that old spark,
   that sense of sharing in the divine purpose,
   testifying to his glory,
   or was that dream destined to die for ever?
It was impossible not to ask it.
But that day, there in the temple, suddenly it all changed –
   faith vindicated,
   hope realised –

for I knew then beyond all doubt
that God had been faithful to his purpose,
his chosen servant there in my arms,
the one who would bring light to the world,
salvation to all.
I saw him with my own eyes,
touched him with my own hands,
and after that I could die happy,
my joy complete,
my faith rekindled,
my soul at peace.

NICK FAWCETT

Meditation of John the Apostle

'Where did it all start?' they ask me.
'Tell us the story again.'
And I know just what they want to hear –
about the inn and the stable,
the baby lying in a manger,
shepherds out in the fields by night,
and wise men travelling from afar.
I know why they ask, of course I do,
for which of us hasn't thrilled to those marvellous events,
that astonishing day when the Word became flesh,
dwelling here on earth amongst us?
Yet wonderful though that all is, it's not where it started,
and if we stop there, then we see only a fraction of the picture,
the merest glimpse of everything God has done for us in Christ.
We have got to go right back to see more –
before Bethlehem,
before the prophets
before the Law,
before time itself, would you believe? –
for that's where it started:
literally 'in the beginning'.
Yes, even there the saving purpose of God was at work,
his creating, redeeming Word
bringing light and love into the world,
shaping not just the heavens and the earth
but the lives of all,
every man, woman and child.
That's the mind-boggling wonder of it –
the fact not just that God made us,

but that through Christ he was determined from the outset
    to share our lives,
    to take on our flesh,
    to identify himself totally with the joys and sorrows,
    the beauty and the ugliness of humankind.
It defies belief, doesn't it?
Yet it's true –
    God wanting us to know him not as his creatures
    but as his children,
    not as puppets forced to dance to his tune
    but as people responding freely to his love;
    and to achieve that he patiently and painstakingly prepared the way,
    revealing year after year a little more of his purpose,
    a glimpse more of his kingdom,
    until at last,
    in the fullness of time,
    the Word became flesh and lived among us,
    full of grace and truth.
It wasn't an afterthought, the incarnation,
    a last-ditch attempt to make the best of a bad job –
    it was planned from the dawn of time.
So next time you hear the story of the stable and the manger,
    of the shepherds gazing in wonder
    and the magi kneeling in homage,
    stop for a moment
    and reflect on everything which made it all possible,
    the eternal purpose which so carefully prepared the way of Christ,
    and then ask yourself this:
    are you prepared to respond to his coming?

NICK FAWCETT

Reflecting on John 1:1-11

This beginning, with the repeated phrase, 'came into being' takes us back to the miracle of life itself – the amazing fact that anything exists at all and not nothing! But the passage does more than celebrate the miracle of biological life, it opens up the mystery of what it means to be, to have a 'soul' – a spiritual and moral centre that responds to God and can give itself away in love. This love is the key to the meaning of the universe. The good news is that this Mystery of Being, of self-transcending love which began everything has lived amongst us, in the man Jesus. John saw his glory and so can anyone see and share in this glory – who believes.

PATRICK WOODHOUSE

Reflecting on Luke 2:22-40

The Presentation of Christ in the Temple . . . takes us back into Jesus' infancy and to two devout old people who had been waiting all their lives for 'the consolation of Israel'. At the heart of the Gospel is the *Nunc Dimittis*, a great cry of fulfilment – at last the consolation has come. The coming means both the consolation of Israel and, for this faithful old man, the end of long years of patient believing. His faith is finally vindicated. The tone is one of triumphant but humble gratitude. Cradling the child in his arms he exclaims, 'My eyes have seen . . . !'

   Prayer can mean long periods of waiting and believing, often in darkness; but in the end, God will always come.

PATRICK WOODHOUSE

Never mind the sheep, look for the baby

Based on Luke 2:8-20

Narrator	Jed and Enoch were shepherds. And Jed was rather a grumpy one – at least on this particular night.
Jed	It's no good, we've got to get out of this business.
Enoch	Oh yes? And what would you do instead?
Jed	I don't know, but not this. All we do is sit out here all night, watching sheep, and we can't even go into the town for a drink, because the people all tell us to go away.
Enoch	Well, you must admit that this isn't the cleanest job in the world.
Narrator	Jed was about to make a rather rude reply when he noticed something strange. The sky was getting light.
Jed	Wow! The night went quickly!
Enoch	That's not the dawn. There's something funny going on.
Narrator	What happened next made Jed wish he'd kept his big mouth shut about being bored! There, before his very eyes, stood an angel. Well, I say 'stood' – 'hovered' might be a better word, because he didn't seem to have his feet on the ground – he was just, sort of, *there*! Jed was terrified! What do you think he did?

* He *covered his eyes*, but he could still hear!
* He *covered his ears*, but then he could still see!
* So he *tried to do both at once*.
     But then he could see *and* hear!

Enoch	Wh-wh-what d'you think we ought to do?
Jed	(*Aside, to audience*) Well! Talk about a silly question! (*To Enoch*) Run like mad! What else!

Angel	Now don't be silly, I'm not going to hurt you. All I want to do is give you a message. Great news – about a special baby who's been born in Bethlehem. His name is Jesus, and he's going to save the world.
Jed	I'm sorry I said life was boring. Can you make it boring again, please? I promise I won't complain any more!
Angel	I'll tell you what; this will prove it to you. Go to Bethlehem, and look for a baby wrapped in swaddling clothes and lying in a cattle feeding trough.
Enoch	Which feeding trough?
Jed	Goodness me, there's thousands of them!
Enoch	That's what I mean.
Jed	Not feeding troughs, you fool – angels!
Narrator	And so there were! The sky was full of angels having a real whoopee of a time! Then, all of a sudden, they'd gone! Just like that! The field was dark again, just as it had been before.
Jed	What do you think we should do?
Enoch	Now who's asking silly questions! Go to Bethlehem.
Jed	We can't do that! Who'll look after the sheep?
Enoch	Never mind the sheep! We've got to look for the baby! After all your complaining about life being boring, then at a time like this you want to count sheep!
Narrator	So they set off for the town. They found Joseph and Mary with their little baby, Jesus. And the baby, just as the angel said, was wrapped in swaddling clothes, and lying in the hay in the feeding trough.
Enoch	Perhaps now you'll stop moaning about life being dull!
Jed	Me? When did you ever hear me complain about that?

MICHAEL FORSTER

The shepherds

Luke 2:8-20

The shepherds watched their flocks by night,
   and saw angels –
   while townsmen, sleeping
   in a noisier, narrower world,
   blinkered against the light,
   deaf to eternal voices,

waking only to complete the daily schedule,
saw and heard
nothing.

And the shepherds,
seeing angels,
did not then disperse the vision
with cool reason,
raising mental barricades
to blot out the light,
but received the message
with unquestioning joy,
open-mouthed,
yet speechless.

And these same poor shepherds,
unembarrassed by the stable
and the Saviour's poverty,
gladly adored him,
overawed by the very lowliness
which would have repelled
those richer in possessions,
but with ragged souls.

So the shepherds,
being ready to receive from God with honest faith,
were as wise in their way
as the bringers of gold, frankincense and myrrh.

PETER DAINTY

Prologue

The stage is set in darkness. Off-stage (this could be prerecorded if possible and played over the PA) an actor speaks:

Narrator 1 In the beginning

The second and third narrators need to speak as an echo, to create an atmosphere and add depth to what is being said

Narrator 2 the beginning

Narrator 3 the beginning

Narrator 1 was the Word

Narrator 2 the Word

Narrator 3 the Word

Narrator 1 and the Word was with God

Narrator 2	with God
Narrator 3	with God
Narrator 1	and the Word was God
Narrator 2	was God
Narrator 3	was God
Narrator 1	He was with God
Narrator 2	with God
Narrator 3	with God
Narrator 1	in the beginning
Narrator 2	the beginning
Narrator 3	the beginning
Narrator 1	through him
Narrator 2	through him
Narrator 3	through him
Narrator 1	all things were made
Narrator 2	were made
Narrator 3	were made
Narrator 1	In him was life
Narrator 2	was life
Narrator 3	was life
Narrator 1	and that life was the light of men
Narrator 2	the light
Narrator 3	the light
Narrator 1	The light shines in the darkness
Narrator 2	the light shines
Narrator 3	the light shines
	On the line 'The light shines' spotlights hit the stage
Narrator 1	but the darkness has not overcome it
Narrator 2	not overcome
Narrator 3	not overcome.
	More lights on stage
Narrator 1	The Word

Narrator 2   the Word

Narrator 3   the Word

Narrator 1   became . . .

A cry of a baby is heard

Narrator 2   flesh.

TONY BOWER

The Wise Men Visit Jesus

Epiphany Sunday

A reading from the Gospel of Matthew (2:1-12)

Jesus was born in Bethlehem, a small town in Judea when King Herod ruled the land. Some wise men from the east travelled to Jerusalem and asked King Herod where they could find the newborn King of the Jews whom they had come to worship.

Herod was greatly troubled because he didn't want anyone else to be king, so he sent for his advisers. 'Tell me where this child, the so-called King, will be born,' he said.

'It has been foretold by the prophets that he will be born in Bethlehem,' they answered.

For the prophets had written:

And you, Bethlehem in Judea,
are not the least important among Judean cities,
for from you a leader will come,
a shepherd for my people Israel!

King Herod sent for the wise men privately, and asked them to tell him exactly when the star had first appeared. Then he said to them, 'I will allow you to search for this child, but you must come back and tell me where to find him. Then I too can go and honour him.'

The wise men set off again on their journey. They followed the bright star until it appeared to stop over a house, where they found Mary with the baby Jesus. They were filled with wonder and joy, and, falling to their knees to worship him, they gave him gifts of gold, frankincense and myrrh.

An angel warned them in a dream not to return to Herod's palace, so they went back to their own country a different way.

This is the Gospel of the Lord
Praise to you, Lord Jesus Christ

KATIE THOMPSON

Introductory material

Epiphany rarely feels as celebratory as the rest of Christmas. It marks fairly closely the end of an old year, the end of holidays from school and work, and the end of decorations and celebrations for another eleven months. Perhaps this comes as a relief, but it can also seem a bit of a letdown after all the excitement. For the western Church, Epiphany celebrates the visit of the magi to the infant Christ, and his revelation to the Gentiles. In other Christian traditions the emphasis is on his baptism and the start of his earthly ministry – the Revised Common Lectionary identifies the first Sunday of Epiphany as the feast day for the Baptism of the Lord. Church calendars may make it more practical to use one of the other Sundays of Epiphany for ecumenical activity (Epiphanytide lasts until Candlemas on 2 February), and Christian Unity is a now major theme of this season, since it contains the Week of Prayer for Christian Unity. This is recognised and marked by most mainstream Churches and has a section of its own later in this book.

On an ecumenical level, Epiphany is a great opportunity for a fresh expression of commitment to working more closely together in mission. In many areas the local Churches now unite every few years expressly to bring the good news of Jesus Christ to their community. Since planning for such events invariably takes many months, Epiphany is the ideal point at which to launch a year of mission and evangelism, even though the focal point will probably lie some way ahead.

At this time of year Methodist congregations hold their annual 'Covenant Service', and in some places like to invite members of other Churches and Christian traditions to share in this act of commitment with them, though the Covenant itself could be used in any service which emphasises discipleship and devotion.

Epiphany carol services and processions are the traditional liturgies for this season, though a major ecumenical celebration in addition to whatever is done during the Week of Prayer for Christian Unity may prove impractical. *The Promise of His Glory* also provides a liturgy for Anglicans to renew their own baptismal promises, though this would be difficult to extend to other traditions with a different view of the sacrament of baptism.

STUART THOMAS

Prayers

Epiphany confession

Loving God,
    you guided the wise men to Bethlehem,
        offering a light for their path,
        and in faith they responded.
    Forgive us that all too often we fall short of their example.
    Gracious Lord,
        have mercy.

You offer us guidance in innumerable ways –
    through the light of your word,
    the illumination of your Holy Spirit,

the fellowship of your Church,
and the encounter of prayer –
yet so often we either fail to hear or refuse to see.
Gracious Lord,
   have mercy.

We are too preoccupied with our own small affairs,
   eyes only for the immediate moment,
   our vision impeded by trivial concerns,
   so we fail to recognise where you are leading us.
Gracious Lord,
   have mercy.

We believe we know just where we are going,
   just what we want from life,
   and exactly how we can get it,
   and we resist any suggestion that we need to think again.
Gracious Lord,
   have mercy.

Loving God,
   forgive us our foolishness,
      our stubbornness,
      our weakness.
Gracious Lord,
   have mercy.

Forgive our pride,
   our lack of faith,
   our closed minds.
Gracious Lord,
   have mercy.

Forgive us for ignoring your guidance,
   for resisting your will,
   and as a result so often walking in darkness.
Gracious Lord,
   have mercy.

Meet with us again we ask,
   and may the light of your love shine in our hearts,
so that we cannot but see it or fail to respond
in grateful praise and joyful service.
Gracious Lord,
   have mercy,
   in the name of Christ.
Amen.

NICK FAWCETT

Intercession

Wise men from distant countries were led to worship Jesus. The light of the living Christ also leads us, and when our lives reflect his light, many others will be drawn to worship the true God who made us and loves us.

Fellow travellers of Christ's Way,
let us pray together for the Church and for the world.

Father, may our Christian witness,
in a confused and nervous world,
shine with a piercing integrity and warmth
that awakens people's hearts to the love of their Creator.
Silence for prayer
Light of the nations:
shine in our lives.

Bless and protect all travellers and pilgrims;
teach us to cherish the beauty of our world
and share its riches.
Silence for prayer
Light of the nations:
shine in our lives.

Help us to see Christ in the eyes of all those we meet,
and delight in giving you glory
by serving others without expecting rewards.
Silence for prayer
Light of the nations:
shine in our lives.

Direct our vision to see
the best practical ways of providing shelter
for the homeless, safe accommodation
for those who live in fear of violence,
and food for the hungry.
Silence for prayer
Light of the nations:
shine in our lives.

May all who have died in faith
be bathed in the everlasting light
of your loving presence,
and may those who mourn be comforted.
Silence for prayer

Light of the nations:
shine in our lives.

In thankfulness, Father,
we offer you our lives.
Silence for prayer

Merciful Father,
accept these prayers
for the sake of your Son,
our Saviour Jesus Christ, Amen.

SUSAN SAYERS

A short prayer

Lord Jesus Christ,
    you have told us to seek and we shall find.
Yet that search is not always easy.
As we look for meaning in our lives,
    there is so much that puzzles and perplexes.
The more we discover
    the more we realise how little we have understood.
Give us the determination of the wise men
    to keep on looking,
    despite all that obscures you,
    until at last we find the journey rewarded
    and discover you for ourselves.
Amen.

NICK FAWCETT

Two Persian prayers

There are two modern prayers by different Persian Christians that I say regularly,
and which are a source of joy and comfort to me. The first says:

Lord Jesus Christ, at your birth
    your ever blessed Mother received on your behalf
    from my ancestors the Magi
    the most valuable gifts they had;
    grant, I beseech of you,
    that I, a Persian of the twentieth century,
    may also, by her holy intercessions,
    find the humble offering of all that I have,
    and all that I am,
    equally received by you,
    now and for all the days of my life.
Amen.

The second one is similar:

Almighty God,
  who when you sent your blessed Son Jesus Christ
  into the world for our salvation,
  didst give to our ancestors the Magi
  the grace and honour of admittance to his presence,
  grant that we, Persians of the twenty-first century,
  may also, like them, be granted the same grace,
  thus entering into the fuller inheritance of our forefathers,
  to the glory of your Holy Name.
Amen.

from *Sharing Ways and Wisdoms* by BARBARA BUTLER

All-age-talk material

LED TO JESUS

```
F O L L O W E D Q J
A P B C F I E D R E
H D R G E S S I M S
X L A E M E N P Y U
B O E K S D E J R S
W G A V E E C H R S
S Z G C L T N O H U
Y T B Y F X I T V T
Z M A N D W T D S H
A N O R N Q G C K E
```

THE WISE MEN
FOLLOWED A STAR
AND GAVE JESUS
PRESENTS: GOLD
INCENSE, MYRRH.

Can you help the wise men
to find JESUS?
Join the stars!

SUSAN SAYERS

The Epiphany of our Lord

Theme: The Wise Men come to Jesus

Tell or read the story of the wise men, with their gifts displayed on the table. (The Palm Tree Bible Stories version is called *Following a Star*.) If possible, have something of real gold, a thurible with incense burning, and some anointing oil. Talk about these things, and how we use them in our worship (or way of showing the 'worth') of our God. How can we give God a present?

Wrap each child in Christmas wrapping paper and give each a label to write and decorate, thread on wool and hang round their neck. At the offering of gifts, let the 'presents' walk up to give themselves. The labels can be collected and blessed before they are returned to the children.

THEY FOLLOWED THE STAR AND FOUND JESUS. Matthew 2:1-12, 19-23

Which way did the star lead them?

A	G	D	E	D	O	R	E	H	F	L	B
W	W	O	L	L	O	F	I	R	X	Q	F
O	B	R	R	O	D	S	D	R	E	A	M
L	W	C	P	A	G	K	H	Y	C	O	E
L	M	V	J	Y	T	T	E	M	E	N	H
O	Z	F	P	I	H	S	R	O	W	N	L
F	R	A	N	K	I	N	C	E	N	S	E
D	A	U	B	W	D	G	I	K	S	Y	J

GOLD   FOLLOW
FRANKINCENSE   STAR
MYRRH   HEROD
WISE   DREAM
MEN   WORSHIP

Following the signs

Aim: For them to explore the link between God's guidance and our willingness to follow.

First have a number of star-shaped cards placed words down. In turn, people select a card and read what it says. They then choose whether to do what it says or not. They will find that these instructions lead them on to another, which again they can choose either to take on board or not. Here are some suggestions for the cards – you can add other particularly relevant ones for your group.

1. Ask Andrew to read you Luke 6:27
2. Work with Sam to find Jeremiah 17:7-8
3. Ask Jane to read you Matthew 18:1-4
4. Work with Ben to find John 6:35

Show a star, and talk about (or read in Matthew 2) how the wise men were not only shown the sign in the sky, but also chose to follow it. The star wasn't always visible; when it wasn't they had to wait expectantly for it, rather than rushing on in the wrong direction. Then read the Gospel for today – what sign was John the Baptist given to guide him?

We are shown guidelines and instructions in our daily Bible reading and prayer life, and also through conversations and events in our life. We decide with our wills whether or not to take notice of them or not.

SUSAN SAYERS

The three kings

Read the story of the three kings [three wise men] from Matthew 2:1-12 or tell it in your own words.

Explore some of the issues in the story:
– How did the kings feel when they reached Herod's palace?
– Were they weary with the journey?
– Did they feel like giving up when the new king was not there?
– Did they trust Herod's invitation to come back to see them again?
– What did they feel like when the star led them to the cattle shed?
– What did they feel about the gifts they had brought?
– How did Herod feel when the kings arrived?
– What was the reaction of Mary and Joseph when they saw the kings?

Encourage the children to imagine themselves as one of the kings, Herod, one of Herod's advisers, Mary or Joseph.

Read or tell the story a second time, giving time afterwards to explore the children's observations.

JILL FULLER

Ending Prayer

Lord, sometimes we feel we must follow our star on a special journey.
Sometimes the way is difficult and the journey long and hard.
Sometimes the journey is full of surprises.
Sometimes the ending is unexpected.
Help us always to be ready, like the wise men, to continue travelling,
  to lay our gifts at the manger and worship the newborn King.
  Amen.

JILL FULLER

Ideas for activities

Have a 'follow-my-leader' game, making a 'conga' type line and going wherever the leader takes them. Now give the leader a star to carry, and everyone follows the star, going over things, round things and through things on the way. Let it lead them to a crib scene, or a picture of Jesus and the wise men, so the children can see what presents have been brought.

SUSAN SAYERS

The gifts

Give each member of the group a piece of paper and a pen. Ask the group if there was any gift that was missing from their Christmas wish list. Is there something that they would like to make sure goes on this year's list? Suggest that they write on the paper the name of one gift that they would like to receive. It doesn't matter at this stage whether it is extravagant or expensive. When they have finished ask them to place the paper out of sight and forget about it for a few minutes.

Read Matthew 2:1-12

The account of the visit to the infant Jesus, by the wise men (or 'Magi') was the fulfilment of a promise that had been made by the prophet Micah, who lived near a village called Gath, about twenty-five miles from Bethlehem. Micah had written, over 800 years before the birth of Jesus, that a Messiah would be born in Bethlehem (Matthew 2:5-6 and Micah 5:2).

The wise men had travelled a great distance over a long time to find the 'king of the Jews'. To this baby they brought gifts of gold, frankincense and myrrh. Each of the gifts has a significant meaning for Jesus.

- Gold is a symbol of something of genuine worth, of great value. It is a gift which was used in the Old Testament to decorate the Temple and was also used as a sign of royalty.
- Frankincense has a sweet odour and was used by the priests in the Temple. One of the main duties of the priest was to make an offering to God of an animal which was sacrificed in place of the people. The Latin word for priest is *pontifex*, which literally means a bridge-builder.
- Myrrh was a perfume used to anoint the bodies of the dead.

These gifts pointed to the mission of Jesus. He was the Messiah, a holy king who is the 'bridge-builder' between us and God. To bridge the gap Jesus was to suffer and die as the ultimate sacrifice. He paid the price. The gifts of the wise men were symbols relating to the greatest gift of all, the gift of Jesus who makes it possible for us to have a relationship with God.

Ask the group to look at the gift ideas they wrote on their piece of paper. Turn the idea around. Suggest that the group might like to think about what gifts they could give to somebody. Encourage them to think of people they know and what those people need. What would improve the quality of their lives? Write the ideas down on the piece of paper, fold it up and place the paper on a plate or in a bag which will be placed in a prominent spot.

PETE TOWNSEND

Reflective material
(sketches, meditations and poems)

Wise men's gifts

Whatever happened to the Magi's gold, Lord Jesus?
Did it fall into the hands of Herod's men,
   when you fled from Bethlehem?
Or maybe it dropped off the back of a camel
   on the road into Egypt
   and was picked up by the greedy fingers
   of a passing merchant?
Otherwise, how does that gold,
   symbol of the whole wealth of the whole world,
   given to you by wise men for safe keeping,
   now come to be in the hands of the minions of Mammon,
   the manipulators of money markets,
   the profiteers and speculators,
   the fraudulent, the affluent and the corpulent?
Surely this is not what it means when it says
   that you became poor, that we might become rich.
Call on new wise men, O Christ,
   to give you back your gold,
   because it's burning holes in humanity.

And what about the frankincense, Lord,
   symbol of religion?
Did your mother drop it in the temple,
   to be claimed by the authorities
   and piped down a succession of priests and prophets,
   crowd-stirrers and heart-throbs,
   its mesmerising smoke wafting by the nostrils

of centuries of idols,
    to the accompaniment of holy turnstile music?
Take back the frankincense, O Christ,
    before we are choked by the stink
    of the worship of false gods.

But the myrrh, the symbol of death,
    and most unlikely of birthday presents,
    you did not lose.
You kept it, without ever needing it;
    for, having died,
    your body could not be found to be embalmed,
    and you could not simply be preserved
    as a fragrant memory.
Instead, your living Spirit strides the world,
    looking for those who are wise enough
    to give you back the incense and the gold.   PETER DAINTY

Brighter than the moon

Lord Jesus Christ,
    you are brighter than the moon,
    more powerful than the sun,
    more beautiful than the stars
    and stronger than the wind.

You are the life-giving water
    that can make gardens
    in the desert.

Take our frail lives
    and fill them with yourself.

So what wherever we go
    parched ground
    will become moist,
    flowers will unfold
    and trees will bear fruit.

Then there will
    be seen in us
    your brightness,
    your power,
    your beauty
    and your strength.

For in you are hidden
    all the secrets of heaven's wisdom
    and all its shining treasure.   MARY HATHAWAY

Meditation of the wise men

We knew it would be worth it the moment we saw the star,
    worth the hassle,
    worth the effort,
    worth the sacrifice.
But there were times when we wondered, I can tell you!
As we laboured over those dusty barren tracks,
    as we watched fearfully for bandits in the mountains,
    as the sun beat down without a break,
    and still no sign of an end to it,
    we wondered, all too often.
We asked ourselves whether we'd got it wrong,
    misread the signs.
We argued over whether we'd taken the wrong turning
    somewhere along the way.
We questioned the wisdom of carrying on as the days dragged by.
And when finally we got to Jerusalem
    only to find his own people had no idea what was going on,
    then we really became worried.
Quite astonishing – the biggest event in their history,
    and they didn't even realise it was happening!
Thankfully they looked it up, eventually,
    somewhere in one of their old prophets,
    and we knew where to go then.
It was all there in writing if only they'd taken the trouble to look –
    God knows why they couldn't see it!
Anyway, we made it at last,
    tired, sore and hungry,
    but we made it.
And it was worth it, more than we had ever imagined,
    for in that child was a different sort of king,
    a different sort of kingdom,
    from any we'd ever encountered before.
As much our ruler as theirs,
    as much our kingdom as anyone's.
So we didn't just present our gifts to him,
    we didn't just make the customary gestures of acknowledgement.
We fell down and worshipped him.
Can you imagine that?
Grown men,
    respected,
    wealthy,
    important,
    kneeling before a toddler.
Yet it seemed so natural,
    the most natural response we could make,
    the only response that would do!

NICK FAWCETT

Order of service

The following outline picks up the themes of revelation and personal commitment to provide a liturgy which can be used by Churches worshipping together at the start of any year, though especially one looking forward to a time of mission and evangelism.

Opening response

The whole earth is covered
with the darkness of sin and despair.
Arise, shine, for our light has come;
the Lord's glory is rising upon us.

The people of the earth are wandering
in deep darkness and confusion.
Arise, shine, for our light has come;
the Lord's glory is rising upon us.

The nations of the earth will come to the light of Christ,
their leaders as they see the brightness of his dawn.
Arise, shine, for our light has come;
the Lord's glory is rising upon us.

Carol

O worship the Lord in the beauty of holiness (HON* 394)

Confession

Lord Jesus Christ,
you reveal your truth to us,
but we fail to understand or obey your will for our lives.
Forgive our stubbornness;
help us to see your glory.

Lord Jesus Christ,
you reveal your compassion to us,
but we fail to show it to others.
Forgive our selfishness;
help us to see your glory.

Lord Jesus Christ,
you reveal your power to us,
but we prefer to trust our own strength.
Forgive our wilfulness;
help us to see your glory.

Lord Jesus Christ,
you reveal God to us

*HON refers to *Hymns Old and New* (Kevin Mayhew)

as Father, Son and Holy Spirit,
perfect in unity,
but we persist in our divisions
and maintain our differences.
Forgive our disunity;
help us to see your glory,
the glory of the Father's only Son,
and to bear witness to the Word
who became flesh and lived among us,
for his name's sake.
Amen.

Absolution

May God in his mercy draw you to himself,
forgive all your sins and pardon your wrongdoing,
and grant you a vision of his glory,
that through you Christ may be revealed
to all the world,
in whose name we pray.
Amen.

Hymn

Faithful vigil ended (HON 118)

Old Testament reading

Isaiah 49:6b-13

Psalm

May God be gracious to us and bless us;
Lord, make your face shine upon us.

May God's power be known on the earth;
Lord, show the nations your saving power.

May God be praised by all people;
Lord, let all the peoples praise you.

May the nations be glad and sing for joy;
Lord, guide them in their ways
and judge them with your righteousness.
May God bless us
with the riches of his creation;
Lord, continue to bless us,
that the ends of the earth may honour your name.

Let all the peoples praise you, O God,
Let all the peoples praise you.
Amen.
(from Psalm 67)

Hymn

God of mercy, God of grace (HON 175)

New Testament reading

1 Peter 2:4-10

Response

How beautiful on the mountains
are the feet of him who brings good news,
proclaiming peace and salvation;
say to the people: 'Your God reigns'.

Burst into songs of joy together,
for the Lord has brought comfort to his people;
say to the people: 'Your God reigns'.

All the ends of the earth will see
the salvation of our God;
say to the people: 'Your God reigns'.

Hymn

How lovely on the mountains (HON 219)

Gospel reading

Matthew 2:1-12

Sermon/Meditation

Procession

The gifts offered could be either twentieth-century equivalents of those offered by the magi, or those which members of the congregation are offering to assist in the mission project which the local Churches are launching. If the former, representatives of three Churches should bring to the altar or Communion table symbolic gold, incense and myrrh. If the latter, invite all members of the congregation to write on a slip of paper what help they might offer to an overall mission event. If each seat has a slip of paper on it when people arrive, these can be collected up by a number of representatives and presented in the same way, or if necessary incorporated into the offering. Quiet music could be played while this happens, or a hymn sung – for example 'At this time of giving' (HON 47). As gifts are offered, the following response could be used:

Whoever sows generously will also reap generously.
Thanks be to God for his indescribable gift.

Intercession

With the wise men
we follow the guiding star to Bethlehem,
bringing gifts to offer to Christ our King.
Lord, receive this offering,
and hear our prayers.

Gold speaks of wealth and power,
kingship and government.
We bring to God the nations of the world
and their leaderships,
those who hold high office
in our nation and local community,
those with responsibility for money,
and those in the public eye, especially . . .
May they place in your hands
the influence and resources at their disposal,
to bring relief to the poor and justice to all.
Lord, receive this offering,
and hear our prayers.

Incense speaks of prayer and devotion,
worship and praise.
We bring to God our Churches
both in this local community
and throughout the world,
that Christians may put aside their differences
and through worshipping
and serving God together
demonstrate the unity which Christ has won
for his people.
We pray especially for . . .
May all Christians proclaim your truth
with one voice
and show your love with one heart.
Lord, receive this offering,
and hear our prayers.

Myrrh speaks of suffering and death,
pain and distress.
We bring to God all who are suffering
through ill-health or depression,
anxiety or grief, ill-treatment or exploitation,
mentioning by name . . .
May they know the peace and comfort
of your presence

in their current distress
and the healing touch of your hand.
Lord, receive this offering,
and hear our prayers.

All of our gifts, all of our life
we offer to the infant king.
As he ministers to us
so may we with our gifts
minister his love and compassion
to our world.
This we ask in his name and for his glory.
Amen.

Alternatively, each bidding can end with '. . . and hear our prayers', the congregation responding by using a well-known Taizé chant, e.g. 'In the Lord I'll be ever thankful' (HON 250) or 'Ubi caritas' (HON 525).

Our Father . . .

Song
Let there be love (HON 298)

Final response
We offer to God the worship of our lips and our lives:
Lord, you have given us this world
and its resources;
make us good stewards
of all you have entrusted to us,
and keep us faithful to our calling.

Lord, you have placed us in families and communities;
make us good neighbours to those around,
and keep us faithful to our calling.

Lord, in Christ you have forgiven all our sins
of thought and speech, action and inaction;
make us willing to forgive those
who wrong us,
and keep us faithful to our calling.
Lord, you have given us eternal life
and the hope of heaven;
make us faithful witnesses
to the joy of your kingdom,
and keep us faithful to our calling.

Lord, you have called us
to show your limitless love
in acts of service and compassion;
make us worthy servants,
**and keep us faithful to our calling.
Accept the worship of our lips and lives,
strengthen us in faith,
and make us one as you are one,
through Jesus Christ our Lord.
Amen.**

Hymn

From the sun's rising (HON 150)

Blessing

God our Father has called us
from darkness into his wonderful light;
**may he shine on our path
and guide our footsteps.
Amen.**

Jesus Christ his Son is the Light of the World;
**may he bring light to our lives
and banish all darkness.
Amen.**

God the Holy Spirit enlightens our minds
and fills us with his love;
**may he shine through our lives
and draw others to the love of God.
Amen.**

The blessing of God Almighty,
Father, Son and Holy Spirit,
be among us and remain with us
today and always. Amen.
or
**The grace of our Lord Jesus Christ,
the love of God,
and the fellowship of the Holy Spirit
be with us all evermore.
Amen.**

Choral music

Coming at the end of the Christmas season, Epiphany itself can still provide a suitable setting for some of the Christmas anthems, especially those associated with the visit of the magi. Harold Darke's setting of 'In the bleak mid-winter' and Peter Cornelius' 'The three kings' spring immediately to mind, while Carols Old and New *has straightforward choral settings of such favourites as 'As with gladness', 'We three kings' and 'The first nowell'. However, there are plenty of options if you prefer to emphasise the themes of mission and evangelism to all people: Handel's great chorus from the Messiah, 'And the glory of the Lord shall be revealed', is particularly appropriate. From* Anthems Old and New *come Ouseley's 'From the rising of the sun', Stainer's 'How beautiful upon the mountains', or Haydn's 'The heavens are telling'. Among more modern compositions, Colin Mawby's 'Let all the world exultant sing' and Christopher Tambling's 'May none of God's wonderful works keep silence' also fit this theme admirably, both from* Thirty New Anthems *(Kevin Mayhew).*

STUART THOMAS

Lent

True Devotion and Worship

God sees us as we are

A reading from the Gospel of Matthew (6:2-6, 16-18)

When you help people, don't 'blow your own trumpet' like people who are only pretending to be good; they want people to say, 'How good you are!' Very good. They get what they want.

When you help people, don't let your right hand know what your left hand is doing; help people without others noticing it. Your Father will notice, and give you what you want.

When you pray, don't make a show of it, like people who are only pretending to be good; they want people to say, 'How good you are!' Very good. They get what they want.

When you pray, go into your own room and shut the door, and say your prayers to God your Father alone. Your Father will notice and give you what you want.

When you fast, don't look sad and make your face gloomy, like people who are only pretending to be good; they want people to say, 'How good you are!' Very good. They get what they want.

When you fast, brush your hair and wash your face; don't let anybody but God your Father see that you are fasting. Your Father will notice and give you what you want.

ALAN DALE

Introductory material

Resolutions for Lent

Faithfully and sincerely living the Christian life means a continual effort to live up to the ideals Christ has set us. Because we so regularly fall short we are constantly picking ourselves up and making a new effort, a new beginning.

Lent is a terrific opportunity to make such a fresh start. This in effect means making resolutions. They should be few, practical and reasonable. A little self-knowledge should be brought to bear. It is quite pointless making great promises, if you know yourself well enough to know that you will not keep them up.

Besides the above there is only one golden rule about Lenten resolutions. Never give up or take up anything that will have an adverse effect upon the family. The classic example is smoking – if Dad's resolution to give up smoking makes him like a bear with a sore head and a 'pain' to live with, he must not do it, at least not during Lent. On the other hand Dad or Mum's smoking may already be very unpleasant and unhealthy for the rest of the family. Then one might give up smoking as a mark of love and respect for those who share the same home.

Having a change of heart does not mean being miserable or making others suffer. If Mum's resolution to help with the church cleaning during Lent takes her away from her own cleaning and household duties or means the house is empty when the children come home from school then she should find something else to do.

Nothing that is done supposedly for the love of God should ever be undertaken if it interferes with our love and responsibility for the family. Our first duty is to love God through the loving service we give to our family.

Fridays of Lent

The final few days of Lent are the climax of these six weeks, and the most important of these days is Good Friday, the day which casts its long shadow over the preceding weeks. All our efforts at self-discipline – saying 'no' to ourselves – are only of any real value if they are linked to Christ's love and obedience, which took him to the cross. It is his obedient love that wins for us the forgiveness of the Father. And he will bless our efforts and raise us up if all that we do in Lent is offered with and through his obedient Son.

In the Church's calendar each week is thought of as the year in miniature. The highlight of the year is Easter Sunday – the highlight of the week is Sunday, when we gather together to recall and celebrate Christ's rising from the dead. In the same way, every Friday we are asked to recall the events of Good Friday.

Fish on Fridays

The 'why' of the old rule about 'fish on Fridays' (really it was abstaining from meat) is not often explained. It became just one of those odd things that Catholics did. The original intention was that each Friday we should recall that this was the day of the week on which Jesus died, and in recalling this that we would mark it with an act of sorrow for sin.

When the obligation to abstain from meat on a Friday was done away with (not a lot of point when two-thirds of the world *never* see meat to eat) we were asked to carry on doing something of our own choosing. The day still needed to be marked out as we always need to express sorrow for sin. Sadly, very few people ever think about it!

The six (seven including Good Friday) Fridays of Lent are a little special and – together with Sundays – can be the focal points of the weeks of Lent. One way to use the day is to link the ancient tradition of fasting during Lent with the concern we should have for the deprived. CAFOD (Catholic Fund for Overseas Development) organises one special 'family fast day' in Lent, but there is no good reason why families cannot make every Friday a 'family fast day'. By going without one full meal or reducing two of the meals, and donating to charity the money we would have spent on feeding ourselves, our own 'no' to ourselves can be a positive 'yes' to the needy.

Friday prayer

The 'table prayer' of Lenten Fridays also offers an opportunity to make these days a bit different. At the principal meal of the day when hopefully most of the family is present, an adapted and simplified Way of the Cross can be used. There are two methods of using it. The first way, in a family where the children are quite young, is to spread the seven 'stations' over the seven Fridays of Lent, one each week. The second method, where the family is older, is to use the whole thing each week (or selected parts: for example the 'stations' that can be found in the Gospels) involving if possible each member of the family round the table. You will need to bring your Bible to the table.

Way of the Cross

This is set out here for use week by week over a period of seven weeks. If it is all to be used at one time, ignore the references to 'First Friday', 'Second Friday' and so on.

First Friday of Lent

1. Jesus is condemned to death

Read John 19:4-11 and 16.

Let us say sorry to God for the times we have talked unkindly and unjustly about other people (and called them names).

Please, God, help us not to judge others. Amen.

Second Friday of Lent

2. Jesus is met by his mother

Tradition tells us that Jesus met Mary on the Way of the Cross. Certainly Mary's great love would have prompted her to be there. This love-poem from the Bible tells us how she would have felt: 'I will rise now and go about the city, in the streets and in the squares; I will seek him whom my soul loves' (Song of Songs 3:1-4).

Let us say we are sorry to God for the times we have upset and hurt those we love most.

Please, God, help us to love and respect our family. Amen.

Third Friday of Lent

3. The cross is laid upon Simon of Cyrene

Read Mark 15:21.

Let us tell God that we are sorry for the times when we have not offered to help other people, especially people in real need.

Please, God, help us to give our help generously
to anyone who needs it. Amen.

Fourth Friday of Lent

4. The women of Jerusalem mourn for Our Lord

Read Luke 23:27-32.

Let us say sorry to God for the times when we have been proud and not admitted that we were in the wrong.

Please, God, help us to be humble
and to ask forgiveness when we have sinned. Amen.

Fifth Friday of Lent

5. Jesus is stripped of his clothes

Read John 19:23-24.

Let us tell God how sorry we are for the times when we have been selfish and pushed ourselves in front of others.

Please, God, help us to strip ourselves of our selfishness. Amen.

Sixth Friday of Lent

6. Jesus is nailed to the cross

Read Luke 23:33-34.

Let us say sorry to God for the times when our hands and feet have led us into sin.

Please, God, help us to be always honest and trustworthy. Amen.

Seventh Friday of Lent

7. Jesus dies on the cross

Read Matthew 27:45-50.

Let us say sorry to God for all the times we have failed in our love for him and not obeyed his wishes.

Please, God, help us to grow in love for you
and give you the obedience you look for. Amen.

TONY CASTLE

Prayers

Thanksgiving and petition

Living God,
    we thank you for this day you have given us,
        a day that reminds us of your mercy,
        your forgiveness,
        your offer of a new beginning for all who truly seek it.
    Search us, O God,
        and lead us in the way of life eternal.

We thank you for this time you have given us,
   this season of Lent which reminds us
   of the need for prayer and reflection,
   discipline and self-examination.
Search us, O God,
   and lead us in the way of life eternal.

We thank you for all this season leads towards,
   the days of Holy Week and Easter
   which remind us of your great love shown in Christ,
   and your great victory won through him.
Search us, O God,
   and lead us in the way of life eternal.

Living God,
   help us to use this day wisely and this season fully,
   so that our faith may be deepened,
   our horizons stretched,
   and our love for you increased.
Search us, O God,
   and lead us in the way of life eternal.

Cleanse us of all that is wrong,
   put a new heart and a right spirit within us,
   and so prepare us to rejoice again at the wonder of your love
   revealed in Christ crucified and risen.
Search us, O God,
   and lead us in the way of life eternal,
   for in his name we pray.
   Amen.   NICK FAWCETT

Intercession

Reconciliation with God. This will involve first admitting our need of God's mercy and forgiveness and then examining our lives in his light to see what needs to be done. God does not simply patch up the bits of us that look bad – he completely renews and restores, giving us the joy and peace of forgiveness.

Let us come before God, our creator and sustainer, with the needs of the Church and of the world.

We bring to your love, O Lord,
all who have committed their lives to your service;
that they may all be one,
bound together by your Holy Spirit.

Silence for prayer

Father of mercy:
hear us with compassion.

We bring to your love all the areas of the world
in which there is hostility and unrest;
that new routes to negotiation
and reconciliation may emerge.

Silence for prayer

Father of mercy:
hear us with compassion.

We bring to your love
the members of our human families
especially any we find difficult
to get on with or understand;
that our love for one another
may enter a new dimension
of warm and positive caring, seasoned with laughter.

Silence for prayer

Father of mercy:
hear us with compassion.

We bring to your love
all who have become hard and aggressive
through years of festering hate or jealousy;
that their unresolved conflicts
may be brought to your light and healed.

Silence for prayer

Father of mercy:
hear us with compassion.

We bring to your love all those, dear to us,
who are separated from us by death;
may we come, one day, with them
to share the eternal peace and joy of heaven.

Silence for prayer

Father of mercy:
hear us with compassion.

We thank you for all your blessings and patient loving,
and especially for coming to save us from our sin.

Silence for prayer

Merciful Father,
accept these prayers
for the sake of your Son,
our Saviour Jesus Christ, Amen.

SUSAN SAYERS

A short prayer

Gracious God,
   deal mercifully with us, we pray.
Give us the courage we need
   to see ourselves as we really are,
   the faith we need to see ourselves as we can be,
   the wisdom we need to discern your will,
   the humility we need to accept your correction,
   and the commitment we need
   to respond to your guidance.
We know our faults,
   we recognise our need for help,
   and so we come to you,
   dependent on your grace.
Gracious God,
   have mercy,
   in the name of Christ.
Amen.

NICK FAWCETT

Reflective material
(sketches, meditations and poems)

From the wilderness

Leader   This is a dry and pitiless land
        for here no flowers blossom
        or birds sing,
        there are no trees
        to give shelter
        from the sun
        or grass to clothe
        the rocks with green.

All   Lord, you are our only hope.
       We cling to you, do not forsake us.

Leader There is no gentleness
in the wind
or joy from the laughter
of children.
The dawn brings no hope
and the evening no comfort.

All Lord, you are our only hope.
We cling to you, do not forsake us.

Leader All those that love me
seem a long way off,
my heart is numb with sorrow
and my eyes are heavy with weeping.
I stumble trying to find
the right path.

All Lord, you are our only hope.
We cling to you, do not forsake us.

Leader I am like a dried-up plant
and my life as meaningless
as dust blown by the wind.
Lord lift me out
of this deep ravine
for I am as helpless
as a little child.

All Lord, you are our only hope.
We cling to you, do not forsake us.

Leader Unless you rescue me
I shall be forgotten
and lost for ever.
Let me find your footprints
and be able to follow them,
for you also walked this wilderness
alone and forgotten,
and you are the only one
who can guide me through.

All Lord, you are our only hope.
We cling to you, do not forsake us.

MARY HATHAWAY

Order of service

A Penitential Service for the beginning of Lent

Outside LEPs (Local Ecumenical Projects), where worship is shared already, ecumenical services are frequently organised to celebrate or mark something, be it a Christian festival, an anniversary, or the launch of a joint mission or project. Somehow lively praise and worship seem more suitable for a large gathering of Christians from different traditions than solemnity and reflection, though there are occasional exceptions, such as a major occasion for grief or concern, whether local or national. Being a penitential season, Lent does not therefore immediately come to mind as a time for ecumenical worship. However, in recent years the observation of Lent has spread far beyond the Catholic tradition and entered the ecumenical domain, notably through inter-church study and fellowship groups.

In large groups or small, within our own tradition or in an ecumenical context, we need to take stock of our spiritual life (individual and corporate) and confess to God those areas which need his forgiveness and healing. Lent is a particularly good opportunity to acknowledge the attitudes and behaviour which promote disunity among Christians, and to take a fresh look at how we are progressing with the work of demonstrating and building up our oneness in Christ through worshipping and serving him together. Since Lent groups are now widely accepted in most places, the service outline for the beginning of Lent also provides for these to be launched corporately. At the other end of Lent, Palm Sunday can effectively be used to round them off.

Mention Lent, and many people will immediately think of having to 'give something up' (some older folk may recall being forced to do so). But while it may be very good for us, physically and spiritually, to abandon our usual indulgences of chocolate or alcohol for forty days, that emphasises only the fasting element of Lent. The study groups remind us that Lent originated as a time of spiritual preparation for those who were to be baptised on Easter Day, as well as those who were to be readmitted to the Church after a time of penitence and reflection following some blatant sin. The liturgical emphasis is therefore on looking forward to Good Friday and Easter Day, the heartland of our Christian faith, and something shared by Christians of all traditions. You may feel it helpful to symbolise the 'fasting' aspect by removing any elaborate decor or banners from the church, avoiding flower arrangements, and considering carefully the style of music to be used. However, not all traditions observe Lent in this way, and any changes may need to be explained in advance.

This following outline service is penitential and contemplative in tone, providing an opportunity for the congregation to reflect, respond and look forward to Holy Week and Easter. Traditionally, the day included the imposition of ashes, but, to avoid offence or misunderstanding, I have suggested an alternative approach.

Opening sentence

The tax collector would not even look up to heaven, but said:
'God, be merciful to me, a sinner.'

Hymn

Dear Lord and Father of mankind (HON 106)

Bidding

Friends, we join together with Christians of all traditions at the beginning of this season of Lent, as we prepare ourselves for the remembrance of our Lord's passion and death, and the celebration of his glorious resurrection. It is a time for personal reflection on our lives; for sorrowing over our sins and honest repentance; for receiving gladly God's promise of forgiveness in Jesus Christ and committing ourselves with fresh resolve to following his way. As we do this in the coming days, we pray that our faith may be strengthened and our devotion deepened.

In our observation of this time of preparation we may spend time in prayer and fasting; we may read and meditate on God's word in the Scriptures; we may discipline ourselves by laying aside familiar comforts in order to focus more clearly on our walk with Christ. We pray now for God's help as we begin our Lenten journey.

Loving God,
we come to you
not knowing how or what to pray,
but bringing you the deepest longings
of our hearts,
which mere words cannot express.
You know our thoughts
before they find shape,
our speech before it comes to our lips,
our intentions before our hands give them form.
Search us this day, O God, and test us,
to remove any wickedness within us
and allay our anxious thoughts.
Give us discernment as we meditate
on your Word,
give us peace as we receive your forgiveness,
give us joy as we deepen our life in you,
and lead us in the way of eternal life,
for the sake of your Son,
our Saviour Jesus Christ.
Amen.

Response

O Lord my God, I cried to you for help
and you healed me.
Sing to the Lord, and praise his holy name.

Hymn

O for a heart to praise my God (HON 361)

Collect for Ash Wednesday

Old Testament reading

Genesis 2:15-17; 3:1-7 or
Isaiah 1:10-18 or
Joel 2:1-2, 12-17 or
Micah 6:1-8

Responsorial Psalm

Lord, your love never fails.
Be merciful to me
and wipe out all my wrongdoing.
Wash away all our sin,
and make us clean from all that pollutes.

Lord, I know well what I have done wrong,
because my conscience troubles me continually.
We have sinned in your sight,
against you alone;
you are justified in judging us.

Lord, only you can cleanse me
through and through;
make me whiter even than the purest snow.
Do not keep looking at our wrongdoing,
but remove it from sight for ever.

Lord, give me deep within a pure heart
and a right spirit;
uphold me with the presence
of your Holy Spirit.
Bring us back to the joy of your saving love
and keep our spirits willing and generous.

Lord, open my lips to declare your mercy,
and to offer you praise and thanksgiving.
You seek from us the sacrifice of repentance and brokenness;
you will never despise or turn away
those whose hearts are contrite.

Hymn
Such love (HON 461)

New Testament reading
Romans 5:12-19 or
1 Peter 3:18-22 or
Matthew 6:1-6, 16-21 or
Luke 18:9-14

Sermon

Liturgy of penitence
Jesus says:

'If you obey my commands you will remain in my love.' Aware of our failure
to keep them, we listen again to the commandments God has given, that they
may be written more clearly upon our hearts.

God says:

'I am the Lord your God.
You are to have no gods other than me.'
Lord, we have not loved you
with all our heart, soul, mind and strength.
Lord, forgive us.

'You shall not make any idol for yourself.'
Lord, we have not worshipped you
in spirit and in truth.
Lord, forgive us.

'You shall not misuse the name
of the Lord your God.'
Lord, we have not worshipped you acceptably,
with reverence and awe.
Lord, forgive us.

'Remember the Lord's Day, and keep it holy.'
Lord, we have not entered
drawn near to you with sincere hearts,
in full assurance of faith.
Lord, forgive us.

'Honour your father and mother.'
Lord, we have not honoured one another,
or looked first to the interests of others.
Lord, forgive us.

'You shall not commit murder.'
Lord, we have not been reconciled
to one another,
nor overcome evil with good.
Lord, forgive us.

'You shall not commit adultery.'
Lord, we have not been pure and blameless
in thought or deed.
Lord, forgive us.

'You shall not steal.'
Lord, we have not been honest in our dealings,
or generous towards those in need.
Lord, forgive us.

'You shall not bear false witness.'
Lord, we have not always spoken the truth in love.
Lord, forgive us.

'You shall not covet anything
belonging to someone else.'
Lord, we have not always been generous
or willing to share.
Lord, forgive us,
and write your law of love on our hearts
that we may love you with all our heart
and our neighbour as ourselves.

Silence

Confession and absolution

God our Father,
you are mighty to save,
but we are weak and sinful,
and have fallen away from your presence.
In your great mercy,
forgive us, O Lord.

God our Father,
you are faithful in every way,
but we are fickle and changeable,
and have put our trust in this passing world.
In your great mercy,
forgive us, O Lord.

God our Father,
you are gracious and forgiving,
but we are critical and self-righteous,
and have not turned to you
in penitence and faith.
In your great mercy,
forgive us, O Lord.

God our Father,
you are eternal and changeless,
but we are earthbound and worldly,
and have not responded
to your forgiving love.
In your great mercy,
forgive us O Lord.

Cleanse us from our sin and guilt
and help us to see more clearly
what you would have us be,
for the glory of your Son,
our Saviour Jesus Christ. Amen.

Almighty God,
whose mercy is on all
who sincerely seek his face,
grant you pardon for all your sins,
time to turn to him and repent,
and strength to walk in his way
of peace and freedom,
through Jesus Christ our Lord.
Amen.

Act of penitence

Give each worshipper a small piece of paper and a pencil before the service starts. After the Liturgy of Penitence, allow a time of silence enabling each person to write down some failing or personal issue that they want to bring to Christ. Invite the congregation to come up and place the slips of paper into a fireproof container situated centrally on a table. Light a taper and set fire to the pieces of paper, allowing them to burn until they are ash.

Prayer before act of penitence

Holy God,
with these ashes
we acknowledge before you
our sins and failings.

May they be a sign
both of our repentance and our mortality,
and a token of your free gift of eternal life
to all who put their trust in you,
through the death of your dear Son
Jesus Christ.
Amen.

Alternative prayer before act of penitence

We come to God in penitence and faith,
recognising his holiness and purity,
and conscious of our own unworthiness.
In penitence we bring before him now
the sins and failings we have written down
to be burned,
reminding us of our need to repent,
and reassuring us that they are forgiven
and completely forgotten.
Holy God,
we acknowledge in your sight
our wrongdoing and weaknesses,
written on these pieces of paper.
As we place them here
may we be reminded of how they have broken
our relationship with you,
and as they are burned
may we know they are blotted out for ever
by your love for us,
as we see it in your Son Jesus Christ,
who died that we might have eternal life.
Amen.

Prayer after act of penitence

God our loving Father,
you make us for yourself,
and our hearts are restless
until they find rest in you.
Make us pure in thought and motive,
unselfish in word and action
strong in purpose and faith.
May our minds know your will,
our hearts respond to it
and our lives enact it,
for the sake of your Son,
Jesus Christ our Lord. Amen.

Hymn

Give thanks with a grateful heart (HON 154)

Intercessions

Lord Jesus,
you sent your disciples out in twos
to take the good news of God's kingdom
to all whom they met.
We pray for all Christian people
working together for the Gospel,
especially in our own area . . .
Help us to overcome our differences
and show by our actions
that you are our one Lord.
Jesus, Lord of the Church,
in your mercy, receive our prayer.

Lord Jesus,
you heard the cry of blind Bartimaeus
and restored his sight.
We pray for those whose lives are impaired
by handicap, disability and disadvantage,
especially . . .
Help us to defeat selfish prejudice
and bring your compassion
to the vulnerable and needy.
Jesus, Light of the World,
in your mercy, receive our prayer.

Lord Jesus,
you heard the last request of the penitent thief
as you hung on the Cross,
and promised him a place with you in Paradise.
We pray for all
whose lives are in confusion and disarray,
who feel unloved and unworthy
and do not know where to turn, especially . . .
Help us to accept those
whom others sideline and reject,
and reassure them of your unlimited love.
Jesus, Friend of Sinners,
in your mercy, receive our prayer.

Lord Jesus,
you wept with Mary and Martha
at the death of your friend Lazarus
and then restored him to life again.

We pray for all
who are enduring illness or infirmity,
anxiety or depression, loneliness or grief,
especially . . . who are known to us.
Help us to be faithful in prayer
and constant in care for them.
Jesus, the Resurrection and the Life,
in your mercy, receive our prayer.

Lord Jesus,
you often took time out
from your work of ministry
to spend time with your Father
in prayer and meditation.
We pray for our times of study and prayer
during this Lent,
especially . . .
Help us to resist the pressures and distractions of our busy lives
and give time to deepening our faith.
Lord Jesus, Teacher and Guide,
in your mercy, receive our prayer.

Lord Jesus,
where two or three come together
in your name
you are present.
Hear and answer these prayers
in accordance with your will,
for your holy Name's sake.
Amen.

Our Father . . .

An alternative congregational response is the Taizé chant 'O Lord, hear my prayer'
(HON 379) *after each bidding.*

Hymn
Father, hear the prayer we offer (HON 120)

Final prayer
> **Lord,**
> **when we are tempted**
> **to put our trust in material things,**
> **help us remember**
> **that we live by the words of life**
> **which come from you.**

When we are tempted to put our trust
in religious rituals and practices,
help us remember
that love for you comes first.
When we are tempted
to seek power and acclaim,
help us remember that you alone
are worthy of worship and honour.
Amen.

Blessing

May God the Father open our minds
to learn more of his grace.
Amen.

May God the Son open our hearts
to respond to his love.
Amen.

May God the Holy Spirit open our hands
to worship and serve him.
Amen.

And the blessing of God Almighty . . .

Choral music

*Musically Lent is a time for restraint and thoughtfulness, not just because it is a season
of penitence and prayer, but also to provide the greatest contrast with the joy and celebration of Easter Day. Allegri's 'Miserere', arguably the most famous of all settings of
Psalm 51, perhaps makes excessive demands for an average church choir (and needs
very fine soloists, too). Tallis' 'Lamentations of Jeremiah' also require much practice.
However, there is plenty of prayerful music well within the compass of most choirs, not
least the lovely compositions of Margaret Rizza, such as 'Silent, surrendered' or 'Fire of
Love'. Any of her* Contemplative Choral Music *pieces would grace a Lent ecumenical
service as a devotional anthem. From* Anthems Old and New *could be selected
Attwood's 'Turn thy face from my sins', Lloyd's arrangement of Stubbs' 'Not for our
sins alone', Oxley's arrangement of Schein's 'O love, how deep' or Wesley's 'Wash me
thoroughly', to mention just four.*

STUART THOMAS

Jesus Overcomes Temptation

Proclaiming the kingdom

A reading from the Gospel of Mark (1:12-15)

The Spirit led Jesus into the desert among the wild animals where he stayed for forty days, and the devil came to tempt him, while angels watched over him.

   Soon after John the Baptist's arrest, Jesus travelled throughout Galilee proclaiming the Gospel and saying to the people, 'The kingdom of God is very near! Turn away from sin and believe the good news.'

This is the Gospel of the Lord
Praise to you, Lord Jesus Christ   KATIE THOMPSON

Introductory material

We are here in the season of Lent, a time which calls us to stop, take stock and reflect on the health or otherwise of our faith. It recalls the temptation of Jesus in the wilderness, and invites us to consider our own response to temptation in turn. It reminds us of his steadfast commitment to the way of the cross, and asks if we are willing to bear the cost of discipleship. It speaks of the prayer and devotion which sustained Jesus during those forty days and nights of testing, and from there urges us to make time and space for God a priority in our own lives. Today we listen to some of the accounts of that time in the desert, exploring what it meant for Jesus, what it meant for John the Baptist, and what it means for us today. We look back, asking that God might lead us forward.

NICK FAWCETT

Prayers

Lent praise

Sovereign God,
   we praise you today
      for the great wonder at the heart of the Gospel –
      your sharing our humanity and enduring our weakness.
   You are sovereign over all,
      yet you became our servant.

You are the holy one of God,
>   yet you were tempted just as we are.
You are the giver of life,
>   yet you endured the darkness of death.
You are the Lord of lords,
>   yet you were crowned with thorns.
You are enthroned on high,
>   yet you consented to be brought low.
In what the world counted weakness
>   you displayed true strength.
Great is your name,
>   **and greatly to be praised.**

We praise you for your love
>   that is able to turn human expectations upside down,
>   and we rejoice in everything this means for us today –
>   that when we are weak, you are strong,
>   when we feel most helpless, you are most powerful,
>   when we can do little, you can do much.
Great is your name,
>   **and greatly to be praised.**

We praise you that your way is not one of coercion but of love,
>   your power transforming from within,
>   never forcing anyone to comply with your wishes
>   but graciously inviting a response.
We thank you that, year after year,
>   generation after generation,
>   you have worked through ordinary flawed individuals like us,
>   to make known your love
>   and to bring nearer your kingdom.
Great is your name,
>   **and greatly to be praised.**

Sovereign God,
>   Servant God,
>   we praise you
>   that, despite everything which conspires against you,
>   everything which frustrates your purpose,
>   your will shall finally triumph,
>   nothing able to overcome your goodness,
>   or to extinguish your love in Christ.
May we live each day in that conviction,
>   bringing honour and glory to you.
Great is your name,
>   **and greatly to be praised.**
Amen.   NICK FAWCETT

Petition

Loving God,
  there are times when our knowledge of your will is flawed,
    when we need the wisdom, humility and courage
    to accept we are wrong.
  Teach us always to be open to that possibility,
    never so full of our own importance
    that we are blind to our weaknesses.
  But there are times too when, like Jesus in the wilderness,
    we have to hold on to what we know is right,
    despite every pressure to the contrary,
    standing firm against popular opinion,
    even when it risks alienating family or friends.
  Help us to know when those times are,
    and teach us to do your will.

  Save us from taking the enticing path of compromise,
    the easy path of capitulation,
    or the cowardly path of leaving decisions to someone else.
  Give us strength, in the day of testing,
    to be true to ourselves and true to you.
  Help us to know when those times are,
    and teach us to do your will.

  In the name of Christ.
  Amen.

NICK FAWCETT

Intercession

We need to build up our defences against temptation.

Father, we pray for all who are going through
a time of temptation at the moment.
Strengthen and protect them all.
Silence for prayer

Your commands, O Lord:
are our delight.

We pray that your church may always
hold true to your truth and love
with your love.
Silence for prayer

Your commands, O Lord:
are our delight.

We pray for those in positions of power
that they may not give way to corruption
but work with integrity.

Silence for prayer

Your commands, O Lord:
are our delight.

We pray for those in our families
and those who live in our neighbourhood,
that we may live in harmony together.

Silence for prayer

Your commands, O Lord:
are our delight.

We pray for those in prison
and those imprisoned by guilt.

Silence for prayer

Your commands, O Lord:
are our delight.

We pray for those who have died through neglect,
mismanagement of resources,
violence and oppression.

Silence for prayer

Your commands, O Lord:
are our delight.

Father, we thank you for the way
you protect and enfold us every moment
of every day.

Silence for prayer

Merciful Father,
accept these prayers
for the sake of your Son,
our Saviour Jesus Christ, Amen.

SUSAN SAYERS

A short prayer

Gracious God,
  we thank you for the time spent by Jesus
  in the wilderness,
  tested there to the limit
  but refusing to be deceived.
Help us to learn from his example;
  to be awake to temptation
  and ready to withstand it;
  to make time to hear your voice
  and reflect upon your word.
Help us to follow you and to do your will,
  regardless of the cost.
So may we grow closer to you
  and stronger in our faith.
Amen.

NICK FAWCETT

All-age-talk material

Jesus in the wilderness

Today is the First Sunday of Lent. Lent lasts for forty days before we celebrate Easter

Write the first letter of each picture in the boxes to find out what the word 'Lent' means

Mark 1:9-15

KATIE THOMPSON

After John the
Baptist was arrested,
Jesus began to preach to
the people. What did he
tell them?

Match the shapes and copy the letters

KATIE THOMPSON

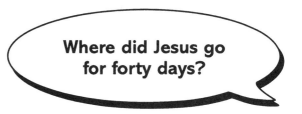

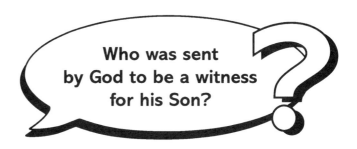

Who was sent
by God to be a witness
for his Son?

Write the first letter of each picture clue to find the answer

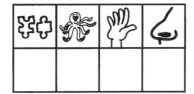

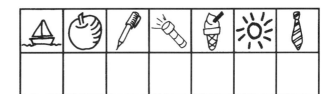

KATIE THOMPSON

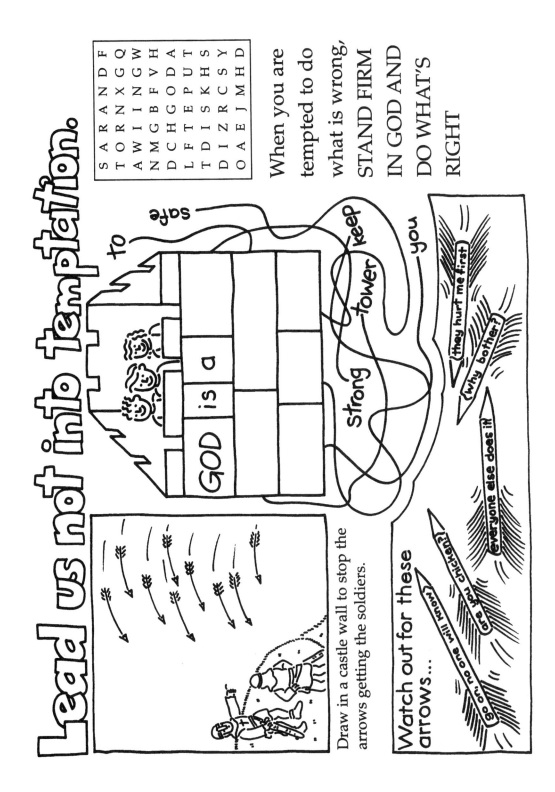

Lead us not into temptation.

S	A	R	A	N	D	F
T	O	R	N	X	G	Q
A	W	I	N	G	W
N	M	G	B	F	V	H
D	C	H	G	O	D	A
L	F	T	E	P	U	T
T	D	I	S	K	H	S
D	I	Z	R	C	S	Y
O	A	E	J	M	H	D

When you are tempted to do what is wrong, STAND FIRM IN GOD AND DO WHAT'S RIGHT

to safe

GOD is a

strong tower keep you

they hurt me first
why bother?
everyone else does it!
go on, no one will know?
are you chicken?

Draw in a castle wall to stop the arrows getting the soldiers.

Watch out for these arrows...

KATIE THOMPSON

Read Mark 1:9-15

Jesus was around 30 years old at the time of his visit to John the Baptist. Jesus had waited for the right moment to begin what he had been sent to do.

- Firstly, Jesus recognised that the time was right, that the moment had come for him to make that decision to leave the comfort of Nazareth and start his ministry.
- Secondly, Jesus wanted to identify with the message of John the Baptist. John was reluctant to baptise Jesus, knowing that Jesus was without sin. But it was important for Jesus to identify with the need for forgiveness of sin. It was also a symbolic act. Jesus was to take on the sins of the world (see John 1:29) which would lead to his death on the cross.
- Thirdly, as soon as Jesus came out of the water, the Holy Spirit came down like a dove. The Holy Spirit was to guide and encourage Jesus for the journey ahead.
- Finally, a voice from heaven said, 'You are my own son.' This was a recognition of Jesus and what he had decided to do. It was a fatherly nod to say, 'Yes, you are mine and I'm really happy with you.' This wasn't a 'pat on the head'. Both God and Jesus knew the way ahead was going to be far from easy but at least Jesus knew that he wouldn't be alone, he had his Father's blessing.

The baptism of Jesus was a 'decision' to go the way that God wanted him to go; it was submitting to his Father, accepting the Holy Spirit as encourager and guide for the way ahead and by following this step Jesus was given his Father's blessing.

Baptism is a way of deciding to start a new journey, of turning away from the actions that separate us from God, receiving God's blessing on our lives and having the Holy Spirit as our encourager.

PETE TOWNSEND

Temptation

You will need a tennis racket, a number of soft, sponge balls or balls of screwed up paper and a large cardboard carton.

First go through the story in 1 Samuel 26, bringing it to life. Ask people what David might have been thinking as he stood there over Saul. What might he have been tempted to do?

Temptations are bound to fly at us from all directions all through our lives. Ask someone to help you to explain this by standing there as a group of people pelts them with balls. Sometimes the temptation is only slight (one ball) such as when you are tempted to kill your sister or brother. You know deep down that though she irritates you you wouldn't really want to do her any serious injury, so your fondness for her acts like a screen (they hold racquet up) and stops the temptation from getting any closer. (Throw ball so that the racquet screens the person.)

Sometimes the temptations fly at us so powerfully and urgently that even with the screen it is difficult to stop them getting to you. (Try this with lots of balls at once.)

What God provides for us is all-round protection. (Let the volunteer crawl into the large carton.) If we make a habit of crawling into God's protection every day, then we will be better equipped to say 'NO!' to temptation. Don't try and fight off temptation on your own.

SUSAN SAYERS

All change

Begin by explaining that to prepare for the talk today you will need everyone in each row to sit in reverse order from how they are sitting at the moment, so that those nearest the centre will end up nearest the sides. Give them a short time to organise that. (This should create mild chaos for a while which gradually settles into order again.) Thank everyone for their co-operation.

What they have just experienced is an important truth – when God prepares his people for his coming, that is bound to cause disturbance.

There they were, sitting comfortably, and then they got messed about by you wanting them aligned differently. The people of Israel were living complacently until Amos came along and challenged the way their lives were aligned. John the Baptist's calling was to alert people to the way they were living and sort themselves out according to God's standards. When our own lives are challenged like this we have to set about checking the way we are living – are we in line with God's commandments and God's values? There may be drastic changes needed (as there were for those sitting on the ends of the rows), or there may be minor changes (as there were for those few who have ended up sitting in the same place as before). But either way we need to get up, spiritually, and take a candid look at the way we speak and spend our time and money; we need to look at our relationships and attitudes, and at the extent to which we allow God to reign in us.

Now, as they realign themselves again in their rows, ask them to do so in silence, opening up their lives to be realigned in keeping with God's will.

SUSAN SAYERS

Reflective material
(sketches, meditations and poems)

Meditation of John the Baptist

It took me by surprise, I don't mind admitting it,
   his going off into the desert like that
   the moment after his baptism.

You see, I thought that was my role,
   to fulfil the words of the prophet –
   'A voice crying in the wilderness:
   "Prepare the way of the Lord."'
And I'd done it well,
   patiently,
   faithfully,
   determined to play my part, come what may.
They'd come in their thousands,
   flocking out to me like there was no tomorrow –
   to be baptised,
   to confess their sins,
   to await the Messiah.
They were ready and waiting,
   eager to receive him,
   hungry for his coming.
And at last we saw him,
   striding down into the water,
   his identity unmistakable –
   not simply Jesus of Nazareth,
   but the Deliverer,
   the Son of God,
   the Saviour of the world!
I was ecstatic, you can imagine.
It was like a dream come true,
   the answer to all my prayers.
And as he came up out of the water
   I was waiting for the next move,
   wondering what would follow.
I'm not quite sure what I expected,
   but something dramatic at the very least –
   a bolt from heaven perhaps,
   a fanfare of trumpets,
   a raising of the standard,
   I don't know –
   but some sign,
   some symbol to let us know beyond all doubt
   that the moment had come,
   the waiting was over,
   and the kingdom was here.
Only what did he do?
Well, like I say, he disappeared.
No pep talk,
   no message for the crowd,
   just off and away without so much as a backward glance,
   and no hide nor hair of him seen for weeks afterwards.

To be frank, I was annoyed at first,
   for it all seemed such an anticlimax,
   but on reflection I can't blame him,
   for I think it took *him* by surprise as much as it did me.
When I recall now how he looked
   coming up out of the water after his baptism,
   so joyful,
   so radiant,
   almost as though he'd heard God rather than me talking to him,
   I just can't believe he had any idea
   that minutes later he'd be making off into the wilderness.
It was like he had no say in the matter,
   as though an unseen hand was guiding him,
   so that the one event progressed naturally from the other –
   a moment of joy –
   a time of trial;
   a wonderful high –
   a desperate low,
   a certainty of faith –
   a wrestling with doubt.
Yet by all accounts it's been the making of him,
   almost as if faith needed to be forged on the anvil of temptation,
   tested to the limit
   before the weight of the world could be hung upon it.
I think I'm beginning to see it now,
   to understand that it wasn't just the wilderness of Judea
   he faced out there,
   but the desert of the soul,
   and he needed to experience both if God was to use him,
   for, strange though it may seem,
   God is often more at work when we don't see it
   than when we do.

NICK FAWCETT

Order of service

Welcome and Notices

Stand a large white cross (card or paper-covered wood) clearly at front of church.

Warm and inviting. Visitors and newcomers should be made particularly welcome.

Introduction to the theme

Short pause, then all stand

Sentence of Scripture and Acclamation

Read sentence without announcing it. With feeling and enthusiasm. Move directly into Acclamation.

'The kingdom of God is near.
Repent and believe the good news!' (Mark 1:15)

Let us give thanks to the God of our Lord Jesus Christ:
who has blessed us in Christ with every spiritual blessing.

Before the world was made, God chose us in Christ:
that we might be holy and blameless before him.

Let us praise God for the glory of his grace:
for the free gift he gave us in his dear Son.

To Father, Son and Holy Spirit:
**give praise and dominion, honour and might, for ever and ever.
Amen.**

Introduction to first hymn begins immediately after Acclamation.

Extended time of sung worship

Hymn and songs linked through instrumental music.

Hymn To God be the glory (*The Source*) or
Song Salvation belongs to our God (*The Source*)
Song There is a Redeemer (*The Source*) or
Song I will offer up my life (*The Source*)

Soft instrumental music continues.

Silence (except for music)

Open worship

The congregation may be encouraged to pray out loud, speak out praise or to share how God has encouraged them. Worship leader may conclude with an appropriate prayer.

(Open to God, open prayer or praise, reflecting, sharing gifts.)

Sit if not already doing so.

Confession

Soft introduction to hymn.

Hymn Here is love (verse 1) (*The Source*)

Soft instrumental music continues in background to prayer.

Let us admit to God the sin which always confronts us:
Lord God, we have sinned against you;
we have done evil in your sight.
We are sorry and repent.
Have mercy on us according to your love.
Wash away our wrongdoing
and cleanse us from our sin.
Renew a right spirit within us
and restore us to the joy of your salvation,
through Jesus Christ our Lord. Amen.

May the Father of all mercies
cleanse us from our sins,
and restore us in his service
to the praise and glory of his name,
through Jesus Christ our Lord.
Amen.

Instrumental music leads into intro to verse 2 of hymn.

Hymn Here is love (verse 2) (*The Source*)

Music ends.

Collect

Almighty God,
whose Son Jesus Christ fasted forty days
in the wilderness,
and was tempted as we are, yet without sin:
give us grace to discipline ourselves
in obedience to your Spirit;
and, as you know our weakness,
so may we know your power to save;
through Jesus Christ your Son, our Lord,
who is alive and reigns with you,
in the unity of the Holy Spirit,
one God, now and for ever.

The Liturgy of the Word

A slide of 'footprints in sand' or 'a child's hand held in father's hand' projected onto the screen during the readings. No announcement of the readings. Should be unbroken time of listening and reflecting.

Reading 1

Short time of silence

Reading 2

Short time of silence

Sermon

The sermon is linked to the theme. Challenging and affirming, giving practical help for discipleship.

Silence (for reflection on Sermon)

Response

Background music plays softly during introduction to Response. As it is the start of Lent, invite the congregation to follow Christ. Perhaps for the first time or in a deeper way. Turning away from old ways or sins, believing with a sincere heart in his forgiveness and all that he offers.

Personal rededication through private prayer

Music continues whilst people respond to Christ privately.
   or
A practical dedication by placing your own ink thumb-print on the white cross at the front of church.

If members of congregation wish to dedicate themselves to Christ then invite them to respond practically by pledging themselves to the cross of Christ, placing their thumb-print on the white cross at the front of church. This would be their own unique pledge as no one else shares their thumb-print identity. Music moves into song of worship to sing during Response.

Song From heaven you came (*The Source*)

Conclude with this statement of dedication.

   The free gift of God is eternal life in Christ Jesus our Lord.
   By his mercy we present our whole lives to God as a living sacrifice.

Short pause
Move directly into prayers without announcing.

Prayers

   Let us sit or kneel to pray:
   Lord, we want to follow you in the way of a servant.
   Give us the strength to let go of our selfish desires
   as individuals and as a Church,
   to deny ourselves for the sake of others.
   Help us to make it our priority to serve you
   by sharing your love in all that we do and say.

Silence

Lord, we'll follow you.
Help us to walk in your footsteps.

Lord, we want to follow you in the way of sacrifice.
May your death on the cross remind us
of all that you gave to bring us forgiveness
and help us to count the cost of truly following you.

Silence

Lord, we'll follow you.
Help us to walk in your footsteps.

Lord, we want to follow you in the way of peace.
We ask that you would give all people the strength
to resist war and hate, to forgive and live in love.
Through your Spirit help your Church to shine
an example of your love and to embrace the lost,
the despised and those rejected.

Silence

Lord, we'll follow you.
Help us to walk in your footsteps.

Lord, we want to follow you in the way of compassion.
Help us to love as you love us.
May we help you in the work of your kingdom
by bringing comfort to the sick and suffering.
We pray now for those who are suffering at this time and ask that you will
give them the healing touch
of your precious hands.

Silence

Show us how we might help them in practical ways, giving them friendship
and support.

Lord, we'll follow you.
Help us to walk in your footsteps.

Lord, we want to follow you to the gates of glory.
You have walked the path from death into glorious life
and now you lead the way to the place
where we can live with you for ever,
joining with all the saints in your endless praise.

Lord we'll follow you.
Help us to walk in your footsteps.
Amen.

Announce hymn whilst music introduction is played in background.

Offertory hymn Breathe on me, breath of God *(The Source)*

Remain standing

Final prayers

God of our pilgrimage,
you have led us to the living water.
Refresh and sustain us
as we go forward on our journey,
in the name of Jesus Christ our Lord. Amen.
The Lord God Almighty is our Father:
he loves us and tenderly cares for us.
The Lord Jesus Christ is our Saviour:
he has redeemed us and will defend us to the end.
The Lord, the Holy Spirit, is among us:
he will lead us in God's holy way.
To God Almighty, Father, Son and Holy Spirit,
be praise and glory today and for ever.
Amen.

Before the final songs offer the opportunity for prayer after the service. Maybe people would like to make their pledge on the cross as they felt unable to respond in front of the whole congregation. Perhaps the worship highlighted a need for prayer or advice.

Song Before the throne of God above *(The Source 2)*

The Grace (sung) *(The Source 2)*

The grace of our Lord Jesus Christ
and the love of God
and the fellowship of the Holy Spirit
be with us for evermore.

Prayer ministry available

Soft music could be played as people leave and whilst prayer continues.

TIM LOMAX

Following Jesus

The cost of discipleship

A reading from the Gospel of Mark (9:2-10)

Jesus led Peter, James and John to the top of a high mountain where they could be alone. While they looked on, Jesus' appearance was transformed as his clothes shone brilliantly white. Then Elijah and Moses appeared before them and began talking to Jesus.

   The disciples were so afraid they did not know what to do or say, until Peter spoke up. 'Master, it is wonderful for us to be here. We could make a shelter for each one of you!'

   At that moment a passing cloud covered them with its shadow, and a voice came from the cloud and said, 'This is my Son whom I love very much. Listen to what he says.'

   Then suddenly they found themselves alone with Jesus, who told them not to tell anyone what they had seen until the Son of Man had risen from the dead. They did what Jesus asked, but discussed amongst themselves what 'rising from the dead' could possibly mean.

This is the Gospel of the Lord
Praise to you, Lord Jesus Christ   KATIE THOMPSON

Introductory material

'If any want to become my followers, let them deny themselves and take up their cross and follow me' (Mark 8:34b). Words of Jesus which, in the euphoria of Christian celebration, we can sometimes forget, yet which lie at the heart of Christian discipleship. The life of service involves cost as well as reward; a price to pay as well as a blessing to receive. Lose sight of that and we are in danger of presenting a lop-sided and ultimately false Gospel. Alongside what we get out of faith we must always remember what Jesus asks us to put in; his call to deny ourselves and put others first, to seek treasures in heaven rather than riches on earth, to be last rather than first, to face trials now in order to help build his kingdom to come. If we expect the Christian life to be plain sailing, then we have not understood the call or listened to the words of the one who called us. Responding in faith will inevitably bring times of challenge . . . but if we are willing to meet the cost we will find the price worth paying, for we will discover life as God intends it to be. 'Those who want to save their life will lose it, and those who lose their life for the sake of the Gospel, will save it' (Mark 8:35).

                                                                    NICK FAWCETT

Prayers

Thanksgiving – the presence of God

Loving God,
worthy of all praise and honour,
we come to offer our worship,
to be still and know that you are God.
Open our eyes to your presence.

You are all good, all holy,
merciful and loving,
faithful and true.
Open our eyes to your presence.

We lift up our hearts with joy,
our voices in thanksgiving,
our lives in adoration.
Open our eyes to your presence.

We thank you for this season of Lent,
this time which invites us to pause and take stock,
to reflect on the things in life which really matter.
Open our eyes to your presence.

We thank you for this time and place set apart week by week,
these special moments when we focus on you
and remind ourselves of your living presence.
Open our eyes to your presence.

We thank you that you want to speak to us,
teach us,
and deepen our relationship with you.
Open our eyes to your presence.

Help us to use this time to hear your voice,
discern your will,
and experience your love.
Open our eyes to your presence.

Loving God,
draw us closer to you,
so that we may return to our homes,
our daily lives and the world around us
with renewed hope, vision, strength and faith.
Open our eyes to your presence.

Through Jesus Christ our Lord.
Amen.

NICK FAWCETT

Confession – the challenge of God

Gracious God,
we thank you for the example you have shown to us in Christ,
the model we see in him of faithful service.
We thank you for the dedication he showed
throughout his ministry;
the fact that he was not prepared to cut corners
or take the easy way out,
but rather confronted injustice and evil
head to head and face to face.
You challenge us to stand up for what is right:
give us the courage to respond.

Forgive us that we so rarely follow his example.
We turn a blind eye to what we know to be wrong,
even bending the rules ourselves.
We go along with the crowd
rather than face being thought different.
We close our eyes and ears to what we would rather not think about.
We make excuses for, and seek to justify, our faults.
We give way to temptation,
promising next time will be different.
We wash our hands of difficult decisions,
claiming it is none of our business.
You challenge us to stand up for what is right:
give us the courage to respond.

Gracious God,
forgive us those times when we have failed to speak up for right,
when we have colluded in wrong,
and when we have lost sight of both.
Renew us through your Spirit,
restore us through your love, equip us through your power,
and so enable us to live faithfully as your people.
You challenge us to stand up for what is right:
give us the courage to respond.

Through Jesus Christ our Lord.
Amen.   Nick Fawcett

Lent petition

Loving God,
we remember today how much Christ loved us,
how much he was willing to sacrifice
and endure for our sakes.
Teach us to follow.

You set before him the need to choose –
    between the way of self and the way of the cross,
    the way of the world and the way of love,
    the way of life that leads to death
    and the way of death that leads to life.
Teach us to follow.

We thank you for the choice he made,
    and all that lay behind it –
    the faith that gave him the inner strength
    to resist temptation and accept your will,
    the courage to take the path of suffering and death,
    the love which guided all.
Teach us to follow.

Forgive us that having received so much from him
    we give so little in return.
We are self-centred,
    putting ourselves before others and before you,
    shying away from sacrifice and self-denial.
Teach us to follow.

We are narrow in our vision,
    more concerned with earthly satisfaction
    than spiritual fulfilment,
    taking the easy, comfortable way
    rather than the way of Christ.
Teach us to follow.

Loving God,
    once more, we pray
     assure us of your constant mercy,
    once more cleanse and renew our hearts,
    once more give us strength, faith and courage
    to follow where you would lead us.
Teach us to follow.

Teach us to hunger and thirst for righteousness,
    knowing that you are able to fill us;
    to trust in you always, come what may,
    knowing your love will never fail us;
    to offer you our worship
    through all we are and all we do,
    knowing you alone are God.
Teach us to follow.

Loving God,
    lead us when our time of trial comes,
        when we are faced by the need to choose,
        and deliver us then from evil.
    Teach us to follow,
        in the name of Christ.
    Amen.

NICK FAWCETT

Intercessions

Following Christ is not always a comfortable place to be.

We call to mind all who are insulted
or persecuted for their faith;
all who speak out
and those who are afraid to.

Silence for prayer

Help us, O Lord:
we put our trust in you.

We call to mind those working for peace,
justice and hope in an aching world.

Silence for prayer

Help us, O Lord:
we put our trust in you.

We call to mind those whose lives
are bound up with ours;
we remember all the families and streets
represented here.

Silence for prayer

Help us, O Lord:
we put our trust in you.

We call to mind those whose bodies
battle against disease or pain;
those whose minds battle against confusion
and depression.

Silence for prayer

Help us, O Lord:
we put our trust in you.

We call to mind those who are dying
in fear or loneliness;
those who have recently passed into eternity.

Silence for prayer

Help us, O Lord:
we put our trust in you.

We call to mind the ways we have been helped
through difficult times,
and have grown to understand more
of your loving care.
And we commend the rest of our life to your keeping.

Silence for prayer

Merciful Father,
accept these prayers
for the sake of your Son,
our Saviour Jesus Christ, Amen.

SUSAN SAYERS

Good news about suffering. In Christ, suffering can become a positive experience; a route to
full life and deeper understanding. In fact, Jesus goes so far as to say it is a necessary part of
our life in him. He will be there with us all through the very blackest, bleakest times.

As children and heirs through adoption, and knowing
that Jesus shares in all our suffering and joy,
let us confide in our heavenly Father
who knows us so well.

Father, into your enlightenment and perception
we bring all whose faith is limited by fear or prejudice;
all whose living faith has been replaced
by the empty shell of habit.

Silence for prayer

Father, give us courage:
you are our only strength.

Father, into the depths of your wisdom
and understanding we bring those with responsibilities,
and all who have difficult decisions to make;
all those in charge of hospitals, schools,
industry and all community services.

Silence for prayer

Father, give us courage:
you are our only strength.

Into your tireless faithfulness we bring any
who rely on us for help, support or guidance;
any whom we are being asked to serve
or introduce to your love.

Silence for prayer

Father, give us courage:
you are our only strength.

Into the gentleness of your healing love we bring all
who are in pain; all those recovering from surgery;
those involved in crippling accidents
or suffering from wasting diseases.

Silence for prayer

Father, give us courage:
you are our only strength.

Into your light and peace we commend
those who have died, especially any dear to us
whom we name in the silence of our hearts.

Silence for prayer

Father, give us courage:
you are our only strength.

Father, we thank you for supporting us
and encouraging us when life is hard,
and for all the exuberant vitality
of the world you have created for us to live in.

Silence for prayer

Merciful Father,
accept these prayers
for the sake of your Son,
our Saviour Jesus Christ, Amen.

SUSAN SAYERS

Short prayers

Loving God,
    through your Son you walked the way of the cross,
    each step leading you inexorably to suffering,
    humiliation and death.
We know it,
    and yet we continue to marvel,
    for such love defies human logic,
    and transcends anything we can give in return.

Open our hearts during this day and this week,
   so that we might glimpse again
   the wonder of your grace.
Give us insight into all it involved,
   all it cost and all it meant;
   and through that same grace, we ask you,
   help us to respond.
Amen.

NICK FAWCETT

Loving God,
   we talk of serving others
   but so often we live for ourselves,
   we speak of self-sacrifice but practise self-interest.
Forgive us for failing to follow Jesus,
   and for distorting the Gospel
   to serve our own purposes.
Remind us afresh
   of the great love you have shown in Christ.
Inspire us through those who responded faithfully to his call,
   and so help us in turn to give as well as receive,
   to bear willingly the cost of discipleship,
   for his name's sake.
Amen.

NICK FAWCETT

Lord Jesus Christ,
   you gave your all so that we might have life.
You counted yourself as nothing
   so that we might rejoice
   in the wonder of your love.
You endured agony of body, mind and spirit,
   so that we might receive mercy
   and know the peace which only you can give.
Help us today to recognise more clearly
   everything you did for us,
   and so inspire us to give a little of ourselves in return.
Teach us to walk the way of the cross,
   and to bear the cost gladly
   for the joy set before us,
   knowing that you will be with us,
   each step of the way,
   whatever we may face.
Amen.

NICK FAWCETT

Lord Jesus Christ,
it is not easy to follow you –
not if we are serious about discipleship.
You call us to a new way of thinking,
a new way of loving,
a new way of living that is more costly and demanding
than we can ever imagine.
Yet though the cost is high the reward is greater,
for in you we find life in all its fullness.
Lord Jesus Christ,
help us to follow.
Amen.

NICK FAWCETT

All-age-talk material

5 score

If anyone wants to follow Jesus what must they do?

Add or subtract letters to find out

ABCDEFGHIJKLMNOPQRSTUVWXYZ

'

| V-2 | K+4 | | A+1 | T-15 | | Q-4 | X+1 |

| G?1 | J+5 | G+5 | R-6 | N+1 | Z-3 | A+4 | Q+1 | | Z-1 | I+6 | S+2 |

| P-3 | H+13 | T?1 | W-3 | | D+2 | D+11 | Z-8 | I-2 | D+1 | S+1 |

| K-10 | A+1 | B+13 | S+2 | X-4 | | B+23 | P-1 | T+1 | V-4 |

| G+8 | V+1 | U-7 | | M+1 | D+1 | F-1 | L-8 | J+9 | | C-2 | H+6 | G-3 |

| B+1 | P-15 | Q+1 | P+2 | Z-1 | | V+3 | S-4 | Q+4 | F+12 |

,

| J-7 | D+14 | C+12 | W-4 | B+17 |

Mark 8:34

KATIE THOMPSON

let your will be done

↑ Start here

Draw (you) doing God's will when it is hard (you could be making up after a quarrel, sharing your sonic or helping with a job at home).

Draw (you) doing God's will when it is nice (you could be playing with friends, making a present for someone or feeding your pet).

He didn't enjoy being killed on a cross.

BUT

Jesus enjoyed making people better.

Start here

SUSAN SAYERS

Let your will be done

You can choose GOOD.

Colour this in your FAVOURITE colours.

Colour this in your WORST colours.

You can choose EVIL.

Cross out the (YES) and (NO) words to read the message:

JYESESUSNODYESIDNONOTYESCHNOOOSE
TYESHENOEASYESYWANOY. HNOECHYESOSE
TNOHEGONOODWAYESYBECNOAUSEYES
HNOELOYESVESNOUS.

Choices

Would you choose a ☐ or a ☐

Would you choose a ☐ or a ☐

Would you choose ☐ or ☐

Part of being human is being able to choose

SUSAN SAYERS

The price is right!

Aim

To emphasise the fact that following Jesus involves cost as well as reward, but that the greatness of his love, beyond all price, deserves a fitting response.

Preparation

Buy three items of confectionery (a packet of Maltesers, a tube of Smarties, a bar of chocolate, for example). Keep a note of how much each item cost.

Prepare three sets of four large eye-catching cards with a different price on each (for example, 26p, 27p, 28p, 29p). Ensure that in each set the correct price is included. The prices should be relatively close to each other, rather than clearly too high or too low.

You will also need nine pieces of blank card and three marker pens for use by your volunteers.

Talk

Tell the congregation that you are going to play your own version of the popular television game, *The price is right!* Ask for volunteers, and select three contestants to 'come on down!'. Give each of the contestants a marker pen and three pieces of card. Hold up the first item and then, after displaying the four prices to choose from, ask them to write down which price they think you actually paid.

After each round hold up the card with the right price. At the end of the game give each of the volunteers one of the items of confectionery.

How many guessed right? For those who didn't, it doesn't really matter for we were talking here about a few pence only. But there are times when knowing how much something might cost us is very important, for we need to decide whether or not we are able to afford it. And that is true not only when it comes to money but in other ways too.

Take, for example, the story of the woman who knelt before Jesus and poured a jar of hugely expensive ointment on his feet – a gift of such enormous value that some of those watching complained about the waste of money.

> Why was this ointment wasted in this way? For this ointment could have been sold for more than three hundred denarii, and the money given to the poor. *(Mark 14:4b-5)*

What they said was quite true, but for this woman her gift was a way of offering not just her money but her whole life to Jesus, for in him she had found a meaning to life which was beyond price.

And Lent reminds us that we too need to respond to the love of God shown in Jesus, which ultimately led him to death on the cross. Here is a love which we can never begin to repay. But if we are serious about following Jesus, there is a cost involved.

> If any want to become my followers, let them deny themselves and take up their cross and follow me. For those who want to save their life will lose it, and those who lose their life for the sake of the Gospel, will save it. *(Mark 8:34-35)*

To follow Jesus will mean sometimes letting go of self-interest, denying our own needs and wishes in preference to someone else's, having less so that others may have more.

What is the cost of following Jesus? In a sense the answer is nothing, for the love of God is free to all, offered by grace alone. But if we truly love Jesus and are serious about following him, then we will want to repay his love through offering our service. There is a price to discipleship, but it is a price worth paying for it leads to lasting happiness, and life in all its fullness.

NICK FAWCETT

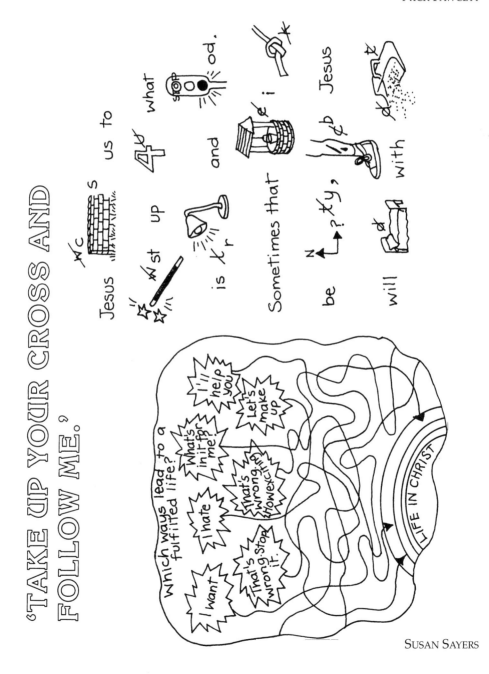

SUSAN SAYERS

This will hurt me more than it hurts you!

Equipment:

pen and paper for each member of the group

Ask the group to close their eyes for a few moments. While they have their eyes closed describe the following scene. Suggest to the group that it would be good if they can visualise the scene as you speak.

It's a really cold miserable day. Dark grey clouds cover the sky and a fine mist is swirling around. As you look ahead there is a large bridge across a deep river. A man is standing on the bridge, staring at the sky. Suddenly the man climbs onto the bridge railings. He is having trouble keeping his balance but this doesn't seem to bother him. He seems in danger of falling off the bridge and into the river far below.

Running over to him, not wanting to frighten him in case he falls, you ask him if he needs any help. Before you can say any more he shouts at you to keep away, threatening to jump if you come any closer.

Now ask the group to write on their pieces of paper what they would say to persuade the man to climb down from the bridge to safety. Discuss some of the responses.

Read Mark 8:31-38

Jesus begins to tell the disciples about suffering, rejection and finally death. But it was only a temporary situation. Jesus explained that three days later he would be alive again.

The disciples had experienced some incredible times and seen Jesus doing amazing things. And then he ruins it by saying it's all coming to an end! What will happen after three days? What will happen to the disciples?

Peter was obviously not impressed. He took Jesus to one side and suggested it wasn't a good idea to talk like that in front of the other disciples. The reason that Jesus got so angry with Peter was that Jesus was being tempted to go in a different direction to the one he knew he should take. Jesus knew that he had to fulfil God's purpose and that a sacrificial death was the only way for human-kind to be reconciled with God. Jesus didn't want to be 'talked out' of the way he was meant to take.

The disciples had seen Jesus do some awesome things but even they didn't know the full extent of what Jesus could do. As the Son of God, Jesus could have defeated anything the Romans or religious groups could throw at him.

Jesus was facing similar temptations to those he overcame in the desert. Did he really want to suffer? Did he really want to waste his life? Did he really want to disappoint all those people? Jesus knew that the only way ahead was for him to pay the ultimate price: his death on the cross.

Ask the group to look again at their responses to the man on the bridge.

What emotions would the group have felt about what the man was attempting to do?

- Was it a waste of life?
- Surely things couldn't be that bad?
- What about the people who cared for him?
- What about the future?

These were all emotions that Peter and the disciples would have felt. Were some of the group's responses similar to what Peter might have said? Can the group begin to understand how Peter would have felt and why he wanted Jesus to stop talking like that?

Although we should value life and not 'throw it away', Jesus knew that our eternal lives depended on him being the final sacrifice so that we could become part of God's family once and for all.

PETE TOWNSEND

Reflective material
(sketches, meditations and poems)

Meditation of Peter

It was a wonderful moment,
   I really thought I'd cracked it.
After all the uncertainty,
   all the questions,
   all the confusion,
   I finally believed I understood who he was.
'You're the Messiah!' I told him,
   and he beamed at me with such delight that I felt my heart would burst.
No one else had grasped it you see,
   not properly.
They wondered, of course,
   but like so many others they were still guessing,
   groping in the dark.
He might as well have been Elijah or John for all they knew.
I was different, and Jesus knew it.
'Blessed are you,' he said, 'for God has revealed this to you and not man.'
What an accolade!
But then it all went wrong,
   just when I felt I'd arrived the bubble burst,
   and with a vengeance!
I suppose I got carried away,
   never stopped to think.

Typical of me, really.
It's just that it came as such a shock,
    him going on like that about the future,
    everything he had to suffer,
    all doom and gloom,
    even talking of death itself.
I wasn't having any of it.
'Not likely!' I shouted. 'No way!'
I meant no harm,
    I just didn't think such things could happen to the Messiah.
But you should have seen his face,
    the anger, the disappointment.
Satan, he called me!
Can you believe that?
Me, his right-hand man,
    the one who'd just hit the nail on the head,
    the pick of the bunch, so I thought –
    Satan!
I was hurt at the time,
    cut to the heart if I'm honest,
    but I can see now, all too clearly, that he was right and I was wrong.
I still had so much to learn,
    so much to understand,
    and I needed a reprimand, a stern hand, if I was to progress any further.
I'd only just begun to glimpse the truth
    and if I'd have had my way
    it would have meant him denying everything he stood for.
He *was* the Messiah but not in the way I meant it;
    he had come to establish his kingdom,
    but in a very different way than we expected.
His was the way of service, of sacrifice, or self-denial,
    offering his life for the life of the world.
I see that now and I marvel at his love,
    but what I marvel at even more is that
    even when I understood him so little
    he understood me so much.

NICK FAWCETT

Meditation of David (based on Psalm 22)

I felt alone,
    utterly abandoned,
    not just by man but by God,
    and I was bereft, desolate,
    broken in body, mind and spirit.

How could it be happening, I asked myself?
Why had God brought me thus far,
   always by my side,
   always there to guide me,
   only to desert me when I needed him most?
It made no sense,
   faith itself thrown into turmoil,
   for it denied everything:
   the love, the purpose, the mercy I'd trusted in so long.
Yet when I cried out in agony of spirit,
   there was nothing –
   not a word,
   not a sign –
   nothing;
   and it was crushing,
   the bleakest, blackest moment of my life.
I wanted to let go,
   give up,
   for surely anything, even the oblivion of death,
   was preferable to this.
Yet somehow I held on.
Despite the emptiness, the awful silence,
   I kept praying,
   remembering all that God had done.
And somewhere, deep within, hope flickered again,
   spluttering,
   tremulous,
   like a smouldering candle,
   a flame caught in the breeze,
   yet alight once more,
   refusing to be extinguished.
It took time, mind you, before the cloud lifted;
   not just days, but weeks, months –
   a long and lonely struggle in the wilderness –
   and I often wondered if I would ever taste joy again,
   my heart dance once more to the familiar tunes of old.
I was wrong, of course,
   for I came through finally,
   stronger and tougher through the experience.
God hadn't forsaken me;
   he'd been there all along,
   right there in the darkness
   sharing my sorrow,
   bearing my pain.

But for a time I'd believed him lost to me,
   I'd glimpsed the agony of separation,
   and it was more terrible than you can imagine.
God save anyone from facing that again.

NICK FAWCETT

Jesus Cleanses the Temple

His death and resurrection foreshadowed

A reading from the Gospel of John (2:13-25)

Jesus went to Jerusalem to celebrate the Jewish Passover. He found the temple in Jerusalem full of people selling cattle, sheep and pigeons, and amongst them sat the moneychangers.

He was very angry and overturned the tables of the moneychangers, scattering their coins everywhere. Using a whip he angrily chased the animals and the merchants out of the temple shouting at them, 'Take all of these things away and stop making my Father's house into a market place!'

The temple priests tried to stop Jesus and asked, 'What right do you have to act like this?'

Jesus answered, 'Destroy this temple and I will raise it again in three days.'

'This temple took forty-six years to build! How could you rebuild it in three days!' they exclaimed.

But the temple which Jesus spoke of was his own body, and after his resurrection from the dead, his disciples would understand what Jesus had said that day. Many people saw the signs Jesus worked while he was in Jerusalem, and they believed in him. Since Jesus knew what was in the hearts and minds of the people, he was careful whom he trusted.

This is the Gospel of the Lord
Praise to you, Lord Jesus Christ

KATIE THOMPSON

Prayers

Thanksgiving and petition

Living God,
    we rejoice that you are a God who is slow to anger
        and full of steadfast love,
        infinitely patient, understanding and merciful,
        always seeking to forgive, to forget, to restore and renew.
    Yet do not let us become complacent,
        for there are times when even your patience
        is tested to the limit
        and your anger blazes against us –
        when we wilfully and stubbornly disobey you,

when our actions, or failure to act, causes harm to others,
when our faithlessness becomes a stumbling block
    to those who seek you.
Forgive us those times,
    and help us put right our mistakes.
Lord, in your mercy,
    hear our prayer.

Living God,
    help us to recognise there are occasions
        when you have no choice but to feel angry,
        and help us to recognise sometimes
        that we should feel the same.
    Help us to know when those occasions are.
    Lord, in your mercy,
        hear our prayer.

Teach us when anger is unjustified, foolish, petty, selfish,
    when it is more about our hurt pride than right and wrong,
    when it says more about ourselves
        than the cause we attribute anger to.
Save us then from the errors it might lead us into –
    thoughtless words, careless deeds,
    and destructive attitudes –
    and help us then to control our anger.
Lord, in your mercy,
    hear our prayer.

But teach us also when we ought to be angry.
When we are faced by anything
    that denies full living,
    that demeans and destroys,
    that feeds injustice or exploitation,
    that cheats, corrupts, wounds or hurts,
    that leads the innocent astray,
    that divides people from one another and from you,
    teach us then to feel a genuine fury
    and to express that with proper passion,
    translating anger into action,
    speaking out against falsehood,
    working to right wrongs,
    overcoming evil with good,
    giving all for your kingdom.
Lord, in your mercy,
    hear our prayer,
    in the name of Christ our Lord.
    Amen.   NICK FAWCETT

Confession

Sovereign God,
   from whom nothing is hidden
      and by whom all things are known,
      forgive us that we so easily and so readily deceive ourselves.
   Have mercy, O Lord,
      and make us new.

We concern ourselves with outer appearances
      rather than with inner reality,
      fooling ourselves into believing all is well
      when in our hearts we know that much is wrong.
   Have mercy, O Lord,
      and make us new.

We turn faith into something we do
      rather than something we are,
      a theory which we learn
      rather than a way of life we put into practice.
   Have mercy, O Lord,
      and make us new.

We talk of following Jesus,
      of committing our lives to him in joyful service,
      but it is ourselves we serve first,
      and our own inclinations that we follow.
   Have mercy, O Lord,
      and make us new.

We know we have done wrong,
      conscious of our weakness,
      yet we run from the truth,
      afraid to face facts,
      excusing or denying our mistakes.
   Have mercy, O Lord,
      and make us new.

Sovereign God,
   forgive us the faults that everyone sees
      and the faults known only to ourselves,
      the weaknesses we cannot hide
      and the weaknesses we conceal from everyone but yourself.
   Forgive us all the ways we let you down
      and betray our calling.
   Have mercy, O Lord,
      and make us new.

Fill our hearts with love,
   our minds with faith,
   our souls with power,
   and our lives with grace,
   so that we may love you better
   and serve you more faithfully.
Help us to see you in all your greatness
   and ourselves as we really are,
   and, through understanding both clearly,
   help us to become the people you would have us be.
Have mercy, O Lord,
   and make us new.

Through Jesus Christ our Lord.
Amen.

NICK FAWCETT

Intercession

Sovereign God,
   we pray for the weak and vulnerable in our world –
      those who feel powerless
      in the face of the massive problems that confront them.
   Help of the helpless,
      reach out to strengthen and support.

We pray for the poor,
   the hungry,
   the diseased,
   the dying.
Help of the helpless,
   reach out to strengthen and support.

We pray for the oppressed,
   the exploited,
   the abused,
   the tortured.
Help of the helpless,
   reach out to strengthen and support.

We pray for the frightened,
   the lonely,
   the hurt,
   the depressed.
Help of the helpless,
   reach out to strengthen and support.

We pray for those who live in lands racked by tension,
    those who face famine and starvation,
    those who are unemployed,
    those who are homeless.
Help of the helpless,
    reach out to strengthen and support.

Sovereign God,
    you have expressed a special concern
        for the bruised, the needy, and the weak of our world.
    May that concern bring strength to all in such need,
        and may it inspire people everywhere
        to work for a more just society,
        standing up for the needy,
        and working for that time when there will be an end
        to suffering, mourning and pain;
        that time when your kingdom will come
        and your will be done.
Help of the helpless,
    reach out to strengthen and support,
    in the name of Christ.
Amen.

NICK FAWCETT

A short prayer

Lord,
    we are not good at showing anger;
    at least, not as it is meant to be shown.
We are ready enough to show our temper,
    easily riled by the most innocuous of things
    and capable, at our worst, of destructive fits of rage,
    but such anger is rarely justified,
    almost always serving merely to give vent to our own feelings
    at the cost of someone else's.
Your anger is so very different,
    for it is not about your hurt but ours.
You see injustice and exploitation,
    and your blood boils for the oppressed.
You see the peddling of drugs and the sale of pornography,
    and your heart burns within you at the innocent led astray.
You see hatred, violence, cruelty,
    and your spirit seethes for those caught up in its wake.

Whatever destroys hope, denies love or despoils life
   arouses wrath within you.
Teach us to share that anger
   and to channel it in your service,
   committing ourselves to do all in our power
   to fight against evil and to strive for your kingdom;
   through Jesus Christ our Lord.
Amen.

NICK FAWCETT

All-age-talk material

He drove the animals and traders out of the temple

How many differences can you find in the bottom picture? Circle the number

6   8   10   12

KATIE THOMPSON

Where do you worship on Sunday?

Draw a picture of your place of worship and the people you see there

KATIE THOMPSON

Jesus said . . .

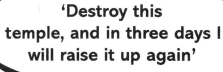

'Destroy this temple, and in three days I will raise it up again'

Which temple did Jesus mean?

John 2:21

Follow the instructions to find out

1. Change A to T
2. Change B to E
3. Change C to H
4. Change D to M
5. Change E to A
6. Change F to W
7. Change G to L
8. Change H to S
9. Change I to P
10. Change J to B
11. Change K to Y
12. Change L to O
13. Change M to I
14. Change N to D

A C B   A B D I G B

A C E A   F E H

C M H

J L N K

KATIE THOMPSON

KATIE THOMPSON

A surprising side

Aim

From the account of Jesus turning out the traders from the temple in Jerusalem, to show that, while anger is typically a destructive emotion, there are times when it is not only understandable but essential.

Preparation

In large, bold letters print or write the following riddle:

My first is in WRATH and not found in MEEK.
My second's in STRONG instead of in WEAK.
My third is in RAGING and not found in MILD.
My fourth is in TEMPER and also in RILED.
My last is in FURY, and also in IRE.
My whole was displayed by our surprising Messiah!

Display this at the front of the church, allowing time before the talk for people to see it and try to work it out (even if this does mean they are not concentrating on the rest of the service!). Ensure that the Bible passage, John 2:13-25, has been read prior to this talk.

Talk

Ask if anyone is able to solve the riddle you have set them. As a clue, tell them that the answer describes how Jesus was feeling in the above passage of Scripture. The answer you are looking for, of course, is ANGER. Run through the riddle and explain how you arrive at this answer.

There are some people who think of Jesus as MEEK and MILD, but the story of him turning out the traders from the temple reminds us that there was nothing WEAK about him. When Jesus saw what was going on in the temple – corruption and exploitation being allowed to continue unchecked – he was filled with WRATH, giving vent to his IRE in a RAGING display of TEMPER, the FURY of which took the traders and moneylenders in the temple by surprise.

Here is a side to Jesus we are not used to, and perhaps one which makes us feel a little uncomfortable; the idea that he could be capable of such STRONG feelings when RILED fitting uneasily with the picture we have of him. Yet it is a side we need to recognise and grapple with, for, although nine times out of ten anger is a destructive thing, there are times when it is right to feel angry. When we see injustice around us, when evil triumphs over good, when the innocent are made to suffer, when unnecessary hurt is caused to others – at times like these it is not only right to feel angry, it is imperative: the only response which will do!

NICK FAWCETT

Anger in the temple!

Jesus was furious when he saw what was happening inside the temple!

Write the PREVIOUS letter of the alphabet on each line to spell out his words in John 2:16

A B C D E F G H I J K L M N O P Q R S T U V W X Y Z A B C . . .

' S
  T U P Q   U V S O J O H   N Z

__ __ __ __ __ __ '
G B U I F S T

__ __ __ __ __
I P V T F

__ __ __ __   __
J O U P   B

__ __ __ __ __ __ !'
N B S L F U

John 2:16

Katie Thompson

Read John 2:13-22

The Passover was an extremely important feast for the Jews. The law stated that every adult male who lived within fifteen miles of Jerusalem must attend the feast.

When the male Jews arrived in Jerusalem and visited the temple, they were asked to pay a temple tax equal to an average day's wage. This tax was to ensure that the temple rituals were carried out each day. But the tax had to be paid in special Jewish currency. Any other coins were considered 'unclean' and not acceptable. To help the pilgrims offer the 'correct' coins, a group of money-changers was available in the temple precincts. The moneychangers charged the equivalent of one day's wage to exchange the pilgrims' coins; that's the wages for two days paid out already and the feast hasn't even started!

The next stage was to offer a sacrifice at the temple. This sacrifice was an offering of thanks for a safe journey or some other event in the life of the pilgrim. A pilgrim could take their own animal into the temple for sacrifice or buy an animal from one of the traders outside the temple. A small animal would cost the equivalent of one day's wages. But the temple rules stated that a sacrificial animal must be perfect. So, any animal that was brought into the temple was inspected for a small fee – about a quarter of a day's wages.

It was almost certain that any animal bought outside the temple would be declared 'impure'. This meant the pilgrim would have to buy one of the 'pure' animals from the stallholders inside the temple. A small animal which cost a quarter of a day's wages outside the temple would cost the same as twenty days' wages from a stallholder inside the temple! So, for a quick trip to the temple, it has cost approximately twenty-two days' wages. Some feast!

If you were rich, the cost of visiting the temple was not a major problem. If you were poor it was a *major* problem. No wonder Jesus was so angry about this social injustice. More importantly, most people would see no more of God's house than the market where they got ripped off. What did this say about God? It certainly gave the impression that God could be bought and that having faith in God was like a market place, the best deals on offer to those who could afford it!

Jesus found some rope and made a whip. He then created a real stir by chasing everyone out of the temple while shouting, 'Don't make my Father's house a market place'.

Jesus was angry because the impression that people got of God was so wrong. The injustice and trading that took place created an unnatural distance between God and his people. It also gave the impression that God and his priests were in the faith business for profit. Jesus knew that before long the greatest sacrifice in history would be made. A sacrifice which was totally 'pure' was to be made at no cost to God's people. He alone was going to bear the cost. Jesus had every right to be angry!

PETE TOWNSEND

Reflective material
(sketches, meditations and poems)

Jesus gets angry

Based on Matthew 21:12-14

Narrator	Dan, the moneychanger, was setting up his stall as usual in the temple, next to Joe, a dove merchant.
Dan	I like it here, Joe – better than being out in the rain.
Joe	Yes. Mind you, our stalls make it difficult for less able people to get in.
Dan	Who cares about them? They've never got any money.
Joe	That's true, and of course in here it's harder for the punters to compare our prices with the ordinary shops.
Dan	You're right. It's a pretty good swindle – and it's legal!
Joe	Just a minute – what's all that noise outside?
Narrator	They listened carefully. It seemed to be some kind of celebration. They could just about make out words like 'Hosanna!' Then Jesus strode into the temple with his friends, and stood looking around.
Joe	He doesn't look very happy – he might cause trouble.
Dan	What! Him? He's a wimp! Talks about 'love' and 'forgiveness' all the time. He's a nobody – ignore him.
Narrator	So they did.

- Dan *counted his money*
- Joe *stroked one of his doves*
- while Jesus *looked from side to side*

Jesus	There are sick and disabled people outside who can't get in, and all the space is taken up by these money-grabbing swindlers!
Narrator	Suddenly, Jesus grabbed a piece of rope which one of the traders had left lying around, and knotted it to make a vicious-looking whip. He went over to Joe.
Jesus	What do you people think you're doing?
Joe	Just a bit of of honest trade, sir. Best prices in town.
Jesus	Best prices for you, you mean.
Narrator	And then, without warning, Jesus grabbed Joe's stall and turned it over. The cages burst open and doves flew everywhere. Then Jesus went over to Dan.

Dan   Now look here, I've got a licence to trade here; I paid a high bribe – I mean tax – for it.

Narrator Jesus wasn't listening. He threw Dan's tray of money on the floor and overturned his table. After that, he drove the animals and all the traders out of the building. By the time the temple police arrived it was all over. Well, nothing changes, does it! Then a wonderful thing happened. Into the temple came a procession of people who had never been in there before. Some couldn't walk and had to be helped by friends; others were blind and had to be guided. They came over to where Jesus was standing, still a little out of breath, and a woman with a stick spoke to him.

Esther   Thank you. We haven't been able to get in before. The traders took up so much room, and all the people bustling about doing their shopping meant that only the really fit people could cope with it.

Jesus   I know, and it makes me angry! Now you're here why don't we do something about that leg of yours?

Esther   I've tried every doctor in the area, but it's incurable.

Narrator Jesus took hold of her hand, and suddenly the woman's leg grew strong again. Jesus moved on to the next person, and soon the temple was full of people laughing, singing and praising God . . . From then on, a lot of new people joined in things at the temple, who had never been able to get in before. They were very happy about it, although Dan and Joe and their friends weren't. But then, you can't please everybody, can you – so why try?

MICHAEL FORSTER

De'ath meets . . . Arthur Angry

Characters De'ath and Arthur Angry

Scene   De'ath, in his smart gear, meets Arthur Angry, who is casually dressed and carrying a large paper bag.

Props   small coffee table
              water jug and two drinking glasses
              two comfy chairs
              large paper bag

De'ath   Delighted to be here once again with all you lovely people. It gives me such a thrill to see you all come here to meet me and my guest. Now, our guest today is someone you may have met at times, some of you may have met him on a very regular basis! It gives me great pleasure – it might not give you the same amount of pleasure though – ladies and gentlemen, Arthur Angry!

Arthur	Hrrumph!
De'ath	Welcome, Arthur. And how are you?
Arthur	Yes!
De'ath	Excuse me – yes?
Arthur	S'right.
De'ath	How are you? Did you have difficulty finding your way here? How's the family?
Arthur	Yes!
De'ath	Is that all you're going to say?
Arthur	Yes!
De'ath	I think we wanted a bit more than a 'yes' to every question. Perhaps you could expand on that a little?
Arthur	No!
De'ath	I see, different word but still just the one?
Arthur	Yes!
De'ath	Come on now. Our audience is eager to hear more about you and what you've been getting up to recently.
Arthur	Yes?
De'ath	For goodness sake! Can't you say more than that?
Arthur	Yes.
De'ath	Then why don't you? Got a problem with your vocal chords, or don't you know more than two or three words?
Arthur	Yes!
De'ath	Well, use them then!
Arthur	OK.
De'ath	OK what?
Arthur	OK.
De'ath	Now look here . . .
Arthur	No! You look here. See this bag? Right! That's my breakfast, that is. How do you think I felt, travelling here on an empty stomach, to be greeted by a sleeping doorman who can't find my name on the guest list and tries to block the doorway to stop me getting in.
De'ath	You're here now.
Arthur	No thanks to your doorman. By the way, he's gone visiting.

De'ath	Visiting? Where?
Arthur	The hospital!
De'ath	You didn't . . . ?
Arthur	I did!
De'ath	Was that necessary?
Arthur	No!
De'ath	Don't start that again!
Arthur	I'll start something in a minute. Just let me get me coat off and I'll show you 'start that again'!
De'ath	I'm so glad you haven't forgotten everything I taught you.
Arthur	You what?
De'ath	It's good to see that you haven't lost the knack of rising to the occasion!
Arthur	You mean you wanted to get me all aggravated?
De'ath	Just my little way of checking to see that you haven't gone soft in your old age.
Arthur	What do you mean, 'old age'? I'll give you 'old age'. Just let me . . .
De'ath	Arthur, Arthur. Calm down. Just for a few minutes anyway. Just kidding, OK?
Arthur	Got me going there you did, good and proper.
De'ath	How is everything these days? Keeping up the traditions, are we?
Arthur	You know me, can't let an opportunity go by without raising the blood pressure.
De'ath	Glad to hear it. Can you see any old friends in the audience?
Arthur	One or two. I'd like to get to know a few more if I can. Anyone like to let their nose greet my fist?
De'ath	Some other time perhaps. Now, any little bits of advice you can share with us?
Arthur	Yes.
De'ath	Oh, not again!
Arthur	Got you!
De'ath	So you did.
Arthur	To answer your question, and using more than three words! I get around quite a lot. You know, making sure that those little insignificant things don't remain that way! Why have a mole hill when, with a bit

of effort, you can have a whopping great mountain! Doesn't make sense to me, to waste so little energy on small things when you might as well go all the way and make it worth your while. People don't forget you then.

De'ath   I'm sure they don't. Thank you very much, Arthur Angry. I hope you've enjoyed yourself.

Arthur   Yes!

Pete Townsend

Meditation of James, the Apostle

He was angry,
   more angry than I've ever seen him,
   more angry than I dreamt he could be.
It was so unlike him, that's what surprised me,
   so different from everything we'd come to expect.
The model of gentleness he'd been up till then,
   always willing to see the best,
   ready to make allowances
   where others rushed in to condemn.
Goodness knows, there'd been provocation enough,
   the way the Pharisees goaded him,
   the scribes heckled,
   the Sadducees found fault,
   but despite everything they threw at him –
   the insults,
   the lies,
   the accusations –
   he never let it get to him,
   somehow keeping his cool
   when all around him were losing theirs.
But not this time.
I could sense it the moment he set foot in the temple –
   not just anger,
   but outrage,
   seething within him before finally boiling over
   in an explosion of fury.
We were stunned by the way he acted,
   not quite sure what to do with ourselves.
I mean, words are one thing,
   but to create a scene like that –
   it just wasn't done.
But here was a face of Jesus we hadn't seen before,
   disturbing yet challenging.

He saw God's house turned into a market-place,
   a centre of extortion, injustice and corruption,
   and suddenly the frustration he'd bottled up for so long
   came pouring out –
   his sorrow and disappointment
   at a world hell-bent on destroying itself
   when salvation was so nearly in its grasp.
It sealed his fate, that day,
   the writing on the wall after such a blatant act of defiance,
   and the funny thing is I think he knew it,
   almost, you might say, timed it to happen that way.
Did he want to die?
I'm not sure of that, for he loved life as much as any of us.
But what he saw there in the temple
   seemed to convince him there was no other way,
   no other course open to him than to tackle evil head on,
   however awful the consequences,
   however great the price.
No wonder he was angry!

NICK FAWCETT

God's Love for the World

The privilege and cost of motherhood

A reading from the Gospel of John (3:14-21)

Jesus said to Nicodemus:

Just as Moses raised up the bronze snake in the desert, so the Son of Man must be raised up, so that everyone who believes in him may have eternal life.

God loved the world so much that he sent his only Son to give eternal life to those who believe in him.

He was not sent to judge the world but to be its saviour. Those who choose not to believe in him have determined their own judgement. The light of the world has come, but many turn away from it and prefer the darkness. Anyone who does wrong is afraid of the light, because their badness will be plain for all to see. Good people are not afraid of the light, because it shows that what they do, comes from God.

This is the Gospel of the Lord
Praise to you, Lord Jesus Christ KATIE THOMPSON

Prayers

Praise

Loving God,
  we praise you that we can put our hand into yours,
    knowing that you will lead, support and hold us
    throughout our lives,
    that you will supply all our needs and far more besides.
  You have touched our lives through your grace.
  In gratitude we respond.

We praise you for our experience of that truth across the years –
    the way you have always held firm to us
    despite our faults and faithlessness,
    never letting go of us even when we let go of you.
  You have touched our lives through your grace.
  In gratitude we respond.

Forgive us that we have let go so often,
   intent on going our own way;
   clinging to what ultimately can never satisfy.
Forgive us for doubting you when times are hard,
   questioning your ability to lead us safely through.
Forgive us for reaching out only when we have need of you,
   expecting you to lift us up from trouble of our own making,
   and to set us on our feet again.
You have touched our lives through your grace.
In gratitude we respond.

Help us to put our hand again in yours,
   in simple trust,
   quiet confidence
   and eager expectation,
   knowing that whatever we face
   and wherever we may find ourselves,
   you will hold us firm.
You have touched our lives through your grace.
In gratitude we respond.

In the name of Christ.
Amen.

NICK FAWCETT

Thanksgiving

Almighty God,
   we thank you for your great gift of love –
      the love which we are able to share with those around us,
      which gives us a sense of self-worth and belonging,
      which enriches our lives in so many ways.
   You have opened your heart to us –
      help us to do the same to you.

We thank you for your love which defies all expression,
      constant, total, inexhaustible,
      flowing out to us like a never-ending stream.
   You have opened your heart to us –
      help us to do the same to you.

Almighty God,
   we thank you for loving us before we ever loved you,
      and for continuing to love us
      even when we fail to love you in return.
   You have opened your heart to us –
      help us to do the same to you.

Deepen our love for you and one another.
Help us to be faithful and true in all our relationships,
   and most especially in our relationship with you.
You have opened your heart to us –
   help us to do the same to you,
   in the name of Christ.
   Amen.   NICK FAWCETT

Intercession

*In the glory of God's presence the covenant of the law is sealed between God and his people;
Jesus himself becomes the sacrifice binding them in the new covenant.*

When following you brings danger, Lord,
or weariness or discomfort,
we long for your help.

Silence for prayer

In the shadow of your wings:
we shall be in safety.

When we watch the violence and selfishness of this world,
its bewilderment and fear,
we long for your peace.

Silence for prayer

In the shadow of your wings:
we shall be in safety.

When we work through our relationships
and feel for those we love,
we long for your guidance.

Silence for prayer

In the shadow of your wings:
we shall be in safety.

When our hearts touch those who suffer,
and know their pain and distress,
we long for your healing love.

Silence for prayer

In the shadow of your wings:
we shall be in safety.

When those we love meet death
and we must let them go,
we long for your mercy and welcome.

Silence for prayer

In the shadow of your wings:
we shall be in safety.

When we see the beauty and wonder
of your glorious creation and of your holiness,
we long for an eternity to praise you.

Silence for prayer

Merciful Father,
accept these prayers
for the sake of your Son,
our Saviour Jesus Christ, Amen.

SUSAN SAYERS

Short prayers

A woman's prayer *by Rachel Mathew*

O God, the giver of life,
  thank you for creating me as a woman
  by allowing me to share your image.
Thank you for the gift of life,
  the gift of my body, my womb,
  which enables me to participate in creating new life.
Thank you for the gift of your sacrificial love,
  which enables me to care and nurture
  children, aged, invalids and nature.
Thank you for breaking your body for all.
By sharing it, I'm strengthened
  when my body is broken and humiliated.
Lord, in the midst of suffering, oppression,
  discrimination and humiliation,
  you are my hope, my strength and my comfort,
  for you suffer with me and have conquered death.
Lord, help me to strive on to nurture life
  in the midst of my struggles against the powers of death.

from *Sharing Ways and Wisdoms* by BARBARA BUTLER

Lord Jesus Christ,
  you told your disciples that the kingdom of heaven
  belongs to little children.
You warned us that unless we can become like them
  then we shall not enter it ourselves.
Teach us what that means.
Help us to be truly childlike in our faith,
  having a child's innocence,
  a child's hunger to learn, and a child's total trust.
Help us, like them, to step out gladly
  into the great adventure of faith.
Amen.

NICK FAWCETT

All-age-talk material

God loves the world

How much do you know about our world? Are these statements true or false?

Tick the True or False box

	T	F
1. The longest river is the Nile	☐	☐
2. The largest ocean is the Indian	☐	☐
3. Earth is approximately 4,600 million years old	☐	☐
4. The largest desert is the Sahara	☐	☐
5. Earth is bigger than Jupiter	☐	☐
6. Ice covers more than one tenth of our planet at any one time	☐	☐

(Answers below)

1. T, 2. F, 3. T, 4. T, 5. F, 6. T

KATIE THOMPSON

God sent his only
Son Jesus to be our

— — — — — — —
7 15 13 11 12 10 8

Solve the problems to find the missing letters

O	$= (6 \times 3) - 6 =$	
A	$= (25 \div 5) \times 3 =$	
U	$= (14 - 7) + 3 =$	
S	$= (17 + 4) \div 3 =$	
R	$= (8 \times 5) \div 5 =$	
I	$= (15 \div 3) + 6 =$	
V	$= (13 + 4) - 4 =$	

KATIE THOMPSON

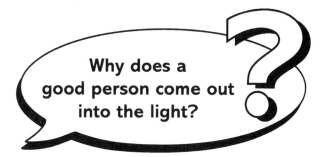

Why does a
good person come out
into the light?

Find the odd word in each set and
write it on the numbered line

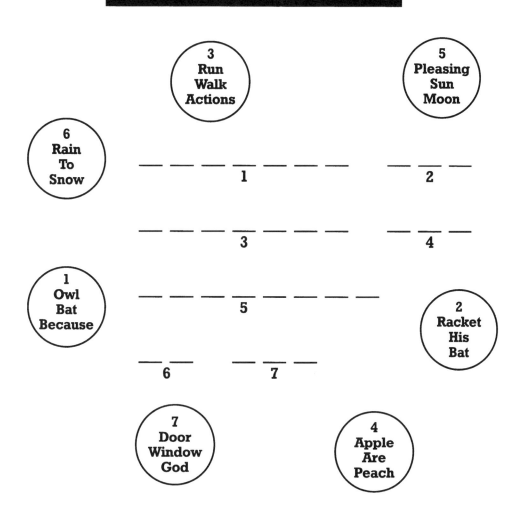

3
Run
Walk
Actions

5
Pleasing
Sun
Moon

6
Rain
To
Snow

_ _ _ _ _ _ _   _ _ _
        1   2

_ _ _ _ _ _ _   _ _ _
        3   4

1
Owl
Bat
Because

_ _ _ _ _ _ _
        5

2
Racket
His
Bat

_ _   _ _ _
 6   7

7
Door
Window
God

4
Apple
Are
Peach

KATIE THOMPSON

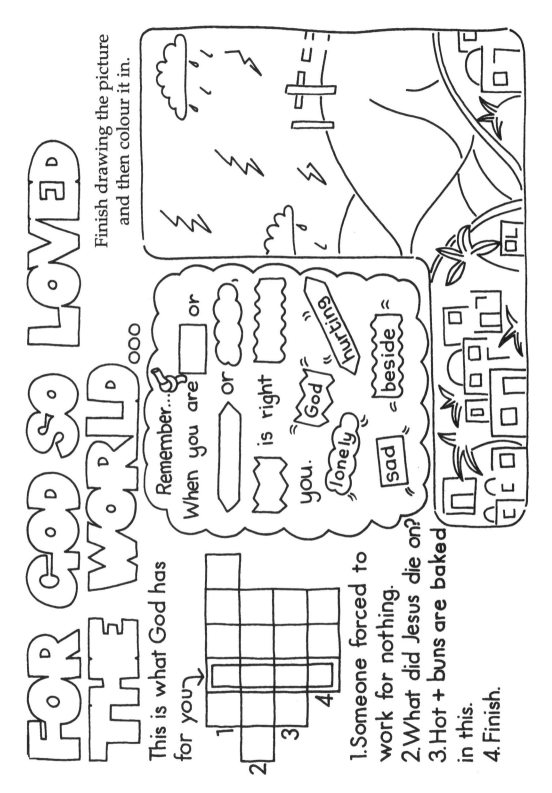

FOR GOD SO LOVED THE WORLD... oooo

Finish drawing the picture and then colour it in.

This is what God has for you

1. Someone forced to work for nothing.
2. What did Jesus die on?
3. Hot + buns are baked in this.
4. Finish.

Remember... When you are ☐ or ▭ or ▭ is right ▭ beside you. God hurting lonely sad

Who did God
send to save us?

Trace the letters and colour the squares with a ★

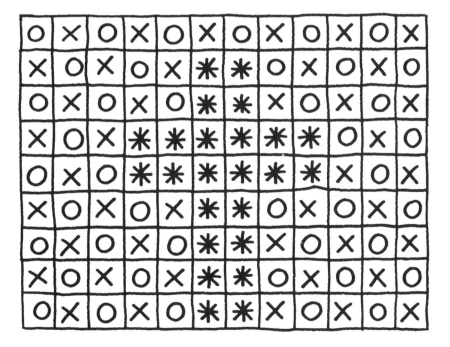

Jesus brings
light into our world and fills us
with his goodness

Draw some of the things you have at
home which give out light

KATIE THOMPSON

Mothering Sunday

Use the code breaker to find out where this brave mother hid her baby

The King of Egypt ordered all new-born Hebrew boys to be killed

	1	2	3	4	5
△	Y	L	N	H	T
○	G	A	B	S	V
□	I	E	R	K	D

$\overline{\square 1}\ \overline{\triangle 3}$ $\overline{\bigcirc 2}$ $\overline{\square 3}\ \overline{\square 2}\ \overline{\square 2}\ \overline{\square 5}$

$\overline{\bigcirc 3}\ \overline{\bigcirc 2}\ \overline{\bigcirc 4}\ \overline{\square 4}\ \overline{\square 2}\ \overline{\triangle 5}$

$\overline{\triangle 4}\ \overline{\square 1}\ \overline{\square 5}\ \overline{\square 5}\ \overline{\square 2}\ \overline{\triangle 3}$ $\overline{\square 1}\ \overline{\triangle 3}$ $\overline{\triangle 5}\ \overline{\triangle 4}\ \overline{\square 2}$

$\overline{\triangle 5}\ \overline{\bigcirc 2}\ \overline{\triangle 2}\ \overline{\triangle 2}$ $\overline{\bigcirc 1}\ \overline{\square 3}\ \overline{\bigcirc 2}\ \overline{\bigcirc 4}\ \overline{\bigcirc 4}$ $\overline{\bigcirc 3}\ \overline{\triangle 1}$

$\overline{\triangle 5}\ \overline{\triangle 4}\ \overline{\square 2}$ $\overline{\square 3}\ \overline{\square 1}\ \overline{\bigcirc 5}\ \overline{\square 2}\ \overline{\square 3}$ **Exodus 2:3**

KATIE THOMPSON

Joseph and Mary the mother of Jesus went to the temple. Which holy man warned Mary that this child would break her heart?

Use the clues to spell out his name

1. 1st letter of

2. 5th letter of

3. 4th letter of

4. 3rd letter of

5. 2nd letter of

6. 1st letter of

KATIE THOMPSON

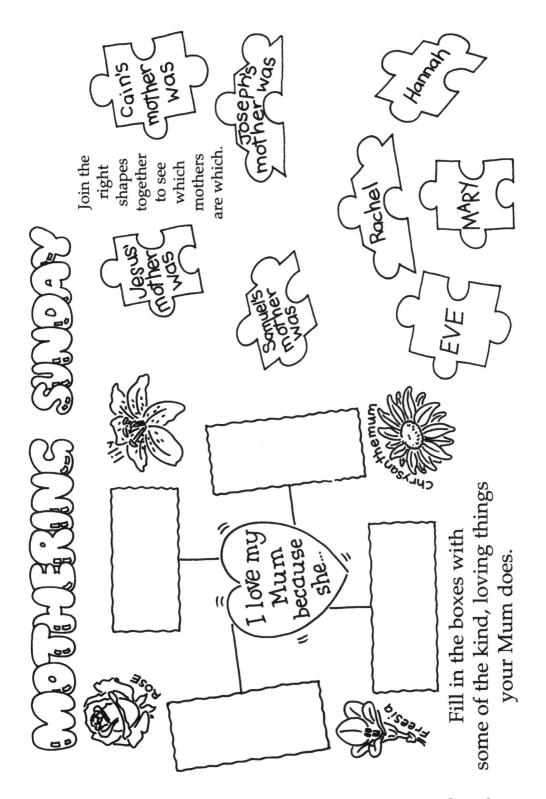

MOTHERING SUNDAY

Join the right shapes together to see which mothers are which.

Cain's mother was

Joseph's mother was

Hannah

Jesus' mother was

Samuel's mother was

Rachel

MARY

EVE

I love my Mum because she...

ROSE

freesia

chrysanthemum

Fill in the boxes with some of the kind, loving things your Mum does.

SUSAN SAYERS

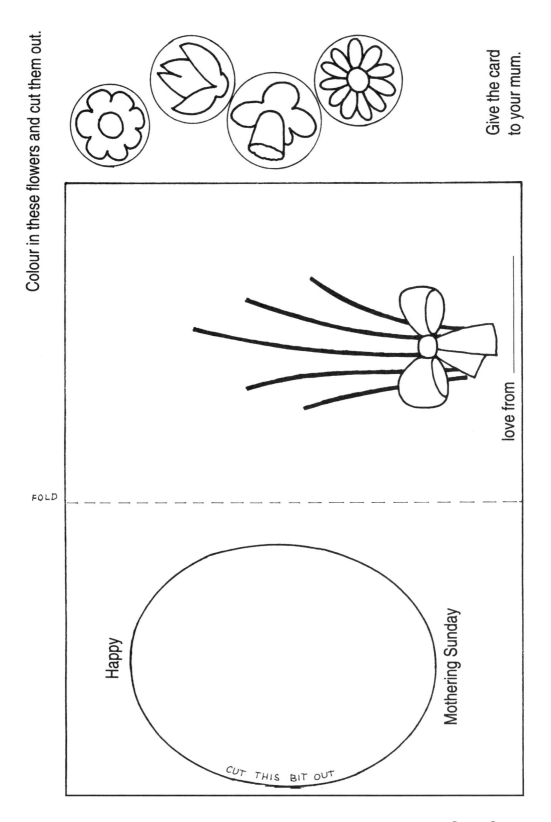

Colour in these flowers and cut them out.

Give the card to your mum.

FOLD

love from _____

Happy

Mothering Sunday

CUT THIS BIT OUT

SUSAN SAYERS

Children of God

Beforehand prepare two chunks of wood, which should be quite different from each other. From each cut a small chip. Also prepare some cards stuck on pea sticks and have a thick felt-tip pen at the ready to write in the signs.

First ask everyone what thing an ant might think of as huge. Then a cat. Then collect some ideas of what they themselves think of as huge. Remind everyone that all of these are contained in the mind of God and he is far greater than we can ever imagine. But let's have a go at imagining what God is like. Write the descriptions on the notices which people can hold up.

Now give out the two chips of wood and show everyone the blocks they came from. Ask a cluster of people round each chip to decide which block their chip came from. How can they tell? – By the way it feels; by its colour; by the grain, etc.

Jesus says that we are to behave in the same way God does – we are to be chips off the old block, and by looking at us and the way we behave, people should be able to recognise that we are Christians. So how will that mean we are to behave? Look again at the notices and they may be able to help us. If God is prepared to love everyone, whether they deserve it or not, then that's how we ought to be. If God is forgiving, we need to be as well. If God is trustworthy, so should we be to one another.

Look at the chips of wood again. If we're honest, we know we don't always behave like God. Jesus suggests that we recognise we are only chips and don't get carried away into thinking we're the block of wood. So long as we don't pretend we know all the answers he will be able to teach us through our lives to become more and more like him.

Susan Sayers

Read John 3:14-21

Within this reading there is one of the most powerful statements in the whole Bible. The verse in John 3:16 is one of the most quoted and also one of the most well known. The verse contains everything we need to know about God's love for us.

- Firstly, we have the amazing statement that God loved the *world*. This tells us that the character of God is love. He doesn't hold grudges or keep a diary of every dodgy event in our lives. God's love isn't just for a race of people, a nation or even a continent; it's for the whole world.

- Secondly, this love was so desperate to build a relationship with the world that he, God, gave the world a gift. The gift, of God's Son, was the only way this relationship between ourselves and God could happen. God gave that which he loved most, his Son, so that he could restore our relationship with him. Prior to the crucifixion of Jesus, a relationship with God was through priests, sacrifice and rituals. With the death and resurrection of Jesus, access to God is for ever available to anyone, anytime, anywhere.

- Finally, this gift doesn't depend on buying a certain number of 'products', as in a supermarket, or taking out a subscription to a magazine, or even joining a club. This gift, and a relationship with the Creator, is available to all those who have faith in Jesus Christ.

The word 'faith' is often difficult to understand. The dictionary states that faith is having trust or confidence. God is asking that we place our trust and confidence in Jesus. The Bible gives us plenty of detail about God keeping his word and doing what he promised. If we see an advert for a car giving us details of the model, engine specification, colour and price, when we go to the garage to see the advertised car we expect to see what was promised. God has a far better reputation than any car dealer! We place our trust and confidence in many things in the hope that we will get what was promised. Having faith in Jesus is not just hoping for what is promised, it's guaranteed. (And that's more than you can say for most car dealers!)

PETE TOWNSEND

Reflective material
(sketches, meditations and poems)

Reflection *by Gabriella Mistral*

We are guilty of many errors and many faults
but our worst crime is abandoning the children,
neglecting the fountain of life.

Many of the things we need can wait.
The child cannot.
Right now is the time his bones are being formed,
his blood is being made and his senses are being developed.
To him we cannot answer, 'Tomorrow.'
His name is 'Today'.

from *Sharing Ways and Wisdoms* by BARBARA BUTLER

Lord Jesus, be welcome in our homes

Lord Jesus, be welcome in our homes
    and dwell in them.

Be a permanent member of our families
    and know all our secrets.

Sit with us at every meal
    and have your own chair by the fire.

Have your own place and possessions
    and your own interests along with ours.

Be at every conversation,
    as you listen to us, may we listen to you.

Have a part in all our plans
    and a voice in all our decisions.

Be there at every argument
    and when the air is heavy with tension.

Be in all our laughter
    and in every whispering of love.

Share our sorrows as well as our joys,
    our good days as well as our bad days.

As we open ourselves to you,
    may you open yourself to us.

Let your beauty, love and peace
    be found among us –

Lord Jesus, be not just a guest
    in our homes but live in them always.

MARY HATHAWAY

Meditation of Andrew, disciple of Jesus

I could have brained those children,
    rushing around like that with their yelling and shrieking,
    shattering our peace and quiet.
We'd had him alone at last,
    just us and Jesus;
    a rare opportunity to sit and listen undisturbed,
    drinking in his every word.
And it was wonderful,
    a truly magical moment,
    until, that is, they turned up –
    those wretched kids ushered forward by their doting parents,
    just so that he could touch them.
Really, how ridiculous!
Superstition, that's all it was –
    no real faith behind any of it –
    just sentimental rubbish,
    nauseating!
So we tried to stop them; you can understand that, surely?
We wanted to get back to the business in hand,
    before we were so rudely interrupted;
    back to more serious matters.

OK, so maybe we were a bit over the top,
   a touch more heavy than the situation demanded,
   but we were angry,
   disappointed.
I mean, could you have concentrated with that row going on?
I couldn't.
Yet did they care?
Not likely!
We fully expected Jesus to back us up,
   send the lot of them packing.
But can you believe this? He didn't!
He actually turned on us,
   and there was anger in his eyes,
   anger touched almost with pity.
'Leave them alone,' he said.
'Let them come to me. What's your problem?'
Well, we didn't know what to say, did we?
It caught us right on the hop.
So we just fidgeted uncomfortably,
trying to cover our embarrassment.
It was so unfair.
We'd meant no harm, after all,
   certainly hadn't meant to upset anybody;
   yet there they were now,
   the kids bawling their eyes out,
   the mums looking daggers at us,
   the dads having a go at everyone –
   what a mess!
I honestly didn't know what to do next.
But thankfully Jesus came to the rescue as always.
He reached out and took the children in his arms, one by one,
   a great loving hug.
And then he lifted them up for all to see.
'These are special,' he told us,
   'More precious than you will ever know – each one treasured by God.'
And you could tell from the way he smiled at them,
   and the way they smiled back at him,
   that he meant every word he was saying,
   and they knew he meant it.
I still feel a bit aggrieved by it all –
   well, you can tell that, can't you?
But I realise now we made ourselves look rather silly that day,
   even childish, you might say;
   and I'm beginning to understand Jesus has no room for the childish,
   only the childlike.

NICK FAWCETT

One great commandment

For a Christian there is only one great commandment, not two. When Jesus was asked which was the greatest of the commandments and he replied with one and then added another, he was talking about the greatest commandments *of the Law*. Matthew's Gospel says so, quite explicitly. These were the two greatest commandments so far, but not the greatest ever to be. But Jesus did not come simply to agree with what had been taught so far; he came to perfect it. I think we as Christians do Jesus a disservice if we take those two commandments as being his own two great commandments. If that was all there was to it, why did he have to come and die on a cross? We had those two already. Luke's Gospel even makes the questioner be the one who comes up with the answer, so who needed Jesus?

The two great commandments of the Law said, 'Love God with all your heart; and love your neighbour as yourself'. Jesus' one great commandment is 'Love one another as I have loved you', which is radically different. The two from the Law start here, on the ground. By my own strength I am to love God one hundred per cent, and my neighbour as much as I love myself, two things I dearly wish to do but two things I am quite incapable of doing for any length of time. [Great effort is needed to climb up towards God before God's love comes back to the one who worships, but] Jesus' one commandment [turned the whole idea on its head: God is pouring love and forgiveness down on us and all we have to do is open our ears and hear the message.] I am to love my neighbour the way Jesus loved me. How did Jesus love me? Without strings, even when he was being crucified. I am to look and see and believe how much God loves me, namely freely. Then love and forgive all others likewise. Jesus' one commandment incorporates the Good News.

GERALD O'MAHONY

Meditation of Mary, mother of Jesus

What was that Simeon said –
  'A sword will pierce your soul'?
I spent so long wondering what that meant,
  tossing and turning on my bed,
  brooding and fretting when I'd a moment to myself.
It seemed such a strange thing to say,
  especially at what was meant to be a time of joy.
We'd only had Jesus a few days,
  and my heart was still bursting with happiness.
We were both over the moon,
  Simeon too, that's the odd thing –
  he was almost dancing with delight.
But then his expression clouded,
  and he gave that awful warning which has haunted me ever since.
I just haven't been able to forget it, try as I might.

Always the question has been there,
    nagging away in the back of my mind,
    even in the brightest moments:
    what did he mean?
And if you'd asked me as little as a week ago
    I still wouldn't have been sure.
Oh, I'd a fair idea by then, of course –
    the fears were mounting up –
    but I'd still kept on hoping,
    praying that I might be wrong.
Now I know though,
    all too well.
My heart is not just pierced –
    it's broken!
For I've stood here today and seen my son die.
I watched him cursed and ridiculed, scourged and beaten.
I watched as they hammered nails through his hands
    and lifted him on to a cross.
I watched as he twisted in agony and cried out in despair.
And a moment ago I watched as they plunged a spear into his side.
At least he didn't feel that –
    thank God he was dead by then –
    but I did.
It thrust deep inside,
    running me through without mercy.
I've never known such pain,
    such agony,
    such horror.
And now life has gone for me too;
    I feel it has nothing left to offer.
Yet he's given me joy,
    no one can take that away.
He was with me for thirty wonderful years,
    everything a son could be –
    not many mothers can say that.
I've had joy,
    and now I have pain.
Maybe that's the way it had to be,
    the way it has to be,
    if there's to be any joy at all.

NICK FAWCETT

Life out of Death

Dying seed brings new life

A reading from the Gospel of John (12:20-33)

Some Greeks who had come to Jerusalem to celebrate the approaching Passover feast came to Philip and asked to meet Jesus. Philip told this to Andrew, and the two disciples went to tell Jesus.

Jesus said to them, 'The time has come for the Son of Man to be glorified. Just as a grain of wheat must die to produce a harvest of many grains, so the Son of God must die so that many can live. Whoever hates his earthly life will keep it for eternal life. If someone wants to serve me, then they must be prepared to follow me. If they do this, then my heavenly Father will glorify them.'

Jesus was troubled because he knew the time for him to die was fast approaching. 'Should I ask my Father to stop this from happening, when it was for this very reason that I have come? Father, glory be to your name!'

Then a voice spoke from the clouds and said, 'My name has been glorified, and will be again!' The crowd heard the voice, but thought it was the sound of thunder. So Jesus said, 'This voice has spoken for your sake. Now it is judgement time for this world; the prince of this world will be overthrown, and when I am raised up I will gather everyone to myself.'

In this way, Jesus revealed how he would die.

This is the Gospel of the Lord
Praise to you, Lord Jesus Christ   KATIE THOMPSON

Prayers

Praise

Loving God,
  we praise you once more for all you have done in Christ,
    for your victory through him over sin and evil,
    darkness and death.
  May that triumph shape our living and our thinking.

We praise you for your love which cannot be kept down,
    whatever it may face,
    whatever may conspire against it.
  **May that confidence inspire us to keep on following you
    through good and bad.**

When life seems hard,
    when good seems frustrated,
    when we feel ourselves in danger
    of being overwhelmed by trials and temptations,
    assure us once more of your power
    that will not be defeated.

When our work seems to bear no fruit,
    when our efforts go unrewarded,
    when our hopes appear unfulfilled,
    teach us to trust in your purpose
    that presses on towards fulfilment.

When the innocent suffer,
    when evil prospers,
    when hatred seems to hold sway,
    help us to keep on believing
    that good will finally win through.

Grant us a deep unshakeable confidence that,
    whatever life brings,
    whatever we face,
    however things seem,
    your will shall be done and your kingdom come,
    through Jesus Christ our Lord.
Amen.

NICK FAWCETT

Confession

Gracious and merciful God,
    as we remember the great love and sacrifice of Christ,
        we come seeking your forgiveness and help.
    In so many ways we have failed you:
        Lord, have mercy upon us.

We have not lived faithfully as your disciples,
    or obeyed your commandments.
We have not loved you as you love us,
    or our neighbours as ourselves.
We have not taken up our cross to follow Jesus.
In so many ways we have failed you:
    Lord, have mercy upon us.

We have been narrow in our horizons,
    weak in our commitment,
    careless in our worship,
    half-hearted in our service.

In so many ways we have failed you:
    Lord, have mercy upon us.

We have preferred our ways to yours,
    and wandered far from you.
We have been concerned with our own advancement
    rather than your kingdom.
In so many ways we have failed you:
    Lord, have mercy upon us.

Gracious God,
    renew our spirits,
        strengthen our wills,
        deepen our faith,
        and send us out forgiven and restored
        to live and work for you,
        in the name of Christ.
    Amen.

NICK FAWCETT

Intercessions

Jesus could only buy us full life by submitting to full death.

Father, we pray for all who follow Christ,
for those whose faith is being tested,
and for those who have drifted away.
Silence for prayer
Into your hands, O Lord:
we place our lives.

We pray for all leaders and advisers,
all meetings and councils,
that right decisions may be made.
Silence for prayer
Into your hands, O Lord:
we place our lives.

We pray for all those we love
and those we find it difficult to love;
for those whose loving is damaged
and those who have no one who cares about them.
Silence for prayer
Into your hands, O Lord:
we place our lives.

We pray for those who are persecuted or imprisoned,
for those locked in fear or hatred
and all who are in need of healing.
Silence for prayer

Into your hands, O Lord:
we place our lives.

We pray for those who have died alone or in fear,
for those who are finding it hard to accept
another's death.
Silence for prayer

Into your hands, O Lord:
we place our lives.

We give you thanks and praise
for bringing us safely to this moment,
and offer you the future, with all that it holds.
Silence for prayer

Merciful Father,
accept these prayers
for the sake of your Son,
our Saviour Jesus Christ, Amen.

SUSAN SAYERS

The victory of the cross. Nothing could look more like failure than the crucifixion, as the promising healer and teacher hung suffering at the mercy of mankind. Yet it was through his anguish and pain, offered in love without sin, that our salvation was secured for ever.

In the presence of God, the giver of all life,
let us lift our hearts and pray.

We pray for all who are training
for ministry in your Church;
may they grow in wisdom and humility,
and be increasingly filled with the life
you have won for us.
Silence for prayer

Lord, breathe into us:
that we may live.

We pray for all areas of bureaucracy
which frustrate and delay the course of useful action;
for areas where anarchy undermines stability;
for areas of political corruption;
that whatever is good may flourish and grow,
so evil is rendered powerless and overthrown.

Silence for prayer

Lord, breathe into us:
that we may live.

We pray for all who are engaged or newly married;
for those coping with family problems,
difficult circumstances or bereavement;
may they lean on your loving presence
which dispels all fear, and brings life and peace.

Silence for prayer

Lord, breathe into us:
that we may live.

We pray that your calming reassurance
will bring peace of mind and spirit
to those worried about the future,
those dreading some difficult event,
and those who are frightened of dying.

Silence for prayer

Lord, breathe into us:
that we may live.

We thank you for the life and example
of all who have lived, worked and died
in the joy of your service; may we one day
share with them eternal life in your presence.

Silence for prayer

Lord, breathe into us:
that we may live.

Father, with thankful hearts we offer ourselves to be
used wherever you need us.

Silence for prayer

Merciful Father,
accept these prayers
for the sake of your Son,
our Saviour Jesus Christ, Amen.

SUSAN SAYERS

A short prayer

If it is possible, make the room dark. Shine a small penlight torch directly on the ceiling above the group. Ask the group to lift their eyes to look at the light. While they do this, read the following prayer:

Jesus, at times it's really difficult,
   really difficult to understand what you mean.
It's even more difficult to do what you say,
   even when we understand.
It's not easy.
I know it's about faith, it's about trust.
Easy to say, but not easy to put into practice.
As I lift my eyes
   allow me to see what you meant
   by dying to live;
   by giving to receive.
Thank you for my choice.
Help me to use my choice,
   rather than ignore it.
You died for me to live.
What more can I say?
Amen.

PETE TOWNSEND

All-age-talk material

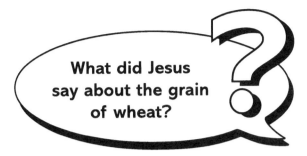

Find his words and read them in the order 1 to 10

Jesus said . . .

John 12:24

KATIE THOMPSON

What does Jesus call EVERYONE to do?

Write the first letter of each word in the boxes to spell out the answer!

John 12:26

KATIE THOMPSON

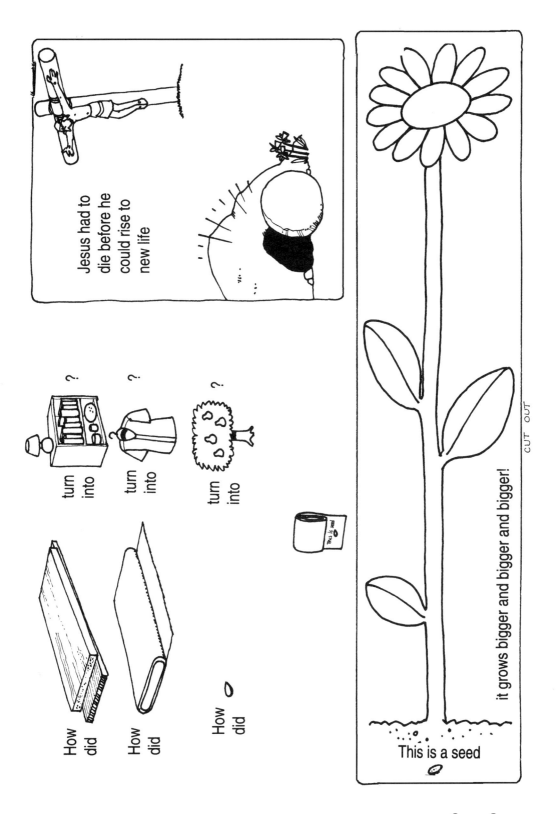

Jesus had to die before he could rise to new life

How did ? turn into

How did ? turn into

How did ? turn into

This is a seed

it grows bigger and bigger and bigger!

CUT OUT

SUSAN SAYERS

Read John 12:20-33

Jesus is speaking in Jerusalem at the time of the Passover (a special Jewish festival). A large crowd had gathered to welcome Jesus into Jerusalem. The crowd had shouted, 'God bless the King of Israel!' Expectations were running high. Miracles had been witnessed, people healed, demons sent packing and the dead raised! Now Jesus declares, 'The time has come for the Son of Man to be given his glory.'

His followers must have given the thumbs up to this statement. About time! Just what we need! We'll show those Romans and those religious snobs in the temple. You can imagine the scene.

But then, before any of this can really sink in, Jesus tells one of his odd stories. 'I tell you for certain that a grain of wheat that falls on the ground will never be more than one grain unless it dies. But if it dies, it will produce lots of wheat' (John 12:24).

What is this bloke on about? Can you imagine the followers' faces now?

One moment Jesus is talking about being glorified and the next about grains of wheat dying! Jesus was telling his disciples that his mission was to die! He was to die to bring glory to the Father and be the sacrifice for humankind. Through his death would come life for everyone.

But Jesus asks his disciples to follow his example: to die to their old lifestyle and allow a totally new life to emerge. His followers must have thought that this was an impossible concept to grasp. To live you must first die? The grain of wheat was simply a grain of wheat until it was 'buried' in the ground. Only when the grain of wheat had 'died' did it develop its potential to grow and become much more than it was before. Only when this process has taken place does the wheat bring life to other people (by being made into flour and then into bread).

If Jesus had been selfish and refused to suffer and die then we could never have a real relationship with God. Jesus gave his life so that everyone could live to have this relationship with God.

We have a choice, whether to hold on to our lives as they are, or give our lives to God. We have the opportunity to become what God has intended for us or to remain inward looking and keep our eyes on the ground. Just as Jesus was lifted up to die, so we can lift up our eyes to see that through his death we can have life.

We have a choice . . .

PETE TOWNSEND

A grain of wheat

Jesus knew that the time was coming for him to suffer and die

Cross out the letters with odd numbers. Write the remaining letters in order on the lines

K T L H S E M N T O I M R E PHS A G S D F CH O H M E
3 2 9 8 7 10 1 9 14 11 6 2 13 12 3 8 5 10 9 2 13 11 14 7 16 5 20 2

P L F Q OR B S T OH A E G FS O E N O J FKGGO D R
9 17 10 21 4 6 13 5 2 11 6 13 8 17 9 4 12 5 10 2 7 8 3 4 1 6 10 5

S T O P B F E D G L O P R F I F I J E D Q
7 12 16 13 2 11 8 3 6 2 18 1 10 7 2 6 8 9 6 8 11

' __ __ __   __ __ __ __   __ __ __

__ __ __   __ __ __   __ __ __

__ __ __   __ __   __ __

John 12:23

__ __ __   __ __ __

__ __ __ __ __ __ __ ,

KATIE THOMPSON

A seed must die to give new life and a rich harvest

These pictures are jumbled up. Can you put them in the right order and number them 1 2 3 4?

KATIE THOMPSON

JESUS DIED BECAUSE HE LOVES US

Q. How can one grain of wheat feed millions of people?

A. If you plant it, it will grow about 30 grains. Each of those grains can grow 30 grains and so on...

MATHS

1 grain grows 30 new grains

30 grains x 30 = 900 grains
900 grains x 30 = 27,000 grains
27,000 grains x 30 = 810,000 grains
810,000 grains x 30 = 24,300,000 grains

24 MILLION, 3 HUNDRED THOUSAND in just 5 years!

Colour this picture of Jesus on the cross. He must love us such a lot!

SUSAN SAYERS

Reflective material
(sketches, meditations and poems)

Meditation of Jeremiah (based on Jeremiah 31:31-34)

You're wasting your time, they tell me,
    chasing an impossible dream –
    one they'd like to believe in, could it possibly come true,
    but hopelessly unrealistic,
    naïve to the point of folly.
And to be honest, I can't say I blame them,
    for when you look at our record,
    our history as a nation,
    there seems as much chance of us mending our ways
    as a leopard changing its spots.
We've tried to be different, heaven knows,
    striven body and soul to turn over a new leaf,
    but somehow we always end up
    making the same mistakes we've always made,
    the spirit willing but the flesh weak.
So, yes, when they hear me speaking of new beginnings,
    a fresh start,
    it's hardly surprising they nod their heads knowingly
    with a wry smile and surreptitious wink.
They've seen it all before, too many times –
    promises made only to be broken,
    good intentions flourishing for a moment
    only to come to nothing –
    what reason to think it should be any different now?
Yet it can be, I'm sure of it,
    not because of anything we might do
    but because of what God will do for us,
    working within,
    moulding,
    shaping,
    like a potter fashioning his clay,
    until his love flows through our hearts
    and his grace floods our whole being.
It sounds far-fetched, I know,
    a wild and foolish fantasy,
    and whether I'll see it in my lifetime, who can say?
But I honestly believe that one day the time will come –
    a day when God breaks down the barriers which keep us apart,
    when through his great mercy we become a new creation,

healed,
restored,
forgiven –
and in that hope I will continue to serve him,
speaking the word he has given,
confident that in the fullness of time it shall be fulfilled!

NICK FAWCETT

Holy Week

Palm (Passion) Sunday

Jesus' entry into Jerusalem

A reading from the Gospel of Mark (11:1-10)

As Jesus and his disciples drew close to Jerusalem, they stopped near the villages of Bethphage and Bethany, and he sent two of his disciples to one of these villages to collect a colt they found tethered there.

'If anyone questions you,' Jesus said, 'tell them that your Master needs it, and will return it immediately.'

They did as he instructed and repeated everything they had been told to say. They brought the young colt to him, and after throwing a cloak on its back, Jesus climbed on, and continued on his journey to Jerusalem.

Many people had lined the road to greet Jesus, and they spread their cloaks on the road before him, and waved branches in the air, as they shouted with joy, 'Hosanna! Blessed is the one who comes in the name of the Lord.'

This is the Gospel of the Lord
Praise to you, Lord Jesus Christ KATIE THOMPSON

Introductory material

Palm Sunday is one of the enigmas in the Christian calendar. It speaks of joy and celebration, and of worshipping Jesus as the King of kings, and yet of course it leads us into the events of Holy Week, the memory of sorrow and suffering, and finally death on a cross. We cannot think of one without the other, and any talk of the majesty of Jesus must be understood in the light of all that followed. The one we serve came to serve others. The Lord of life endured the darkness of death. The way to the throne involved the costly path of sacrifice. It is easy enough to sing Christ's praises and acknowledge him as Lord; it is a different matter to take up our cross and follow him. Yet that is the homage he asks of us and the challenge this day brings. As we offer today our glad hosannas let us ask ourselves if we are ready also to offer ourselves in his service.

NICK FAWCETT

For resources on the Passion of Christ, see Maundy Thursday and Good Friday

Palm Sunday, coming both at the end of the forty days of Lent and the start of Holy Week, encompasses penitence and the passion of our Lord as well as the immediately obvious element of celebration and rejoicing. In most places it will also mark the end of Lent study groups and the beginning of the drama of Holy Week. Palm crosses and processions spring readily to mind, and are accepted by most mainstream denominations, forming a welcome part of our own LEP's (Local Ecumenical Projects) observation of Holy Week. However, a large-scale event involving several Churches is probably best arranged for an evening. Our own Churches Together group has for some years used this as a way of drawing the Lent studies to a conclusion, and at the same time allowing some of the practical fruits of these to be used in the worship. Music groups, drama groups, flower arrangers, painters and writers have all made their contribution to the service. It is worth pointing out that to do this successfully requires a church building which can be adapted to such a variety of uses.

STUART THOMAS

Prayers

Praise – the King of Glory

Lord Jesus Christ,
   we greet you today as the Word made flesh,
     before all,
     beyond all,
     within all –
     the one in whom all things have their being,
     yet entering our world of space and time,
     sharing our humanity,
     experiencing the joys and sorrows of flesh and blood,
     living and dying among us
     so that we might share in the joy of your kingdom.
   Blessed is the king who comes in the name of the Lord!
Hosanna in the highest heaven!

We greet you as the Messiah,
     the Son of David,
     King of Israel –
     Servant of all,
     Saviour of all,
     anointed for burial,
     crowned with thorns
     and lifted high on a cross –
     your kingdom not of this world.
   Blessed is the king who comes in the name of the Lord!
Hosanna in the highest heaven!

We greet you as Lord of the empty tomb –
  the risen Christ,
  victorious over death,
  triumphant over evil,
  the one who has gone before us,
  whose Spirit walks with us now,
  and who will be there to greet us at our journey's end –
  Jesus Christ, the pioneer and perfecter of our faith.
Blessed is the king who comes in the name of the Lord!
Hosanna in the highest heaven!

We greet you as the King of kings and Lord of lords,
  the ascended and exalted Lamb of God,
  ruler of the ends of the earth,
  enthroned in splendour,
  seated at the right hand of the Father,
  worthy of all honour and glory and blessing –
  the King of Glory!
Blessed is the king who comes in the name of the Lord!
Hosanna in the highest heaven!

Lord Jesus Christ,
  we greet you today with joyful worship and reverent praise.
  Hear our prayer
    and accept our homage,
    for we offer it in your name and to your glory.
  Amen.

NICK FAWCETT

Confession – the King of Love

Lord Jesus Christ,
  we claim to be your followers,
    and we declare that you are the Lord and King of our lives,
    but all too often our actions deny our words.
  When you look at our lives,
    the weakness of our faith
    and the frailty of our commitment,
    you must grieve over us
    as surely as you wept for Jerusalem long ago.
  You offer us salvation,
    joy, peace and fulfilment,
    yet we so easily let it slip through our fingers.
  King of Love,
    have mercy upon us.

We thank you that your kingdom is not of this world,
  that you rule not as a dictator but as a servant,
  winning the hearts of your people,
  inspiring devotion through who and what you are.
If you dealt with us as we deserve,
  then our future would be bleak,
  none of us able to stand before you,
  for day after day we break your commandments,
  betraying your love,
  ignoring your guidance,
  our faith fickle,
  our allegiance poor.
King of Love,
  have mercy upon us.

Forgive us all the ways we fail you,
  through thought, word and deed.
Forgive our limited understanding of your greatness
  and the narrowness of our vision.
Forgive our inability to grasp the values of your kingdom,
  still less to base our lives upon them.
We want to bring honour to you,
  but so often we do the opposite.
King of Love,
  have mercy upon us.

Lord Jesus,
  we come before your throne,
  throwing ourselves upon your grace,
  and asking you to receive our worship,
  despite its weakness;
  to accept our service,
  despite our many faults.
Rule in our hearts
  and use us for your glory.
King of Love,
  have mercy upon us.

In your name we ask it.
Amen.

NICK FAWCETT

Petition

Father God,
>   we thank you for this day –
>>   for all it recalls,
>>   all it means,
>>   all it says to us.
>   **Speak to us now as we worship you.**

>   Teach us, through our reading and reflection on your word,
>>   through our hymns and prayers,
>>   through our meeting with one another and with you,
>>   to understand more
>>   of what Palm Sunday signified and signifies.
>   **Speak to us now as we worship you.**

>   Help us to picture Jesus riding into Jerusalem,
>>   in triumph yet humility,
>>   to a welcome yet also rejection,
>>   to a crown but also a Cross.
>   **Speak to us now as we worship you.**

Father God,
>   may this day lead us
>>   to a deeper understanding of your kingdom,
>>   a greater awareness of your love,
>>   and a clearer sense of your purpose,
>>   yesterday, today and tomorrow.
>   **Speak to us now as we worship you,**
>>   **through Jesus Christ our Lord.**
>   **Amen.**   NICK FAWCETT

Intercession

Lord Jesus Christ,
>   you entered Jerusalem in quiet humility,
>>   taking the form of a servant,
>>   even to the point of death on a cross,
>>   emptying yourself so that we might be filled.
>   Come again now
>>   **and establish your kingdom.**

>   Come afresh to our troubled world,
>>   with all its needs,
>>   its tensions,
>>   its problems,
>>   and its evil.
>   Come again now
>>   **and establish your kingdom.**

Bring healing where there is division,
   love where there is hatred,
   hope where there is despair,
   joy where there is sorrow,
   confidence where there is fear,
   strength where there is weakness,
   healing where there is sickness,
   life where there is death.
Come again now
   and establish your kingdom.

Lord Jesus Christ,
   reach out to your Church and world,
      despite the weakness of our faith,
      and the rejection of so many.
   May your will be done on earth
      even as it is in heaven.
   Come again now
      and establish your kingdom,
      for in your name we pray.
      Amen.   Nick Fawcett

Short prayers

Place a palm cross in the centre of the room. Give each member of the group a
piece of paper and a pen. Ask them to write on the piece of paper an issue or situation that is causing trouble or giving them concern. The issue or situation may
or may not involve the group member directly. When each member has written
an issue or situation which they are concerned about, ask them to fold the paper
and place it by the palm cross. When everyone has placed their piece of paper
by the cross, read the following prayer:

Lord, trouble seems to have a habit of getting under my skin.
It itches and aggravates,
   and the more I scratch it, the more it itches.
How does trouble find me?
I certainly don't go looking for it,
   it seems to find me wherever I am.
It's not always my fault,
   well, sometimes maybe, but not every time!
Please help me to see things your way,
   because my way sometimes misses the point
   or makes the trouble worse!
I need to see things your way,
   because I have the knack
   of sometimes missing the obvious

or making up my mind
without knowing all the facts.
You seemed to know what you were doing
on the way into Jerusalem.
Even though others thought it odd
that a king should ride a donkey.
But you had other thoughts in mind,
beyond what could be imagined
by your closest friends.
Prince of Peace, take my troubles
and bring your peace instead.
Amen.

PETE TOWNSEND

Lord Jesus Christ,
you had no interest in serving yourself,
only in serving others;
you did not desire your own glory,
only the glory of him who sent you,
and because of that God has highly exalted you,
giving you the name that is above every name.
Teach us today the true nature
of kingship, service and authority,
and so help us to honour you as you desire,
through loving God with heart, mind and soul,
and loving our neighbour as ourselves.
So may we build your kingdom,
until you return in glory
and gather all things to yourself.
Amen.

NICK FAWCETT

Lord Jesus Christ,
servant of all,
friend of all,
saviour of all,
ruler of all,
receive our worship.
To you be glory and honour,
praise and thanksgiving,
this day and for evermore.
Amen.

NICK FAWCETT

All-age-talk material

Think and Look Ahead

What do we call the week between Palm Sunday and Easter Sunday?

Write the first letter of each clue in the numbered boxes

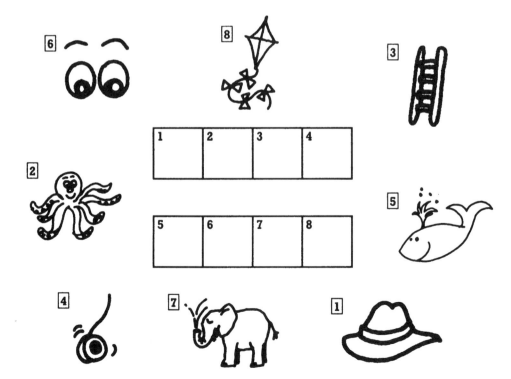

1	2	3	4

5	6	7	8

KATIE THOMPSON

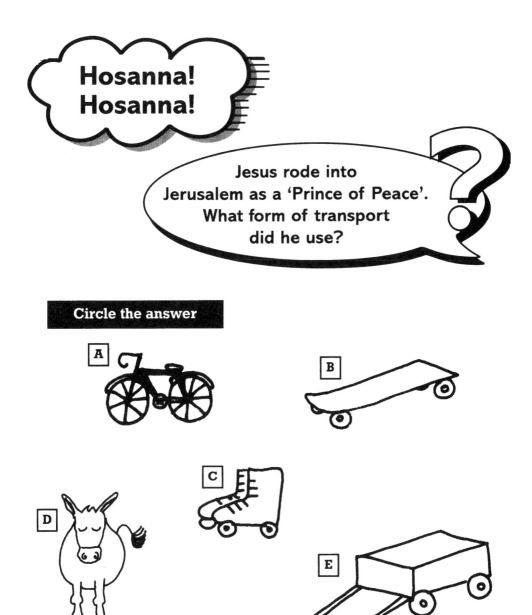

KATIE THOMPSON

The way of humility

Aim

To contrast the way of self-denial exemplified by Jesus with the way of self-interest so often seen in the world.

Preparation

Select some slogans from television advertisements (suggestions are given below, but these will have already begun to date). Arrange the names of the products in a column down the left side of a display board. Print your selected slogans in large, bold letters and attach magnetic tape or Blu-Tack to the back of each, ready for later use.

Bounty – A taste of paradise
Carlsberg – Probably the best lager in the world
Kwik-Fit – You can't fit quicker than a Kwik-Fit fitter
British Airways – The world's favourite airline
Flake – Only the crumbliest flakiest chocolate
Kellogg's – The original and best
McVities – Bake a better biscuit
Duracell – Looks like and lasts like no other battery
Vauxhall – Once driven, forever smitten
Mars Bar – A Mars a day helps you work rest and play
Mr Kipling – Makes exceedingly good cakes
Pedigree Chum – Nine out of ten top breeders recommend it
Milky Way – The snack you can eat between meals
McDonald's – A visit to McDonald's makes your day
Tesco – Every little helps

Talk

Ask the congregation how many of them watch the advertisements on television. Tell them you are going to test today how well these advertisements have achieved their aim. Read through the list of products on the display board, then ask if anyone can match the appropriate slogans to each one. Invite suggestions, and insert the slogan next to the product when the correct answer is given.

Our examples were just some of the extravagant claims advertisers make for the things they sell. Each claims to be the best product on the market. And most of us at some time or other have probably met people rather similar: full of their own importance, convinced they know it all, and looking down their noses at others – the sort of people we might describe as too full of themselves by half! Compare their attitude with the one we see in the reading from Philippians:

Do nothing from selfish ambition or conceit, but in humility regard others as better than yourselves. Let each of you look not to your own interests, but to the interests of others. Let the same mind be in you that was in Christ Jesus, who, though he was in the form of God, did not regard equality with God as something to be exploited, but emptied himself, taking the form of a slave, being born in human likeness. And being found in human form, he humbled himself and became obedient to the point of death – even death on a cross. *(Philippians 2:3-8)*

If anyone could have claimed to be special, it was Jesus! He alone could claim to be better than others, for he was without sin, the Son of God, able to offer eternal life, forgiveness of sins, reconciliation with God, everything anyone can ever need for fulfilment and happiness in life. Just imagine the sort of build-up he could have given himself to impress the crowds and win their support. And yet, throughout his life, we see only humility, putting himself last and others first, pointing away from himself to the Father, offering his life for the life of the world.

In the example of Jesus there is a challenge for us today. Are we like those advertisements, blowing our own trumpets, full of ourselves and our own importance – what we are, what we've done, what we want, what we know and what we think? Or are we ready to learn from Jesus and follow in his footsteps, taking the path of self-sacrifice and self-denial. Which way will we choose?

NICK FAWCETT

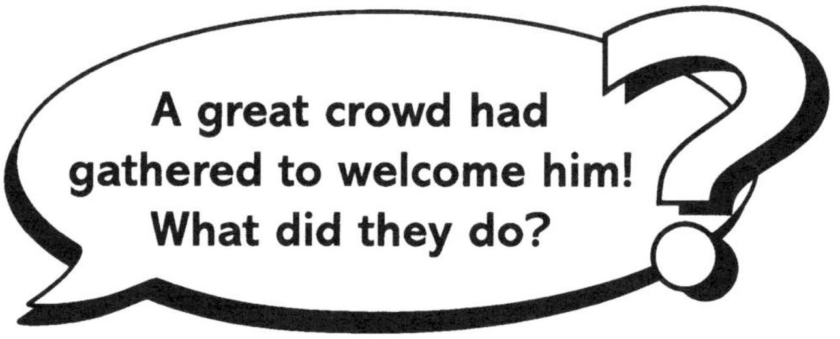

A great crowd had
gathered to welcome him!
What did they do?

Follow the arrow to find out

L	O	M	B	E	Y	H	(T)
D	A	R	E	S	R	E	S
N	O	H	F	P	C	D	A
D	G	E	T	L	O	K	R
R	E	N	T	N	S	A	G
Y	F	M	H	I	M	D	B
R	O	E	F	E	L	P	S

'T ← ↓ ↖   ↙ ↓ ↗ → ↘ ←

← ↙ → ↘ ↑ ↙   ↑ ↙   ↖ ↖ ↗

← ↙ ↑ ←   → ↙ ↓

→ ↙ → ↗ ↓ ← ← ↓   → ↙ → ↗

↗ ↓ ↙   → ↗ ↓ → ↗ ↘'

Mark 11:8

KATIE THOMPSON

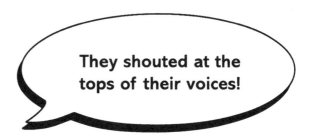

Use the code cracker to read their words from Mark 11:9

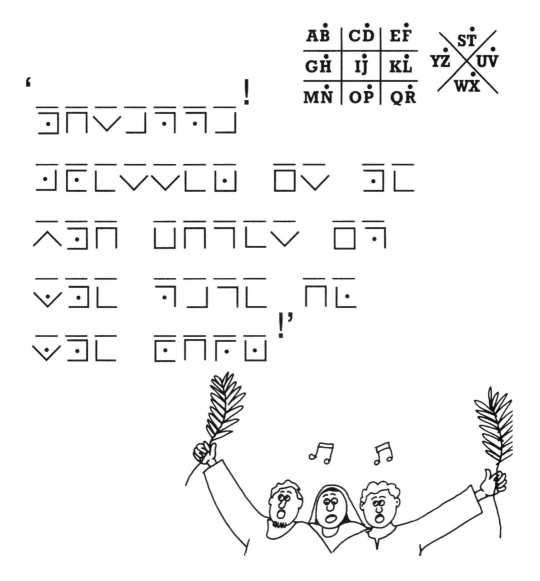

KATIE THOMPSON

They shouted at
the tops of their voices!

Use the code to see what they shouted

A = ☀   N = ☁   H = 💧   O = 🌧   S = 🌈

_ _ _ _ _ _ _ !

Jesus entering Jerusalem

Encourage the children to bring large leaves or branches to wave in the procession, or colourful streamers. They may also join in the crowd sections of the Gospel if they are in the church at this point.

If not, read *Jesus on a Donkey* (Palm Tree Bible Stories) which tells the story of Jesus entering Jerusalem, and then help the children make a model of that ride. Use a large tray as the base, with hills of crumpled paper under a green towel. The track is a strip of brown or beige material.

Houses can be made from
white paper like this:

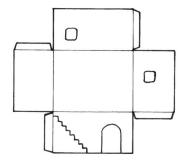

and palm trees from
green paper like this:

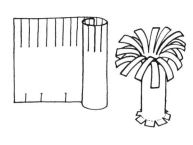

Have a farmyard model of a donkey and make plasticine figures waving real leaves. Pieces of material cut out can be laid on the path in front of Jesus.

Display the finished model where the rest of the congregation can see it.

SUSAN SAYERS

Ideas for activities

Tell them the story very simply (with the children acting it out), and then play some children's praise tapes, dancing and singing along to them, and waving pom-poms or streamers. If the church has a procession through the streets today the children can join in, waving their streamers and playing instruments.

SUSAN SAYERS

A Stand up model to make

1. Colour the picture of Jesus riding on a donkey.

2. Cut out the shaded bits at the side.

3. Fold along the fold lines.

4. Stand your model up like this:

CUT OUT

CUT OUT

SUSAN SAYERS

The King of Glory rides on a donkey into Jerusalem

Readings

Psalms 61, 62; Jeremiah 7:1-11 or Exodus 11; Luke 19:29-end or Mark 14.

Aim: To bring the events of the readings to life for children.

If you have access to one of the videos about Jesus' life, show them the section of the entry into Jerusalem and the cleaning up of the temple. Or they can act this out, with everyone involved, either as vendors or crowd members. Afterwards talk together about how different people felt when Jesus came in and started protesting, overturning tables and so on. If possible, join in with an all-age procession, leading the singing or dancing for one or two of the songs.

Discussion starters

1. Our society believes in allowing everyone the freedom to do more or less what feels right for them, so long as it doesn't interfere with others. Where does this view start to clash with Christian values and beliefs?

2. Why did Jesus feel so angry with the moneychangers in the temple, and why do you think he decided to deal so forcibly with them?

SUSAN SAYERS

Readings

Psalms 61, 62; Jeremiah 7:1-11 or Exodus 11; Luke 19:29-end or Mark 14.

Aim: To see the contrast between the joy of the entry into Jerusalem and the anger of Jesus at the abuse of the temple.

First make the pom-poms –

Then use them either in an all-age procession, or in a time of singing and dancing on their own.

Then tell the story of Jesus throwing out the moneychangers, acting it as you tell it, explaining how the temple was being misused and then literally overturning a few tables and spilling everything on to the floor. The shock of seeing and hearing this really helps them realise the depth of Jesus' concern to put things right.

SUSAN SAYERS

1. Cut a handful of lengths of different coloured crepe paper

2. Fold it in the middle

3. Put two rubber bands on it like this

Hosannah! Hosannah! Hosannah!

SPOT THE DIFFERENCE

Draw in the faces in the crowd.

me

house

den

thieves

prayer

you

What did Jesus say to the money changers in the temple?

"My ☐ is a ☐ of ⬡ have 〰 it a ⬦ of 〰."

SUSAN SAYERS

Jesus finds a donkey

Announce to the group that you are going to a party during the week and you are a bit unsure what to wear. Can the group make any suggestions? Ask the group what they would wear if they were going to a really smart party. Make a list of the types of outfits and accessories. What kind of vehicle would each member of the group like to arrive in at the party? Would they invite the press and photographers to record the event of the year? Which magazines or newspapers would they like to see themselves in?

PETE TOWNSEND

Read John 12:12-16

The Passover Feast was an important part of Jewish culture. At least once in their life each male Jew would try and attend the Feast in Jerusalem. There would have been several hundred thousand people gathered in Jerusalem. The atmosphere would have been one of great expectancy and excitement.

Jesus rode into Jerusalem to be met by a huge crowd of people all shouting and waving palm branches. It must have been an amazing sight!

Immediately before arriving in Jerusalem, Jesus had performed yet another miracle by raising Lazarus from the dead. The chief priests were already plotting how to get rid of Jesus. They were also trying to figure out how to kill Lazarus!

Two main features of the entry into Jerusalem stand out:

Firstly, Jesus rode into Jerusalem as a wanted man. Not wanted as a liberator or saviour by the priests but wanted by them as a criminal. Even the disciples were taken up with the idea that Jesus had at last come to claim his place as King of the Jews. The people greeted Jesus with a cry of 'Hosanna' or 'hooray', which roughly translates as 'please save us'. This was a shout of praise to God but it would have made the chief priests even angrier than before, as it was also a shout acknowledging that Jesus was in some way connected with God; worse, that he was a 'saviour'!

Secondly, Jesus rode into Jerusalem on a donkey! This act fulfils the prophecy from the Old Testament book Zechariah (9:9-10). Zechariah writes that everyone in Jerusalem should celebrate and shout 'your King has won a victory and he is coming to you . . . riding on a donkey' (verse 9). We may not think that riding a donkey gives the impression of a king! In Old Testament times, if a king were going to war, he would ride a horse. But if the king rode a donkey it meant he came in peace. Jesus made a significant statement. He rode into Jerusalem as a king of peace; not to liberate the world by force but by peace.

Even though Jesus knew that he was considered a threat to the chief priests (see verse 19) and that he would die a criminal's death, he rode a donkey to make the most profound statement.

God didn't send his Son into the world to condemn its people but to save them (see John 3:17). The Prince of Peace rode a donkey knowing that he would die a violent death at the hands of soldiers for a crime he didn't commit.

Ask the group to consider the entry of Jesus into Jerusalem. Picture the scene with the excited crowds all waving palm branches and shouting.

- What do they think the disciples and followers of Jesus thought?
- Did they think a major change was about to take place?
- Did they think that Jesus was going to cause a revolt against the Romans?

PETE TOWNSEND

Reflective material
(sketches, meditations and poems)

The entry into Jerusalem

The story of Palm Sunday and the triumphant entry of Jesus into Jerusalem is very well known to us. It's a story that is full of joy and hope as the crowds welcome Jesus.

However, it's another of those occasions when I find myself wondering what the people on the edge of events must have thought. Today, if the average churchgoer saw a load of people tearing down branches from the trees in the park, he or she would be much more likely to brand them as hooligans and vandals, than to join them in welcoming the latest prophet. Similarly, those of us who are parents would be singularly unimpressed by our offspring if the excuse for ruining their new coat was that they used it to carpet the road so the prophet's donkey could walk on it. And yet we hear these things every Palm Sunday and sit in silent approval.

This sketch takes a light-hearted look at these events and puts a slightly different slant on them.

One of the following passages should be read, immediately before the sketch takes place: Matthew 21:1-11, or Mark 11:1-10, or Luke 19:28-40.

Enter Rachel and Salome (they can stand or be seated).

Rachel   He's gone and done it this time, Salome.

Salome   Gone and done what, Rachel?

Rachel   It! It! He's gone and done it!

Salome   I think I've got that much. What I mean is, what is 'it'?

Rachel   He's only gone and got himself arrested, that's all.

Salome   Arrested for what?

Rachel   Wilful and criminal damage; that's what!

Salome	Wilful and criminal damage? That doesn't sound too serious to me. I thought he must have murdered someone.
Rachel	Murdered! I'll murder him when I get hold of him, if they ever let him out. You should have seen the state of his coat when he got home. It looked like some great donkey had walked all over it, and it was his best one.
Salome	Has he got two coats then?
Rachel	No, that's why it was his best one.
Salome	What was this wilful and criminal damage?
Rachel	He only vandalised the municipal palm trees. You know, them nice ones on Mount of Olives Boulevard.
Salome	That doesn't sound too serious. Surely he'll get off with a fine?
Rachel	Not with his record, and not with the company he keeps. He's already been accused of blasphemy, no less. He only got off because that Jesus character bamboozled the Pharisees. But how long can he keep that up? They're a right clever lot them Pharisees, you know.
Salome	Oh, I know, dear. Do you know, one of them told me, well, actually, told my Zech – they don't talk to women, you know – anyway, he told my Zech he had worked out you could get thirteen million, seven hundred and fifty nine thousand, one hundred and forty six and a half cherubim on a half shekel.
Rachel	What would you want to do that for?
Salome	Search me, dear, but it shows how clever them Pharisees are. So what do you think will happen to your lad?
Rachel	I think they'll send him to one of those new tough sandal camps they're setting up.
Salome	They're very tough those, so I've heard.
Rachel	It might do him good though. I mean, throwing your best coat on the floor for a donkey to tread on, cutting down perfectly good palm branches and yelling 'Hosanna! Hosanna!' all over the place. Like a bunch of Nazareth United supporters after they've lost.
Salome	Cheer up, Rachel, it might not be as bad as you think.
Rachel	It's ever since he started hanging around with that Jesus character. Before that you at least knew where you were. He was always a bad lad, but he was a decent bad lad. Now he's got no respect for authority and says stupid things about forgiving people, loving them and stuff like that. I mean, where would we be if we all went round forgiving people and loving them? It would be the end of the world as we know it.

Salome   I know what you mean, dear. But you mark my words, that Jesus will come to a bad end and no mistake. He's one of those 'here today and gone tomorrow' characters. In a few weeks' time he'll be yesterday's news.

Rachel   I hope you're right, dear. I just hope my poor Reuben has got him out of his system by the time he gets out. After all, we don't want all this resurrecting in the future, do we?

Salome   No fear of that, dear. I think it's safe to say we've heard the last of that Jesus character.

Rachel   I do hope so.

Salome   Come on, let's go and see what the courts have to say. You never know, Caiaphas might be having one of his lenient days.

Rachel   I doubt it, but you never know.

Exit Rachel and Salome.

DAVID WALKER

Meditation of one of the owners of the colt ridden by Jesus

Hello, I thought, what's going on here?
And you can hardly blame me,
    for there I was, minding my own business,
    when suddenly these fellows I've never clapped eyes on
    appeared from nowhere and, cool as you like,
    started to make off with our donkey!
In broad daylight, too, that's what I couldn't get over –
    bold as brass,
    without so much as a by-your-leave!
Well, you can imagine my surprise, can't you?
Hardly the kind of goings-on you expect in a quiet village like ours.
So I asked them straight, 'What's your game?'
And that's when they spoke those special words:
    'The Lord needs it.'
Not the fullest of explanations, admittedly,
    but it was all I needed,
    for straightaway it all came flooding back –
    that day when Jesus came by
    and for a wonderful few moments I met him face to face.
No, you won't have heard about it,
    for it wasn't the sort of encounter to hit the headlines –
    no stunning healing or unforgettable miracle needed in my case,
    but he touched my life as surely and wonderfully as any,
    offering a new direction,
    a fresh start from which I've never looked back.

Quite simply, he changed my life,
  and though I'm not the sort to shout it from the rooftops
  I wanted to respond nonetheless,
  to show Jesus how much he meant to me,
  how much I valued what he'd done.
This was it,
  the chance I'd been waiting for,
  my opportunity to give something back at last.
Hardly earth-shattering stuff, I grant you –
  the loan of a donkey –
  but that didn't matter;
  the fact was that Jesus had need of me –
  it was all I needed to know.
He arrived soon after, and I followed him to Jerusalem,
  where the crowds were waiting to greet him,
  wild with excitement,
  shouting their praises,
  throwing down their cloaks in welcome –
  and, small though it had been, I knew I'd done my bit
  to make that great day possible.
Never forget that, whoever you are,
  however little you think you have to offer,
  for some day, some time, your moment will come –
  a day when your contribution to his kingdom
  will be requested in those lovely words:
  'The Lord needs it.'

NICK FAWCETT

Order of service

Introductory sentence

In this is love, not that we loved God but that he loved us, and sent his Son to be the atoning sacrifice for our sins (1 John 4:10).

Opening response

  We do not preach the Gospel with words of human wisdom, lest the cross of Christ be emptied of its power. The message of the cross makes no sense to those who are perishing,
  but to us who are being saved
  it is the power of God.

God has made foolish the cleverness of the scholar and philosopher,
for the world cannot know God
through wisdom.

Through the folly of what is preached,
God is pleased to save those who believe.

The foolishness of God is infinitely wiser than human wisdom;
his wisdom is infinitely greater
than human strength.

Hymn

Ride on, ride on in majesty (HON 435)

Confession and absolution

At the start of Holy Week we come to the cross of Christ in sorrow and penitence
for the sins which he bore there.
Lord Jesus,
we turn to you in faith,
repenting of our wrongdoing
and seeking your pardon.
Merciful Lord, forgive and heal us.

We have acted in our own strength,
and not put our trust wholly in you.
Merciful Lord, forgive and heal us.

We have been arrogant and proud,
and not humbled ourselves before you.
Merciful Lord, forgive and heal us.

We have acted out of self-interest,
and not shown your love or compassion to those in need.
Merciful Lord, forgive and heal us.

We have lived as though you had no part in our lives,
and not acknowledged you as Lord.
Merciful Lord, forgive and heal us.
Turn our failings into strengths,
and our weaknesses into opportunities
for the sake of your kingdom.
Amen.

May the God of forgiveness
show you his mercy,
forgive your sins, and bring you to eternal life,
through Jesus Christ our Lord.
Amen.

Hymn

My song is love unknown (HON 346)

Prayer at close of study groups

God our Father,
at the close of our time of reflection and study
we thank you for new insights into your love,
new bonds of fellowship forged,
and renewed strength to continue walking
in the way of Christ.
Make us stronger in faith,
draw us closer to you and each other,
and deepen our knowledge and experience
of your love and grace
as we see it revealed
in the death of our Saviour on the cross,
in whose name we pray.
Amen.

First reading

Isaiah 50:4-9a

Introduction to presentations

This should be as brief as possible, and those responsible for each group should be aware of the time limits imposed. It may be helpful to give some background information for the benefit of those who have not taken part in any groups, not least on how they relate to the theme of the Lent studies. It should also be clear how they fit in with the rest of the liturgy. Three examples only are given here, though more can be added as appropriate. However, time will be limited; the more time given to presentations, the less will be available for other elements of the liturgy – and don't forget to take into account the hidden time lost between each item, which can increase greatly without anyone noticing!

Drama group

Song

My Lord, what love is this? (HON 345)

Second reading

Matthew 21:1-13

Music group

Song

You are the King of Glory (HON 570)

Third reading
Philippians 2:1-11

Dance group

Song
Brother, sister, let me serve you (HON 73)

Meditation

Intercessions
We bring our prayers to Jesus,
despised and rejected,
saying, Lord of love,
hear our cry.

Lord Jesus,
criticised, mocked and condemned as a criminal,
we pray for all who suffer ill-treatment
or ridicule for their faith,
especially . . .
May they stand firm in their faith
and remain joyful in their faith.
Lord of love,
hear our cry.

Lord Jesus,
arrested wrongly and tried unfairly,
we pray for all who suffer
as a result of injustice and oppression,
especially . . .
May they be given courage and patience
to be true to themselves and you.
Lord of love,
hear our cry.

Lord Jesus,
jeered at by crowds and flogged by soldiers,
we pray for all
who suffer physical or mental abuse,
especially . . .
May they receive comfort and assurance
in their troubles
and relief from persecution.
Lord of love,
hear our cry.

Lord Jesus,
nailed to the cross in cruel pain,
we pray for all who suffer in mind or body,
especially . . .
May they receive healing and peace from you,
the wounded healer.
Lord of love,
hear our cry.

Lord Jesus,
utterly alone as you died,
we pray for all who suffer isolation
or the loneliness of grief,
especially . . .
May they find in you the faithful friend
who will never let them down.
Lord of love,
hear our cry
and bring to our lives
the wonder of your healing
and the joy of your salvation,
to the glory of your name.
Amen.

Hymn

I, the Lord of sea and sky (HON 235)

Prayer for Holy Week

Lord,
the paradoxes of your passion and death
bewilder us:
the King of Glory is crucified
with common thieves;
the one who knew no sin
takes our sins upon himself;
the Lord of life dies in agony;
the scene of humiliating defeat
becomes the place of final victory
over sin and death.
By your life may we live for you;
by your death may we die to sin;
by your resurrection may we rise
to eternal life
for your holy name's sake.
Amen.

Final response

As we run the race set before us,
keep us firm in faith and steadfast in hope.

As we continue our earthly pilgrimage,
keep our eyes fixed on Jesus.

As we look for the coming of your kingdom,
we pray together,
Our Father . . .

Blessing and dismissal

STUART THOMAS

Maundy Thursday

Jesus, for ever at our service

Jesus washes his disciples' feet (John 13:1-10)

The country where Jesus lived is a really hot country. People had to walk for miles along dusty tracks. This meant that their feet soon became dirty, sweaty and very smelly. The custom was that if you were a guest in someone's home, your feet would be washed, normally by one of the least-important servants. What a horrible job, especially if there were large numbers of guests.

One day, Jesus and his friends hired an upper room for a meal, but of course this meant that there was no servant to wash their feet. I can imagine some of the older disciples trying to persuade one of the younger ones to go round and wash everyone's feet. Of course no one would want to volunteer to wash thirteen pairs of dirty, smelly feet!

Suddenly Jesus got up, took off his outer garment, tied a towel around his waist and started to wash his friends' feet. They were really embarrassed! Jesus was their leader. He was a really important man, a great teacher. He could perform fantastic miracles like walking on the water and making blind people see! He was the greatest person any of them had ever met and yet here he was, washing their dirty, smelly feet!

Simon Peter couldn't keep quiet. 'You are not going to wash my feet! Never!'

Jesus said, 'If I do not wash your feet you will no longer be my disciple.'

'Oh, wash my hands and my head, too!' answered Peter.

'If you have had a bath, you are completely clean, except for your feet!' replied Jesus.

Peter was amazed that such a great man as Jesus was prepared to do such a horrible job, but by being prepared to become like a servant Jesus showed that he was a truly great man.

Round-up

One day you may write a book, or a play, or become a famous singer or sports person, and people may say that you are really great. But remember, truly great people are those who go out of their way to serve and help others.

Prayer

Lord, thank you that we don't have to be famous to be great, but that we need to be prepared to help others in whatever way we can. Amen.

JOHN HARDWICK

Matthew 26:26-29

The Last Supper

During the supper, Jesus took the loaf, blessed it, broke it, and gave it to his friends. 'Take it,' he said. 'This is my very self.'

He took the cup, said Grace, and gave it to them; they all drank from it. 'This means my death,' he said. 'I am dying to bring everyone to God, as the Bible says, "from the least of them to the greatest". I am sure of this: I shall drink no more wine until that day when I drink it fresh in God's Kingdom.'

When supper was over, they sang a hymn; then they walked out to the Olive Hill outside the City, on the road to the village where he was staying.

ALAN DALE

Introductory material

As a devout Jew, Jesus celebrated the Jewish festival of Passover. At his last Passover he gave us, for the very first time, the sacrament and sacrifice of the Eucharist. By so doing he placed himself for ever at our service.

If your family cannot attend evening worships, then before the evening meal you could have an extended grace, your own little service. This would, of course, be adapted according to the ages of those present.

Mum or Dad can ask one of the children, 'What is special about today? What happened on the first Maundy Thursday?' Trying to build on the answer, whatever it might be, Mum or Dad continues: 'Holy Communion isn't something just for ourselves'.

'He got up from the table (*if Mum is speaking then Dad can get up – this is especially easy if the family is eating in the kitchen and can match the words with actions*), filled a bowl with water and put a towel over his arm. Then he went round and washed the feet of his friends – including Judas who was just about to go out and betray him.' (*The parent with bowl and towel may match actions with words and take off socks and briefly wash the family's feet.*)

When the parent has sat down: 'Only after Jesus had shown his love in this way, by serving his friends, did he take the bread, bless it and give it to them.'

The little service can finish with a simple prayer such as:

We thank you, Lord Jesus,
for your example of humble service
and for the gift of yourself in the Eucharist,
the breaking of bread.
May we follow your example of loving service
by helping one another.
May we always be grateful
for all the gifts we receive from you.
Amen.

TONY CASTLE

Prayers

Approach

Loving God,
  we come before you,
    in worship, praise, thanksgiving and remembrance.
  Open our hearts to the presence of Christ,
    and lead us in his way.

We come recalling that last week in the life of Jesus
    and all it teaches us of him –
    his faithfulness to the last,
    his willingness to take the Way of the Cross,
    his courage in the face of opposition, suffering and death.
  Open our hearts to the presence of Christ,
    and lead us in his way.

We come consecrating our lives to his service,
    committing ourselves to his cause.
  Open our hearts to the presence of Christ,
    and lead us in his way.

We come thankful for all he has done
    and continues to do,
    celebrating his great love.
  Open our hearts to the presence of Christ,
    and lead us in his way.

We come acknowledging him as our Lord and Saviour,
    and desiring to be his true disciples.
  Open our hearts to the presence of Christ,
    and lead us in his way.

Receive now this time of worship that we offer to you,
    and speak through it so that we may grow in faith
    and be strengthened in your service.
  Open our hearts to the presence of Christ,
    and lead us in his way,
    for in his name we ask it.
    Amen.   NICK FAWCETT

Confession

Lord Jesus Christ,
  once more we remember that last week
    before you faced the cross –
    your pain and hurt as you faced betrayal,

denial, rejection and abandonment,
and we confess that we have added to your pain.
Lord Jesus Christ, have mercy upon us.

Through our thoughts, words and actions,
so often we have deserted you when you needed us most.
Lord Jesus Christ, have mercy upon us.

Through our lack of thought, our failure to speak,
and our reluctance to act,
so many times we have denied
the faith and love we declare.
Lord Jesus Christ, have mercy upon us.

We have cared too much for the good opinion of others.
We have been fearful to contemplate the true cost of discipleship.
Like lost sheep we have gone astray.
Lord Jesus Christ, have mercy upon us.

Yet you have called us to be your Church.
You have forgiven us, cleansed and restored us,
giving your own life for our sakes.
Receive our thanks.
Receive our praise.
And help us to follow you more faithfully,
for in your name we pray.
Amen.

NICK FAWCETT

Petition

Loving God,
we look back today to Jesus in the wilderness,
faced with the temptation to compromise,
forced to choose between the easy and the demanding path,
the way of the world or the way of costly sacrifice.
Speak through the example Christ has given,
and help us to listen.

We remember today Jesus in Jerusalem,
the shouts of the crowd still ringing in his ears,
their welcome still fresh in his memory –
once more faced with the temptation to compromise,
forced to choose between the easy and the demanding path,
and we remember how he chose the costly way,
the way of suffering, humiliation and death.
Speak through the example Christ has given,
and help us to listen.

Loving God,
   forgive us that we lack the same courage,
      the same faith,
      the same commitment,
      the same love.
   Speak through the example Christ has given,
      and help us to listen.

   Forgive us that so often we choose the easy option –
      conforming to this world's expectations
      rather than risk rejection or confrontation,
      more concerned with present happiness and earthly success
      than the things which bring eternal fulfilment.
   Speak through the example Christ has given,
      and help us to listen.

Loving God,
   we thank you that through the love of Christ
      we are assured of your mercy,
      accepted as we are with all our faults and failings,
      daily renewed by his Spirit.
   Inspire us then, by his example,
      to serve you more faithfully and love you more deeply,
      even as you have loved us.
   Speak through the example Christ has given,
      and help us to listen,
      for in his name we ask it.
   Amen.

NICK FAWCETT

Intercession

Lord Jesus Christ,
   we remember today that you were broken not only for us,
      or even for many,
      but for all.
   We rejoice that your love isn't for the select few but for everyone –
      young and old,
      rich and poor,
      male and female,
      black and white.
   So then we pray for our world in all its need.
   May your grace bring hope;
      may your love bring healing.

We pray for all who feel broken today –
    shattered by disappointment, tragedy and bereavement;
    overwhelmed by poverty and hunger, disease and deprivation,
    crushed by injustice, oppression, imprisonment and violence –
    all those who have been broken in body, mind and spirit,
    battered by the circumstances and events of life.
May your grace bring hope;
    may your love bring healing.

We pray for those who long for wholeness –
    delivery from physical pain, sickness and disease,
    freedom from fear, anxiety and depression,
    an answer to inner emptiness and spiritual longing,
    the opportunity to be at peace with you, their neighbour
    and themselves.
May your grace bring hope;
    may your love bring healing.

Lord Jesus Christ,
    broken for all,
        reach out now to our broken world
        and teach us to reach out in turn.
Show us where you would have us serve,
    teach us what you would have us do,
    and use us to fulfil your purposes.
May your grace bring hope;
    may your love bring healing.

To the glory of your name.
Amen.

NICK FAWCETT

Short prayers

'If it be possible, take this cup from me.'
Lord, how often have we heard those words?
The desperate cry of Jesus as,
    in the darkness of Gethsemane,
    he faced up to the horror of the Cross.
He knew all too well what the future held,
    and was terrified by it.
Yet he was able to say,
    'Not my will, O God, but yours.'
And it wasn't simply courage that led him to do that,
    still less some superhuman reserve
    by virtue of being your Son –

it was his love for you,
and his love for us.
Loving God,
help us as we worship you tonight
and recall the torment that Jesus went through,
to appreciate the magnitude of what he did.
And so in turn may we learn
the true meaning of love,
for you, for ourselves, and for others.
Amen.

NICK FAWCETT

Lord Jesus Christ,
we have eaten the bread and drunk from the cup,
and so once more proclaimed your death.
Now let us go back to the world
and proclaim your death there,
through the people we are
and the lives we live.
May we make known your love,
make real your compassion,
make clear your grace,
and so make nearer your kingdom,
until you come.
Amen.

NICK FAWCETT

Lord Jesus Christ,
we have broken bread,
we have shared wine –
and we have done it,
together with your people across the centuries,
in remembrance of you.
You promise that the time will come
when we share with you
in your Father's kingdom;
a time when your will shall be done
and all things be made new.
Until then, may the memory of your great sacrifice
shape our lives,
and guide our footsteps,
to the glory of your name.
Amen.

NICK FAWCETT

Lord Jesus Christ,
   you knew one of your disciples would betray you,
   another deny you,
   and the rest forsake you,
   yet still you went to your death.
You know that we are no better
   and that, with far less reason,
   we continue to betray, deny and forsake you today,
   yet still you love us.
Despite the weakness of our faith
   and the poverty of our discipleship,
   you go on caring,
   faithful to us no matter how faithless we may be to you.
Accept our thanksgiving,
   and give us strength to show our gratitude
   through staying true to our calling,
   wherever the path may lead,
   for your name's sake.
Amen.

NICK FAWCETT

Reflective material
(sketches, meditations and poems)

Who's the greatest?

Aim

People often look up to pop stars, TV stars, or sports people. They think that famous people are great people. The Bible says great people are people who serve others (Mark 10:43).

Puppet sketch

Micky   Two new boys joined our class today. They are brothers, Gary and Gordon Bennett. In fact they are twins, almost identical.

John   What are they like?

Micky   Gary appears to be a real cool dude; tells great jokes, a fast runner and excellent at football. All the girls think he's cute!

John   What about Gordon Bennett?

Micky   He was a little shy today and his jokes weren't funny. He came last in a running race we had and he is absolutely useless at football!

John   Seeing as they are almost identical twins, do the girls think Gordon is cute as well?

Micky	No! They think Gary is much better looking! In fact within one day Gary has become the most popular person in school! They all think he's great! But I don't!
John	Micky, you're not jealous because he's so popular, are you?
Micky	No! But he did pinch my chair during dinner. I got up for a second and when I came back he was sitting in my chair!
John	Oh, dear!
Micky	During a game of football, he was on the other team. He got the ball and dribbled round our team, but I managed to tackle him fair and square. He didn't like that and when no one was looking he tripped me up, kicked me really hard and laughed at me!
John	Oh, dear!
Micky	No one else noticed, but then he came at me with the ball again. I got ready to tackle him when suddenly he pushed me. I went flying! He laughed and then everyone joined in! Then they carried on with the game, leaving me on the ground with a cut knee.
John	What? No one helped you?
Micky	Yes, Gordon did. He helped me get up and took me to the first-aid teacher, to get a plaster.
John	What, Gordon? Gary's twin?
Micky	Yes. He's a great guy. Anyone who will stop playing football to help someone else is pretty great, I reckon. A mate you can rely on!
John	What about Gary?
Micky	He's not as great as he thinks he is. It's a shame he's not more like Gordon. Bye!

JOHN HARDWICK

Meditation of John the Apostle

We were there in the upper room,
   just us and Jesus,
   the night drawing in,
   the end drawing near.
We knew it,
   he knew it.
There could be no doubt any more, not for any of us;
   no question of a last-minute reprieve.
We'd seen Judas sneaking out, darkness in his eyes,
   and we knew it wouldn't be long before the vultures descended,
   hungry to devour their prey.

We wanted him to run for it;
   back to Nazareth,
   back to Galilee,
   back to the safety of the wilderness,
   anywhere but there in Jerusalem.
But he wouldn't listen, of course,
   wouldn't even consider it.
So we stayed with him,
   nervous,
   fearful,
   one eye over our shoulders, but determined to do our best for him.
He was under no illusions;
   he knew full well what was coming –
   an ugly, agonising death.
And it was getting to him,
   eating away inside,
   that much we could all see.
When he broke bread, he was trembling,
   clearly petrified about what lay ahead;
   and as he shared the wine, there was a sob in his voice,
   a tear in his eye.
Yet then he spoke,
   softly,
   gently,
   almost as if in a dream,
   and we realised he was praying –
   not for himself,
   but for us!
Not for his own life,
   but for the life of the world!
Yes, I know that sounds hard to believe, but it's true, honestly.
I was there, remember;
   I heard him.
It wasn't his death that was troubling him,
   it was the fear that we wouldn't stay together,
   that somehow we'd become divided,
   even end up fighting among ourselves.
God knows why he thought that,
   but you could see how worried he was,
   how much our unity meant to him.
It was his dying wish in a way,
   his last request –
   that we should stay together:
   one people,
   one faith,
   one God.

I'm sure he needn't have worried, least of all at a time like that.
All right, so we've had our differences since then, I admit it –
 we don't always see things the same way,
 and maybe once in a while we might even have fallen out –
 but I honestly can't imagine anything major coming between us, can you,
 not in the long run?
After all, we're his disciples, aren't we, each one of us?
All called by him,
 all confessing the same Lord,
 and what could ever be more important than that? NICK FAWCETT

Meditation of Matthew

He was scared, that much is certain.
I've never seen him like it before.
He'd always seemed so sure,
 so confident,
 so at ease with himself,
 even when he talked about death
 and he'd done that often enough.
I really thought it didn't worry him, the way he'd spoken,
 but this time it was different,
 so different.
We'd just finished supper,
 and he'd seemed strangely preoccupied throughout,
 so we weren't surprised when he suggested going out for a little air –
 a stroll to clear our heads, that's what we expected.
But then he asked us to pray for him,
 and off he went alone into the darkness.
Gone for ages it seemed,
 and when he came back you should have seen him.
Shaking like a leaf he was,
 eyes wide with fear,
 sweating buckets,
 a right old state.
We were shocked, I can tell you.
It made us nervous just to look at him.
And the tone of voice he used with us,
 just because we'd dozed off for a few minutes.
I know he was hurt, but I ask you, it was past midnight!
Three times he went off,
 and each time he came back the same –
 terrified.
He was scared, make no mistake.
It wasn't as easy as we all thought.
Not easy at all. NICK FAWCETT

Meditation of the temple policeman

Why didn't he escape while he had the chance? –
    that's what I can't work out.
He had only to melt away into the shadows,
    slip quietly off into the darkness,
    and we'd have missed him for sure,
    our quarry once again slipping through our fingers.
Right fools we'd have looked then!
But, luckily for us, it didn't work out that way.
Don't ask me why, for I still can't make sense of it,
    but for some reason he actually came looking for us,
    determined, apparently, to give himself up.
Was he fed up, perhaps, with the constant harrying,
    the knowledge that we were always there,
    plotting behind his back,
    waiting for the chance to bring him down?
Some have said so,
    yet he'd never appeared troubled before,
    our attentions, seemingly, of no importance to him.
Whatever it was, though, the fact is he took the initiative,
    and we were taken aback,
    such assurance the last thing we'd expected.
You should have seen us,
    enough men and weapons to bring down an army,
    and there he was surrendering without a murmur,
    even rebuking that hot-headed disciple of his
    for taking a swipe at Malchus.
It was astonishing,
    yet that's how it continued –
    no argument,
    no resistance,
    no attempt to defend himself –
    not even when he stood before Pilate, his life on the line.
He submitted willingly,
    almost eagerly,
    like a lamb led to the slaughter.
Well, we achieved what we were sent to do.
We got our man where we wanted him,
    nailed for all to see on a cross.
Yet somehow it doesn't feel right,
    the whole business leaving a strange taste in the mouth,
    for the truth of the matter is this:
    we didn't take his life from him as we'd planned –
    he gave it to us!

NICK FAWCETT

Meditation of Judas Iscariot

Oh God, what have I done? What have I done?
The man I called my friend,
    taken before Caiaphas,
    tried by the Council,
    condemned to the most dreadful of deaths,
    and all down to me.
I've tried telling myself that it's not my fault,
    that it's the priests,
    Herod,
    Pilate to blame,
    anyone but myself.
They're the ones who want him dead after all.
They're the ones who pronounce the sentence,
    so why accuse me?
I've tried telling myself that my part was irrelevant,
    that if I hadn't betrayed him someone else would,
    that it was only a matter of time,
    that all I did was bring things to a head –
    so why condemn me?
I've tried telling myself I had no choice,
    that I had to bring him down to earth,
    make him see reason,
    stop the crowds getting carried away.
All for the best possible motives –
    so why judge me?
I've tried telling myself it's what he wanted,
    even that I've been used,
    an innocent pawn in God's cosmic plan,
    a helpless puppet dancing to his tune,
    made in such a way that I had no choice –
    so why blame me?
But I do, that's the trouble;
    I do blame myself.
It's not others I'm worried about;
    it's me.
For I know, despite all my excuses,
    that there's no escaping my responsibility.
It's there before me, every second, every moment,
    deep in my heart –
    the doubt,
    the fear,
    the greed,
    the selfishness,
    which sent him to his death with a kiss.

Oh God, what have I done? What have I done?
God forgive me, forgive me.
For I can't forgive myself.

NICK FAWCETT

Judas

The writings and documents of the Church over the centuries have never said that Judas is in hell. That in itself is remarkable, since it is only relatively recently that Christians who committed suicide were allowed a Christian burial in a Christian cemetery. The Roman Catholic *Order of Christian Funerals* currently in use dates from 1970 and is the first one I have come across with official rites and prayers for those who have killed themselves, though the sympathetic attitude to individuals goes back much longer than that, of course.

What has always upset me, and still does to some extent, is the way Jesus says, 'For the Son of Man goes as it is written of him, but woe to that one by whom the Son of Man is betrayed! It would be better for that one not to have been born.' But does he only mean Judas? The saying is placed by Mark at the Last Supper, just before Judas betrayed Jesus, but we know the Gospel writers often chose their own setting for a saying of Jesus that might have been spoken at some other time. The saying about betrayal does not use our word 'man', meaning 'male person'; it uses the word *anthropos*, which means 'member of the human race'. Perhaps the best way to take the saying is to see each one of us as capable of betraying Jesus. I know I am quite capable of it. I am only worthy to carry on because I am a child of God, not just a human child.

Consoling in this respect is the way Jesus says elsewhere: 'Those who are ashamed of me and of my words in this adulterous and sinful generation, of them the Son of Man will also be ashamed when he comes in the glory of his Father with the holy angels.' Peter was ashamed of Jesus at the fire in the high priest's courtyard, yet Jesus did not disown him, then or ever.

GERALD O'MAHONY

Good Friday

The Way of the Cross

The Last Days

In the Garden   John 18:1-12

Jesus left the house with his friends and crossed the Kidron Brook to the other side of the valley. They came to a garden and went inside. They knew it well, for Jesus and his friends had often met there.

Judas knew this, and he led a detachment of Roman soldiers and a company of Jewish police straight to the spot. They were fully armed and carried lanterns and torches.

Jesus stepped out to meet them.

'Who do you want?' he asked.

'Jesus from Nazareth,' they answered.

'I'm the man you want, then,' said Jesus.

At these words, they stepped back and fell on the ground.

'Who do you want?' asked Jesus again.

'Jesus from Nazareth,' they repeated.

'I've told you – I'm the man you want,' he said. 'If it's me you're after, let these men go.'

Peter drew his sword and struck at a slave of the High Priest and cut off his right ear.

'Put your sword up,' said Jesus. 'Do you want to stop me facing what God the Father has set before me?'

The soldiers then arrested Jesus and handcuffed him.

Before Annas   John 18:13, 15-27

The soldiers took Jesus before Annas, the most powerful man in Jerusalem City. He was not the High Priest of the Jewish people. Caiaphas was the High Priest that year; Annas was his father-in-law.

Now Jesus had a friend whose name we do not know. He was not one of the 'Twelve', but belonged to one of the most important families in Jerusalem; the High Priest knew him well. He was the 'other friend'.

Peter and the 'other friend' followed Jesus along the road. When they got to the courtyard, the 'other friend' went straight in with Jesus; Peter was left standing outside at the door. The 'other friend' came back and had a word with the girl on duty at the door and then took him inside.

'You're one of this fellow's friends, too, aren't you?' the girl asked Peter.

'Not I,' said Peter.

It was a cold night, and the slaves and court officers had lit a charcoal fire. They were standing round it, trying to keep warm. Peter joined the crowd round the fire; he wanted to get warm too.

The High Priest asked Jesus about his friends and what he stood for.

'What I have had to say,' said Jesus, 'I have said openly for everybody to hear. I have talked in the Meeting Houses, and I have talked in the Temple to Jewish people from all over the world. I have not been plotting in back rooms. Why ask me questions now? Ask the ordinary people in the villages and in this city. They heard me. They know what it was I talked about.'

One of the court officials standing near him gave him a slap on the face.

'Is that the way to talk to the High Priest?' he said.

'If I did something wrong,' said Jesus to the officer, 'prove it. If I didn't, why hit me?'

Annas had Jesus handcuffed again and sent to Caiaphas.

Peter was still standing near the fire, getting warm.

'You are one of this fellow's friends too, aren't you?' said some of the men by the fire.

'Not on your life,' said Peter.

Now it happened that one of the court officers standing there was a relative of the man Peter had slashed with his sword.

'I saw you in the garden with him, didn't I?' he asked.

'No, you didn't,' said Peter. At that moment, somewhere in the distance a cock crowed.

Before the Roman Governor   John 18:28-31, 33-40; 19:1-16a

It was now Friday, the day before the Great Feast.

Just before dawn Jesus was marched into the headquarters of Pilate, the Roman Governor.

The Jewish leaders stayed outside the building (it was 'unclean' to them because it belonged to foreigners, and, if they had gone inside, they would not have been allowed, by Jewish law, to take part in the Great Feast). So Pilate came outside.

'What's the charge against this man?' he asked.

'He's a criminal,' they said. 'Would we have brought him here if he wasn't?'

'Well, take him off and deal with him yourselves,' said Pilate. 'You've got your own laws and law courts.'

'But we can't pass the death sentence,' they replied.

Pilate went back into the building and had Jesus brought before him.

'So you're the Jewish King, are you?' he said.

'Are those your own words?' asked Jesus. 'Or are you just repeating what other people have told you?'

'Do I look like a Jew!' said Pilate. 'You've been brought here by your own leaders. What have you been up to?'

'I'm no nationalist,' said Jesus. 'My men would have been out on the streets fighting, if I were – they wouldn't have let me be arrested so easily. My "kingdom" has nothing to do with that sort of thing.'

'So you *are* a "king", then,' said Pilate.

'The word is yours,' said Jesus. 'I was born to defend the truth. Anybody who cares for the truth knows what I am talking about.'

'What is truth?' said Pilate.

And with that he went outside again.

'As far as this court is concerned,' he told the crowd, 'there is nothing this man can be charged with. I've been in the habit of setting one prisoner free for you at the Feast. What about letting "the Jewish King" go free this year?'

The crowd broke into a roar.

'Not this man, but Barabbas!'

(Barabbas was one of the terrorists in the Resistance Movement.)

So Pilate had Jesus flogged, and the soldiers – as was often their custom with prisoners – made sport of him. They made a crown out of some thorn twigs and crowned him with it, and dressed him in a soldier's purple cloak. Then they kept coming up to him, saluting him with 'Long live Your Majesty!' and slapping him on the face.

Pilate went out to the crowd again.

'Here he is,' he said. 'I'm going to bring him out to you to make it clear that there is nothing this court can charge him with.'

Jesus was brought outside, still wearing the mock crown and the purple cloak.

'There's the man!' said Pilate.

When the Jewish leaders and their officers caught sight of him, they started shouting.

'The cross! Let's have him on the gallows!'

'Take him and put him on a cross yourselves,' said Pilate. 'He's done nothing this court can deal with!'

'But we've a law of blasphemy,' they answered, 'and by that law he ought to be executed – he claims to be equal with God himself!'

That last sentence frightened Pilate. He went back again into the building.

'Where were you born?' he asked Jesus.

Jesus didn't speak.

'I'm the Governor, you know – why don't you say something?' said Pilate. 'Don't you know I can set you free or have you executed?'

'You would have no power over me at all,' said Jesus, 'if God had not given it to you. The man who handed me over to you is more guilty than you.'

From that moment Pilate made up his mind to set him free.

But the shouting of the crowd went on.

'If you let this man go, you're no friend of the Emperor! Anybody who calls himself a king is an enemy of the Emperor!'

Pilate heard what they were shouting.

He brought Jesus outside again, and took his seat as Governor and Judge at the place called 'The Pavement'. It was now just midday.

'Here's your "King"!' he said.

'Take him away! Hang him on a cross!' the crowd shouted.

'So it's your "King" I'm to hang on a cross?' he asked.

'The Emperor is the only King we've got!' they shouted back.

Pilate handed him over for execution.

At Skull Hill   John 19:16b-35, 38-42

The soldiers marched Jesus off, and, with his own cross on his shoulders, he went out of the building to Skull Hill, a place quite near the city. And there they hung him on the cross. Three men were hung on crosses that day – Jesus in the middle, the other two on either side of him.

Pilate had a notice written out in three languages, Jewish, Roman and Greek: JESUS OF NAZARETH, THE JEWISH KING. He had it fastened on the cross. Crowds of citizens read it.

'Don't put THE JEWISH KING,' the Jewish leaders protested to Pilate. 'Put – HE SAID HE WAS THE JEWISH KING.'

'It stays as I wrote it,' said Pilate.

When the four soldiers had carried out their orders, they picked up the clothes of Jesus and made four bundles, one for each of them. Then they picked up his tunic. This was one piece of cloth, woven from top to bottom, not made up of several pieces.

'We mustn't tear it up,' they said. 'Let's toss for it.'

That is what they did.

All this time, his mother, his aunt Mary, the wife of Clopas, and Mary from Magdala were standing near the cross itself. Jesus caught sight of his mother – and the friend he loved dearly standing by her side.

'Mother,' he said, 'take my friend as your son.'

'Take my mother as your mother,' he said to his friend.

And from that time, his friend took her into his own home.

'I am thirsty,' said Jesus.

A full jar of sour wine had been put nearby for the guard. The soldier soaked a sponge in it, stuck it on a javelin and put it up to his mouth. Jesus drank it.

'My work is done,' he said.

His head dropped, and he died.

The Jewish leaders did not want the bodies on the crosses to stay there over the Saturday, the Holy Day of the Jews, especially since this was a very important Saturday, the first day of the Great Feast. They asked Pilate to have the men's legs broken to make them die quickly, and then to have the bodies taken away.

This is what the soldiers began to do. They broke the legs of the two men hanging on either side of Jesus, one after the other. They went up to Jesus, but they found that he was already dead. They didn't break his legs, but one of the soldiers jabbed a lance into his side, and water and blood flowed out. (This is what happened; it is the evidence of an eye-witness who can be trusted.)

After all this, two men went to Pilate – Joseph from the village of Arimathea (he was a member of the Jewish Council; he had kept his friendship with Jesus a secret, for he was afraid of what the Council might do) and Nicodemus (who, as we have told, first met Jesus at night).

Joseph asked Pilate to let him take the body of Jesus down from the cross, and Pilate agreed. So his friends came and took his body away, and wrapped it in linen sheets with spices which Nicodemus had brought, more than seventy pounds weight of perfume mixture. (This is the Jewish method of burial.)

There was a large garden nearby. In it there was a new tomb – nobody had yet been buried there.

It was now getting on for six o'clock in the evening, the time when the Holy Day began. The tomb lay near at hand; so they put Jesus there.

ALAN DALE

Introductory material

For the modern Christian family there is a certain tension between Good Friday as the 'holy day' and as the public holiday. On the only other occasion when a sacred day and a secular holiday come together – Christmas Day – everyone is more or less in step. However, on Good Friday the secular world is coolly indifferent to the sacred meaning of the day. If parents are serious about the Faith then there will be no question about where the emphasis will be. From the very beginning of the day it should be experienced by the family as different and special.

Good Friday breakfast

Lots of families replace their breakfast toast on this day with toasted hot cross buns. As it is a bank holiday, with a little organisation the family can all eat breakfast together. Whoever leads the grace should draw everyone's attention to the hot cross buns with some suitable comment, for example:

Dear Father,
even the food we eat today
reminds us how special and important this day is.
Your Son's great love and obedience
took him to death on the cross;
please deepen our love of you
and help us to be obedient to your commandments.
May we always be grateful for the food we eat
and all the gifts you give us.
We ask this through Jesus,
who lives and reigns now and for ever. Amen.

While we recall what happened on the first Good Friday so that we may better appreciate Jesus' great love for us, we must keep in mind that Jesus is with us here and now. His resurrection gave us his continuing presence for ever. So, while we recall the sad events of that day and express sorrow for our sin, we must remember that we have him with us even as we recall those events!

Way of the Cross

Today, in some form or other, the story of Jesus' Passion should be followed in a devotional way. It is true that the family will hear the Passion read at the afternoon liturgy, but something additional might be attempted. This could be:

- a service of the Way of the Cross, arranged in the parish church
- a family version of the Way of the Cross
- a public procession of witness
- a simple retelling by parents for their children.

Those who have lived through the cold and gloom of winter really appreciate the beauty of spring. Those who have suffered the loneliness of a wakeful night greet the morning light with relief and joy.

In a similar way only those who have taken Lent seriously and died spiritually with Christ on Good Friday can experience the resurrection joy of Easter.

A public procession of witness

In some places a united procession of witness is organised on Good Friday by the local Churches. It usually involves the carrying of a large wooden cross through the streets in the middle of the day. Sometimes the procession takes the form of a Way of the Cross, with regular stops for a meditation on the Passion, a Scripture reading and a prayer. Not everyone finds it easy to take part but it really is a terrific opportunity for the family to proclaim their Faith. It is a wonderful annual lesson for the children, showing them the need to be courageous in witnessing to their Faith.

Telling the story

It is hard to improve upon an old-fashioned recounting of the Passion in one's own words. As the story is one of supreme love and sacrifice it is very fitting for it to be told in a family group. Mum or Dad knows enough of the story to put it across without having to read it (the Gospel Passion will be read during the afternoon liturgy).

Pictures are a different matter. They are a great help to both the parent in telling the story and the children in listening. One of the best sets of pictures available is those from the film *Jesus of Nazareth*. They can be obtained as slides, but the book of the same name – the text is by William Barclay – has over twenty excellent pictures on the Passion. Remind the children, before showing them the photographs, that these are not real photos of Jesus and his friends but pictures from a film. After the 'telling' – and naturally the inevitable questions – the younger members can be encouraged to draw a picture or use playdough or building bricks to depict a part of the story.

Family fast day

For the adults, Good Friday is a day of fasting and abstinence. But there is no more suitable day in the year for the whole family to do without a little. Before the main meal of the day the grace should reflect this:

> Almighty Father,
> today we are thinking
> about the wonderful love of your Son
> which took him to the cross.
> That love reminds us
> that we often fail in our loving.
> To express our sorrow
> for the hurt we have caused you
> we are trying to do without a little today.
> Please accept the love
> we are trying to express in this way
> and may the money we save
> and give to the needy uplift them a little.
> We thank you for all the good things
> we have received from your hand,
> especially the food we are about to share. Amen.

TONY CASTLE

Holy Week

The three very special days of the week we call 'holy' – Thursday, Friday and Sunday – are the pinnacle of the Church's year. Everything else in the year either builds up to these three days or looks back to them. They are rather like the Holy Trinity – three but one: three days making up one event – the 'passover' of Jesus. Parents really need to read and think about all this in order to be able to help their children understand and join fully in the celebration of Easter.

The three days actually are:

Maundy Thursday evening to Good Friday evening	Last Supper and death of Jesus
Good Friday evening to Saturday evening	Burial and 'silence' of grave
Saturday evening to Easter Sunday evening	Resurrection

- Jesus offers himself
- The offering is accepted
- The offering (Jesus) is given back to us

TONY CASTLE

Were you there when they crucified my Lord?' So asks that lovely and powerful hymn so often sung on or around Good Friday. The answer of course is that we weren't. But in the pages of Scripture we can read the testimony of those who were – those who experienced first-hand the grief, the horror, the pain, and the anguish of watching Jesus nailed to the cross. Today we listen again to their testimony, and we seek to get behind their words through asking what else each might have said to us about that day given the opportunity.   NICK FAWCETT

Prayers

Praise – a man like us

Gracious God,
   we praise you for the astonishing love we recall today,
     the love you showed to all humankind
     through your coming, living and dying among us in Christ.
   We thank you for being willing to endure so much for our sakes –
     to face the mental agony,
     the physical torture
     and the spiritual torment involved in the cross.
   But, above all, we praise you that you did that
     through a person as human as we are,
     experiencing the same temptations,
     torn by the same fears,
     sharing the same joys and sorrows,
     suffering the same pain.
   You became one with us:
     may we become one with you.

   We thank you for the assurance this brings –
     the knowledge that you understand
     the trials and tribulations we go through;
     the worries, concerns, doubts and problems
     which confront us each day.
   We thank you for the inspiration this brings –
     the example in Christ of humanity at its most selfless,
     courageous,
     compassionate
     and loving.
   We thank you for the challenge this brings –
     the call to follow in his footsteps,
     to take up our cross,
     to deny ourselves and to offer our service.
   You became one with us:
     may we become one with you.

You could have disassociated yourself from our sinfulness,
   yet you identified with us fully.
You could have demanded we pay the price for our folly,
   but you chose rather to pay it yourself.
You could have lectured us about the importance of love,
   but instead you demonstrated what love really means.
You experienced humanity at its worst
   and revealed it at its best,
   opening up a new dimension of life
   for all who will receive you.
You became one with us:
   may we become one with you.

Gracious God,
   you became human,
     flesh and blood like us.
Accept our praise
   and receive our thanksgiving,
   through Jesus Christ our Lord,
Amen.   Nick Fawcett

Petition – light in our darkness

Lord Jesus Christ,
   you came to our world as light in its darkness,
   bringing life and love,
     hope and forgiveness.
Lighten our darkness, Lord, we pray.

You came not to condemn, but to save,
not to judge, but to show mercy,
   and to do that
   you willingly endured darkness for our sakes –
   the darkness of loneliness and rejection,
   of betrayal and denial,
   of suffering and humiliation,
   of fear and death,
   of all our human sinfulness
   pressing down on your shoulders.
Lighten our darkness, Lord, we pray.

Lord Jesus Christ,
   forgive us that, despite all you have done,
     we so often walk in darkness,
     preferring our way to yours,
   betraying our convictions,
     abandoning our responsibilities,
     and denying our faith through the way we live.
Lighten our darkness, Lord, we pray.

Teach us to walk in your light
   and to follow where you lead,
   knowing that in you
   is the Way, the Truth and the Life.
Lighten our darkness, Lord, we pray,
   for in your name we ask it.
Amen.

NICK FAWCETT

Thanksgiving

Gracious God,
   you have done so much for us,
      giving us a world rich in wonder
      and filling our lives with so much that is special.
Receive our thanks.

But above all today we come to thank you
for your most precious gift of all –
   the great love you have shown to us in Christ.
Receive our thanks.

In him you came and lived amongst us,
   fully part of our world.
Through him you revealed your grace, your mercy,
   your will, your kingdom.
By him you identified yourself
   with the sin and suffering of our world,
      opening the way through his death and resurrection
      to forgiveness and eternal life.
Receive our thanks.

Gracious God,
   you have given to us without counting the cost,
      not just a little but all.
Receive our thanks.

You emptied yourself,
   taking the form of a servant,
   sacrificing your only Son for our sakes.
Receive our thanks.

And the wonder is you ask so little in return –
   you make no extortionate demands,
you set no stringent conditions to your love,
   you ask simply that we love you in return.
Receive our thanks.

Gracious God,
　　teach us to offer you our willing and joyful discipleship,
　　　and to play our part in working for your kingdom.
　　Receive our thanks,
　　　for the sake of Jesus Christ our Lord.
　　Amen.

NICK FAWCETT

Intercession

Lord Jesus Christ,
　　we remember today
　　　how your concern throughout your ministry
　　　was not for yourself but for others –
　　　the vulnerable,
　　　the distressed,
　　　the sick,
　　　the despised;
　　　all those who were marginalised in society –
　　　downtrodden,
　　　oppressed,
　　　rejected.
　　You came as the man for others:
　　　come again to our world today.

　　We remember how you had a special place in your heart
　　　for the poor,
　　　and so we pray for the millions suffering still
　　　under the yoke of poverty
　　　with all the attendant misery that involves –
　　　victims of failed harvests, natural disasters and civil wars,
　　　crying to us for help,
　　　begging for food to stave their hunger,
　　　homes to house their children,
　　　resources to build a better future,
　　　an opportunity to start again
　　　free from the shackles of debt.
　　You came as the man for others:
　　　come again to our world today.

　　We remember how you suffered at the hands of others,
　　　and so we pray for all who endure violence and cruelty,
　　　all who are wounded in body, mind and spirit
　　　by acts of inhumanity.
　　We pray for victims of racism and discrimination,
　　　of verbal and physical bullying,
　　　of assault and abuse,

    intimidation and torture,
    terrorism and war.
  You came as the man for others:
    come again to our world today.

Lord Jesus Christ,
  you lived for others,
    you died for others
    and you rose for all.
  Help us to live in turn as your people,
    seeking to serve rather than be served,
    to give rather than to receive.
  Teach us to reach out in love
    and so to make real your compassion
    and represent your body here on earth.
  You came as the man for others:
    come again to our world today.

  We ask it in your name.
  Amen.

NICK FAWCETT

Short prayers

Lord Jesus Christ,
  living as we do in the light of Easter
  we can lose sight sometimes of the darkness of Good Friday.
But for those who were part of it there could be no mistake,
  no escaping the awfulness of seeing you
  hanging there upon that cross.
For them it was their darkest hour,
  what seemed like the end of all their dreams,
  and for a time their faith swung in the balance.
Yet even there, especially there, you were at work,
  bringing your love to all.
Lord Jesus Christ,
  teach us that even when life seems dark,
  your light continues to shine.
Amen.

NICK FAWCETT

Lord Jesus Christ,
  no matter how often we hear it,
  how often we picture it,
  we can barely begin to imagine
  what you went through
  on that first Good Friday.

We know you suffered,
   we know you died,
   but we cannot comprehend
   the agony you experienced,
   or the terrible sense of isolation
   you must have felt on the Cross.
Lord Jesus Christ,
   we cannot imagine it, but we need to try,
   for only then can we recognise
   how much you loved us.
So we come today,
   to listen again to the words of Scripture,
   and to try and get behind them
   to the events of that day.
Lord Jesus Christ,
   help us through this service to stand ourselves
   by the foot of the Cross,
   and to realise afresh the incredible truth
   that you died for us!
Amen.

NICK FAWCETT

Gracious God,
   we fail you, we deny you,
   we abandon and betray you,
   yet still you love us, still you have mercy,
   nothing able to exhaust your grace.
So we come,
   with all our faults and weaknesses,
   all our doubt and disobedience,
   seeking again your renewing touch
   upon our lives.
Help us to stand again before the cross
   and to receive the forgiveness you so freely offer,
   so that our lives may speak of your goodness
   and honour you through all we are and all we do.
Amen.

NICK FAWCETT

All-age-talk material

Jesus suffered for us

Ask two people to come out and stand at least three metres apart. Ask one of the people to walk down to reach the other. Was there any problem in that? (Hopefully not.) Now ask both people to get to you, only this time with one condition – they mustn't move. Can they do it? (No, it's impossible.) If they want to get across to reach you they will have to go on a journey to do it. Is the journey easy or difficult? (They can try it to find out.) They probably did that with no trouble at all.

But suppose the journey is made very difficult? (Tie all four ankles together with a scarf and walk away from them.) Can they get to you now? (Let them try.) As they are moving along explain that they can certainly do it, but only by using a lot more effort, and with quite a struggle. Stop them halfway and explain how being crucified was like a terrible journey that Jesus had to make to rescue us. In the middle of his journey people shouted at him to come down from the cross and save himself from the suffering.

Ask the people if they would be capable of untying the scarf and walking free. So could Jesus have come down from the cross, so why didn't he? He did it because there wasn't any other way to rescue us apart from accepting all the chains of our sin and carrying them for us, even though it made his journey so difficult. So instead of opting out, he carried on (the people can carry on too) until the journey was finished so we can all be set free (untie the legs of the volunteers).

SUSAN SAYERS

HE DIED THAT WE MIGHT BE FORGIVEN.

Hebrews 10:9-12

SUSAN SAYERS

Reflective material
(sketches, meditations and poems)

The feeling of being on your own or rejected seems to happen about as often as you put milk on your cornflakes. In other words, that feeling of being alone in a crowd is part and parcel of life. But does that mean we should just put up with it and concentrate on breathing?

Like many things in life, it's how we react to issues and situations that dictates the way we feel and deal with the tripwires of life.

Although Jesus knew that death on the cross was essential for the restoring of the relationship between God and his people, this knowledge didn't make the feeling of desolation and rejection any easier to deal with. Jesus was absolutely confident that his father loved him, yet, at that precise moment of agony on the cross, that confidence didn't dull the pain.

In many ways, if we stood back and looked at the issue or situation calmly, we would know that we have people who care for us and want the best for us but, at that exact moment of hurt, it feels as if nothing else counts, nothing can stop us feeling such pain, and the last thing we feel is calm . . .

The victim of crucifixion would be made to carry the horizontal beam of his own cross through the streets of the city. After a vicious whipping, the victim was really is no fit shape to carry a heavy, roughly hewn lump of wood around. However the victim made it to the place of crucifixion, it was there that the next stage took place: hammering nails through the hands and the feet fastened to the wooden upright. The pain was intense.

It was the custom of some wealthy women to offer the victims a drink of drugged wine which would deaden the pain. To refuse the drugged wine was to experience the full agony of every nerve-jangling sensation of pain.

PETE TOWNSEND

Reflective prayer

Inner

(Place a candle in the centre of the room. Sit or stand facing the candle as you read the prayer.)

Lord,
    here I am
    with eyes wide open,
    staring, gazing,
    just watching
    as time flickers by.
After a while
    things seem to blur,
    as the encroaching darkness
    bleeds into my reality.

It's all around me,
   prodding at my consciousness,
   nudging at my senses,
   threatening to overwhelm me.
It would be so easy
   to peer into the darkness,
   allow it to cover my eyes,
   cloud my being
   and envelop me
   in its clinging sightlessness.
I'm frightened, Lord.
The darkness
   hides the day.
It hangs over me
   like a storm cloud
   blotting out the sun.
Let the light of your love
   shine into my life,
   pushing away the shadows,
   turning night into day
   and tearing the fear
   from my eyes.
Let the warmth of your love
   hug me,
   embrace my being,
   turning the shivers of cold
   into a glow
   of reflected love.
Lord,
   be with me
   as I walk through each day.
Allow my life
   to reflect the sun.

Outer

(Light a second candle and place it next to the first.)

Lord,
   where there is darkness
   let me bring
   the light of your life.
Where there is hatred
   let me bring
   your peace.

Where there is hurt
  let me bring
  comfort.
Where there is crying
  let me bring
  hope.
Lord,
  be with each of us,
  allow us
  to be your light
  in a world
  that often seems
  engulfed,
  cloaked
  in darkness.
Lord,
  wherever we are,
  help us to be
  your voice,
  your heart,
  your love.
Protect us
  as we try to bring
  light
  into the dark places.
Be with us
  each step of the way
  so that the shadows
  will disappear
  wherever your people
  call out your name.

PETE TOWNSEND

The last throw of the dice
Mark 12:1-8; John 19:28-30

The last move in the game
  was very like the first
  in some things;
  his death was like his birth –
  poor, weak, naked, in the dark,
  stared at by animals,
  innocent victim of ignorance,
  his body linen-wrapped
  and laid to rest;
  and still there was no room.

But it was different too;
   a *public* humiliation –
   the crowds had gathered
   for the finish;
   not excited shepherds
   with light in their eyes,
   but scowling spectators,
   bored soldiers
   and stone-faced priests;
   and no angel music,
   but the hate-filled howlings
   of a callous mob;
   no prickling straw,
   but piercing thorns and nails;
   no precious gifts,
   but a sponge full of bitter wine;
   and no wise worshippers,
   but weeping women and empty disciples
   and Mary with a breaking heart.

So the last stake was raised,
   and the dice that God threw at Bethlehem
   came to rest on Calvary –
   the game of his love
   to win a world.

PETER DAINTY

Woman, behold your son

Then Pilate handed Jesus over to be nailed to a cross. Jesus was taken away, and he carried his cross to a place known as 'The Skull'. In Aramaic this place is called 'Golgotha'. There Jesus was nailed to the cross, and on each side of him a man was also nailed to a cross. Pilate ordered the charge against Jesus to be written on a board and put above the cross. It read, 'Jesus of Nazareth, King of the Jews'. The words were written in Hebrew, Latin and Greek. The place where Jesus was taken wasn't far from the city, and many of the Jewish people read the charge against him. So the chief priests went to Pilate and said, 'Why did you write that he is King of the Jews? You should have written, "He claimed to be King of the Jews."' But Pilate told them, 'What is written will not be changed!' After the soldiers had nailed Jesus to the cross, they divided up his clothes into four parts, one for each of them. But his outer garment was made from a single piece of cloth, and it did not have any seams. The soldiers said to each other, 'Let's not rip it apart. We will gamble to see who gets it.' This happened so that the Scriptures would come true, which say:

   'They divided up my clothes and gambled for my garments.'

The soldiers then did what they decided.

Jesus' mother stood beside the cross with her sister and Mary the wife of Clopas. Mary Magdalene was standing there too. When Jesus saw his mother and his favourite disciple with her, he said to his mother, 'This man is now your son'. Then he said to the disciple, 'She is now your mother'. From then on, that disciple took her into his home.

John 19:16-27

So close, Mary

Watching life fade is something that nobody wants to see. But looking up at a life that means so much to you is an experience you never want to happen. It's all happening so close yet so far away. The frustration of being close enough to see the sweat bead on his forehead yet too far away to wipe them away is agony. And now, the life that means so much doesn't think of his own suffering but wants to make sure that his mother will be cared for. While his body cries out to have his mother's arms around him, to comfort him, he ensures that she has arms to comfort her.

Character   Mary, Jesus' mother is standing alone. She is feeling emotionally desolate.

Scene   Mary is standing apart from the crowd. She needs to be alone to grieve as only a mother can. The lighting is sombre, casting dark shadows. Her clothes are an expression of her heart: blue and lifeless.

Props   Spotlight with different coloured gels (blue, green, red), clothing dark, possibly blue, with head-scarf made of reflective material.

This is to be performed as a monologue. The only interaction is between the actor and the lighting. The overall feeling is to be intimate, a heart expression of Mary.

Start with lighting dark. Single colour to highlight Mary (blue).

Mary stands slightly to one side and facing across the stage. She looks into the distance.
The last few days have been awful. It's impossible to describe the feeling in your stomach. As if something is tearing your insides, clawing at your heart, draining your life away. *(Slight pause)*

I always knew something like this would happen. I'd put it to the back of my mind, not wanting to think about it, not giving the thoughts space to develop, to take form in my head. *(Sigh)* It's easier to get through each day by dismissing them as leftovers from some nightmare, some ghost of a memory that is best left at the edge of consciousness. *(Take deep breath)*

But now reality has arrived like a thunderstorm on a summer's day. The nightmare has arrived. Those thoughts which had been buried in the deepest recesses of my mind *(Hand held to side of head)* have now stormed into the light of day. *(Change lighting to brighter colour, e.g. yellow)*

(Look upwards, still with hand on side of her head) Looking at him is too painful. There is my son *(Hand moves from side of head and points vaguely in front of her)* whose birth was a miracle, whose life had taken form cocooned from the world

within me, and now the world is taking him from me. His was the life which I had cradled in my arms *(Fold both arms across body)*. *(Lighting colour: green)* His was the life which I saw grow each day. *(Arms move from body and open downwards as if welcoming a small child)*

His was the life which had fulfilled everything a mother could hope for. His is the life which is draining away before my eyes *(Hands move to cover eyes. Head is lowered)*. *(Lighting colour: red)*

(Lift head and hold hands out in a questioning manner) Why have they done this to him? Was it so wrong to want the best for him? *(Pause)*

It's a mockery of life! I want to reach out to him *(Slight move forward with one hand)* and wipe his forehead, to wipe away the blood from his face, to hold him, hold him so tight. *(Hand moves across body in clutching motion)* Why? Why this? *(Move whole body to face audience)*

Why does everybody just watch? They know he shouldn't be suffering like this. If only I could reach out to him, to touch him. *(Pause)*

He looks so weak, so much pain. *(Gentle stroke of the head)* He had so much to give and now they're taking everything! *(Lighting colour: blue)*

(Angry voice) THAT'S MY SON YOU'RE KILLING! Let me hold him, let me feel his breath against my cheek, let me comfort him. *(Shoulders sag)*

This heat is unbearable. He's thirsty. *(Look around)* Someone, let him drink, please! Hasn't he endured enough? *(Turn head upwards)*

Heaven above, can't someone help him? Surely it wasn't supposed to be like this?

(Move head gradually from one side of the audience to the other) Look at all these faces, what are they waiting for? Didn't his life mean anything? Can you stand by and watch the last breath escape his lips without the least touch of guilt?

(Long pause. Thrust head forward) YOU'RE WATCHING MY CHILD DIE! *(Pause)*

How long can this go on? Whose heart will break first? It feels as if my own life is fading as I watch. My blood runs cold through my veins. I have no strength left, I can't go on. *(Sign and turn to face distant side of stage)*

How can he go on? How can I watch my son go through such agony? *(Lighting colour: merge blue with red)*

Why does he deserve to die this way? He hasn't hurt anyone. He wasn't interested in their politics. Is this what life is all about? *(Hands held open in question)* Is this the politician's answer? I don't care who's right and who's wrong. I care that my son's life is fading as each second passes. *(Pause. Head tilted towards the floor)* *(Lighting colour: blue)*

His life is precious to me. If no one else in the world loves him, I do! *(Head turned towards audience)* *(Lighting colour: red)* Why does this have to happen? *(Head bowed)*

There is a legend which tells that Mary, the mother of Jesus, had woven a seamless outer garment as a gift for her son. It was the custom for a Jewish mother to give her son a special gift when he left home (see John 19:23).

Seeing the special garment being gambled over by the four Roman soldiers must have been especially difficult for Mary to deal with. Not only was her son dying in front of her eyes but his clothes meant nothing more to the soldiers than an excuse to play dice. Mary must have thought it particularly insensitive on the part of the soldiers to make it so obvious that her son's life was now worthless in the eyes of the law. But, Mary's gift held a special significance.

The garment is said to be a single, seamless piece of cloth. This is the exact description for the outer garments worn by the High Priest. The priest's main function was to act as the go-between or liaison between God and the people. The Latin for priest is *pontiflex*, which literally means *bridge-builder*, and the priest was acknowledged as the person to build the bridge between God and his people.

From the beginning of his ministry Jesus had worn the symbol of a *bridge-builder*. At the cross Jesus became the ultimate sacrifice and bridge-builder between God and the people. Although deeply distressing for Mary, the death of Jesus was essential for the relationship between ourselves and God to be restored.

An added agony for those being crucified was the flogging they received prior to being nailed onto the cross. Although already in pain as a result of dragging their cross through the streets and the nails being driven into their hands, the victim's back was an open would laid against a piece of rough hewn wood ('. . . though my back is like a field that has just been ploughed' Psalm 129:3).

The flogging most often associated with crucifixion was known as *verberatio*. The leather whip would be made up of several thongs fitted with pieces of jagged lead and sharpened bone. The flogging would be carried out by a soldier who would flog the victim until either the soldier was exhausted or the officer told him to stop.

PETE TOWNSEND

Meditation of Pilate

'Truth!' I said. 'What is truth?'
No, I wasn't trying to be clever,
    despite what some people may tell you.
I really meant it,
    for I'd encountered so many over the years
    convinced they had the answer,
    each swearing blind that they knew best,
    party to some special knowledge denied to others.
Well, they couldn't all be right, could they? –
    and, the way I see it, none of them were.
Some were downright crazy,
    others well-intentioned but misguided,
    a few with genuine insights to offer,
    but not one of them had the truth,
    the whole truth and nothing but the truth.

Life just isn't like that – black and white –
  and anyone who thinks otherwise is potentially dangerous,
  all the makings of a dictator or fanatic –
  believe me, I've trodden that road myself.
So when this Jesus fellow trotted out the same old refrain
  you can understand my being sceptical.
Quite simply, I'd seen it all before.
Or at least, that's what I thought;
  only it soon became apparent that there was more to this man
  than met the eye,
  something quite out of the ordinary.
I'd expected him to launch straightaway into some diatribe,
  to tell me, as they always do, why he was right and I was wrong.
But he didn't.
He just looked at me with an expression that left me mystified,
  unlike anything I'd seen before.
None of the usual cocktail of fear and bravado,
  laced with a liberal dash of resentment,
  not even the remotest suggestion of it.
Instead there was what seemed like pity, concern,
  even compassion –
  as though he was genuinely disappointed I didn't understand,
  as though he longed for my eyes to be opened,
  as though he actually cared about the way I responded.
It threw me completely, I don't mind admitting it;
  after all, I was the one conducting the trial, not him.
At least, that's how it should have been,
  yet it didn't feel that way.
It was as though my life was being weighed there in the balance,
  and found sadly wanting.
Ridiculous, a man in my position . . .
  to feel I had to answer to some Judean nobody,
  but, try as I might, I just couldn't shake the feeling off,
  and the more I tried to wriggle off the hook,
  the more hopelessly impaled I became.
Do you *still* ask 'What is truth?'
I don't, for I know the answer now –
  I saw it there that day in the eyes of that man,
  and I wish to God I hadn't, for it's haunted me ever since –
  the knowledge that for the first time in my life
  I had the chance to make a stand,
  to commit myself to something which really mattered,
  and I let it slip through my fingers
  for fear of the consequences.

I held the difference between life and death in my hands that day,
    his fate in my hands,
    and I decided finally on death.
The trouble is I'm not sure whose fate we're talking about –
    his, or mine?   NICK FAWCETT

Meditation of Mary, mother of Jesus

He was thinking of me, even then!
I couldn't believe it –
    despite everything he was going through,
    the awful, stomach-churning agony
    which seemed to pierce my very soul,
    he was concerned more about my welfare than his.
Yet I shouldn't have been surprised –
    it was so like Jesus,
    the way he'd been from a boy,
    always putting others before himself.
I'd dared to hope that just this once it would be different,
    that for the first time in his life he'd look after number one.
Why not?
Would it have been so wrong?
He'd given enough already, hadn't he?
Scarcely a moment to himself,
    the crowds always with him,
    clamouring,
    calling,
    pleading,
    demanding –
    enough to break any lesser man.
And, as if that wasn't enough,
    his enemies had been there stalking him,
    unable to conceal their hatred,
    watching his every move,
    waiting for their moment.
He knew what they were up to,
    yet he'd continued without a murmur of complaint –
    always having time,
    always ready to respond,
    nothing and no one outside his concern.
I saw him so many times just about all in,
    drained to the point of exhaustion,
    and I can't tell you how much it troubled me,
    to see my wonderful lad pouring himself out
    in a constant act of sacrifice,
    pushing himself to the very limit.

But it was useless to argue –
   I tried it sometimes and he simply smiled at me
   in that gentle way of his,
   knowing I understood full well that there was no other way.
He was right, I knew that,
   and I knew equally there was no way
   he'd come down from that cross,
   but I could still hope, couldn't I,
   still pray I might be wrong?
He was thinking of others even then,
   not only me, but a common thief hanging there beside him,
   my fellow-women, sobbing their hearts out,
   even those who'd hounded him to his death –
   thinking, in fact, of everyone
   except himself.

NICK FAWCETT

Meditation of John the Apostle

He was groaning,
   a sound like I'd never heard before,
   a sound I never want to hear again –
   awful,
   stomach-churning,
   indescribable –
   the sound of unimaginable pain,
   of overwhelming sorrow,
   of utter isolation.
And I could watch it no longer.
I thought I was ready for it,
   prepared for the worst,
   for I knew he had to die.
But I wasn't ready,
   not for this;
   I never realised people could suffer so much,
   that anything could be quite so terrible.
But I know now,
   and I'm telling you straight,
   I'd have felt sorry for anyone facing that –
   a robber,
   a mugger,
   even a murderer!
My heart would still have bled for them.
But to see Jesus there,
   a man of such gentleness and compassion,
   a man who had always loved and never hated,
   a man who had brought healing to the sick

and wholeness to the broken,
   it all but finished me.
What had he done to deserve this?
What crime had he committed?
What was it about him that aroused such passion,
   such devotion,
     yet such loathing?
I prayed that God would finish it,
   put him out of his misery,
   but still the torment continued,
   still they mocked him, delighting in his pain.
I knew he was suffering, but even then didn't realise how much,
   not until he lifted his head and I saw the despair in his eyes,
   not until he spoke and I heard the wretchedness in his voice:
   'My God, my God, why have you forsaken me?'
Then I realised,
   and my blood ran cold.
He felt alone,
   totally alone,
   abandoned by everyone he'd loved and trusted,
   even by God himself.
He could cope with the rest –
   he'd even expected it –
   but God?
It was the final torture,
   the ultimate agony,
   a pain beyond words.
He was groaning, a sound like I'd never heard before,
   a sound which suddenly I understood,
   and a sound I could listen to no longer.

NICK FAWCETT

Meditation of James, the Apostle

He was dead, and I still can't believe it.
I kept on hoping it was all a bad dream,
   that any moment I'd wake up and find we were back together again;
   there on the mountainside as he preached to the crowd,
   there in the boat as he stilled the storm,
   there on the road as he healed the sick,
   there in the upstairs room as we shared supper.
But I didn't wake up and I knew then it was no dream – it was real.
Yet still I couldn't accept it;
   I was waiting for another miracle,
   waiting for him to come down off the cross
   and wipe the smile off their faces,
   waiting for God to do something, anything to put a stop to this madness.

I still can't understand it.
Why did he have to die?
Why the waste of such a beautiful life?
It doesn't make any sense to me.
But it did to him, that's the extraordinary thing.
He warned us of it often enough,
    told us it had to happen,
    even said we should welcome it.
Well, it's happened now,
It's over.
I witnessed his last gasp,
    I heard his last cry,
    I watched them drive the spear into his side,
    I was there when they cut him down, limp and lifeless,
    and I saw the stone rolled against the tomb.
I still can't believe it,
    but I've seen it with my own eyes.
He was dead.   NICK FAWCETT

Order of service

Among the most popular ecumenical activities of the last decade has been the Good Friday procession or 'walk of witness', which takes place in many towns during the morning, often to enable those Churches which do so to keep their *three-hour vigil*, starting at 12 noon. In a busy shopping area this can be a powerful witness to the secular world, but many Christians are unable to participate because they have to work themselves. In any event, in many locations a procession would be impractical or have little impact. In the more Catholic tradition, the three-hour vigil would be kept, but this is now often reduced to 'the last hour', a devotional reflection on the cross.

Our LEP has adopted an ecumenical approach to the three-hour vigil, and, while it needs a bit of fine-tuning, both traditions have found it helpful. Broadly, the first hour is devotional and reflective; the second is unstructured, but with visual material at various points in the worship area, which can be used for personal meditation on the passion; the third is more liturgical. A children's workshop runs in parallel with the first two hours, enabling parents to take part in the liturgy if they wish, but also, in the second hour, enabling the ministers to spend some time with the children, and lead them in a short time of worship. The final hour enables the children's leaders to share in formal worship as well. However, there is no reason why two churches fairly close to each other should not work out a similar pattern. The following outline shows one way of handling the first and third hours, but that should not detract from the importance of the time spent with the children – it is quite feasible to link their themes with those the adults have been considering.

The First Hour

Opening response

Jesus himself bore our sins in his body
on the tree,
so that we might die to sin
and live for righteousness.
By his wounds we have been healed.

The punishment that brought us peace
was upon him.
By his wounds we have been healed.

Hymn

There is a green hill (HON 499)

Prayer

Glory be to you, Almighty Father,
for your limitless and pervasive love
with which we are confronted on the cross.
We feel ashamed and unworthy
to stand in your presence,
and acknowledge our failure to respond
to your gracious act of sending your Son
to bring us back to you.
Lord, have mercy.
Lord, have mercy.

Glory be to you, Lord Jesus, Son of God,
humiliated and crucified King of kings,
for your perfect obedience in going to the cross
to win us freedom from sin and death.
We feel sorrowful and contrite
at the sins which nailed you there,
and ask you to forgive and restore us
to the path which leads to eternal life.
Christ, have mercy,
Christ, have mercy.

Glory be to you, Holy Spirit of God,
for your persistent troubling of our conscience,
and your reassurance that on the cross
love has conquered the power of evil and death.
We feel joyful that your grace
has won our forgiveness,
and praise you for the hope
which is set before us.

Lord, have mercy,
Lord, have mercy.

Through the cross of Christ
may God have mercy on us,
pardon us, and set us free,
that we might be strengthened in faith
and kept in eternal life.
Amen.

Lord Jesus,
remember us in your kingdom as we pray:
Our Father . . .

Hymn
My song is love unknown (HON 346)

Readings
Lamentations 5:15-22; John 19:17-30

Hymn
Come and see (HON 88)

Reflection/Meditation
As we read the accounts of Jesus' arrest, trial, crucifixion and burial, we see a cast of characters watching, participating and reacting to the events leading up to the cross. In viewing them we see ourselves reflected: our words which aren't translated into action; our refusal to acknowledge Jesus through fear of other people; our determination to prove we're right; our vain attempts to sit on the fence.

There's Peter, sitting by the fire, trying to keep warm – and keep his head down. Full of fine words when things are going well, he's already got into trouble by injuring a servant's ear, so now he's playing safe and keeping it all at arm's length. His protestations that he'll never deny his master are soon to be tested and found wanting. Not that we'd ever do such a thing . . . But too often we try to keep out of trouble, and make sure we're not really associated with Jesus. It's easy to say all the right words in church, but the acid test comes when we engage with the world for the rest of the week. The soft option is to pretend we're being reasonable, and open to all views. The tough option is openly to follow the way of Jesus, the suffering Servant.

Then there's Nicodemus, the religious leader who came to Jesus by night so no one would see him and tell the tabloids. He knew in his heart that Jesus was someone special whose words rang true, whose life matched them. He recognised, however dimly, the words and work of God in this wandering rabbi. Yet only after Jesus' death does he take any risk by offering to help with Jesus' burial. So much of our behaviour is conditioned by our fear of other people, their reactions, their scorn, their rejection, their condemnation. If we are to follow the way of Jesus, we can't keep our heads below the parapet in case someone disapproves. Our response to his love means potentially accepting the sneering, the abuse and the rejection which he endured.

On the other hand we can look at Caiaphas and his fellow priests, all totally convinced that they're doing the right thing and preserving the true religion of Israel. It never occurs to them that their actions run counter to all that God is and does. We condemn the grossly unfair trial and unjust sentence, yet have to recognise the pride and arrogance within us which is determined to be proved right at all costs, even if others have to suffer. In complete contrast, Jesus never condemns, but looks with sorrow on the whole system in Jerusalem which rejects his Father's love in the belief that it alone is right.

Finally, what of Pilate, whose ritual ablutions have never exonerated him for his part in Jesus' death? He thought he could stand aside from it and push the responsibility elsewhere, but his refusal to make a decision didn't remove his name from the narrative. Jesus just won't let us sit on the fence and be objective, because he's not a Greek philosopher but our Saviour.

The characters of the Good Friday story make us face our own response to the cross: the pain and agony of the dying Jesus; the jeering of the crowds; the fear of the authorities; the apparent defeat of all that is good and pure and holy. Yet, if we want to share in the victory of the cross, we must share too in its suffering. In responding to the love poured out on that civic rubbish tip, where three Roman gibbets were hastily erected, we rule out arrogance, pride, cowardice and apathy.

Hymn

Were you there when they crucified my Lord? (HON 540)

Intercessions

As our Saviour lays down his life for us on the cross, we bring to him our thanksgiving and requests, saying,
Lord of love, hear our prayer;
let our cry come to you.

Lord Jesus,
on the cross you were willing to forgive
those who mocked and jeered at you.
We pray for those who refuse
to recognise you as King or own you as Lord,
who despise what is good
and rejoice in the unworthy, especially . . .
May their eyes be opened
to see your dying love,
and their hearts to respond
to its transforming power.

Lord of love, hear our prayer;
let our cry come to you.

Lord Jesus,
on the cross you asked the disciple you loved
to care for your mother.
We pray for those whose grief or loneliness
make them feel vulnerable and disadvantaged, especially . . .
May they know the strength and comfort
of your eternal presence
through the care and compassion
of the Christian community.
Lord of love, hear our prayer;
let our cry come to you.

Lord Jesus,
on the cross you forgave a common criminal
crucified with you,
and offered him a place in your kingdom.
We pray for those
who feel unworthy and rejected,
who are left on the margins of society,
especially . . .
May they know your acceptance and welcome
through the ministry of your people.
Lord of love, hear our prayer;
let our cry come to you.

Lord Jesus,
on the cross a Roman centurion recognised
what others failed to see
and praised God.
We pray for those whose faith is growing,
who are at a key point
in their spiritual journey,
especially . . .
May they move onwards in the Christian life
as they learn more of your love
and enter more fully into your risen life.
Lord of love, hear our prayer;
let our cry come to you.

Lord Jesus,
on the cross you were obedient to your Father
in facing death to win for us eternal life.
May we be strengthened
to follow your example

of selfless love and service.
Lord of love, hear our prayer;
let our cry come to you.
As your love dwells in us
so may we love one another
for the sake of Jesus Christ,
our crucified Lord.
Amen.

Hymn

When I survey the wondrous cross (HON 549)

Closing response

Lord of the joyful procession,
may we worship you wholeheartedly.

Lord of the upper room,
may we dine with you for ever.

Lord of the desolate garden,
may we watch and wait with you.

Lord of the unjust sentence,
may we pursue justice and peace.

Lord of the cruel cross,
may we be willing to suffer with you.

Lord of the empty tomb,
may we rise with you to eternal life.

Blessing

The Second Hour

The minister(s) now go to where the children are working on material connected with the Good Friday theme. Meanwhile the worshippers are free to stand or sit by the various displays and meditate on the significance of what they have seen and heard. We mix traditional visual symbols, such as icons, a purple robe, a copy of a painting of the crucifixion, with modern images, such as a collage of suffering built up from press pictures. Appropriate quiet music is played in the background. Each year the children have a different approach. One particularly effective idea was to take the fourteen Stations of the Cross and produce a 'news report' on each of them, to pull together into a 'documentary' of the events of the first Good Friday. The act of worship is very informal, but aims to help the children make sense of what they have been doing in the wider context of the day. Kidsource *has some excellent songs for this kind of children's event: 'There on a cruel cross' (328), 'I will offer up my life' (186), 'Jesus, thank you for the cross' (214), 'I'm special' (162) and 'God never gives up' (83) are particularly suitable.*

The Final Hour

Silence

Opening prayer

Lord Jesus Christ,
on the cross at Calvary
your hands were ripped by cruel nails,
hands that stretched out
to offer healing, comfort and acceptance.
Make our hands open
to the pain that comes from serving you,
open to reach out with your love
to the broken and needy.
Lord, we offer you our hands.

Lord Jesus Christ,
as you hung on the cross
your feet were pierced,
feet that approached the despised,
and walked alongside those
condemned as sinners.
Make our feet willing to go where you lead us,
unafraid of sneering or rejection.
Lord, we offer you our feet.

Lord Jesus Christ,
on the cross your side was torn open
with a soldier's spear,
your body freely given up
for love of those who did not love you.
Make us strong to withstand opposition and ridicule,
knowing your love overcomes
the power of evil.
Lord, we offer you our bodies.

Lord Jesus Christ,
as you died in agony on the cross
your heart was broken
by the rebellion and rejection
of your own people,
by our sin which nailed you there.
Make our hearts clean and pure,
dedicated to your service
and filled with your love.
Lord, we offer you our hearts and lives
to be a living sacrifice.

Old Testament reading

Isaiah 52:12-53:12

Hymn

My Lord, what love is this (HON 345)

New Testament reading

Hebrews 4:14-16, 5:7-9

Hymn

Meekness and majesty (HON 335)

Gospel reading

Luke 23:13-49

Meditation

In the first hour of the vigil the meditation looked at how some of the characters in the passion narrative responded to the events leading up to Jesus' crucifixion. Here we see how some of them respond to Jesus himself, as he hangs in agony on the cross.

One character who plays a large part in all the Gospel accounts is Pontius Pilate. He tries hard to pretend it's 'not my problem', but even his unwillingness to make a decision has its consequences. He knows the decision to release Barabbas, a political terrorist, is totally against all principles of justice, Jewish or Roman, but for a quiet life he lets it through. John records that the authorities wanted the inscription above Jesus' head to be changed, to say 'this man claimed to be the King of the Jews', but Pilate now refuses to budge. His response to Jesus is by no means one of opposition, but rather of ambiguity. Perhaps deep down he recognises that here is a man of such authority as he's never before encountered.

Luke alone tells of the 'penitent thief', a common criminal crucified by chance alongside Jesus, who condemns his friend for joining in the laughter and insults against Jesus. His comment indicates that he too is aware, however dimly, that he is in the presence of true kingship. His response is hardly dramatic, while his final request contains no expectation of forgiveness or pardon. Yet Jesus at once offers him a place in his kingdom; even the act of recognising who Jesus really is opens up a chink through which God's love and grace can come flooding through. The other criminal is unmoved, and, though quite unaware of it, the abusive and sarcastic crowd of onlookers stand just as much under condemnation as he does.

Typically, Luke also highlights two foreigners. Simon of Cyrene was perhaps just a large, strong man who happened to be nearby when the cross needed to be carried. We know little about him, but he seems to have carried out his duty without complaint, though as a member of an ethnic minority he may well have felt exploited. And after Jesus' death a Roman centurion, equally despised by true Jews, shows far greater understanding of the identity and mission of this extraordinary victim of a gross miscarriage of justice than do his fellow countrymen. No wonder Jesus wept when he saw Jerusalem.

None of these characters would have fitted in with the Jewish authorities – only one of them was a Jew, and he was from the bottom of the social pile. Yet, as Luke shows us, their part in the events was significant enough to warrant being written down. It's easy to write people off because they don't quite 'belong', or conform to the norms of a particular group. But if we're to follow the way of Jesus, we have to welcome and accept those who may well have been written off or rejected by others. And while it may gall those who've been going to church most of their lives, God's love needs only the tiniest gap in our self-defence system through which to start pouring in . . . God's grace can overcome and transform even the murkiest past and the darkest character.

Hymn

O sacred head surrounded (HON 389)

Good Friday Litany

(during which a simple wooden cross can be brought to a central position)

Lord of the cross of shame
we feel your pain.

Lord,
in the desolation of this earth
through our greed and exploitation,
we feel your pain.

Lord,
in the refugee camps and shanty towns
we feel your pain.
Lord,
in the streets which are home
to unloved and unwanted children
we feel your pain.
Lord,
in the courts which hear only the voice
of the rich and powerful
we feel your pain.
Lord,
in the prison cells and torture chambers
we feel your pain.
Lord,
in the killing fields,
heavy with death and despair
we feel your pain.

Lord,
in the barricaded streets and riot-torn cities
we feel your pain.
Lord,
in the cry of the abused child,
in the sigh of the lonely elderly
we feel your pain.

Lord of the cross of forgiveness,
have mercy on us.
We have been greedy and selfish;
have mercy on us.
We have shut our eyes to need and poverty;
have mercy on us.
We have been unkind and uncaring;
have mercy on us.
We have been unfair in our judgements;
have mercy on us.
We have not acted as peacemakers
and bridge-builders,
have mercy on us.
We have turned away from the cry of pain
and the plea for help;
have mercy on us.

Lord of the cross of glory,
we share in your victory.

STUART THOMAS

Easter

Easter Day

The victory of love over evil and death

A reading from the Gospel of Mark (16:1-7)

Early on the Sunday morning, the day after the Sabbath, some of the women made their way to the tomb to anoint Jesus with burial spices. They were Mary, the mother of James, Mary of Magdala and Salome.

On the way there they had been wondering how they would roll back the heavy stone which covered the entrance to the tomb, and when they arrived they were surprised to see that someone had already done this.

Going into the tomb, they were amazed to find a young man, dressed in white, sitting there. Seeing their expressions of surprise, he said to them, 'You have come to find Jesus who was crucified, but he is not where they laid him. He is risen! Go back to Peter and his disciples and tell them he is going ahead of them to Galilee, and, just as he said, you will see him there.'

This is the Gospel of the Lord
Praise to you, Lord Jesus Christ   KATIE THOMPSON

A reading from the Gospel of John (20:1-9)

Before sunrise on the Sunday morning Mary of Magdala went to the tomb. As she reached the entrance, she saw that the stone had been rolled away and the tomb was empty. She ran to the disciples saying, 'They have taken the Lord from the tomb and we don't know where they have put him!'

Peter and another disciple, John, ran to the tomb and found it just as Mary had described, with the linen burial cloths lying on the ground. The cloth which had been wrapped around Jesus' head lay rolled up separately from the other pieces of cloth. Peter went into the tomb first, followed by John.

Until this moment they had not understood the Scriptures which had said, 'He must rise from the dead.' But now they saw, and they believed.

This is the Gospel of the Lord
Praise to you, Lord Jesus Christ   KATIE THOMPSON

Introductory material

'This is the day,' we sing on Easter Sunday. The day of love's triumph over sin and death. Everything about Easter Sunday speaks of triumph. Eastern Christians call it that 'unique and holy day, king and lord of days, feast of feasts, solemnity of solemnities'. It is so important a day for Christians that, having prepared for it for forty days, the next forty days are spent celebrating it! From Easter Sunday until Ascension Day, 'Alleliua' is our song as 'the day' is continually celebrated. When those forty days are up, the celebration of Our Lord's resurrection continues – every Sunday: the first day of the week is our weekly remembrance of the day he rose.

There is a neat catch question to ask children if you discover that they are learning about the Ten Commandments. You can ask, 'Which of the Ten Commandments do Christians break?' The answer is the fourth commandment, 'Remember to keep holy the Sabbath day'. Those commandments were drawn up for the Jewish people and the fourth one refers to their holy day, which, of course, is Saturday. Jesus said that he had not come to sweep away the Jewish laws, but to fulfil them. This is one example where God still wants us to retain the idea behind the law, but on a different day. Christians, of course, keep Sunday holy, the first day of the week and the day Jesus rose from the dead.

Sundays

With so many jobs to do around the house, outside or on the car, it is difficult for adults to think of Sunday as a 'holy' day. But that is what it is, if being a Christian means anything to us. It is also a family day when families have the opportunity . . . to be together and do things together.

There should be two highlights to the day, both to do with 'family'. As members of God's family we meet together with other family members to share a meal, offer a sacrifice and celebrate Jesus' continuing presence with us. Sunday Mass is just that. There are too many of us to get *round* the altar table literally, but that is what we would do if it were possible. We listen to God's word and share from the table of the Lord.

The Passover meal is the centre of the Jewish year – the Last Supper meal of Jesus has become the centre of the week for Christians: 'The Eucharist is a family meeting, a meeting of the large family of Christians. Every altar will always be a table round which gathers a family of brothers and sisters', in the words of Pope John Paul II.

The second highlight of Sunday is our own private family meal together – Sunday dinner. There can be no more important regular family event each week than this. It is so vital to the happy, balanced life of the family that parents should gently but firmly insist that the whole family will always be together for Sunday dinner.

All through human history sharing a meal has always been seen as a very significant event. 'Going out for a meal' is still one of the most accepted ways to celebrate an anniversary or birthday. Think too of wedding receptions, birthday parties, and so on; they all involve a meal and togetherness. In most societies around the globe sharing a meal together denotes special bonds of friendship.

If you want to strengthen your family life then eat together as often as you can – daily if possible. The family table is the place for sharing and serving one another. Talking, sharing ideas, asking advice, passing on news, all take place round the table. It is difficult to think of every Sunday dinner as a celebration but good habits can be formed to make it clearly special and different. If a tablecloth is not used during the week then using one on Sunday will add to the sense of occasion. Laying the place settings with care, arranging a simple flower display or a decorative centrepiece: these simple little things can mark the meal as different.

The resurrection symbols

Here are a few symbols of the resurrection that the children might like to draw, and which give you further opportunity to explain what we are celebrating.

The Butterfly. It is not only children who find it fascinating how the caterpillar goes into a cocoon (a type of tomb) where it seems to die, then emerges to a new life as a beautiful butterfly. It is a terrific symbol of Christ's death and resurrection. Rather than skip over this symbol quickly, it might be an idea to have a more detailed home project based on different butterflies and their life cycles. Don't forget to point out the symbolism; it is a most valuable way of tying in God's creation with his work of re-creation.

The Phoenix. This was a very popular symbol of the resurrection with the early Christians. They used it on burial stones and in their writings. The first Christian writer we know of who used the ancient legend about a mythical bird was Clement of Rome. Around ad 98 he records the legend in his letter to the Corinthian Christians and applies it to the resurrection of all Christ's faithful followers. Later it was applied to Christ's own resurrection.

According to legend, the phoenix was a bird that lived for 500 years, then built itself a funeral pyre for a nest and burnt itself to death. When the ashes cooled, the bird rose again from the ashes to start a new life.

Lamb and Flag. At the time of Jesus lambs were sacrificed in the Jerusalem temple as part of an act of worship. Jesus was described by John the Baptist as 'the Lamb of God': the lamb that would be sacrificed to take away the sins of the world. Only this lamb was victorious, rising to a new life. The standing lamb therefore represents Jesus and the flag is the sign of his triumph.

Easter and 'the teens'

That agonising period of development which we call, in modern jargon, 'the teens', is a time of discovery, and not only for the young person! This time of self-discovery includes searching for what is real and what is true: 'They look for independence and are reluctant to conform. Sometimes they wish to reject past traditions and even reject their faith.' That was Pope John Paul II, speaking at York, on his first visit to Britain. He showed that he knew and appreciated this period of questioning that adolescents have to go through on their way to adulthood.

Parents often feel that they have personally failed if a son or daughter, nurtured in the Faith, suddenly and sullenly refuses to go to Mass. Parents have to be fair to themselves and realise that this rebellion is natural and even quite healthy. Young people need time and support as they sort out priorities in their minds, and find their way to a more mature faith and commitment.

TONY CASTLE

Easter decorations

Children, especially young ones, learn better through what is seen taking place in the home than by words spoken at school, at church or even in the home. So to help the children look forward eagerly to Easter – as indeed they do to Christmas – things need to happen and be seen to happen!

We have no tradition in this country of decorating our homes for Easter but there is no reason why we cannot start our own family tradition. Children are never going to discover the importance of Easter as the pinnacle of the Church's year if it remains uncelebrated in the home. With the season of spring reflecting the theme of new life, the ideal preparation is to take a walk in the countryside or perhaps a park. Primary school children will almost certainly have been talking about spring and new life at school. But pre-school children too will take delight in being shown the daffodils in flower and the new fresh green buds appearing on the trees and bushes.

A few bunches of daffodils arranged with a selection of twigs in bud collected on your county walk (not from the park, of course!) make a simple and effective arrangement. The children are usually on school holidays for a few days before the festival and can be organised to decorate the house in fitting fashion. Most young children like to have the opportunity to show off their drawing and painting skills. Scenes from nature, showing new life appearing, pictures of Easter eggs, pictures of the open tomb, of Jesus appearing to his friends – there are plenty of subjects. But definitely no Easter bunnies! They have absolutely no relevance to or connection with Easter.

The emphasis of the pictures should be joyful and positive, but if a child insists on drawing a crucifixion scene, use it as an opportunity to talk about the death of Jesus. Take care to emphasise that the sad part, when Jesus seemed to be beaten by death, was followed by the most important part of all – his coming alive in a new and special way. That new way of living makes it possible for him to be with us now and for ever as our friend. Then encourage the young artist to show the victory of Christ by adding yellow and orange rays shining out from the cross to all parts of the world.

Easter candles

In some primary schools children learn how to make Easter candles from paper. These are extremely simple and most appealing. Any home could make a number to stand among the flowers on the mantelpiece, or the window sill. They can be as large or small as the paper supply allows.

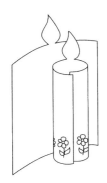While the smaller candles appeal especially to the five- to eight-year-olds, the older children might like to co-operate on a larger project – a huge family Easter candle. Most households have a half-used roll of wallpaper in the attic, garage or understairs cupboard (if not, a neighbour will surely help). The idea is identical to the above, except this one is to be 4 or 5 feet tall and made to stand on its own in a dignified corner of the living room, lounge or hallway. It might be best placed in a decorated tub or box. If older children are involved the candle should bear a closer resemblance to the Easter candle in the parish church, by adding a decorated A and Ω (Alpha and Omega) and the year's date.

Easter cards

If we are serious about the importance of Easter and what it means, we should make an effort to send cards. There is never a very good selection in the shops for the obvious reason that there is little demand! The children could use their leisure time and talent throughout Holy Week to produce home-made ones.

Easter eggs

If it were not for Easter eggs, most children would not realise that there was anything special about the Easter bank-holiday weekend. At first glance eggs seem to have no link with Our Lord's death and resurrection but in fact they can be a most useful teaching aid. The first and most important rule about Easter eggs and their symbolism is that within the family no Easter eggs are to be given or eaten before Easter Day. (The 'Day' – 'this is the day the Lord has made' – begins with the end of the Easter vigil.) Families with young children tend to produce the eggs *after* breakfast (for obvious reasons!) on Easter morning. After breakfast, which should ideally be of boiled eggs, Mum and Dad can make something of the occasion by presenting the eggs with an accompanying explanation of their symbolism.

The adult needs only an ordinary hen's egg (hard boiled) to illustrate the explanation, and can follow the general outline of the following:

'Why do we have chocolate eggs as a present today?' (Even if an older child remembers a previous year's explanation and gives a correct answer, still proceed with the following for the sake of any younger child.)

'Can you imagine for a moment a space ship landing from outer space? The landing site it chooses is a wide, pebbly beach. After a few minutes a hatch opens and out steps a strange-looking little space traveller. He looks around at the scenery. There's no one in sight. Bending down, he picks up one of the round/oval stones. He weighs it in his hands, then tests it with a little calculator-like box in his left hand. It's smooth, cold and lifeless. He looks around at a beach full of lifeless stones. Our space traveller walks up the beach to a bank of grass. After inspecting that, he sees in the distance a farmhouse and its barns and outhouses. He walks cautiously towards the buildings. Halfway there he almost steps on a cluster of brown, oval, stone-like objects. "More stones," he thinks, but when he picks one up it's warm. He runs his little machine over it and finds, to his surprise, that there is life inside what looks and feels like a stone.' (The storyteller now shows the egg in their hand and says, 'Eggs really do look and feel like stones.')

'As the space traveller holds the egg in his hand it cracks, once, twice, three times, and as he watches, a little chick pushes its head out into the world. You can imagine the surprise of the space traveller; new life from what looked like a stone. It is a perfect example of what happened on the first Easter morning. The stone, behind which Jesus had been buried, looked cold and dead, but suddenly new life burst out of it – Jesus was alive. The risen Jesus came out of what seemed a cold, dead stone to new life.'

Such a story can bring out the symbolism and relevance of the chocolate Easter egg.

TONY CASTLE

The Triumph of Love

Introductory thoughts

If you wake in the middle of the night and look out of the window, it is almost as though the whole world has closed down. It's dark and silent – as silent as the grave. For the sick, nights can be long and very trying, but there is always the hope of the coming of light and the dawning of a new day.

If you take a country walk in midwinter, the trees seem dead and the country-side is bleak, but there is the hope and happiness of spring to look forward to. When someone we love dies, everything seems to close down – it seems to be night-time and wintertime all rolled into one. But our Christian faith tells us at such a time that there is life after death; the light and happiness of a future resurrection gives us hope.

- At the dawn of each day light triumphs over darkness.
- Each year spring triumphs over winter.
- In every person's life love can triumph over death.

In the first two, nature takes its course; in the third the co-operation of the human person is required. Love *can* triumph if it springs from a lively faith. And the basis of that faith is Christ's own triumph over suffering and death.

At the time of Jesus and throughout the lives of the apostles, the Roman Empire, which was the political power in their lives, celebrated 'triumphs'. When a general returned to Rome after a great land or sea victory there was a massive triumphal procession through the streets of Rome. The victorious general's chariot was decorated with wreaths of laurel announcing that he was the victor.

The early Christians did not hang up crucifixes in their homes as we do. When they portrayed the cross it was without the naked figure of Christ. It was shown as a triumphant sign with a laurel wreath around it. Christ had died but had risen victorious – Christ, the victor over death.

Our drawing shows the victor's laurels surmounting the cross and round the CHI-RHO sign. That comes from the Greek letters Xp (in English CHR) and is shorthand for Christ. So the picture – from a fourth-century sculpture – says, 'Christ, the victor, has triumphed over the cross'.

Escape stories

A very good preparation for the children's understanding of Holy Week and the 'passover' of Jesus is a good escape story; an escape from imprisonment to freedom. Sometimes newspapers carry such stories, often with accompanying pictures and drawings. A popular Second World War film, *The Great Escape*, tells the story of how determined British soldiers and airmen tunnelled under a wire fence to escape imprisonment. The following story describes an escape to freedom over the Berlin Wall in the 1970s:

> John and Michael were well aware that over seventy people had been killed trying to escape over the Berlin Wall but they were determined to try. With the help of a friend who lived in West Berlin they worked out a plan. First they searched for a tall block of flats on their side of the wall. It had to face a house that was not quite so tall on the west side of the wall. When they had found number five Schmoller Strasse, they needed a fibreglass bow, steel arrows, 100 metres of fishing line and some quarter-inch steel wire.
>
> They hid in the top of the house for fifteen hours until conditions were just right. At 5am a signal flashed by torch from the house on the other side. They opened a window and fired the arrow with the line attached over the house opposite. The arrow sailed over the house to where their friend was waiting. He pulled in the line with the cable attached to it and secured it to the back of his car. Each of the escapers had to wait for the moment when the Communist guards in their observation towers were looking the other way. Then, hitched to a pulley made to run down the wire, Michael, followed by John, sailed over the 'death wall' to the house on the other side, passing over from the closed-in unhappiness of East Berlin to joy and freedom in the West.

It was very like the great escape of the Israelites from the slavery of Egypt. That event has been celebrated by the Jewish people every year since it happened, right up to this day.

This escape story could be used in discussion with the family, although basing the discussion on a topical story straight from the newspaper would be better. To help get the idea of 'passover' across to the younger family members it might be useful to make a chart, something like this.

John and Michael feel closed in and unhappy in East Berlin	Escape over the 'death wall'	Freedom and new life in the West
Moses and Israelites very unhappy slaves in Egypt	Escape through the waters of 'Sea of Reeds'	Freedom and new life in Promised Land
Jesus unhappy at our slavery to sin	Escape for us through Jesus' death	Freedom from effects of original sin – new life as children of God

You can well imagine John and Michael's joy and excitement at escaping and how they would celebrate every year the anniversary of their escape, their 'passing over' the 'death wall'. So every year the Jewish people celebrate their 'passing over' all those centuries ago. It is important for an understanding of so much in the Christian way of life (especially baptism and the Mass) to realise that it was on the very festival of the Passover that Jesus went out to his death and passed over to the risen life.

TONY CASTLE

The greatest change of mood in the Christian Year comes as the excitement and celebration of Easter bursts in on the darkness of the preceding days and weeks. The Early Church was quite clear that Easter was the Church's most important festival, and despite the best efforts of the retail trade and others, the hype and frenzy of Christmas has not altered this in any of the mainstream churches. The programme for Easter Day itself is therefore likely to be well fixed in every Church diary, so other than in full-blown LEPs this may not be the most convenient day to organise an ecumenical service. However, there may be scope for using one of the Sundays of Eastertide to join together in an Easter Praise service.

Where Lent as a season is best suited to a more structured and reflective approach to worship, Easter lends itself to spontaneity and joyful praise. The last three decades have seen a great increase in the number of Churches incorporating a 'praise service' into their programme, often on a Sunday evening. While the initial impetus for this came from the Charismatic Renewal, other factors have kept it going: the inclusion of newer worship songs, the need to use a worship group, and, not least, the desire to let the breeze of God's Holy Spirit blow away some of the long-established dust and cobwebs of more formal liturgy! The television programme *Songs of Praise* has also proved enduringly popular, and established a format for worship which has appealed even to Churches where there are reservations about adopting unstructured praise services. As a result, there are plenty of 'Praise and Prayer', 'Celebration Praise' and 'Songs of Praise' services which owe little to the traditional worshipping practices of the mainstream Churches, but provide a common approach for most of them. This may not go down too well among liturgical purists, but it provides a simple and widely accepted style for ecumenical worship.

However, simplicity is often more difficult to achieve than might appear on the surface. There may be less formality, but some kind of structure is essential if the service is to be meaningful to all present and draw them together into worshipping the risen Lord. An overdose of unfamiliar, brand-new worship songs, excessive use of someone's in-house jargon, or plain uncertainty about what is going to happen next, all create a sense of unease in any congregation, not least one drawn from several different traditions. Spontaneity is especially tricky to handle. It requires a delicate balance between allowing people to express their worship in a personal, informal way, without this either degenerating into liturgical anarchy, or becoming the exclusive preserve of those who are familiar with it, to the exclusion of everyone else. Times of 'open worship' therefore need to be balanced with more set patterns that enable everyone to participate. Music can also become an issue in these less structured services. They offer an excellent opportunity to learn some of the very good new hymns and worship songs now available, but these need to be practised and taught in a way that enables everyone to sing, and balanced with better-known items. Most important of all, an act of worship needs a sense of direction and purpose if those taking part in it are to feel they have been inspired and challenged.

STUART THOMAS

We are here to rejoice. We are here to give thanks. We are here to worship God, the giver of life. For today we remember that day which transformed the course of history and which across the years has transformed countless human lives. Easter Day – the day on which evil, sorrow and suffering, even death itself, were finally defeated; a day that makes every day and every moment a new beginning. Listen again to the words of Scripture, and listen also to reflections upon those words. Enter as best you can into the experience of those who witnessed the empty tomb and the risen Christ. For the message they heard, the good news they celebrated, was not just for them but for us, and for all!

NICK FAWCETT

Prayers

Praise – life from death

Lord Jesus Christ,
    it seemed like the end of everything –
        the hope you had brought gone for ever –
        for you were dead,
        laid in a tomb,
        a stone sealing the entrance.
    Your followers had watched you suffer,
        heard you draw your last breath,
        watched as a spear was thrust into your side
        and sobbed as your body was taken down from the cross,
        limp and lifeless.

It was over,
   finished,
   no possibility of change.
Except suddenly the stone was rolled away,
   the tomb was empty,
   you were there speaking words of peace,
   you were alive!
Risen Lord,
   lead us from death to life.

For us, too, death can seem the end of everything –
   the end of all our hopes,
   all our striving,
   all our dreams;
   the last enemy which one day each of us must face,
   no matter who we are or what we do.
Risen Lord,
   lead us from death to life.

For many the death of someone close to them
   seems the end of everything –
   the joy they had known,
   the love they shared,
   the life they had built together,
   all lost for ever.
The present seems devoid of meaning,
   the future empty of hope,
   while the past serves only to remind them of their pain.
Risen Lord,
   lead us from death to life.

We praise you, that despite appearances,
   death is not the end of everything –
   for the victory you won was not just for you but for all,
   the enemy defeated,
   the grave conquered,
   the future assured.
You are the resurrection and the life,
   the one who leads us not just now but throughout eternity,
   nothing in heaven or earth,
   in this world or the next,
   able to separate us from your constant love.
Risen Lord,
   lead us from death to life.

Lord Jesus Christ,
>we praise you for the message of Easter,
>>the assurance that life is not in vain,
>>that love is not blotted out,
>>that faith is not futile.
>We praise you that death is not the end but a new beginning,
>>a gateway to heaven,
>>a door on to untold blessings you hold in store for us.
>Receive the worship we offer you this day,
>>and teach us to live each day
>>in the light of your Easter triumph.
>Risen Lord,
>>**lead us from death to life.**

For your name's sake.
Amen.   NICK FAWCETT

Praise and confession

Living God,
>we are here in the name of Christ.
>We are here to celebrate once more his resurrection,
>>to rejoice once more at his victory
>>over evil, hatred and death,
>>to give thanks once more
>>for his living presence with us now and always.
>Lord of life,
>>**hear us.**

>Receive our praise,
>>our worship,
>>ourselves as we come before you.
>Fill us with joy and wonder
>>as we hear again the message of the risen Christ,
>>and as we recognise his presence among us
>>through his Holy Spirit.
>Lord of life,
>>**hear us.**

Living God,
>we are here in the name of Christ.
>We are here to confess our faults and failings,
>>to acknowledge our unworthiness of your love,
>>to seek your mercy and forgiveness,
>>and to ask for renewal in our lives.
>Lord of life,
>>**hear us.**

Receive our confession,
   our penitence,
   ourselves as we come before you.
Cleanse and restore us through the love of Christ,
   and strengthen us through the inner power
   of your Holy Spirit.
Lord of life,
   hear us.

So may we serve you better,
   and live to your glory.
Lord of life,
   hear us,
   through Jesus Christ our Lord.
Amen.

NICK FAWCETT

Petition

Lord Jesus Christ,
   there are times when life seems a mystery,
      when we can make no sense of anything,
      not even our faith,
      when the events of life confuse and trouble us
      so that our minds are in turmoil
      and our confidence is destroyed.
Help us to know you are with us at such times.
Speak again your word of peace,
   and may our souls find rest.

Remind us of the experience of your followers
   on that first Easter day –
   how you came to them in their confusion –
   each still reeling from the shock of your death,
   struggling to come to terms with the suffering you had endured,
   and the apparent triumph of evil over goodness –
   and how you restored their faith,
   rekindling their joy,
   reviving their vision
   and renewing their commitment.
Speak again your word of peace,
   and may our souls find rest.

We thank you for your promise to be with us always,
   to the end of the age,
   and we rejoice that we experience the fulfilment of those words
   through the living presence of the Holy Spirit.

Whatever storms may confront us,
   whatever trials we may face,
   we know that you will always be there,
   meeting us in our confusion to quieten our hearts.
Speak again your word of peace,
   and may our souls find rest.

We thank you that the day will come
   when your victory will be complete
   and your will accomplished –
   a day when the puzzles that confound us will be resolved,
   when the forces that conspire against your kingdom will be overcome
   and when harmony will be established among the nations –
   a day when you will speak your word to all.
Speak again your word of peace,
   and may our souls find rest.

Lord Jesus Christ,
   meet with us when life is hard and our faith is weak,
      and grant the assurance that, despite appearances,
      your purpose continues unchanged,
      your strength remains undiminished
      and your love is indestructible.
   Speak again your word of peace,
      and may our souls find rest.

We ask it in your name.
Amen.

NICK FAWCETT

Intercession – joy from Sorrow

Lord Jesus Christ,
   we remember the trauma
      which your suffering and death brought to your followers,
      a grief which went beyond words
      and which seemed beyond healing.
   We recall how Peter wept bitterly
      when he realised he had denied you as you predicted;
      how women sobbed on the way to the cross,
      and as they watched you die;
      how Mary broke down in the garden, overwhelmed with grief –
      each one a symbol of the desolation and despair
      so many felt at your death.
   But we recall also how Peter rejoiced
      as, three times, you repeated your call,
      how your followers celebrated

as you stood among them, risen and victorious,
how Mary's heart soared with wonder as you spoke her name.
Gracious Lord, wherever there is sorrow,
grant your joy.

We pray for those who suffer today –
all who endure constant pain,
who wrestle with illness,
who are victims of violence
or whose bodies are broken by accident or injury.
Gracious Lord, wherever there is sorrow,
grant your joy.

We pray for those who feel betrayed today,
cheated by loved ones,
deceived by those they trusted,
hurt by those they counted as friends,
or let down by society.
Gracious Lord, wherever there is sorrow,
grant your joy.

We pray for those who grieve today,
their hearts broken by tragedy and bereavement,
their lives torn apart –
many for whom tears are a constant companion,
laughter and happiness like some distant memory.
Gracious Lord, wherever there is sorrow,
grant your joy.

Lord Jesus Christ,
reach out into our world of so much pain,
heartache and sadness.
May your light scatter the shadows,
your love lift the burdens,
and your grace bring life in all its fullness.
Gracious Lord, wherever there is sorrow,
grant your joy.

We ask it in your name.
Amen.

NICK FAWCETT

Short prayers

Jesus of Bethlehem,
be born in us today.
Jesus of Galilee,
touch our lives with your presence.

Jesus of Gethsemane,
　　strengthen us in times of trial.
Jesus of Calvary,
　　have mercy upon us,
　　for we do not know what we do.
Jesus of the empty tomb,
　　lead us from light into darkness,
　　from death into life.
Jesus of eternity,
　　the Word made flesh,
　　the King of kings and Lord of lords,
　　walk with us until our journey's end,
　　and to you be glory
　　this day and for evermore.
Amen.

NICK FAWCETT

Lord Jesus Christ,
　　it was not just you who was broken
　　that day you hung on a cross;
　　it was your disciples too,
　　their hearts broken just as surely,
　　their dreams and hopes snuffed out,
　　their faith cut from beneath them
　　and laid to rest.
It was not just you who rose again
　　that day you emerged from the tomb;
　　it was your disciples too,
　　their hearts beating once more
　　with joyful anticipation,
　　their vision for the future reborn,
　　their faith rekindled,
　　bursting into unquenchable flame.
Come to us now where we are broken –
　　where love has died,
　　where hope has faded,
　　where faith has grown cold.
Reach out and touch us
　　in body, mind and spirit,
　　and help us to walk in the newness of life
　　which you alone can bring.
In your name we ask it.
Amen.

NICK FAWCETT

Living God,
   we praise you for the great truth of Easter –
   the message that your love will not be defeated.
When human evil had done its worst,
   despite every effort to frustrate your purpose,
   still your will triumphed!
The stone was rolled away, the tomb was empty,
   Christ had risen!
May that truth fire us each day with new hope,
   new confidence, and new enthusiasm,
   knowing that whatever obstacles we may face
   and whatever may fight against us,
   there is nothing that will finally be able to stand
   in the way of your purpose.
Amen.

NICK FAWCETT

All-age-talk material

Luke 24:33-34

JESUS IS ALIVE!

EARLY on SUNDAY MORNING the WOMEN went to the TOMB. They found the STONE had been ROLLED AWAY. An ANGEL told them that JESUS was ALIVE again, just as he had PROMISED! Mark 16:1-8
Find these words in the wordsearch.

SUSAN SAYERS

Jesus is with us.

Who else has ever risen from the dead?

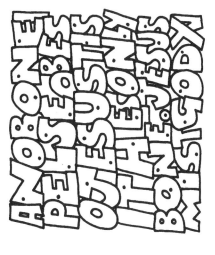

Can you see your own back?

Yes | No

How do you know you have a back if you can't see it?

I can feel it | Oh, help – I have no back!

Can you see Jesus?

Yes | No

How do you know he's here?

I have seen him in the gospels | I see him in the lovely world | He helps me and listens to me

Jesus

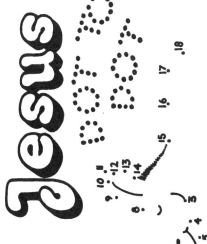

At first you can only see dots. Then you can see the picture.

Now 👏 and point to where the 👉 goes. Open 👀. Are you right?

SUSAN SAYERS

Art and craft

Prepare for an Easter procession. (Explain to the congregation that you are going to invite them to follow the children in acting out the journey to new life. Everyone is invited to join in, but if (as will almost inevitably be the case) there are those who would find it difficult, they are free simply to stay seated and use the time to pray for people who, in real life, are going through this experience. Now get the children to lead the procession, as you have planned it. If the procession is able to go outside the worship area of the church for a time, then perhaps you could arrange for the organist or the music group to strike up a triumphant tune when they return.) You will need a processional cross – if the church has one you might be able to use that, or if not make a simple one from two lengths of wood. Don't make it too big or heavy – for this service it needs to be clear that it isn't a burden but a symbol of liberation. Plan where the procession will go, and designate a child to lead it (but point out that they're all going to be leaders – they're going to lead the congregation on a journey to new life!) If the route takes you through a few doors that's all the better. This can be done very simply, or it could be made more powerfully symbolic if your building and resources are appropriate. For example, would your circumstances lend themselves to the idea of having some black curtains hung over the door leading out of the church? Another refinement would be to have a screen, using either a sheet of tissue-paper or just a few strips that could be taped across the doorway by which you will return – then you would be able to go through the dark curtains of 'death' and burst through the barrier on the way back, symbolising the breakthrough to new life! However simple or complicated you make it, keep the central point in mind: the journey to new life.

Draw or paint a picture of the women at the empty tomb.

This is the key picture, but you might want to do others in addition to it, such as:

- the women preparing to set out in the early dawn
- the women running to tell the others about Jesus' resurrection

MICHAEL FORSTER

Art and craft

Prepare in advance some ugly 'graffiti': Use large pieces of paper (flipchart pages would be good) and keep a second copy of each for yourself. Don't be afraid of using some common offensive symbols like swastikas – it will enhance the point about God's redemptive creativity! Get the children to work on them in groups, using whatever medium you think is appropriate – paint, crayons, felt-tips, collage, etc. – to turn your dreadful scrawls into something beautiful.

You can explain that this is what God did when Jesus was crucified. He didn't destroy the cross and put something nicer in its place, but he transformed the cross, with all its pain, into a sign of life and hope. Prepare a large, ugly cross – either a picture or a model – for the congregation to transform at the service, and have ready some brightly coloured cards.

Put up the copies of your 'graffiti'. Draw attention to the 'graffiti'. Not very nice, is it? Then cover each one with the children's transformed version. Emphasise to the congregation that they didn't destroy what you had done, but *used* it and *transformed* it – which is just a tiny illustration of what God did . . .

Divide the congregation into groups. Ask them what are the 'signs of death' in your locality that need to be transformed by God's life and love into 'signs of life'. Perhaps it's environmental – waste ground that becomes a haven for nefarious goings-on. Could the council be persuaded to turn it into a sensory garden for blind people – perhaps with some help from church people? Or it may be lack of leisure facilities – could the Church help there? Ask them to write down the life-giving ideas they think of on the coloured cards. (This is a time for dreaming dreams, so don't let them worry about the details, just the vision!) After a time, call the groups to order and get one or more representatives from each group to tell the congregation their ideas and then stick or pin their cards onto the cross, transforming it from stark, deathly ugliness to a sign of life and hope for the community. The cards can be kept after the service and used by the Church's organisations and committees to focus on mission ideas, so that the 'body of Christ' may be a sign of Jesus' kingship of life and love.

Draw or paint a picture of the empty tomb, with the cross in the background.

This is the key picture, but you might want to do others in addition to it, such as:

• Jesus on trial before Pilate
• The women coming to the tomb
• The angel at the open tomb

Put up the copies you kept of your 'graffiti', and set the large cross at the front. Draw attention to the 'graffiti'. Not very nice, is it? Then cover each one with the children's transformed version. Emphasise to the congregation that they didn't destroy what you had done, but *used* it and *transformed* it – which is just a tiny illustration of what God did in the story that's about to be read.

MICHAEL FORSTER

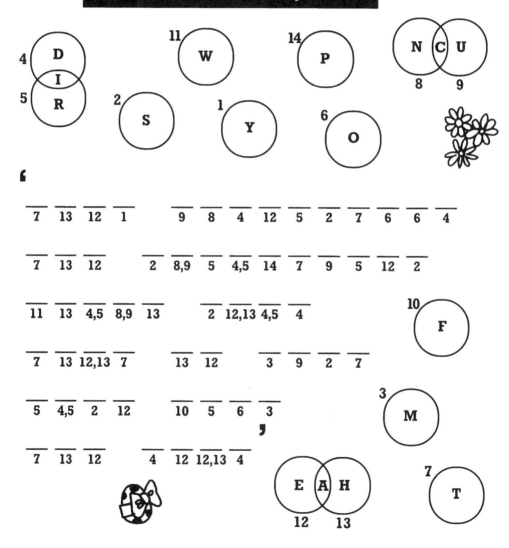

KATIE THOMPSON

Easter is a time
for celebrating new life!

**Can you find these Easter symbols hidden
in the wordsearch puzzle?**

LAMBS   EGGS   FLOWERS   BUNNIES   CHICKS

J	C	H	I	C	K	S
C	L	M	N	P	R	E
H	S	G	G	E	A	I
B	R	P	W	B	S	N
E	E	O	S	E	G	N
I	L	A	M	B	S	U
F	L	B	M	S	E	B

KATIE THOMPSON

Write the first letter of each picture to see!

Katie Thompson

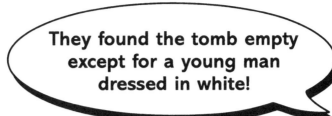

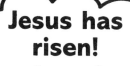

How many  can you find in the picture?

Circle your answer

KATIE THOMPSON

Jesus has risen!

What are these women carrying and why?

Use this code to find the answer!

P E T C U S O I N A J
1   2   3   4   5   6

$\overline{3,4}$ $\overline{1}$ $\overline{4,5}$ $\overline{2,3}$ $\overline{1,2}$ $\overline{3,4}$ $\overline{2}$ $\overline{4}$

$\overline{5,6}$ $\overline{5}$ $\overline{4}$ $\overline{4,5}$ $\overline{5}$ $\overline{2}$

$\overline{6}$ $\overline{1,2}$ $\overline{3,4}$ $\overline{3}$ $\overline{3,4}$

Mark 16:1

KATIE THOMPSON

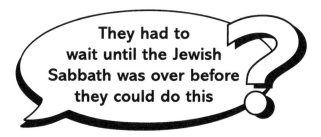

Solve the clues to find which day they went to the tomb. The first letter of each clue will spell the answer out.

1. Something which twinkles in the night sky

2. The opposite of over

3. The eleventh month of the year

4. This follows night

5. A snake that's good at maths!

6. Buttercups are this colour

KATIE THOMPSON

When they arrived, the tomb was empty except for a young man dressed in white who told them . . .

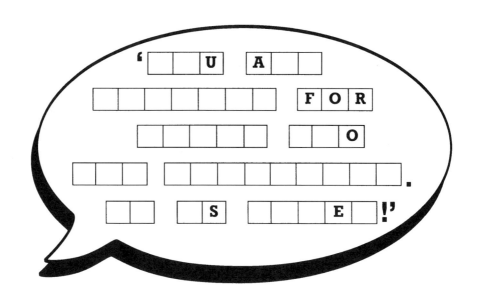

Unscramble the mixed-up words to read what he said in Mark 16:6

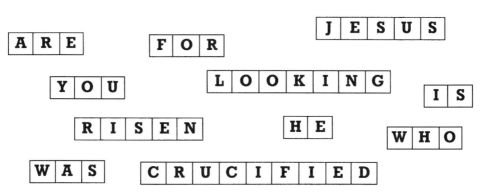

KATIE THOMPSON

A miraculous change!

Aim

To illustrate the great transformation which Easter brought about in the life of the disciples and the life of the world [start by reading John 11:25-26].

Preparation

On pieces of card or paper, and in large, bold characters, write or print the following letters:

A A C D E E E E F H H I I I L M N N O R R R S T T T U

Attach a small piece of magnetic tape to the back of each, and arrange them on a board as follows:

ISNT THERE A MIRACLE HERE   FIND OUT

Talk

Read out the words displayed on the board, then ask the congregation if anyone can spot what the 'miracle' might be? Suggest that they might like to change things around to arrive at a very different message, reminding them of the words of Jesus in the reading shared earlier. When the right answer is given, or if it is clear no one is going to guess it, rearrange the letters on the board to spell out the following:

I AM THE RESURRECTION AND THE LIFE

From one message to another – an astonishing transformation, yet not half as astonishing as the miracle we celebrate today: the resurrection of Jesus Christ from the dead. To the disciples and followers of Jesus the events they had witnessed in the days leading up to Easter spoke only of death, tragedy, sorrow and disaster. There seemed nothing left to hope for, no reason to expect any change in their situation. They had watched Jesus suffer and die, then seen him buried in a tomb and the stone rolled against the entrance. The adventure of faith was over, and all their dreams with it.

But suddenly it was all turned around. Three women went to the tomb and came back with the news that Jesus was not there. Two men on the road to Emmaus declared that Jesus had met them on the way and broken bread with them. And then, as the disciples huddled together in the upper room, Jesus appeared amongst them, risen and victorious. It seemed too good to be true, but it wasn't – Jesus was alive!

'I am the resurrection and the life.' That's what Jesus told his followers. And that's what he tells us today. It is a miracle which some find difficult if not impossible to accept, and which many across the centuries have argued fiercely over. We can't prove it any more than they can, but we can find out the truth for ourselves, for the risen Christ is constantly waiting to meet with each one of us and transform our lives in turn. We need simply to respond, to put our trust in him and give him space to work. Do that, and we will find a miracle not just in the words of Scripture but deep within our hearts – life changed for ever!

NICK FAWCETT

Read John 20:1-18

After the reading the first question might be: What's love got to do with it? The popular way to consider this passage from the Bible is to think about the stone being rolled away from the tomb.

The common way to cover a tomb in those times was to cut a large groove in front of the tomb opening and wheel a large circular stone along the groove to close the tomb entrance. The authorities had taken the further precaution of 'sealing' the large circular stone on Jesus' tomb to try and make sure no one could get in.

None of Jesus' friends could visit the tomb on the Sabbath (our Saturday); to do so would break the Jewish law.

Mary Magdalene gets up as early as she can, before 6am, and goes to the tomb of Jesus. Once there she finds the stone rolled away and the tomb appears empty. Mary immediately runs and tells Peter and John that someone has taken Jesus from the tomb.

A while later, Mary is standing by the tomb alone, weeping. Mary has followed Jesus ever since he set her free from evil spirits. Mary is distraught. Not only have the authorities killed Jesus, either someone has robbed the grave or the authorities have taken his body away to avoid any further problems with the followers of Jesus.

Inside the tomb are two angels who ask Mary why she is crying. Mary's response is extremely personal: 'They have taken *my* Lord (not *our* Lord). And *I* (not *we*) don't know where they have put him.'

Immediately Mary senses someone is behind her and she turns around. Mary is standing by the tomb entrance and looks into what little light there is available at that time of the morning. Through her tears and the dull light she can make out the shape of a man who she assumes is the gardener. It isn't until Jesus speaks her name that the light of recognition dawns. The person who she thought lost is now in front of her! She is overwhelmed. But Jesus comforts her and reassures her that he isn't going anywhere straight away so there is no need to 'hold on' to him; he isn't going to the Father straight away.

Mary, although very sad, was able to recognise the voice of the Lord she loved so much. Even though all the evidence seemed to underline her grief, her love enabled her to hear Jesus speak. Mary was able to 'see' through her tears, her grief, her fear and hear the voice of Jesus speaking her name with love.

Is our relationship with Jesus one which allows us to 'see' through all the garbage and hear what he has to say to us?

PETE TOWNSEND

Reflective material
(sketches, meditations and poems)

Playlet: The Great Abyss

Set the scene, either using a convenient doorway or a makeshift screen. Set up a sign saying, 'The Great Abyss' in sinister, Gothic-style writing.

Enter Guide and a party of children

Guide   Well, children, welcome to the Wonderful Life Themepark – I'm your guide for the day. We want you to enjoy yourselves.

Child 1   *(Pointing to door)* What's that?

Guide   Oh, you don't want to know about that.

Child 1   Yes, I do.

Child 2   Me, too.

Child 3   Me, three.

Guide   Well if you must know, it's – well, it's – the Great Abyss.

Child 1   He means death.

Guide   *(Shudders)* Please don't say that word.

Child 3   Why?

Guide   We don't talk about it, here. It's not polite.

Child 2   Oh, you mean like sex, politics and religion.

Guide   *(Brightening visibly)* Oh, you can talk about religion.

Child 2   Don't want to.

Child 1   Want to talk about the Great Abyss.

Guide   Well, you can't. It's not done. Anyway, it's a terrible place – really horrible and frightening. No one who's gone there has ever come back.

Child 3   Well, if no one's ever come back . . .

Child 2   . . . how d'you know it's horrible and frightening?

Guide   *(Angrily)* Don't ask silly questions! Just take my word for it: it's a horrible place, no one ever comes back, and polite people don't talk about it.

Enter, Jesus, through the door from the Great Abyss, with 'wounds' visible on his hands, and wearing a 'Big J' badge.

Jesus   Don't talk about what?

GUIDE passes out from the shock

Child 1   Have you just come from . . . there?

Jesus   Oh, there's nothing there to be frightened of.

Child 3   What happened to your hands?

Jesus   That's a long story.

Child 2   What d'you mean, 'There's nothing there to be frightened of'?

Child 3   The guide said no one ever came back.

Child 1   Can we go there?

Jesus   Hey, one at a time! There's nothing to be frightened of, but it's true that people don't come back from there to this place.

Child 3   You just have.

Jesus   That's another long story. Look, it's a one-way door, so you really don't want to go through it until the right time.

Child 2   When's the right time?

Jesus   The point is not to let it spoil your enjoyment of the rest of the Wonderful Life Themepark. You'll see people go through there occasionally, and it's always sad because you know they're not coming back. But you don't actually need to be frightened of it.

Child 1   But we are allowed to talk about it?

Jesus   Why not? Since you're not afraid of it, what harm can it do? And now you've seen me you're not afraid, are you?

Child 2   Um – I don't think so.

Child 3   But we'll just stay in the park and enjoy it for as long as we can.

Jesus   Good idea. Oh, and *(indicates GUIDE)* when he comes round, tell him what I said, won't you?

MICHAEL FORSTER / SIMON SMITH

Dying for Easter

Easter, with its message of suffering and death in order that salvation might be restored to humanity, is a challenge both to the world and to the Church. Conventional wisdom does not sit easily with such precepts. We live in a society that believes in retaliation, the justifiable use of force, and that corporal punishment is the ultimate weapon in the correction of behaviour. These are views that find as wide a credence in church congregations as they do anywhere else.

And yet, these views surely have to find some challenge from the message of Easter. If Jesus proclaimed a message of love that was superior to all other powers, and lived out that message in the practicalities of his daily life, must it not challenge those of us who claim to be his followers to do the same?

But none of this seems easy or straightforward when we look at the world around us. This sketch seeks to highlight these issues and, in a light-hearted way, to show the dichotomy between the Gospel message and the normally accepted wisdom of the age.

Enter George.

George   (*To audience*) I'm right fed up! All I ever seem to do is work, work, work! More hours, greater efficiency, fewer staff, increased work-load! Can't afford to give you a wage rise this year. Profits are down, costs are up, and the high rate of the pound is hitting exports. On and on and on, excuses, reasons, but it's always the workers who pay in the end.

Enter Bill.

Bill   Hi ya, George! How's tricks?

George   I'm fed up, Bill! All this working, it's getting me down. I mean, what's it all for? Where does it get us in the end?

Bill   Cheer up, at least you've got a job. There are plenty more who would be happy to take yours if you don't want it.

George   That's the trouble, that's why they get away with it all the time.

Bill   Get away with what?

George   Fleecing us! Paying us peanuts while they make their profits and live in style.

Bill   Cheer up, you old misery! You've got the summer to look forward to. A fortnight in Benidorm, isn't it?

George   Oh great! Two weeks drinking warm beer, the kids complaining they're bored, the missus telling me what a nice body the waiter has and how Spanish men are much more considerate than we are, and evenings spent listening to some drunken bloke from West Hartlepool singing 'Una Paloma Blanca!' What have I got to complain about? I only work all year for that!

Bill   Oh dear, you have got it bad. Never mind, Easter is coming; at least you'll get a day off.

George   Wonderful! Do you think there is anything in this Easter lark?

Bill   I dunno. Our Mary says there is. She's gone all religious, you know; prays, reads her Bible, goes to church! The other three are OK, they're still quite normal. I don't know where we went wrong with Mary.

George   I expect she'll grow out of it; they usually do.

Bill	She came in yesterday and said, 'I've got an Easter egg for the Vicar.' I said, 'That sounds like a fair swap.' I don't think she was very amused though.
George	I don't understand it anyway. What's the point of getting yourself killed? I mean, it can't do you any good, can it?
Bill	Mary says you have to be prepared to die in order to be born again, whatever that means. She says that we have to be prepared to suffer, if necessary, for the truth.
George	It makes no sense to me. I'm all for a bit of retaliation; you know, 'An eye for an eye and a tooth for a tooth', that's my motto.
Bill	I couldn't agree more, George. There are far too many of these 'do-gooders' about nowadays. Look out, here comes one now.
	Enter Vicar.
Vicar	*(To Bill)* Hello, you're Mary's dad, aren't you?
Bill	That's right, Vicar, and this is my mate George.
Vicar	*(Shakes hands)* How do you do. She's a lovely girl, Mary, such an enquiring mind, you must be very proud of her.
Bill	Absolutely, Vicar! I was just telling George here how pleased I am about Mary going to church and all, wasn't I, George?
George	*(Coughs)* Um . . . er . . .
Bill	Precisely!
Vicar	Perhaps we might see you in church this Easter.
Bill	I don't think so, Vicar. We were just saying, we're not much on this suffering lark. Seems a bit stupid getting yourself killed. Not much of a future in that, is there?
George	It's life you see, Vicar. It will get you nowhere if you let people walk all over you. I'm all for giving as good as I get. Get your retaliation in first – that's my motto.
Bill	I agree! We were just saying the problem with the country today is, people have gone soft. Youngsters have got no respect. They want a good clip round the ears, if you ask me. Too many 'do-gooders', that's the problem.
Vicar	In my experience there are only three kinds of people: 'do-gooders' of which there are few; 'do-badders' who seem equally scarce in number; and 'do-nothings' who appear to be in abundance.
George	Very clever! Give them a good thrashing, I say; that will teach them not to be violent.

Vicar   But, don't you see? Jesus was prepared to suffer, even to die, to show there is no greater power than love. Without his death Jesus couldn't have been raised and without his resurrection we couldn't have been set right with God.

Bill   Still sounds confusing to me. Dying in order to live. What kind of sense does that make? It would be a poor world if we all went round doing that kind of thing, and no mistake.

Vicar   Look, come to church with Mary and find out more. At least come at Easter, it can't do you any harm, can it?

Bill   I suppose not, but I can tell you now, you're not going to change my mind.

Vicar   I won't have to, we can leave God to do that.

Bill   I don't fancy his chances.

George   I'll say one thing for Easter though, Bill.

Bill   What's that?

George   At least we get an extra day off work.

Bill   And very welcome it is too.

George   After the way I've been feeling lately, I'm simply dying for Easter.

Vicar   I think you'll find that's been done already.

Exit All.

DAVID WALKER

We know that death is not the end
  but the beginning of Life.
We know ourselves not to be
  the children of a moment,
  but pilgrims of eternity.

WILLIAM BARCLAY
from *You're Never Alone* by E. Rundle

Christian people believe in the strong love of God . . .
  that love does not answer all questions,
  nor does it protect us from the bad times.
But from experience, ours, and others,
  we perhaps begin to learn that it is strong
  and it will see us through.

N. COLLINSON AND D. MATTHEWS
from *You're Never Alone* by E. Rundle

Reflecting on John 20:1-18

We will not see unless we search, not hiding from sorrow. Peter and the beloved disciple run, and Mary who stands alone weeping bends down and 'looks in'. 'For whom are you looking?' – the words of Jesus, almost his last in this Gospel, echo his first to Andrew – 'What are you looking for?'

At the beginning and at the end, faith will always be a search for that which is lost. And the search may well take us into and through the darkness of our sorrows.

Easter is about seeking – and finding, and being found, as we are eternally known by name: 'Mary'. And as we are known, so we come to know – a knowledge too deep for words – that God is, and we are, and in him always will be. The Father of Jesus who raised him, is our Father too. And will raise us also. Alleluia.

PATRICK WOODHOUSE

Drama: He's alive!

Narrator	Jesus' enemies thought they'd won when they saw him nailed to the cross, but they couldn't have been more wrong. Even there, Jesus showed that love can be stronger than hatred. He never cursed anyone – he even prayed for the people who were torturing him – and he comforted the criminal who was dying on the cross next to him. And the last words he said were words of faith.
Jesus	Father, I commend my soul into your care.
Narrator	Standing at the foot of the cross was a tough soldier – a hard man, who'd seen a lot of death – and even he couldn't help being impressed.
Soldier	What a man! He truly was a completely good man!
Narrator	Standing further away were some of the women who were friends of Jesus. They'd never left him, even at the most dangerous moments, but had stayed there to show they cared.
Passer-by (male)	You ought to go home. This is no place for women.
Joanna	Well, someone has to be here to share his last moments with him – we're not going to let him die alone.
Narrator	Joanna was there with Mary Magdalene and another Mary, the mother of James, who all felt the same way. When they finally knew Jesus was dead, she turned to Mary Magdalene.
Joanna	Let's go and see where they bury him.
Magdalene	Yes – then we can come back later to pay our respects.

Narrator	Stealthily, not wanting to attract attention, they followed the men who were burying Jesus. They saw him placed hurriedly in a hole in the hillside, with a big stone rolled in front to seal it.
Mary	After the religious festival's over, we'll come back and make sure he's given a *decent* burial.
Narrator	So it was that, early on the Sunday morning, the same women – Joanna, Mary Magdalene and the other Mary who was James' mother – all met with jars of spice and perfume to go to Jesus' grave.
Magdalene	How are we going to move that big stone away from the grave?
Mary	I don't know – let's worry about that when we get there.
Joanna	A lot of people would say we were mad, anyway, but these things matter. Jesus always cared about other people, so now we're going to do the right thing by him.
Narrator	They walked silently in the early dawn light until they came within sight of the tomb, and they stopped in amazement and horror.
Joanna	Someone's opened it already. The stone's been rolled away.
Magdalene	Someone's up to no good. Can't they just let him rest in peace?
Narrator	Slowly, they moved nearer to the tomb and peered in. It looked very spooky, but as their eyes became used to the low light they saw something that made them stop in their tracks. Nothing. Jesus' body wasn't there. They were staring open-mouthed at one another when suddenly the place was filled with light, and two men in dazzling white clothes stood in front of them.
First man	Why are you looking in a grave for someone who's alive?
Second man	Jesus isn't here – he's risen from the dead!
Narrator	The women were terrified, but gradually the truth sank in as the men continued talking.
First man	Remember what he told you while he was with you before – how he'd be killed by his enemies but would rise again on the third day?
Second man	Well, this is it!
Narrator	Suddenly, everything fell into place. Of course – God had raised Jesus to new life, just as Jesus had said that he would. The women didn't know whether to laugh or cry for joy!

Magdalene	Fancy us being the first to know!
Joanna	Not so surprising. After all, we stayed with him – and we're here now.
Mary	Come on! We've got to tell the others.
Narrator	What a sight they were – stumbling over tree roots, tripping over the hems of their skirts, and laughing joyfully all the time, as they ran to where they knew the disciples were hiding.
Mary	He's alive! he's alive! Really, he is – just as he promised he would be!
Narrator	At first, none of the men believed them – they thought they'd been dreaming or something. But they hadn't – and soon the whole world was going to be buzzing with the Good News: Jesus is alive!

MICHAEL FORSTER

Risen Lord

Leader	You who transformed the world in your rising, giving it new light,
All	Risen Lord, we praise you.
Leader	You who broke down the barriers, going beyong the things we thought we knew, destroying our illusions of the dark,
All	Risen Lord, we praise you.
Leader	You who changed the course of the river of life so that its waters flowed across the edge of heaven and into time,
All	Risen Lord, we praise you.
Leader	You who stretched our minds to take us out beyond ourselves, our safe assumptions and our own proud reasonings,
All	Risen Lord, we praise you.
Leader	You who shattered all our dreams – to bring us to a more beautiful reality,
All	Risen Lord, we praise you.
Leader	You who lift us up so that we can be with you in glory to see all things from where you are,
All	Risen Lord, we praise you.

Leader   You who scatter our small darkness
        that we may reflect your radiance as from lesser stars,

All   Risen Lord, we praise you.

Leader   You who shine upon our beings here in time and in eternity –
        light beloved and most glorious,

All   Risen Lord, we praise you.

MARY HATHAWAY

Meditation of Salome

You'd have thought we'd be pleased, wouldn't you? –
    over the moon at the news that he had risen.
And we were, later,
    once we finally took it all in.
But at the time it wasn't pleasure we felt,
    it was sheer, unadulterated fear.
Can you blame us?
I don't think so,
    for it's not every day you find a tomb empty, is it? –
    not often that you go to anoint a body
    only to find it's disappeared!
Yet that's what happened to us –
    early that morning,
    the dew still wet on the grass,
    mist still rising,
    the three of us making our way to the tomb,
    suspecting nothing,
    expecting nothing,
    simply going to pay our last respects.
It was shock enough finding the stone rolled away,
    our stomachs lurching at the sight of it,
    and when we finally plucked up the courage to look inside,
    to find not Jesus but this man we didn't know from Adam,
    well, we could scarcely suppress a scream!
Who was he?
Why was he there?
What did he want?
And, most important of all, where had he taken our Lord?
The questions crowded in upon us,
    our minds reeling in confusion.
He may have been calm
    but *we* weren't!
We felt faint with disbelief,
    dizziness growing by the second,

wanting only to get out and as far away as possible;
    so when he told us to go back to the disciples,
    believe me, we were only too happy to oblige.
Did we tell them what we'd seen?
Well, what do you think? Would *you* have done?
We knew all too well the response we'd get,
    our words dismissed as so much nonsense –
    and that's just what happened
    when they finally forced it out of us,
    for, try as we might, we simply couldn't hide our confusion.
We weren't just scared,
    we were terrified,
    trembling as though we'd seen a ghost,
    and with good reason,
    for we honestly thought we had!

NICK FAWCETT

Meditation of Peter

They said he was alive! Can you believe that?
All right, I know they were upset, cut up about what had happened,
    but then we all were, each one of us.
We'd all loved him,
    all believed he was someone special,
    all hoped he was the one we were waiting for.
And we were crushed by what had happened, utterly devastated.
We understood how they felt.
But you have to face facts, don't you?
It's no good burying your head in the sand
    and pretending the worst hasn't happened.
There's no point trying to fool yourself when you know the truth full well.
And we knew, believe me, all too well.
We'd seen him crying out in agony,
    we'd heard him draw his last breath,
    and we'd been there when they laid him in the tomb.
At a distance, true – keeping well out of sight, just in case,
    but he was dead, there's no question about that.
So what were they playing at, those women, claiming he's alive?
They didn't seriously expect any of us to swallow it, surely?
I guess they'd finally gone over the edge, lost their marbles?
Women! We might have guessed they'd go under in a crisis.
No wonder Jesus stuck to men for his disciples –
    clear-headed, realistic, down to earth, sensible.
Jesus alive! We'd like to believe it, of course we would.
But it's nonsense, any fool can see that.

Version for three voices

Peter	They said he was alive! Can you believe that?
John	All right, I know they were upset, cut up about what had happened.
James	But then, we all were, each one of us.
Peter	We'd all loved him.
John	We'd all believed he was someone special.
James	We'd all hoped he was the one we were waiting for.
Peter	And we were crushed by what had happened, utterly devastated.
John	We understood how they felt.
Peter	But you have to face facts, don't you?
John	It's no good burying your head in the sand and pretending the worst hasn't happened.
James	There's no point trying to fool yourself when you know the truth full well.
Peter	And we knew, believe me.
John	We'd seen him crying out in agony.
James	We'd heard him draw his last breath.
Peter	And we'd been there when they laid him in the tomb.
James	At a distance, true – keeping well out of sight, just in case.
John	But he was dead, there's no question about that.
Peter	So what were they playing at, those women, claiming he's alive?
John	They didn't seriously expect any of us to swallow it, surely?
Peter	I guess they'd finally gone over the edge, lost their marbles?
James	Women! We might have guessed they'd go under in a crisis.
John	No wonder Jesus stuck to men for his disciples – clear-headed, realistic, down to earth, sensible.
Peter	Jesus alive! We'd like to believe it, of course we would.
John	But it's nonsense, any fool can see that.

NICK FAWCETT

Meditation of Mary Magdalene

I'll never be able to say what it meant to me,
   after the horror and the heartache,
   the darkness and the despair,
   to hear that wonderful, astonishing news –
   Jesus, alive!
I'd lived in a daze until then,
   unable to take in the horror of what I'd seen,
   the anguish and the agony which he'd borne
   with such quiet dignity and awesome courage.
He'd warned us to expect the worst,
   and I suppose in our hearts we'd known what was coming
   but we'd refused to accept it,
   hoping against hope there might be some other way,
   a path less costly, less awful for us all.
But as we walked that morning to the tomb,
   all such thoughts were gone,
   buried along with our Lord,
   life dark, cold, empty,
   bereft of meaning.
We were blind to everything in our grief,
   scarcely aware even of the ground starting to shake
   or light flooding around us,
   but when we reached the stone, rolled away from the tomb,
   we saw that all right,
   and for a moment we just stood there gazing in confusion,
   not knowing where to turn or what to say.
That's when it came, the news that took our breath away:
   'He is not here.
   He has been raised.
   Come, see the place where he lay.'
We scarcely dared to look at first, afraid it might all be a dream,
   but finally we found the courage,
   and it was true,
   he was gone! –
   just the grave clothes left to show he'd been there.
You can imagine how we felt,
   our hearts pounding with excitement;
   but there was more to come,
   things yet more wonderful,
   for even as we ran to tell the news,
   skipping with sheer delight,
   we saw him ahead of us –
   Jesus, the man we knew and loved,

arms outstretched in welcome,
    waiting to greet us in his old familiar way.
He had risen, just as we'd been told,
    death unable to hold him!
Only it wasn't just Jesus who rose that day,
    it was all of us:
    for there in the garden life began again,
    life which we thought had died in us for ever –
    hope reborn,
    faith renewed,
    love rekindled,
    joy restored –
    and we knew now these could never be destroyed –
    the proof was there before us!

NICK FAWCETT

Additional Easter Material

Resurrection appearances

A reading from the Gospel of John (20:19-31)

On the Sunday after Jesus had died, his disciples gathered together in a locked room, hidden away for fear of being arrested.

Suddenly Jesus appeared in the room with them. 'Peace be with you,' he said, and he showed them the wounds in his hands and his side.

The disciples were overjoyed to see their master again.

'As my Father sent me, so I am sending you,' he said. Then, breathing on them , he said, 'Receive the Holy Spirit, and know that whoever you forgive, I will forgive also!'

The disciple called Thomas was not with the others when Jesus had appeared, and because he had not seen him with his own eyes, he did not believe that Jesus was alive.

A week later Jesus appeared to them again and, greeting them with the words, 'Peace be with you', he showed his wounds to Thomas, and said, 'See the wounds in my hands and side, touch them and doubt no longer, Thomas.'

At once Thomas answered, 'My Lord and my God.'

Jesus said to him, 'You believe because you have seen me with your own eyes. Blessed are those who have not seen and yet believe.'

The disciples of Jesus saw many other marvellous things done by Jesus which are not written down here. What has been included in this book has been written so that you may believe that Jesus is the Christ, the Son of God, and that through this belief in him you will have life.

This is the Gospel of the Lord
Praise to you, Lord Jesus Christ   KATIE THOMPSON

A reading from the Gospel of Luke (24:35-48)

The disciples who had met Jesus on the road to Emmaus were telling the others what had happened, and how they had recognised Jesus in the breaking of bread. Suddenly Jesus appeared among them, and at first they were terrified, because they thought that they had seen a ghost!

Then Jesus said to them, 'Peace be with you.' Seeing that they were still scared, he added, 'Do not be afraid. Why do you doubt what you can see? Look at my wounds and see that I am not a ghost. Touch me, a ghost has no flesh or bones as I have!'

They were overjoyed but still filled with disbelief, so Jesus asked them for something to eat and they watched as he ate some grilled fish.

Then he began to explain the Scriptures to them, and finally they understood what Scripture had said about the Messiah suffering and rising after three days; and how, starting in Jerusalem, the message of repentance and forgiveness should be preached in his name to all the nations.

Then Jesus said to them, 'You are my witnesses because you have seen all these things happen.'

This is the Gospel of the Lord
Praise to you, Lord Jesus Christ   KATIE THOMPSON

Introductory material

'They came to him, took hold of his feet, and worshipped him.' . . . 'They said to each other, "Were not our hearts burning within us while he was talking to us on the road?"' . . . 'She turned and said to him in Hebrew, "Rabbouni!" (which means Teacher).' . . . 'Thomas answered him, "My Lord and my God!"' . . . 'Jesus came and stood among them and said, "Peace be with you." . . . Then the disciples rejoiced when they saw the Lord.' The Christ who came, the Christ who comes, risen and victorious! Together, let us welcome him with thanksgiving and join the celebration!

NICK FAWCETT

Prayers

Praise: Strength from weakness

Lord Jesus Christ,
   we are reminded today
      of how your followers must have felt as Easter dawned –
      women walking sadly to the tomb,
      disciples trudging wearily home along the Emmaus Road,
      Apostles gathered together behind locked doors –
      all of them, to a man or woman, devastated,
      stunned by what had taken place,
      overwhelmed by sorrow and confusion.
   Gracious Lord, sovereign yet servant,
      in weakness you are our strength:
      receive our Easter praise.

We recall how they had looked forward
      to the coming of your kingdom,
      convinced that the day was near,
      refusing to believe, despite your warnings,
      that any harm could befall the Messiah.

We think of their sense of helplessness
   as they saw you taken before Pilate,
   whipped and ridiculed,
   nailed to a cross,
   laid in a tomb.
It looked as though you were powerless to resist,
   as though faith in you had been misguided and trust misplaced,
   for instead of glory they saw only humiliation,
   instead of a crown of victory, a crown of thorns.
Gracious Lord, sovereign yet servant,
   in weakness you are our strength:
   receive our Easter praise.

We praise you that at the empty tomb,
   on the Emmaus Road
   and in that room locked against the world
   you demonstrated that you were not defeated but victorious,
   your purpose not destroyed but gloriously fulfilled.
The events of Good Friday were seen for what they were:
   not a hideous mistake or an unseen catastrophe
   but an integral part of your sovereign plan,
   the ultimate expression of your love
   through which you brought life to all.
Gracious Lord, sovereign yet servant,
   in weakness you are our strength:
   receive our Easter praise.

We recall then, finally, how your followers must have felt
   on the day of resurrection –
   women running back to tell the news,
   disciples returning from Emmaus rejoicing,
   Apostles gazing in wonder as you stood there among them.
We recall how tears of sorrow turned to tears of joy,
   how eyes closed to the truth were opened at the breaking of bread,
   how minds clouded by doubt were illuminated by faith.
New purpose, new confidence, new faith
   emerged in lives which had seemed broken;
   your triumph was complete.
Gracious Lord, sovereign yet servant,
   in weakness you are our strength:
   receive our Easter praise.

Lord Jesus Christ,
   crucified yet risen,
     servant of all yet King of kings and Lord of lords,
     hear our prayer
     for your name's sake.
   Amen.

Assurance

Living God,
    we come to you on this day of celebration,
        conscious that there is so much in our lives
        that is uncertain,
        so much we cannot predict,
        so much we neither know nor understand.
Assure us of the victory you have won in Christ.

Remind us once more through this season
        that in all the changes and chances of this world
        you are an unchanging rock,
        an unfailing deliverer,
        and an everlasting hope.
Assure us of the victory you have won in Christ.

Remind us, as we continue to celebrate Easter in the days ahead,
        that your love continues through all things,
        your power is supreme over all things,
        and your presence is with us in all things.
Assure us of the victory you have won in Christ.

Give us this day
        a sense of your greatness,
        a recognition of all you have done,
        and a confidence in all you shall do.
Assure us of the victory you have won in Christ.

Living God,
    be among us now, we pray, through the risen Christ.
    Help us to hear his voice,
        to offer him our service,
        and to offer you our praise.
Assure us of the victory you have won in Christ.

We know that our hope is in you and you alone.
Help us to accept that,
    to live in that assurance,
    and so to follow wherever you might lead us.
Assure us of the victory you have won in Christ,
    for in his name we ask it.
Amen.

NICK FAWCETT

Thanksgiving

All-loving and all-powerful God,
　　we thank you for this day and all it means –
　　　　the assurance it brings that your love is stronger
　　　　than anything else in heaven or earth –
　　　　stronger than evil,
　　　　than all human powers,
　　　　than sorrow and suffering,
　　　　than death itself.
　　Accept our thanks for this day.
　　Accept our thanks for everything.

　　We thank you that in our world of so much pain and sorrow
　　　　you have shown that hope and faith is not in vain.
　　Your purpose is always at work,
　　　　giving meaning to our seeking and striving after good.
　　Accept our thanks for this day.
　　Accept our thanks for everything,

All-loving and all-powerful God,
　　accept our praise for all you have done in Christ –
　　　　a mystery before which we stand in awe,
　　　　a wonder before which we bow down in praise,
　　　　a truth in which we live and move
　　　　and have our being.
　　Accept our thanks for this day.
　　Accept our thanks for everything,
　　in the name of the living and risen Christ!
　　Amen.   Nick Fawcett

Praise and intercession

Loving God,
　　we praise you for this day of celebration,
　　　　this day of praise,
　　　　this day of thanksgiving,
　　　　a day that changes the way we think,
　　　　the way we act,
　　　　the way we live –
　　　　that changes everything.
　　Lord of life,
　　　　hear our prayer.

　　And so we pray now for change in our world,
　　　　for change in all those places where there is human need.
　　We pray for the poor, the homeless,
　　　　the sick and the hungry.

Lord of life,
>   **hear our prayer.**

We pray for the victims of war, for refugees,
>   for divided communities and countries,
Lord of life,
>   **hear our prayer.**

We pray for the sorrowful, the fearful,
>   the troubled in heart and mind.
Lord of life,
>   **hear our prayer.**

We pray for the oppressed, the persecuted,
>   the imprisoned and the exploited.
Lord of life,
>   **hear our prayer.**

Living God,
>   may the truth of Easter
>   break into each and every one of these situations,
>   bringing help and healing,
>   strength and support,
>   comfort and courage,
>   hope and help,
>   faith and freedom,
>   love and life,
>   the change that you alone can bring.
>   Lord of life,
>   **hear our prayer,**
>   **through Jesus Christ our Lord.**
>   **Amen.**

NICK FAWCETT

Intercession

The life-giving presence of the risen Lord. The disciples began to realise that Jesus was present with them whether they could see him or not. We, too, experience his spiritual presence among us and welcome him with joy.

Dear friends in Christ, as we gather here in the presence of the living God,
let us ask for his help and guidance in the Church and in the world.

We join in prayer with all other worshipping Christians;
give us an increasing love and affection
between individuals and groups in every parish
and denomination;
increasing open-heartedness,
outreach and generosity of spirit.

Silence for prayer

Unchanging Lord:
we pledge ourselves to your service.

We pray for the breaking down of suspicion,
double standards and hypocrisy in our world;
that the nations may work together
to conquer the problems of food and water distribution,
so that our planet's resources are shared and not wasted.

Silence for prayer

Lord, breathe into us:
that we may live.

We pray for the homes and families represented here,
with all their particular joys and sorrows,
needs and resources;
that our lives may be practical witnesses to our faith.

Silence for prayer

Unchanging Lord:
we pledge ourselves to your service.

We pray for those involved in medical research,
and all who suffer from diseases
which are as yet incurable;
for any who are too weak or exhausted to pray;
for any who are desperate or suicidal.

Silence for prayer

Unchanging Lord:
we pledge ourselves to your service.

We pray that all who have died in faith
may rise to new life in glory.

Silence for prayer

Father, we thank you for your immense compassion,
understanding and encouragement throughout our lives.

Silence for prayer

Merciful Father,
accept these prayers
for the sake of your Son,
our Saviour Jesus Christ, Amen.

SUSAN SAYERS

Short prayers

Lord, I don't understand philosophy,
    I can't get my head around psychology,
    and theology leaves me cold.
I'm not trying to make trouble,
    or cause anyone a problem.
I just want to be honest,
    well, as honest as I can be.
Don't get me wrong,
    I'm not saying I know it all,
    I'm glad I don't,
    know it all, I mean.
I want my faith to be real,
    not based on some second-hand account,
    or a set of rules which make me choke.
If I'm going to believe in you,
    properly, not some Sunday saint,
    or weekday wonder,
    but real, like a proper relationship
    between two hearts,
    then help me see the truth
    of who you are,
    and what you mean to me.
Amen.

PETE TOWNSEND

Lord Jesus Christ,
    we thank you that you meet us day by day,
    just as you met your disciples
    in the days following your resurrection.
We thank you that your victory of good over evil,
    of love over hate, of life over death
    continues to make such a difference to our lives,
    just as it did to theirs.
We thank you that for us too
    you turn weakness into strength,
    fear into confidence, and doubt into faith.
And we praise you that for each of us
    there is always the assurance of a new beginning
    when it seems like the end,
    new hope where there seems only despair.
Amen.

NICK FAWCETT

All-age-talk material

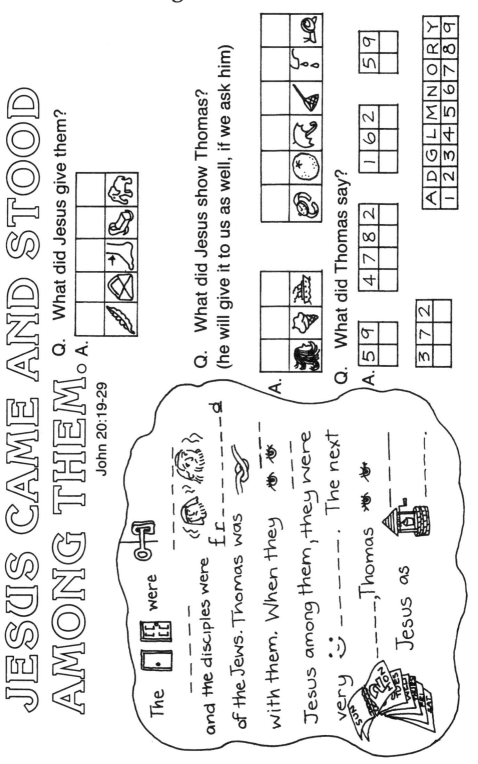

JESUS CAME AND STOOD AMONG THEM.

John 20:19-29

The [ ] [ ] were _ _ _ _ _ and the disciples were fr _ _ _ _ _ d of the Jews. Thomas was _ _ _ with them. When they [ ] [ ] Jesus among them, they were very :-) _ _ _ _ _ . The next _ _ _ _ _ , Thomas [ ] [ ] Jesus as _ _ _ .

Q. What did Jesus give them?
A.

Q. What did Jesus show Thomas?
(he will give it to us as well, if we ask him)
A.

Q. What did Thomas say?
A. 5 9   4 7 8 2
   3 7 2

1 6 2   5 9

A	D	G	L	M	N	O	R	Y
1	2	3	4	5	6	7	8	9

SUSAN SAYERS

Read the Emmaus section of *Jesus is Risen* (Palm Tree Bible Stories) which captures the atmosphere very well [or any other suitable account]. Talk about the story with the children:

– why do they think the disciples couldn't believe Jesus had risen?
– do they sometimes wonder if it is all true, and then later feel certain of Jesus being with them?
– talk about having expectations (for Christmas presents, for instance) which make us feel let down when they are not what we had in mind.
– when have they been surprised by God acting in their lives?

Teachers can give great encouragement in faith by being prepared to talk about some of their own surprises and disappointments; the children are then brought into contact with the real, living faith, rather than history. Help the children make this pop-up scene of Jesus breaking bread.

SUSAN SAYERS

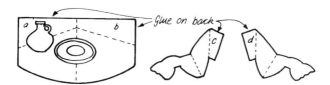

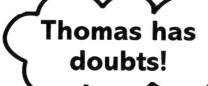

Thomas has doubts!

John 20:19-31

The door was locked and bolted because the disciples were afraid!

How many padlocks can you see? Write the number in the box

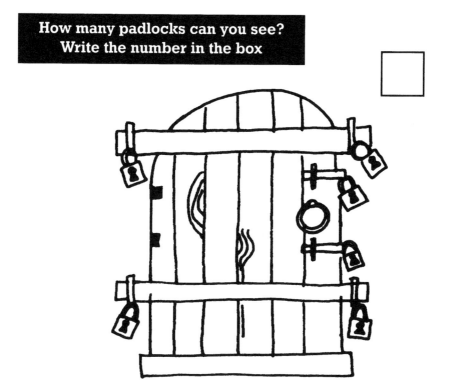

KATIE THOMPSON

At first Thomas would not believe that Jesus was alive. What did he say when Jesus showed him his wounds?

Use the code to find Thomas' words

CODE CRACKER

O (1)   N (3)   Y (5)   A (7)   L(9)

M (2)   G (4)   D (6)   R (8)

KATIE THOMPSON

Complete the joyful faces in the picture

'Peace be with you!'

John 20:20-21

KATIE THOMPSON

KATIE THOMPSON

Read John 20:19-31

Thomas the Twin is often referred to as 'Doubting Thomas'. The term is more often than not used more as an insult than a compliment. But Thomas had already shown a willingness to follow his faith in Jesus by his actions (see John 11:16). Thomas was willing to give everything for his belief in Jesus. So his 'doubt' was not so much to do with unbelief as with his inability to understand what had happened.

Thomas wasn't with the other disciples when Jesus appeared. All that Thomas knew was that Jesus had been crucified, the body of Jesus had 'disappeared' (had the authorities taken it?) and the disciples were afraid of what the Jewish leaders might do to them! It isn't clear why Thomas was not with the other disciples. He may have been on an errand or maybe he just wanted to be on his own for a while after all the events of the previous days. Thomas may have questioned in his own mind those events and how they affected what he believed. Knowing that the person you had seen raise people from the dead was now dead himself would cause doubts in anybody's faith!

The news that Jesus had appeared to the disciples was not enough for Thomas. He may have thought that they had all drunk too much wine or it was the result of a bit of wishful thinking. His doubts needed more than a second-hand account of something that might have happened.

A whole week went by during which Thomas must have thought 'I told you so!' But Jesus has a way of getting to the point and he made sure Thomas was around when he next dropped in on the disciples. This time Thomas need not rely on a second-hand story or gossip. He could have said, 'Nice stunt, Peter! Who's the actor?' But the facts were there before his eyes. His doubts vanished when he saw the risen Jesus. He could have then mumbled an apology and crept to the back of the room. His response was incredible: 'You are my Lord and my God.' No one else is recorded in the Gospel as acknowledging Jesus in this way. Thomas was honest about his doubts. He didn't pretend or keep his thoughts to himself. Instead he chose to face his questions and doubts. When he was faced with the truth he went all the way and left no one in any doubt about who he thought Jesus was.

Can we be as honest as Thomas about our doubts? Are we able to stand out from the crowd and admit we are not sure about something?

Give each group member a pencil and a piece of paper and ask them to write three statements about themselves on the piece of paper. Suggest that they make one statement true, one statement totally over the top and one statement believable, but not absolutely true (not necessarily in that order).

Ask each member of the group to read their 'statements'. Can the rest of the group decide which is true, which over the top and which is almost true?

If the group guess the 'almost true' statement, what made them doubt the truth of the statement? Was it a lucky guess or did something make them question the statement?

PETE TOWNSEND

Reflective material
(sketches, meditations and poems)

I'll believe it when I see it

Based on John 20:24-29

Narrator	After Jesus had risen from the dead, Mary Magdalene ran and told his friends all about it. But none of the men believed it. Then, as they were arguing, Jesus was suddenly standing among them! They were terrified!

- They *covered their faces*
- They *peeped between their fingers*
- Then they *covered their faces again*

They thought it must be a ghost! Then he spoke to them.

Jesus	Don't worry, I'm not a ghost. Here, come and take hold of my hand, just to prove that I'm real.
Narrator	Very gingerly, Peter took Jesus' hand.
Peter	It's true! It really is him!
Narrator	Then everyone went wild! They all crowded round Jesus, asking questions.
Jesus	The important thing is that God has brought me back to life. Your job is to go and tell everybody that – not argue about how he did it!
Narrator	Then, all of a sudden, he was gone! His friends had never been too sure what Jesus was going to do next. But now he seemed to be able to come and go as he liked.
Peter	No one's ever been able to pin Jesus down. He's not just alive, he's *free* as well!
Narrator	Just then, Thomas came in. He could tell that everybody was excited.
Thomas	What's going on?
Philip	Jesus has been here; he's alive.
Thomas	Pull the other one, Philip!
Narrator	Peter and Philip simply couldn't convince him.
Thomas	I'll tell you what: if you can see him, and touch him, I'll believe he's alive. But not until!
Philip	Why? Don't you trust your own friends?

Thomas   Not a lot! Remember when you told me the easy way to count sheep was to count the legs and divide by four?

Philip   And you actually tried it!

Thomas   Laugh if you like, but you're not catching me again.

Narrator   With that, Thomas went home. A week later Jesus appeared again, and this time Thomas was there, and he was overjoyed!

Thomas   It's true! My master – alive!

Jesus   You've seen me, and now you can believe. It's going to be harder for people who don't see me. You've got to go and help them.

Narrator   Some of the disciples used to tease Thomas after that, because he had doubted what they had told him. I expect he probably said that they had no room to talk – they didn't believe it, either, when the women first told them. They had to see before they believed, just like Thomas. And of course, he would have been quite right, wouldn't he?

MICHAEL FORSTER

Reflecting on John 20:19-31

The terror and fear leading to doors slammed, locked and bolted, is dispelled by the greeting 'Peace be with you', spoken again and again into the heart of panic.

But the emphasis is on the wounds teaching us that only when we are vulnerable, and share the burden of our hurt and pain does Christ live amongst us.

Faith in the resurrection of Jesus Christ is never a triumphant crusade, but the opening up in love and acceptance of hearts that are hurt and afraid, so bringing peace, and removing sins.

PATRICK WOODHOUSE

Meditation of Cleopas

We met him, there on the Emmaus road,
   and still we didn't understand –
   can you believe that?
Despite the testimony of the women and the apostles,
   the empty tomb,
   the vision of angels,
   still we couldn't take it in!
I suppose we'd made up our minds that it was finished,
   come to terms with the fact that our hopes had been dashed,
   and we just couldn't bring ourselves to think any different
   for fear of yet more disappointment,
   yet more broken dreams.

Condemn us, if you like,
   but remember this:
   we'd seen him hanging there on the cross,
   contorted in agony,
   we'd watched in desolation as he drew his final breath,
   and we'd been there, tears streaming from our eyes,
   as they cut him down and laid him in the tomb.
You don't forget that in a hurry, I can tell you.
So when this stranger appeared out of the blue
   we thought nothing of it –
   why should we? –
   the possibility of him being Jesus was the last thing on our minds.
Even when he interpreted the Scriptures for us,
   explaining why the Messiah had to suffer and die,
   still we didn't suspect anything –
   even though our hearts burned within us with inexplicable joy.
But when we sat together at table,
   and he took bread and broke it,
   then even *we* couldn't miss it,
   the extraordinary, incredible truth –
   it *was* Jesus,
   Christ crucified and risen,
   there by our sides!
We'd thought the adventure was over,
   but it had only just begun.
We'd thought there was nothing left to us but memories,
   but suddenly the future beckoned, rich with promise.
The night had ended,
   a new day was dawning,
   life was beginning again –
   and we marvelled at the sheer wonder of his grace,
   for, of course, *we* didn't meet *him* that day,
   despite what we'd thought;
   he met us!

NICK FAWCETT

Meditation of Andrew

We still hadn't seen it, you know,
   not even after he stood there among us, alive and well.
We still imagined that his death had been a ghastly mistake,
   an unforeseen catastrophe,
   which somehow, miraculously, God had put right,
   salvaging triumph from disaster.

Perhaps some of us had an inkling –
    Peter, James, John –
    but not me, I'm afraid;
    I was convinced he'd snatched victory from the jaws of defeat.
Only, of course, I couldn't have been more wrong,
    as I learned that day when Jesus opened the Scriptures,
    and opened, along with them, our minds.
It took some doing, believe me,
    for I was a slow learner,
    but slowly it sunk in –
    the mind-boggling truth that it was all there:
    suffering,
    death,
    resurrection,
    each foretold,
    each purposed long before,
    each part of God's saving plan.
I was staggered,
    overwhelmed,
    for it was everywhere,
    the words leaping out at me from the pages –
    the prophets,
    the psalms,
    the law,
    all pointing to him –
    and I marvelled at the realisation that for so long,
    so many years,
    God had been building up to that one moment,
    that astonishing expression of his love –
    his Son on a cross!
The shadow of death had been the cradle of life,
    the descent into darkness the dawning of light!
Unseen,
    unnoticed,
    our God had been there,
    in the worst of moments as well as the best,
    enfolding all in his mighty hand.
And I glimpsed for a moment the awesome truth:
    that he'd brought us joy,
    not despite the sorrow
    but through it –
    the only way such joy could be.

NICK FAWCETT

Meditation of James

I thought I'd seen a ghost.
   no joking, I really did.
Oh, I shouldn't have done, I realise that –
   not after everything Jesus had said,
   and certainly not after the reports we'd heard
   from those who'd seen him –
   but we were still struggling to take it in,
   more troubled than happy at the news,
   afraid something spooky was going on.
And when suddenly he appeared, popping up out of nowhere,
   I was absolutely petrified.
Well, we all were, let's be honest,
   though none of us would admit it publicly.
We nearly jumped out of our skins when we saw him,
   and though we composed ourselves afterwards,
   tried to look as though we'd been expecting him all along,
   we couldn't fool Jesus.
He'd seen our faces,
   taken in our reactions at a glance,
   and in his eyes I caught both surprise and disappointment.
'Why are you frightened?' he asked us.
   'Why do you doubt so much?
   Look and see, is it me, or isn't it?'
Yet it wasn't as simple as that,
   not even after we'd seen his hands,
   touched his feet,
   felt his side.
We knew it was him, but we still couldn't quite believe it
   despite what our eyes were telling us.
It was too good to be true, I suppose.
We were afraid to trust ourselves,
   afraid it might all be wishful thinking, seeing what we wanted to see.
We didn't want to raise our hopes only to have them dashed again,
   so we simply stood and gawped.
Yet there could be no denying it,
   not when he ate with us,
   talked with us,
   laughed with us.
It was almost like it had been before,
   him and us together,
   and we knew then that somehow,
   in a way we couldn't quite understand,
   he'd come back to us!

Yet it wasn't quite how it used to be –
   there was something different,
   something about him we couldn't quite put our finger on.
It was Jesus all right,
   unquestionably the man we had loved and followed,
   and he was there by our sides, flesh and blood as we are.
But we realised that though he'd come back to us
   we would have to let him go,
   have to part again.
There could be no return to what had gone before,
   no turning the clock back and pretending nothing had happened.
It was the end of a chapter,
   a chapter we had wanted to go on for ever.
Yet it was also the beginning of another,
   the turning of a new page,
   with no knowing where it might lead.

NICK FAWCETT

Order of service

Evening Praise

Opening response

We meet together in the presence of the living God;
we have come to worship him.
With angels, and the whole company of heaven,
we have come to worship him.
With rivers and mountains, stars and planets,
and the whole of creation.
we have come to worship him.

We meet together in the presence of the risen Christ;
we have come to exalt him.
With the apostles and saints,
we have come to exalt him.
With the Church in every age
and Christians in every nation,
we have come to exalt him.

We meet together in the presence of the life-giving Spirit;
we have come to praise him.
With psalms, hymns and spiritual songs,
we have come to praise him.
With joy and gladness in our hearts,
we have come to praise him.

Hymn

Jesus is Lord (HON 270)

Confession and absolution

Living Lord,
raised from death, victorious over evil,
we confess to you our sins and wrongdoing.
By your mighty power,
raise us with you to eternal life.

Living Lord,
by your death and resurrection
you have destroyed the clutches of sin.
Forgive us when we yield to temptation,
and by your mighty power,
raise us with you to eternal life.

Living Lord,
by your death and resurrection
you have won for us freedom and new life.
Forgive us when we allow guilt and fear to dominate our lives,
and by your mighty power,
raise us with you to eternal life.

Living Lord,
by your death and resurrection
you have opened the way to eternal life.
Forgive us when we live without thinking
about our home in heaven,
and by your mighty power,
**raise us with you to eternal life
and set our minds on the things which are above,
where you reign for ever.
Amen.**

Almighty God,
who raised our Lord Jesus from the dead,
forgive all you have done wrong,
and raise you from the death of sin
to the life of righteousness,
through Jesus Christ our Lord.
Amen.

Alternative confession

Praise the Lord, O my soul,
and do not forget his benefits.
Lord, have mercy;
Lord, have mercy.

He forgives all my sins
and heals all my diseases.
Christ, have mercy;
Christ, have mercy.

He redeems my life from the pit,
and crowns me with love and compassion.
Lord, have mercy;
Lord, have mercy.

Song

We will lay our burden down (HON 538)

First reading

Isaiah 65:17-25 or Acts 10:34-43 or 1 Corinthians 15:1-11 or 1 Peter 2:19-25

Songs and hymns

Chosen from:

All heaven declares (HON 14)
Alleluia, Alleluia, give thanks to the risen Lord (HON 24)
Led like a lamb (HON 294)
Jesus, Jesus, holy and anointed one (HON 271)
We believe *(The Source 541)*
For this purpose *(The Source 111)*

Second reading

Matthew 27:62-28:10 or Luke 24:13-35 or John 20:19-29 or John 21:1-14

Songs and hymns

Chosen from:

In the tomb so cold *(The Source 234)*
He is Lord (HON 204)
He has risen *(The Source 155)*
Be still, for the presence of the Lord (HON 53)
Jesus, we celebrate your victory *(The Source 299)*

Time of shared reflections and insights

In the context of ecumenical worship it can be very stimulating to hear the fruits and insights of others' meditations. However, opening this to the congregation runs the risk that one or two folk with bees buzzing in their bonnets will seize the opportunity to hold forth at length. To try and avoid this, you could invite a couple of people in advance to share their thoughts for a minute or so, thus setting a pattern for others. Alternatively, you could either suggest specific subjects for contributions, or invite people to group in threes or fours to exchange their ideas, though this may be restricted or precluded both by the building and the numbers present. Whichever you prefer, it would be wise to indicate a clear time limit at the outset.

Hymn

I, the Lord of sea and sky (HON 235)

Time of open thanksgiving and intercession

Response after each section

Risen Master,
receive our prayer.

Alternatively use the Taizé song 'The Lord is my song' (HON 487) as a response.

Our Father . . .

Final prayer

For the power which rolled away the stone from the tomb,
Risen Master,
receive our praise.

For the love which called Mary by name in the garden,
Risen Master,
receive our praise.

For the joy which energised the disciples
to run and tell their friends the good news,
Risen Master,
receive our praise.

For the strength which helps us day by day to walk by faith,
Risen Master,
receive our praise.

For the hope which reassures us of eternal life,
starting now,
Risen Master,
receive our praise.
Transform us by your risen power,
restore us with your undying love,
and strengthen us by your Spirit ever with us,
through Jesus Christ our Lord.
Amen.

Closing hymn

Thine be the glory (HON 503)

Blessing

May God the Father,
who raised our Saviour Jesus Christ
from death,

give us freedom from sin and death,
to live by faith instead of fear.
Amen.

May Christ, the Son of God,
who was obedient even to death on a cross,
give us freedom and hope,
to live in the light of eternal life.
Amen.

STUART THOMAS

Ascension

Ascension Day

Jesus is glorified

A reading from the Gospel of Mark (16:15-20)

Jesus said to his disciples:

> Go out and proclaim the Gospel to the whole world. Whoever is baptised and believes in me, will be saved; whoever does not believe in me will be damned. Whoever believes in me will be recognised by what they are able to do through the power of my name. They shall chase out devils; speak in tongues; poison will not harm them and the sick will be healed.

When he had finished speaking to them, Jesus left his disciples and took his place in heaven at God's right hand.

The disciples did everything Jesus had commanded, and provided signs for all to see, so that they might know that the Lord was indeed with them.

This is the Gospel of the Lord
Praise to you, Lord Jesus Christ

KATIE THOMPSON

Introductory material

Although Ascension Day always falls on a Thursday, because it is exactly forty days from Easter Sunday (see Acts 1:3), it is an important, if generally unnoticed, festival. Ascension Day is one of the earliest of the Christian holy days to be celebrated, dating from the late fourth century, well before Christmas Day!

While theologians may debate what actually happened at the Ascension, the meaning is clear; it marks the final appearance of the risen Jesus to his friends, and his return to his Father. That is what we celebrate. For centuries – up until 1970 – this was symbolised by the public extinguishing and removal of the Easter (Paschal) candle from the Church. While this is no longer done in church, it does suggest an idea for the home. If the Easter candle suggestion was followed, then the candles can be moved onto or near the table for the evening meal. After a suitable grace and a word of explanation, the candle(s) are extinguished – by cutting the flame off with scissors if they are made of paper or card, or blowing out a candle lit especially for the occasion.

TONY CASTLE

Prayers

Approach

Lord Jesus Christ,
  we greet you this day as King of kings and Lord of lords –
    we proclaim your greatness,
    we acknowledge your authority,
    we celebrate your exaltation,
    we rejoice in your triumph.

Living Lord,
  open our eyes to the meaning of this day –
    broaden our vision,
    enlarge our understanding,
    widen our perspectives,
    deepen our faith.

  Accept us now as your disciples,
    inspire us through your Holy Spirit,
    lead us in your service,
    equip us for all you would have us do,
    and so may we live to your glory
    and bring your kingdom nearer.
  In your name we pray.
  Amen.   NICK FAWCETT

Praise and confession

Lord Jesus Christ,
  risen and ascended,
    the Word made flesh,
    before all, in all, and beyond all,
    for the lives you have given us,
    and the gift of life eternal,
    we praise you.

  For all the beauty,
    the complexity,
    the variety,
    and the wonder of life that surrounds us,
    we praise you.

  For all the opportunities,
    the challenges,
    the experiences,
    and the achievements life offers us,
    we praise you.

For all the things we can think and do,
  see and touch,
  hear and feel,
  smell and taste,
  we praise you.

Lord Jesus Christ,
  Lamb of the world,
    suffering servant,
    heavenly King,
    for the love that surrounds us each day,
    through family and friends,
    the fellowship of the Church
    and the inner presence of your Holy Spirit.
    we praise you.

  For all the care,
    the support,
    the understanding,
    and the friendship we enjoy,
    we praise you.

Lord Jesus Christ,
  Lord of lords,
    Prince of Peace,
    King of kings,
    for your greatness that fills the universe,
    your power and majesty,
    holiness and righteousness,
    justice and mercy.
    we praise you.

  For the way you have brought our world into existence,
    the way you have worked through history,
    the way you have shared our humanity,
    and the way you continue to build your kingdom,
    we praise you.

Lord Jesus Christ,
  Lord of all,
    forgive us that we have not lived our lives to the full –
    we have taken its wonder for granted,
    we have failed to appreciate its potential,
    and we have lost sight of the abundant, eternal life you offer.
  For offering us life despite all that,
    we praise you.

Forgive us that we have not responded fully
　　to the love shown to us –
　　we have allowed it to be poisoned
　　through discord and division,
　　we have starved it of nourishment
　　through failing to offer our love in return,
　　and we have closed our hearts to all you would offer us.
For loving us despite all that,
　　we praise you.

Forgive us that we have not begun to grasp your lordship –
　　we have not kept our sense of awe and wonder before you,
　　we have let our vision become stilted,
　　and we have offered worship that is half-hearted,
　　reflecting our weakness rather than your glory.
For calling us despite all that,
　　we praise you.

Lord Jesus Christ, our Lord and Saviour,
　　open our hearts as we worship you to the fullness of life,
　　　　the fullness of your love,
　　　　and a fuller understanding of your greatness,
　　　　and so may we truly confess you
　　　　as King of kings and Lord of lords.
For all you are, all you have done,
　　and all you have yet to do,
　　we praise you,
　　this day, and for evermore.
Amen.   NICK FAWCETT

Intercession

Jesus has ascended into heaven. With his ministry complete, and death conquered, Jesus takes his place at the right hand of God. No longer tied by time and place he reigns in glory.

Trusting in Christ's victory over all evil,
let us pray to the Father for the world and the Church.

We pray for all who witness to Christ
in spite of danger and persecution;
all who work to bring others to know and love you;
that in your strength they may be blessed,
encouraged and bear much fruit.

Silence for prayer

King of glory:
reign in our hearts.

We pray for those who have never received
the good news of your saving love;
for those areas where violence and terrorism
make normal life impossible;
that the Spirit of Jesus, the Prince of Peace,
may filter through to increase love
and understanding, respect and goodwill.

Silence for prayer

King of glory:
reign in our hearts.

We pray for our families
and those with whom we live and work;
for particular needs known to us personally;
that in everything we do,
and every minute we live,
your name may be glorified and your will be done.

Silence for prayer

King of glory:
reign in our hearts.

We pray for the sick and the dying;
that their trust in you may deepen
until their fears are calmed
and they can look forward with real hope
to meeting their Saviour face to face.

Silence for prayer

King of glory:
reign in our hearts.

We pray for those who have died;
may they wake to the joy of eternal life with you.
We offer you thanks and praise
for your constant love and kindness,
and especially for the joy of your salvation.

Silence for prayer

Merciful Father,
accept these prayers
for the sake of your Son,
our Saviour Jesus Christ, Amen.

SUSAN SAYERS

Short prayers

Living God,
   today is Ascension Day,
   the day we remember how Jesus departed
   into heaven,
   a day which reminds us that one day
   he will return in glory.
We come then to reflect on what that means –
   to recall that mysterious event so long ago,
   to look forward to that cataclysmic event
   some time in the future,
   and to ask what this says to each of us,
   here and now.
Open our ears.
Open our minds.
Open our hearts.
And so may all we see and hear
   and think and feel today
   give us a deeper insight into the wonder
   of all you have done for us in Christ,
   and a greater sense of all you have yet to do.
Amen.

NICK FAWCETT

Baby of Bethlehem, born in a stable,
   we worship you.
Child of Nazareth, full of grace and truth,
   we acknowledge you.
Man of Galilee, teacher, preacher, healer, redeemer,
   we praise you.
Son of David,
   coming in humility to claim your kingdom,
   we greet you.
Suffering servant, bruised, beaten, broken,
   we salute you.
Lord of the empty tomb, risen and triumphant,
   we honour you.
King of kings, exalted by the side of the Father,
   we adore you.
Jesus Christ, our Lord and Saviour,
   receive the homage we offer,
   to the glory of your name.
Amen.

NICK FAWCETT

All-age-talk material

Aim: To help the children understand why Jesus had to go away.

Show the children what looks like a blank sheet of paper, but is in fact invisible writing. (You can use lemon juice for this or an invisible writing pen, widely available from toy shops.) Explain that there is a hidden message on the paper, but they won't be able to receive the message unless something happens first.

Now make the message visible, either by using the other part of the invisible writing pen, or by warming the sheet of paper with a hair drier if it is written in lemon juice. The word that emerges is POWER.

Go over the resurrection appearances and how the disciples saw Jesus going away from them so that he was no longer visible to them. We couldn't receive our message until something happened to the paper. The disciples couldn't receive God's power – the power of his Spirit – unless Jesus left them in that particular time and place. Now he would be available to every person in every country in every age, including us!

Let them experiment with writing secret messages and making them visible again. Then give them a fresh sheet of paper on which they write in invisible ink: JESUS IS HERE. This is one for their family to discover at home.

SUSAN SAYERS

Jesus says goodbye to his friends.
One day he will come back.

1. Shut your eyes and make the world disappear.
2. Open your eyes – Hello world!

Did it go away when you shut your eyes?

We can't see Jesus but he is always there.

CUT OUT

CUT-OUT

Colour background and figures; cut out and stick to picture.

SUSAN SAYERS

JESUS WILL COME AGAIN IN GLORY.

Acts 1:11

H	A	E	G	J	O	R	D	P	J
Z	I	R	N	I	S	T	I	E	F
B	D	S	E	N	P	W	S	A	W
S	E	C	V	T	S	U	C	H	T
D	S	Y	A	O	S	L	I	A	B
Q	S	K	E	Q	A	N	P	U	Q
H	E	P	H	G	E	M	L	I	H
N	L	X	I	K	D	E	E	C	W
A	B	B	A	N	R	M	S	P	N
S	J	T	O	D	V	L	Y	O	C

AS JESUS BLESSED HIS DISCIPLES HE WAS TAKEN UP INTO HEAVEN

Find this in the wordsearch.

SUSAN SAYERS

The Ascension of Christ

Daniel 7:9-14; Ephesians 1:15-end; Luke 24:45-end

It is not widely known that children are still entitled to take time off from school on Ascension Day in order to go to church. If you decide to have a special children's service, make out a form for the children to take into school and use the occasion to witness through courtesy and goodwill.

Keep the service simple and involve the children in the planning, reading, singing and decorating.

For the Sunday after Ascension, start by showing the children a bright cut-out sun, then cover it from sight with a cut-out cloud. Is the sun still there? Show that it is. We do not always see it because it is sometimes hidden from view, but we know it is always there. How?

Talk about life and growth and light and warmth. If we shut ourselves in where the sun cannot reach us we couldn't survive. Can we see Jesus? No. Then what do we mean when we say he is alive? Where is he?

Read them an account of the Ascension as told in Acts. His friends had seen him a lot after he had come back to life on the first Easter Day, and now, like the sun behind a cloud, he is hidden from sight for a time. (Show a bright card with JESUS written on it, and put the cloud in front.) But he is just as much alive as before. As our King he reigns over everything – people, animals, the sun, the stars, the universe!

Ask some children to draw and colour flowers and trees, some animals and people, some stars and planets, mountains, seas and weather. Then mount all their work on a big collage banner, with OUR GOD REIGNS written over the top. This can be carried into the church in procession.

SUSAN SAYERS

Reflective material
(sketches, meditations and poems)

Meditation of James

We thought we'd lost him.
After everything we'd been through
    we thought we'd lost him.
And it was dreadful.
It had been terrible enough the first time –
    watching helplessly from the shadows as he was crucified,
    as he was cut down from the cross,
    as they laid him in that tomb.
We'd believed it was all over –
    the end of a wonderful adventure –
    and we were devastated,
    inconsolable.
Only then he came back.
Astonishingly,
    incredibly,
    he came back!

And we were together once more,
   almost like in the old days,
   life suddenly magical again,
   even more than it had been before.
Until he left us –
   by our sides one minute,
   gone the next!
We couldn't work it out at all,
   just stood there,
   gazing up at the clouds,
   tears streaming down our faces.
He'd left us to face the world alone,
   abandoned us when we needed him most.
Why?
How could he do it?
That's what we kept on asking.
But then a strange feeling came over us.
I can't explain it;
   it was almost like a voice from heaven.
And when we looked at each other again
   we somehow knew he hadn't gone,
   not really.
Even though we wouldn't see him again,
   even though we wouldn't be able to talk with him as we used to,
   we knew he was there with us;
   there in Jerusalem,
   there in Galilee,
   there in Judea and Samaria,
   there in all the world, wherever we might choose to go.
And we knew he would be with us every moment,
   every day,
   constantly by our side,
   even in death itself,
   waiting to receive us and welcome us home.
We thought we'd lost him,
   and for a moment it was dreadful.
But the fact was we had to lose him
   before we could really find him.

NICK FAWCETT

Pentecost

Pentecost Sunday

The gift of the Spirit

A reading from the Acts of the Apostles (2:1-11)

The disciples had gathered together in Jerusalem to celebrate the Feast of Pentecost and to wait for the Holy Spirit that Jesus had promised to send.

   One day, as they were praying together, the room was suddenly filled with the sound of a powerful wind which roared through the house. Then, what looked like small tongues of fire appeared and spread out to touch each one of them. So it was that they were filled with the Holy Spirit.

   At once, in their excitement, they rushed outside to tell everyone what had happened to them. As they began to speak, they were amazed to find that everyone listening to their words could understand them! People from different regions and countries were astounded to hear these men preaching to them in their own native languages.

This is the Word of the Lord
Thanks be to God   KATIE THOMPSON

A Whitsun wonder (Acts 2:1-41)

Jesus had promised his disciples that his death would not be the end of him. He would return in his Spirit, to be with them in a far more intimate way than he could have been before. Luke describes the young Church's first charismatic understanding of this, and its first impact.

Fifty days after Jesus was raised from the dead,
his friends had gathered together.
Suddenly,
as if a storm of wind and fire had burst upon them,
they were all filled with the Holy Spirit of Jesus.
All of them began to talk in a new way,
as God gave them the power to speak out boldly.

Jewish people from all over the world
had come to Jerusalem for Whitsun,
from north, south, east and west,
even from as far away as Rome.
They thought these friends of Jesus were drunk,
they acted so strangely.

Peter told them, 'No, we're not drunk;
it's only nine o'clock in the morning!
What has happened to us is what the Bible promised,
that God's Spirit would come upon everyone.'
Then he told them the good news about Jesus.
Three thousand asked to be baptised.

H. J. RICHARDS

A reading from the Gospel of John (15:26-27, 16:12-15)

Jesus said:

> I will send the Spirit of truth from the Father to be my witness, just as you who have been with me from the beginning will also bear witness to me. There is still much to tell you, but for now you have heard enough. The Spirit will guide you to the truth, and help you to understand all that is yet to come. Through him I shall be glorified, just as the Father is glorified, since all that is mine comes from him.

This is the Gospel of the Lord
Praise to you, Lord Jesus Christ

KATIE THOMPSON

Introductory material

The giving of love

Introductory thoughts

Many families now have home computers. If you want to get the most out of such an electronic device you have to learn basic computer language. You need to understand the symbols and icons used, how to give instructions to the computer and understand what it says.

The same thing goes for learning to drive. If you want to be a competent driver and pass your driving test you must know and understand the road signs. The 'language' of the road consists not just in road signs shown in the Highway Code but also in the experience of how other people drive.

So many 'languages' exist in addition to the obvious spoken word. Another example, from day-to-day relationships between people, is what we call 'body language' – the messages people convey to one another by the way they stand, sit and walk, or what they do. This is particularly true in the family:

> 'Don't you look at me like that!' the parent says to the sullen child.

> 'Stop lounging around and get your bedroom tidied up,' says an exasperated mother to her teenage daughter.

> 'This is for you,' the young child says, handing her mother a dandelion.

In the words of the catchphrase, 'It's not what you do, it's the way that you do it'.

Pride brings disunity

There's a rather neglected little story in the first book of the Bible – Genesis 11:1-9. It goes like this:

> At that time, some while after Noah's rescue through the ark, there was only one language spoken by all the people on earth. Then they had a very proud idea: 'Let's make a name for ourselves by building a town and a tower reaching right up into the heavens.' God, however, was not pleased with their idea and while they were busy building, he confused everything and everyone by giving them many different languages. They stopped building because they could no longer communicate with one another.

From that moment on, the Bible tells us, every tribe and people had their own language. As there was now no single language, God himself used signs and symbols to communicate with the human race. And throughout history that is how God has made himself known – except to a few very special people.

God 'speaks' through signs

Of the signs God has used, fire immediately springs to mind but also the wind. There's the beautiful story of Elijah in 1 Kings 19:9-14. The prophet experiences the presence of God not in a strong wind, nor in the earthquake, nor in lightning but in a gentle breeze!

In our lives today God makes his loving presence and his actions known through the words of Scripture and the sign-language of the sacraments. If we want to understand what God is saying to us we must learn what the 'language' means and how to use it.

Each feast has its symbols

Each of the Church's feasts has its symbols and signs. Christmas has the baby, the supreme sign of God's love. Epiphany has the Magi with their gifts, showing that God's love is not just for one group of people but for everyone. Easter has the special candle and the waters of baptism.

Pentecost, described in Acts 2:1-4, is especially rich in God's sign language:

> When Pentecost day came round, they had all met in one room, when suddenly they heard what sounded like a powerful wind from heaven, the noise of which filled the entire house in which they were sitting; and something appeared to them that seemed like tongues of fire; these separated and came to rest on the head of each of them. They were all filled with the Holy Spirit, and began to speak foreign languages as the Spirit gave them the gift of speech.

And, full of energy and courage, the apostles rushed out into the crowded streets to speak about Jesus as Lord and Saviour. All the foreigners from every corner of the Roman Empire, gathered in Jerusalem for the feast of Pentecost, were amazed to find that they could understand what was said. It was the tower of Babel story in reverse! The Spirit brought unity as the Church began to be built.

The special message of Pentecost

The signs of Pentecost are wind and fire:

> *Wind:* Now that we have the everyday use of electricity, we forget how the wind was once used as a source of energy. Ships were propelled by wind and windmills ground grain and drew up water; so the blowing of the wind was a sign of the arrival of energy and power.

> *Fire:* In our more luxurious lives we fail to realise how important fire was in simpler, more rudimentary times. It was essential for heating, cooking and lighting in the home. It was a symbol of warmth, purification and illumination. Fire also arouses widely different emotions – a cosy glow when seated round an open fire in the winter and terrifying fear when a building catches fire.

At Pentecost the Holy Spirit came as a source of great energy and power and in that power the apostles immediately went out to proclaim Christ. Pentecost, then, is the birthday of the Church and the time when we are all reminded of our Christian call to be missionaries. The Apostles were transformed by the coming of the Spirit. The fire symbolised how the Spirit warmed their hearts and cleansed their minds. Suddenly they understood who their friend Jesus really was and what they must do – and out they went to do it.

The Jewish festival of Pentecost

Long before the time of Jesus, the Jewish people had celebrated the feast of Pentecost, as they still do today. It is a celebration of the first picking from the harvest fields – rather like the harvest festival we have later in the year. It is also closely linked to the Passover. After Passover they counted fifty days and on the fiftieth celebrated Pentecost (the word means 'fiftieth' in Greek). It was on that day that the Jewish people celebrated the Covenant (or agreement) that God had made with Moses, their leader. It was the spirit of the Covenant, their loyalty to God, that united them.

The Christian Church actually begins with the 'passover' of Christ at Easter. But only with the coming of the Holy Spirit (while the Apostles, as good Jews, were celebrating the Jewish feast) does it really come alive. Pentecost is the completion or fulfilment of Easter. It is always thought of as the birthday of the Church.

'Giving of Love'

Our first chapter, 'The Coming of Love', spoke of the great revelation, through Jesus, that God is love. At Christmas we celebrate that wonderful event when God came into our world as one of us. Our second chapter was about the Epiphany and was entitled 'The Showing of Love' because the word Epiphany means 'showing'. The chapter covering Lent and Holy Week was called 'The Offering of Love' because Jesus' love for us prompted him to make the offering of himself on our behalf to the Father. Because the Father accepted his offering, Easter is a time of great triumph. So that chapter was called 'The Triumph of Love'.

This present chapter is entitled 'The Giving of Love' because true love shows itself in its impulse to give, and perfect love gives perfectly and completely.

The Holy Spirit is understood to be the spirit of love between the Father and the Son in the intimate love of the mysterious Holy Trinity. It was the giving of that same spirit of love that instantly transformed fearful men into energetic preachers and missionaries. It was the fire of love given to their hearts that warmed them and burned out of their minds their misunderstandings about Jesus and his message.

Pentecost – the neglected festival

As the fulfilment of Easter and the birthday of the Church, this day is one of the most important in the year. It is certainly more important than Christmas, yet it is rather neglected. This might be because of the time of the year – warmer weather and holidays in the air; it might be because the symbols of the feast are not so easy to understand; it could be because the secular bank holiday weekend of Whitsun gets confused with the Christian Whit Sunday, or it may be because its importance has never properly been understood and no tradition has been built up. For whatever reason, Pentecost tends to get overlooked. Our parish churches could do more to mark the Church's birthday and to encourage the celebration of the occasion in the home.

Practical suggestions

Which name, Whitsun or Pentecost?

A worthwhile little project to set the children as part of their preparation for Pentecost is to ask them to find out – from school or their local priest, from the library or books around the home – what is the meaning of the two names given to this time in the Church's year. It is amazing how few Catholics know what either word means or how to use it.

First, it has to be said that both titles do apply to the self-same day. As we said above, the name 'Pentecost' comes from the Jewish tradition and means 'fiftieth day' since the Passover. The word 'Whitsun' is a shortening of 'Whit Sunday' and is totally of Christian origin. In the early Church the period from Easter to Pentecost, during which Easter continued to be celebrated, was the time when people who had prepared throughout Lent to be received into the Christian community were baptised.

In our part of the world, Northern Europe, it became more common and popular to have the baptisms at or near Pentecost day. (This may have been because of the climate – the candidates for baptism had to strip off!) In England the feast became known as 'White Sunday'. This was because of the white clothes worn after their baptising by the newly received converts. Naturally in time this was broken down to 'Whit Sunday' and 'Whitsun'.

Children and symbols

Pentecost is a perfect time to introduce or reintroduce the children to signs and symbols. Here are some symbols that are associated with the festival. Get the children to draw and colour them.

The Descending Dove. This symbol is associated with the times the Holy Spirit appeared during our Lord's life, for example at his baptism (Matthew 3:16).

Tongues of Fire. Seven are drawn to symbolise the seven gifts of the Holy Spirit that are a result of his coming (Acts 2:1-4).

Windmill. The wind is not easy to illustrate but the children might like to draw a windmill, or instead make this paper windmill. It could be decorated with the two symbols from above.

Love is

As Pentecost is the time when we recall the giving of the Spirit of Love to the Church, the table prayer for the principal meal can be based on the theme of love in the family. You have probably seen cartoon pictures and cards captioned, 'Love is . . .' Examples are:

'Love is sharing problems with each other',
with a picture of Daddy and Mummy sitting talking.

'Love is giving the children swimming lessons',
with a drawing of Daddy holding a child up in the water at the local pool, while another child sits on the edge.

It might be possible to acquire two or three suitable samples. Show them to the family in the week before Whitsun and suggest that they draw a picture for each member of the family on this theme of love. For example, one of the children might draw Mum cuddling a child with the caption, 'Love is giving us a cuddle when we don't feel very well'. Or for Dad there might be a picture of a car with two feet sticking out from underneath, with the words, 'Love is making the car safe for us all'. Mum and Dad could enter into the fun and draw a suitable picture (matchstick people are good enough!) for each of the family. The cartoons are hidden until the morning of Pentecost day, and then placed, folded, at each person's place for breakfast. The grace might be something like:

Today we recall that wonderful moment
when the Holy Spirit, the Spirit of Love,
came upon the apostles.
They were filled with energy and fired by love.

May that same Spirit fill us with energy
in God's service and love for one another.

Then everyone opens up their pictures and enjoys a laugh when the secrets are revealed! The cartoons might be used to decorate the kitchen for the following week and be a talking point for neighbours and friends who call.

Children love candles and especially blowing them out. Later in the day at the principal meal – if candles are available – everyone can have one by their place at table. At grace time Mum or Dad says something along these lines:

At birthday parties there's usually a birthday cake with candles. Today is the birthday of the Church. When we were baptised we became God's people, members of his Church. We are the Church and the candles in front of us are like the ones we were each given when we were baptised. Today it is a birthday candle. (*The candles can now be lit.*) Your candle flames are like the tongues of fire which were seen over the heads of the Apostles on the first Pentecost day. Let us be quiet, just for a moment, and ask the Holy Spirit to come and fill our hearts with the fire of his love. (*Short pause.*) Now let's blow out our candles.

When the Apostles had received the Holy Spirit they rushed out to tell everyone about Jesus. We are missionaries, too, and in our own little way we must try and make God's love known. So now we say, 'Thank you, God, for the love we share in this home and family. Thank you, too, for the food which comes from your loving hand.' Amen.

If Mum has led the above, Dad might like to finish off with a reading of the following passage. If Dad led the table prayer, perhaps the eldest child could read it. (It's not appropriate for Mum to read it out!) It needs to be introduced with a remark like, 'A 14-year-old girl was asked at school to write about a missionary she knew, and this is what she wrote':

A missionary I know

When I was asked to write about a missionary I knew, a few people crossed my mind, such as Mother Teresa. Then I stopped and thought, 'I can't write about one of these great people because I don't really know them. It's true I've heard their names and read and been told about them, but I don't know what they're like.'

The person I think is a missionary, and a good one, is my mother. This may sound peculiar but surely you don't have to be ordained to be a missionary. My mum's mission is to be a housewife and a mother to me and my family. My mum has never been selfish and put herself first before her family. I have never been starved or been without her endless love. Just like the famous missionaries, my mother has needed a lot of courage. She could easily have gone off shopping or to a party with friends and left me, but she didn't. She made the supreme sacrifice of thinking about me before herself. I am very lucky to have a missionary mother.

If there are teenage children in the family an interesting exchange of ideas might develop over the meal after that school essay!   Tony Castle

Prayers

Praise

Mighty God,
    we remember this day, with awe and wonder,
        the events of that day of Pentecost long ago
        which so transformed the lives of the apostles.
    Move in us, we pray.

    We remember how in the space of a few moments
        their experience was revolutionised –
        their expectations turned upside down,
        their attitudes changed for ever;
        one moment consumed by fear,
        the next radiating confidence;
        one moment uncertain of the future,
        the next sure of their calling;
        one moment wrestling with doubt,
        the next full of faith;
        one moment hiding behind locked doors,
        the next preaching boldly to the crowds.
    Move in us, we pray.

Mighty God,
    you came through your Spirit
        and life was never the same again.
    Come to us, breathing new fire into our hearts,
        new energy into our lives,
        new life into our souls.
    Transform our fear, anxiety and doubt,
        filling us with confidence and faith.
    Move in us, we pray.

    Open our minds to new horizons, new experiences
        and a new way of looking at life,
        and so may we live by the Spirit,
        bearing rich fruit to your glory.
    Move in us, we pray,
        through Jesus Christ our Lord.
    Amen.

NICK FAWCETT

Confession

Holy Spirit,
    we remember today how, on the day of your coming,
        there were many who mocked,
        pouring scorn on the disciples' experience,
        claiming they had drunk too much wine,
        or that they were simply out of their minds.
    You come still today:
        forgive us for being closed to your life-giving presence.

We remember how you re-ignited their faith
    and empowered them for service,
    so that they flung open the locked doors
    behind which they had been hiding,
    and went out among the crowds,
    boldly witnessing to their faith
    and declaring their allegiance to Christ.
    You come still today:
        forgive us for being closed to your life-giving presence.

We remember how you worked in the life of the early Church,
    prompting,
    guiding,
    cleansing,
    invigorating,
    opening doors to the Gospel,
    and raising up men and women ready to make it known
    through word and deed.
    You come still today:
        forgive us for being closed to your life-giving presence.

We remember how you have worked in subsequent generations,
    equipping,
    enabling,
    teaching,
    inspiring,
    breathing new life into age-old structures,
    bringing fresh insights into established tradition,
    and firing your people to imaginative ventures
    built on the foundations of the past.
    You come still today:
        forgive us for being closed to your life-giving presence.

We remember how you took ordinary, uneducated people,
    and used them in the most extraordinary of ways;
    how you took those who had miserably failed you,
    and gave them courage to endure suffering and death
    for the sake of faith.

We rejoice that you are able to use ordinary people
 like us here and now,
  provided we are ready to see beyond our own limited horizons,
  and to overcome our fears, doubts and prejudices.
 You come still today:
  forgive us for being closed to your life-giving presence.

Holy Spirit,
 you are always moving,
  daily seeking to lead us into truth,
  constantly striving to break through the walls we erect against you.
 You want to deepen our faith,
  enrich our experience,
  strengthen our commitment,
  and enlarge our vision,
  yet, time and again, we allow a lack of expectation
  to frustrate your purpose.
 You come still today:
  forgive us for being closed to your life-giving presence.

Hear this and all our prayers through Jesus Christ our Lord.
Amen. NICK FAWCETT

Petition

Mighty God,
 come to us through your Holy Spirit,
  filling us with peace.
 Give us a love for all and a desire to serve,
  humility of mind and gentleness of soul.
 Nurture your grace in our hearts.

Mighty God,
 come to us through your Holy Spirit,
  setting us on fire with love for you.
 Fill us with a burning desire to work for your kingdom,
  and cleanse us of all that is impure
  and unworthy in our lives.
 Kindle a flame of faith in our hearts.

Mighty God,
 come to us through your Holy Spirit,
  breathing new life into our souls.
 Fill us with energy and enthusiasm in the service of Christ,
  and sweep away all in our lives
  that keeps us from living as your people.
 Instil a sense of expectation in our hearts.

Mighty God,
   forgive us that we so easily limit the Spirit,
     receiving its blessing for ourselves
     but failing to pass it on to others.
   Forgive us that we so readily quench the Spirit,
     resisting that which challenges and disturbs.
   Forgive us that we are so often closed
     to the movement of your Spirit,
     shutting it out by the narrowness of our vision.
   Come as the dove, the fire, and the wind,
     opening our lives to the peace, the power
     and the inspiration you would give us.
   Open our lives and touch our hearts,
     through Jesus Christ our Lord.
   Amen.
                                                    Nick Fawcett

Intercession

The Holy Spirit is poured out on the disciples like a rush of wind and with tongues of fire. Ever since, God's Holy Spirit has enriched and empowered all who open their hearts and minds to receive it.

In wonder let us come before the almighty
and everlasting God, to pray in the Spirit of Christ.

We pray for every Christian;
that each may be more receptive to the Holy Spirit,
until each worshipping community is charged
with the vitality and love of the living Christ.

Silence for prayer

Loving Father:
let your Spirit live in us now.

We pray for the world and its leaders;
for its mistakes and tragedies,
misunderstandings and confusion;
may your active Spirit bring
order, serenity and hope.

Silence for prayer

Loving Father:
let your Spirit live in us now.

We pray for a deepening of our own faith,
more understanding of your will,
a clearer awareness of others' needs
and a greater desire to give our lives away.

Silence for prayer

Loving Father:
let your Spirit live in us now.

We pray for those whose lives are darkened by guilt,
resentment or despair;
for those who live violent and cruel lives,
and for all who are ill, injured or abused.

Silence for prayer

Loving Father:
let your Spirit live in us now.

We pray for those who have died in the faith of Christ,
especially . . .

may they enjoy life with you for ever.

Silence for prayer

Father, in grateful thanks for all
your blessings in our lives,
we relinquish our will to yours.

Silence for prayer

Merciful Father,
accept these prayers
for the sake of your Son,
our Saviour Jesus Christ, Amen.

SUSAN SAYERS

Short prayers

Gracious God,
    we thank you for those extraordinary moments
    we occasionally experience
    which change our lives,
       giving us joy and fulfilment we never imagined possible.
We thank you especially for the great gift of your Holy Spirit –
    an experience which transformed the lives of the apostles,
    which has changed the lives of countless believers across the centuries,
    and which has power to reshape our lives here and now.
Open our hearts, our minds and our souls to your living presence
    so that we shall know your life-changing power for ourselves.
Amen.

NICK FAWCETT

Spirit of God,
    refining like fire,
    free as the wind,
    gentle as a dove,
    come among us.
Cleanse our hearts,
    liberate our souls,
    bring peace to our minds,
    and send us out with power
    to proclaim the kingdom of God,
    in the name of the living Christ.
Amen.

NICK FAWCETT

God of all,
sometimes in the earthquake,
sometimes in the storm;
sometimes in the still, small sound
we hear your voice,
proclaiming, whispering,
softly urging your will.

Attune our ears to hear
and our hearts to listen.
Give us discernment
and a new understanding.
Then incline our wish and will,
to joyfully and obediently
do your bidding
when we leave this place.
Amen.

SUSAN HARDWICK

All-age-talk material

Mighty winds

This Prayer Focus is to help the children to explore the mystery of a force which cannot be seen and yet which has remarkable effects.

Collect together all the words you can which describe types of wind or the effects of the wind: draught, current, icy blast, sirocco, monsoon, trade wind, zephyr, sea breeze, gale, gust, squall, hurricane, whirlwind, cyclone, tornado, blizzard, cooling, refreshing, chilling, biting.

Collect together words which describe the sounds of the wind: whisper, moan, howl, screech, scream, whistle, sing, hum, sigh.

Collect together words which describe the effects of the wind which we can see: flap, windswept, blow, swirl, turn, hurl.

Discuss ways in which the wind is productive: drying washing, sailing ships, kites, windmills, wind power.

Discuss ways in which the wind is destructive.

Reflect with the children on the mystery of the wind which cannot be seen and yet which has remarkable effect.

Can they think of other things which can only be seen by its results?

Ending Prayer

We give thanks for the mystery of the wind;
for the movement of the clouds in the skies;
for the refreshment of gentle breezes on
    hot sunny days;
for the power and strength of the wind.
Help us to be more aware of things which
    we cannot see but which change our lives.
Amen.

JILL FULLER

The Holy Spirit gives life. Colour the flames to bring this picture to life!

I will pour out my Spirit. (Joel 2:28)

The Holy Spirit helps us to understand things more clearly. So use the key below to colour this picture and discover a message.

1=Blue   3=Red   5=Green

2=Brown   4=Pink   6=Light Brown or Yellow

WORDSEARCH

Find the following words in the grid below: COMMUNICATE, WAITING, FIRE, WIND, NEW LIFE, SPIRIT, POWER, PROMISE, GOOD NEWS, JESUS, BROKEN BARRIERS.

```
G O O D N E D S P I R C
N M B A R R I E R S O O
I M R O M I S E P U K M
T U O M M U N I C S E M
I N K G O O R N E E N U
A I E W I I N D O J E N
W I N D T X G O O D N I
N C W E P R O M I D E C
E W S N W L I F E N W A
E R B A R R I E D E S T
W I L N D P R O M I S E
L I F F E F I R E W O P
```

MICHAEL FORSTER

Power for living

Aim

To bring home the fact that the Holy Spirit is the source of power for Christian faith and discipleship.

Preparation

On separate pieces of card, write or print the following in large, bold characters:

gas	light
diesel	engine
steam	locomotive
hydroelectric	dam
horse	power
solar	panel
wave	barrage
petrol	pump
wind	mill
nuclear	reactor
oil	well
coal	mine

Arrange those in the first column down the left-hand side of a display board, and place the words in the second column randomly on the right-hand side, taking care not to form a matching pair.

Talk

Ask the congregation what all the words in the left column on the display have in common (they are all forms of power). Invite suggestions as to which of the words on the right match those on the left (note, that 'engine' and 'locomotive' fit with both 'diesel' and 'steam'). As each answer is given insert this next to its matching pair (as above).

These are just some of the forms of power we depend upon in our daily lives, and if any were to run out we would soon notice the difference. So great is our demand for power that one of the great quests of our modern age is to discover an unlimited source of renewable energy.

But for us as Christians there is one source of power more important than all of these, and that is the power first promised by Jesus to his disciples at the end of his earthly ministry:

See, I am sending upon you what my Father promised; so stay here in the city until you have been clothed with power from on high. *(Luke 24:49)*

This was the power of the Holy Spirit which was to come suddenly and unexpectedly upon the Apostles on the day of Pentecost, transforming them from uncertain and fearful believers to fearless ambassadors for Christ. And it is that same power which is promised to us and each and every believer. In the words of the Apostle Paul:

> I pray that, according to the riches of his glory, he may grant that you may be strengthened in your inner being with power through his Spirit. *(Ephesians 3:16)*

Whoever we are, however weak or powerless we may feel, God, through his Holy Spirit, is able to take us and use us in ways beyond any we can ever imagine. That is the promise Pentecost reminds us of year by year: God's gift of power for living!

NICK FAWCETT

Many people from
different countries could hear
the disciples preaching in their
own languages!

**Find these places hidden in the
wordsearch puzzle! Circle them**

JUDEA   MESOPOTAMIA   CAPPADOCIA   ASIA
PONTUS   EGYPT   LIBYA   PHRYGIA   ROME

B	C	A	P	P	A	D	O	C	I	A
J	A	M	C	O	P	R	S	E	B	I
U	L	A	I	G	Y	R	H	P	F	I
D	P	M	K	C	A	P	S	O	E	P
A	I	M	A	T	O	P	O	S	E	M
E	B	N	S	P	R	O	S	E	M	A
D	E	P	I	Y	M	B	M	I	Y	A
U	S	J	A	G	C	O	S	B	B	Y
J	P	R	L	E	R	R	I	E	S	E
P	O	N	T	U	S	L	L	Y	M	G

KATIE THOMPSON

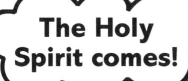

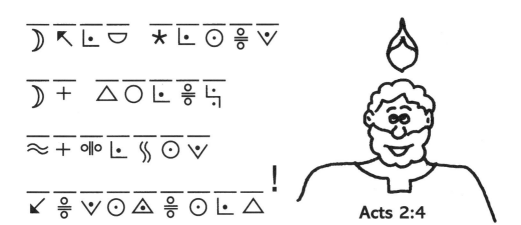

KATIE THOMPSON

Even people
from different countries
could understand the
disciples' words

How many people from each country can you see?
Circle the number

Everything the Spirit tells us comes from

Use the picture code to fill in the letters and find the answer

CODE

$*$ = J

◇ = S

⊕ = U

SS = E

$*$	SS	◇	⊕	◇

KATIE THOMPSON

I will pour out my Spirit on all my people

If someone comes to you hoping to find God's love, would they find you full or half full or empty?

If you want to be filled with God's Spirit, this is what to do...

God has known it, by asking for it to be...

R = red
Y = yellow
O = orange

Which holds most?

Number them in order

When the Spirit came to the disciples it looked like this

SUSAN SAYERS

Ideas for activities

Help the children to make or decorate some shakers and jangly instruments and then have some lively songs and dances, using taped music and live percussion if you can stand noisy rejoicing.

SUSAN SAYERS

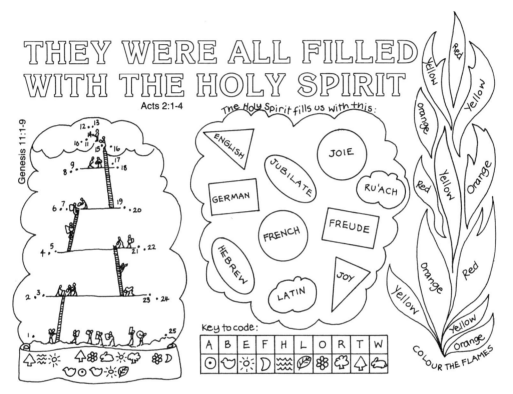

SUSAN SAYERS

Acts 2:1-21

It wasn't only the followers of Jesus who were gathered in Jerusalem. Pentecost was an important Jewish festival, celebrating the wheat harvest. Jerusalem would have been filled with Jews gathering together to celebrate Pentecost (see verse 5).

The Lord's followers had gathered together in one place, most likely to join in the celebrations of the festival. Then came the unexpected!

Although Jesus had made it clear that, after he had gone, he would send a 'comforter' or 'counsellor', his followers were not sure how this would happen. All the followers knew was that Jesus had told them to wait in Jerusalem until the Father gave them the Holy Spirit (see Acts 1:4). Suddenly, a sound of a mighty wind filled the house where the Lord's followers were gathered. The word for 'wind' and 'spirit' are the same in Greek, the language in which most of the New Testament was written. To the amazement of the Jews who had travelled from most of the known countries, the Lord's followers began speaking their languages (see verses 8-11).

The Holy Spirit was given to speak about the wonderful things that God had done, to give the Lord's followers encouragement that they were not alone and to give them the power to live a Christian life.

The Lord's followers had met together in Jerusalem unsure of what the future held for them. They didn't know how they could fulfil what Jesus had asked them to do when he told them 'go to the people of all nations and make them my disciples, baptise them in the name of the Father, the Son and the Holy Spirit' (see Matthew 28:19).

Now, on the day of Pentecost, they had been given the gift of the Holy Spirit. The Jews from many countries had heard the Lord's followers declare what God had done and now the followers knew that God was with them wherever they went. They now knew that God keeps his promises. He wasn't going to leave them alone and without the help that they needed to do the things that Jesus had asked them to do.

How does this relate to us? God has promised us the gift of his Holy Spirit to help us live our lives as Jesus wants us to. The Holy Spirit also allows us to listen to God and hear the truth about Jesus. We have access to a source of power which allows us to face questions like:

- Why do I exist?
- What does God want?
- Where is my life going?

This same source of power also gives us the strength we need to work through those questions.

Ask the group to think about the experience of the Lord's followers when they were gathered together in Jerusalem.

- What do the group think the followers were expecting? Anything?
- When they heard the sound of a mighty wind, do you think the followers would have been just a touch frightened, scared, shocked?
- How do they think the Jews would have felt when they heard so many languages being spoken by the followers?

PETE TOWNSEND

Reflective material
(sketches, meditations and poems)

Meditation of Peter

I don't know who was the more surprised,
    us, or them?
They were bewildered, certainly,
    unable to make head or tail of what was going on,

amazed to hear us speaking to them in their own language
and wondering what on earth it all could mean.
But if anything, our astonishment was the greater,
each of us scarcely able to believe what was happening.
Yes, I know we'd been told to expect it,
the promise given by Christ himself,
but as to what it meant,
what it actually involved,
we'd no idea until that incredible moment
when the Spirit came.
No warning,
no tell-tale signs,
just bang! –
and our lives were changed for ever.
Truthfully, I never thought I had it in me,
to get out there and speak fearlessly for Christ –
and as for sharing in his ministry,
continuing where he had left off,
the very idea seemed ridiculous.
Only that's what happened –
gifts beyond our wildest imagining,
power beyond our most fantastic dreams,
a joy that burned unquenchably within us
and a sense of purpose which nothing could contain.
We were no longer on our own, gazing wistfully to the heavens –
Christ was with us,
and in a way more wonderful than he'd ever been before;
not just by our side,
but in our hearts,
filling our whole being with his presence.
It was more than we'd ever expected,
more than any of us had dared hope for,
and we had to pinch ourselves to be sure it was true.
But it was,
and I tell you what,
impossible though it seems,
I shouldn't wonder if God has more yet in store,
new experiences of his love,
new expressions of his purpose,
not just for us but for everyone,
his Spirit poured out on all, just as the prophet said –
nothing will surprise us now!

NICK FAWCETT

Drama: God breaks the language barrier

Narrator The friends of Jesus had a wonderful story to tell. For a time, they'd thought it was all over – the people who hated Jesus had had him killed, but God raised him from the dead and gave him new life – and he'd been seen by all his close friends before he went back to heaven. But they had a promise that he'd always be with them, and he'd told them to tell the whole world the good news that he was alive – and Peter was getting impatient.

Peter So what are we waiting for? We've got to do as he said – tell the world. And instead we're all sitting here together, just praying!

Narrator Peter always was the one who went at everything like a bull at a gate – head down, mouth in gear, brain in neutral!

Andrew Jesus also told us to wait until we get the power we need. I don't know what he meant, but I'm sure we'll know when we get it.

Peter But, Andrew, this is the great festival – there are people from all over the world here, and we've got to tell them so they can go home and tell their friends. That's right, isn't it, Thomas?

Thomas Fine – and just how are you going to talk to foreign visitors when none of us can speak any of their languages?

Narrator Peter had to admit, Thomas had a point – but before he could answer, something really strange started happening. It sounded like a gale blowing through the room – but the air was completely still. It got louder and louder, but still they didn't feel anything. Philip, another of the friends, knew something important was going on.

Philip Didn't Jesus say that God's Spirit was like the wind? Didn't he say something about it blowing and you never knew where it came from or where it went?

Peter Oh, heaven save us, he's getting all intellectual!

Narrator Peter knew all about nets and fish, but he would never have called himself a deep thinker.

Nathanael He's right, though – that's exactly what Jesus said, and it's *exactly* what's happening now.

Peter Never mind the theories, Nathanael. We've got to get out and *do* something. On second thoughts, just get out – the room's on fire!

Philip (*Calmly*) You know, I do believe he's right – the room *is* on fire. This is very interesting.

Peter Never mind interesting – let's get out!

Philip But it's not burning, is it? Lots of fire, but nothing's burning.

Narrator	He was right. Gradually the panic subsided, but Peter was still agitated.
Peter	What's going on? I can't remember anything like this before.
Philip	Yes you can. Moses – the burning bush – it was on fire but it never got burnt. Don't you see?
Narrator	Peter didn't see. But Nathanael did.
Nathanael	This is the Holy Spirit Jesus promised us! Just like Moses – God's giving us the power we need to go and do his work. Oh, I say – where's everybody gone?
Narrator	When Nathanael got outside he was amazed. Peter was rattling on nineteen to the dozen – nothing strange in that, but he was telling someone from Libya about Jesus – in Arabic. Then he heard Andrew speaking Latin – he'd buttonholed a Roman merchant who just couldn't wait to hear more about Jesus. Just then, a woman came up to Nathanael.
Woman	What's this all about?
Nathanael	I'm really very sorry, but I don't speak Turkish. You'll have to ask someone else.
Woman	I don't understand.
Nathanael	Well, it's really simple enough: I don't speak your language – go and ask someone who does.
Woman	But if you don't speak my language, how come I'm understanding every word you're saying?
Narrator	She was right! Everyone was amazed. The good news about Jesus was being spread to all the foreign visitors *in their own languages*.
Nathanael	So this is God's Holy Spirit at work. Impressive. *Very* impressive!

MICHAEL FORSTER

Holy Spirit

Acts 2:1-4, John 3:8

The Spirit is a lively wind –
  breathtaking
  for those who breathe
  the stale air of mechanical worship;
  but for sails unfurled
  and wings spread wide
  he comes as driving energy,
  uncontrollably bracing.
He only destroys cobwebs
  and dead branches.

The Spirit is a lively power –
   not available
   to bolster up our empires,
   but unpredictably exploding
   in surprising places,
   strengthening weak knees
   and faints hearts,
   and giving secret growth
   to mysterious fruit.
He only destroys
   the rotten enemies
   of our souls.

The Spirit is a lively jester –
   embarrassing,
   with outrageous gesture,
   stiff respectability;
   tumbling over dignity
   in multi-coloured guises,
   impudently prodding
   deadly faces
   into joy and laughter.
He only destroys
   our pomp and vanity.

The Spirit is a lively bee –
   buzzing elusively
   through our solemnities.
He's not pinned down by resolutions,
   but flies in dizzy revolutions
   round our cultivated plots.
Sweet gifts he brings
   of his own making;
   and when he stings,
   his heart is breaking.

PETER DAINTY

Order of service

Pentecost always seems a particularly suitable time for ecumenical worship. Perhaps at Pentecost we are more aware that the Early Church was divided on the basis of location rather than denomination; perhaps church diaries tend not to be so full as at the other major festivals; or perhaps our awareness that the Spirit makes us one becomes more acute. Few will argue that the Church needs the fresh breeze of God's Spirit to disperse the staleness and blow away the sameness of its rituals and procedures, but it needs to be open for that to happen. When better than at Pentecost? Spontaneity and joy in worship are the keynote at Pentecost (though why restrict these to one Sunday a year?), but however much scope is given for open worship, some semblance of a framework is still necessary if the service is to involve several different traditions, not all of whom may feel comfortable with a less structured approach.

As with the less formal services for Easter and Ascension, considerable sensitivity and skill are required of those leading the act of worship: first, to ensure that Christians of all traditions feel included and able to worship God in that context; and second, to keep the proceedings under control so that no one individual or group can dominate or manipulate events for their own ends. The amount of freedom that can be given to *ad hoc* choice of hymns and songs will depend, as before, on the scope and flexibility of the musical resources, but however unspontaneous it may seem, do keep a few items up your sleeve that you know the musicians can play! If possible, try to order the songs and material to create times of quiet and reflection among the exuberance and anticipation, and break up the blocks of singing with readings and prayers. A clear time limit and end point are also helpful, so that those who need to leave may do so without feeling embarrassed.

Opening response

The Lord says, 'I will pour out my Spirit
on all people'.
We live in him and he in us,
because he has given us his Spirit.

When the Spirit of truth comes,
he will guide you into all truth.
We live in him and he in us,
because he has given us his Spirit.

We are all baptised by the one Spirit
into one body.
We live in him and he in us,
because he has given us his Spirit.

Opening hymn

Come down, O Love divine (HON 90) or Father, Lord of all creation (HON 122)

Confession and absolution

Spirit of God,
we acknowledge your transforming power,
and confess our lack of faith.
Forgive and renew us;
fill us with your strength.

Spirit of God,
you came on the disciples as wind and flame,
giving them your power and authority.
We confess that our lives
show little of your power
and our witness little of your authority.
Forgive and renew us;
fill us with your power.

Spirit of God,
you come to bestow your gifts and blessings on the Church.
We confess that we have been satisfied
with the earthbound poverty of our lives.
Forgive and renew us;
fill us with your life.

Spirit of God,
you come to equip your people for witness and service.
We confess that we have resisted
your gentle yet insistent leading.
Forgive and renew us;
fill us with your love.

Spirit of God,
you come to make your people one in the risen Lord.
We confess that we have maintained barriers
and tolerated division.
Forgive and renew us;
fill us with your unity.
Release our lives from self-interest and guilt,
and our tongues to declare the praises
of Jesus Christ our Lord.
Amen.

Almighty God,
the Father of all mercies,
pardon and forgive all your sins
and by his Spirit make you one in him,
and with each other.
Amen.

Songs

Two or three chosen from:

For I'm building a people of power (HON 135)
Gracious Spirit, Holy Ghost (HON 184)
Holy Spirit, we welcome you *(The Source 181)*
I give you all the honour (HON 230)

I love your presence *(The Source 216)*
Spirit of the living God (HON 454/455)
The King is among us (HON 483)

First reading

Romans 8:14-17 or
Acts 2:1-21

Songs

Two or three chosen from:

Bind us together, Lord (HON 60)
Filled with the Spirit's power (HON 131)
Jesus, restore to us again *(The Source 295)*
Lord, we long for you *(The Source 337)*
O breath of life (HON 356)
O thou who camest from above (HON 416)
Silent, surrendered *(The Source 456)*

Second reading

1 Corinthians 12:3b-13 or John 14:8-17

Time of open reflection

As mentioned previously in the Easter service, the value of this time, intended for sharing of insights and prayer, depends very heavily on the leader enabling everyone present to share in it, rather than allowing one group or section to dominate the proceedings. If, as is likely, the tone of the service is basically joyful and exuberant, it would be wise to make this time quieter and more devotional, maybe incorporating some reflective songs and/or readings, provided time allows. As a response to a prayer or group of prayers, the song 'Alleluia' (HON 23) could be used, with words adapted to the context. The Lord's Prayer forms a suitable conclusion, joining together both the spoken and unspoken prayers offered previously.

Final hymn or song

Chosen from:

The Spirit lives to set us free (HON 494)
God's Spirit is in my heart (HON 180)
Angel voices, ever singing (HON 33)
Lord, the light of your love (HON 317)
Jesus is Lord (HON 270)

Final prayer

May God our heavenly Father
give us his Spirit of peace and unity.
Amen.

May Jesus Christ his Son
give us joy and confidence
as we walk by faith with him.
Amen.

May the Holy Spirit
make us one in worship, fellowship and mission
and guide us in the path of righteousness.
Amen.

STUART THOMAS

Trinity

Trinity Sunday

The mystery and wonder of the Godhead

A reading from the Gospel of Matthew (28:16-20)

The eleven apostles set off for Galilee to meet Jesus where he had arranged. When Jesus appeared before them on the mountain, several of the Apostles fell to their knees and worshipped him; but some doubted.

Then he said to them:

I have been given authority over everything in heaven and on earth, and by this authority I am sending you out to all peoples to teach them everything I have taught you. Make them my disciples and baptise them in the name of the Father, the Son and the Holy Spirit. Remember that I will never leave you; I am with you until the end of time.

This is the Gospel of the Lord
Praise to you, Lord Jesus Christ   Katie Thompson

Introductory material

The first Sunday after Pentecost is called Trinity Sunday. The feast dates from the Middle Ages and has been particularly popular in England since the time of St Thomas à Becket.

Remembering that we were each baptised 'in the name of the Father and of the Son and of the Holy Spirit', and that we usually commence our prayer with the sign of the cross and those words, in the family we might like to try the following to mark the day. At Sunday dinner, or the meal when the family are together, place a suitable small bowl full of water in the centre of the table. The parent who is going to lead the grace before the meal draws the bowl to the attention of everyone and in a few simple words reminds the family of the Christian significance of water as the sign of new life. A blessing can be asked on the water. These words might be appropriate:

Almighty God,
we recall today that you have revealed yourself
to us as a trinity of persons – Father, Son and Holy Spirit.
We ask your blessing on this water;
may it remind us of our baptism
and the promises made at that time
to reject evil and to love and dedicate ourselves
to the good. Amen.

The parent then asks each member of the family to make a sign of the Trinity with the thumb and first two fingers of the right hand. Each of those round the table can then form a 'clover' figure of three, and dip the three fingers into the water and make the sign of the cross, with the usual accompanying words.

TONY CASTLE

Prayers

Praise

Great and loving God,
  we greet you this day with praise and wonder.
  We greet you as the creator of the ends of the earth,
    sovereign over space and time,
    greater than we can ever imagine.

Gracious and living Christ,
  we greet you this day with joy and thanksgiving.
  We greet you as our Lord,
    our friend,
    our Saviour.

Mysterious and mighty Spirit,
  we greet you this day with awe and worship.
  We greet you as our guide and inspiration,
    our source of strength and comfort,
    a living inner reality.

Almighty God, Father, Son and Holy Spirit,
  we greet you this day,
    and we praise you that you are here
    to greet us and everyone,
    today and every day,
    here and everywhere.

  Help us to meet with you,
    and grow closer to you,
    through this time of worship.

  Help us to glimpse your glory,
    and make it known,
    through all we say and do,
    to the glory of your name.
    Amen.

NICK FAWCETT

Petition

Loving God,
> we thank you that you are here among us
>> as we join to worship you –
>> here as a loving Father watching over his children,
>> as our Lord yet also our friend in the person of Jesus,
>> as an ever-present reality
>> through the daily experience of your Holy Spirit.
> Forgive us that we have lost sight sometimes of your living presence,
>> and open our eyes afresh to all that you are
>> and everything you are doing.
> Meet with us now, in all your glory,
>> **and help us to meet with you.**

Father God,
> we recognise our need of you,
>> and we acknowledge our emptiness deep within.
> We have chased after illusory fulfilment,
>> turning our backs on where true happiness lies.
> Help us to recognise everything you have given us
>> if only we could but see it –
>> the wonder of your love,
>> the constancy of your care
>> and the greatness of your mercy.
> Teach us to put our trust in you,
>> and to seek your kingdom and righteousness,
>> and so fill us again with hope, joy and peace.
> Meet with us now, in all your glory,
>> **and help us to meet with you.**

Gracious God,
> you have made yourself known to us in Christ,
>> demonstrating the immensity of your love
>> and the awesome extent of your mercy,
>> yet still sometimes our faith grows cold.
> You have offered us a new beginning,
>> renewal and redemption through his life-giving sacrifice,
>> yet still, time and again, we go astray.
> Draw closer to us through the risen Christ,
>> and inspire us with a vision
>> of what life can be like through his grace.
> Meet with us now, in all your glory,
>> **and help us to meet with you.**

Living God,
    inspire us now through the living presence of your Holy Spirit,
      so that we may walk boldly into this new day,
      with new faith and purpose.
    Help us to forget ourselves and to look outwards,
      so that we might bring light to those for whom life seems dark.
    Teach us to live this and every day
      in the warmth of your presence,
      illuminated by your radiance,
      refreshed by your cleansing touch
      and renewed by your power.
    Meet with us now, in all your glory,
      and help us to meet with you.

Loving God,
    Father, Son and Holy Spirit,
      help us to be aware of your presence amongst us –
      to see you, hear you, know you and love you,
      and so may we offer you fitting worship and service.
    Help us to understand you are with us
      not just here but everywhere,
      not just now but always,
      and so may every part of our lives reflect your grace
      and proclaim your goodness.
    Meet with us now, in all your glory,
      and help us to meet with you.

    Through Jesus Christ our Lord.
    Amen.

NICK FAWCETT

Short prayers

Place an oil burner in the centre of the room. Light the burner and use a light fragrant oil . . . Read the following prayer:

Lord, allow your Holy Spirit to fill this room.
Lord, allow your Holy Spirit to be in my life.
Lord, allow your Holy Spirit to show me your love.
Take my worries and doubts,
    take my insecurities and fear,
    take my hurt and pain.
Heal me, love me and keep me.
Amen.

PETE TOWNSEND

Almighty and everlasting God,
  we are here before you.
Grant us a glimpse of your awesome presence,
  and help us to worship you with reverent praise.
Father God,
  we are here before you.
Grant us a sense of your everlasting arms
    surrounding us,
  and help us to trust always in your loving purpose.
Lord Jesus Christ,
  we are here before you.
Grant us grace to hear your call,
  and help us to follow in your footsteps
    wherever that might lead.
Holy Spirit,
  we are here before you.
Grant us openness of heart, mind and spirit,
  and help us to know your peace and power.
Almighty and everlasting God,
  Father, Son and Holy Spirit,
  we are here before you.
Grant that we may know you better,
  and help us to live and work for you,
    this day and always.
Amen.

NICK FAWCETT

Mighty God,
  beyond all space and time, greater than our minds can fully grasp,
  ruler over all that is and has been and shall be,
  we worship you.
We worship you as the God made known to us in Christ,
  a God all good and wholly other,
  and yet a God who loves us as a father loves his children,
  a God who has shared our humanity.
We worship you as the God we experience within us,
  the God who fires our imagination and sets our hearts aflame
  through the Spirit of Christ.
Mighty God,
  help us to catch a sense of your greatness,
  opening our hearts and minds to your presence
  made known through Father, Son and Holy Spirit.
Amen.

NICK FAWCETT

All-age-talk material

> We believe in
> the three persons of God.
> Who are they?

Match the shapes

KATIE THOMPSON

We will have everlasting life if we do what?

Draw an X through the squares with a •

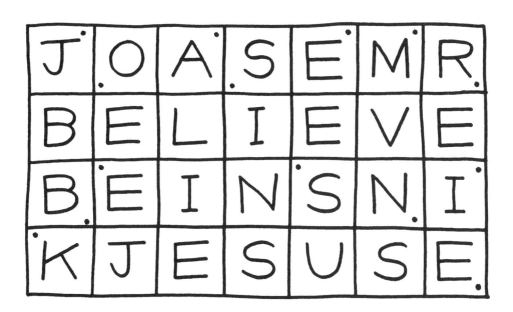

KATIE THOMPSON

Find the opposites below to spell out the answer

The opposite of QUIET is

The opposite of LOW is

The opposite of DARK is

The opposite of QUICKLY is

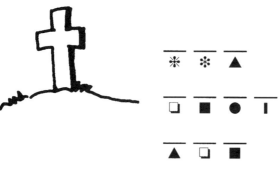

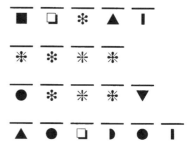

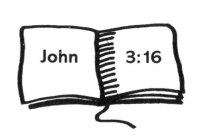

KATIE THOMPSON

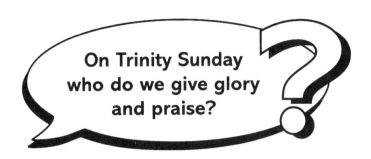

On Trinity Sunday who do we give glory and praise?

Fit the pieces in the puzzle

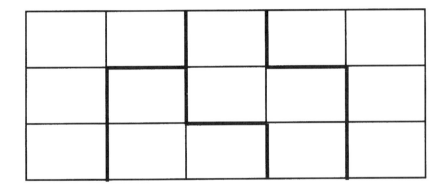

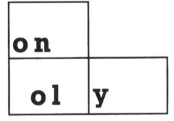

KATIE THOMPSON

Jesus spoke
to a Pharisee called
Nicodemus about the
Son of God

Follow the instructions to find his words

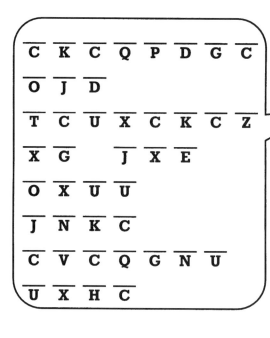

1.	Change the letter C to E	
2.	Change the letter D to O	
3.	Change the letter G to N	
4.	Change the letter J to H	
5.	Change the letter K to V	
6.	Change the letter P to Y	
7.	Change the letter Q to R	
8.	Change the letter T to B	
9.	Change the letter U to L	
10.	Change the letter X to I	
11.	Change the letter Z to S	
12.	Change the letter E to M	
13.	Change the letter O to W	
14.	Change the letter N to A	
15.	Change the letter H to F	
16.	Change the letter V to T	

KATIE THOMPSON

Describing the Trinity

Aim: To explore how the Trinity came to be expressed as such.

Begin by having a juggling session, using light scarves, juggling balls or rolled-up socks or anything else 'jugglable'. Make sure there are enough for everyone to have a go, and see if anyone can manage to keep three balls going at once. Enjoy their performance.

Have the doxology written up so everyone can see it. They may well have come across this during worship; say it together now. Look into the meaning to discover how many people are being worshipped in this prayer. Encourage discussion about what the Trinity explains, and point out that in a way this is like trying to juggle with ideas about God. We are attempting to hold all our knowledge of God at once, so as to keep as close to the truth as possible.

Look at Peter's sermon after the coming of the Holy Spirit, to see how the idea is expressed of God being three persons yet one God.

Work out together what you believe about God the Father, God the Son and God the Holy Spirit, and form this into a chant, rap or set of responses that could be used in worship as a statement of faith.

SUSAN SAYERS

Describing God

Begin by asking a couple of volunteers to take part in a guessing game. Give one person a note with the name of an animal written on it. This person tries to describe the animal to the other person, who has to guess what the animal is. If you have access to an OHP or flipchart you could get the second person to draw what they hear being described. You could have two or three goes at this, or you could ask everyone in the congregation to pair up and play the game. The way you do it will depend on the expectations and nature of the congregation!

Now fix a cardboard pair of rabbit ears on a volunteer and explain how we all tend to describe things in terms of what we know already. We would probably describe a rabbit as being furry with long ears because our own ears are short, and we are generally lacking in fur. Ask for suggestions as to how a rabbit might describe a human? (It might be something like a bald rabbit with very short ears.)

It's even harder trying to describe someone we have never seen, like God. It's difficult, but we do our best by looking at the world he has created and picking up clues from this. What can we tell about God by (a) looking at his creation? (Write these qualities up for everyone to see.) (b) Looking at Jesus? (Write these qualities too.) (c) Looking at the working of the Holy Spirit? (Add these qualities.)

When we worship the Trinity we are remembering all these qualities in the God we love.

SUSAN SAYERS

SUSAN SAYERS

Father, Son and Holy Spirit

Begin by exploring relationships in the group, asking the children to stand in the 'daughter' ring, if they are daughters and the 'son' ring if they are sons (use lengths of wool, or hula-hoops to make the rings). Now ask the sisters and brothers to go to other rings, such as cousin, grandchild, friend and nephew. Some children will have changed rings several times.

Sit the children in a circle and show them a picture of someone they all know about – it may be the Queen; or a photo of one of their teachers, perhaps. Work out together all the different things the person is, such as mother, daughter, woman, sister, grandmother, queen, horse rider. Write all these down beside the picture.

Now show them a poster with the word GOD in the middle. Uncover the first picture of trees, mountains, animals and flowers.

What is God? He is our Father, the Creator.

Uncover the second picture of Jesus, healing and teaching.

What else is God? He is Jesus Christ.

Uncover the third picture of wind and fire and the disciples full of joy.

What else is God? He is the Holy Spirit.

Just as they are themselves, although they are also sisters, friends and cousins, so God is God, although he is also Father, Son and Holy Spirit. Give each child a triangle of coloured card. They write GOD in the middle and Father, Jesus and Spirit at the three corners to take home with them.

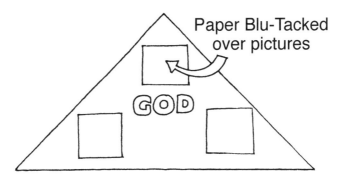

SUSAN SAYERS

God's children

In his letter to the church in Rome, Paul says ' . . . we must not live to satisfy our own desires. If you do, you will die!' Strong words, but what was he getting at? We each have a desire to be accepted, to be appreciated and to be acknowledged as individuals. We can try various ways to gain acceptance, appreciation and acknowledgement by the way we act or the way we dress. Sometimes our feeling of acceptance means liking the type of music that our peer group likes or adopting the same style of dress or 'look'.

To a certain extent there is nothing wrong with all this; it's a part of life. The problems occur when we go to desperate lengths to be accepted, appreciated and acknowledged. We can sometimes spend most of our time trying too hard to be somebody that everybody will like. It can become our main driving force. It can consume every moment we have. That is when we start to die inwardly.

Paul was saying that if we put all our effort into trying to be accepted by other people and follow whatever desires we have, then we lose sight of who we really are.

One of the Old Testament kings, Solomon, wanted to search for what would make him happy. He said, 'I wanted to find out what was best for us during the short time we have on earth' (Ecclesiastes 2:3).

Money was not a problem and so he bought the best wines available and created a huge royal cellar. He set out to drink as much as he could and more.

Then he decided to be a bit more creative and built houses, planted vineyards, created gardens and orchards and accumulated vast wealth, became famous and got whatever he asked for.

Not satisfied with that, he decided to check out his sexuality. He eventually acquired so many wives that to see a different wife each day would have taken two years!

After all that Solomon sat back and had a think. 'Then I thought about everything I had done . . . and it was simply chasing the wind. Nothing on earth is worth the trouble' (Ecclesiastes 2:11).

We don't have to go to such extreme lengths to find acceptance, appreciation and acknowledgement. Nothing can fill the God-shaped hole in the middle of our being. We can try filling it with possessions, exotic substances or try and ignore it all together. The Holy Spirit will always make us aware of God's love for us. He accepts us for who we are. God isn't bothered with what we may think of as imperfections. He loves us as a father, and we become his children (Romans 8:15-16). If we accept that God loves us anyway, then our desires can be influenced by the Holy Spirit. We don't have to fit the moulds that other people might want us to fit. The important thing is that God loves us as we are; no matter what.

PETE TOWNSEND

Reflective material
(sketches, meditations and poems)

God is simple

God is simple. This is a technical term in Catholic philosophy and theology, meaning that wherever God is, the whole of God is. God is single-fold, God cannot be divided up into parts.

The great consolation of that for human beings is that they can say, 'I have the whole of God's attention, all the time.' If God is behind my eyes, looking out with me and sharing the scene, how intimate that makes our union! If I raise my eyes above the head of the person I am speaking to, and look at the pictures on the wall beyond, God and I know what picture, and what feature of what picture, I am looking at. Nobody else does. And this in spite of the fact that the same God is the force behind the whole universe of stars.

God is simple even though God is Trinity. I can with truth look out at my world and say, 'Father, only you and I can see this scene. We can see Christ everywhere, and your Spirit goes out to him everywhere in love.' Or else I can look out and say, 'Jesus, nobody knows the trouble I feel except you. Help me to see God everywhere and in all things. Share with me your trusting love-in-return for the Father who will make all well.'

God knows all my thoughts as I think them, and shares my memories with me. We experienced together the events that I now call to mind, and now we remember them together.

Every tiny atom in the universe has the simple presence of God as we do, but we human beings have the enormous privilege of awareness.

GERALD O'MAHONY

Reflecting on John 14:23-29

Read back a few verses – particularly to verse 15: 'I will ask the Father and he will give you another Advocate to be with you for ever . . . he will be in you.' This passage suggests an extraordinary intimacy at the heart of the contemplative life. The breathtaking promise is that somehow the very life of the Trinity will come and 'make our home' within those who love God.

If we can begin even to glimpse this then the Peace of verse 27 is, of course, totally ours. But how do we glimpse it, how do we comprehend it?

Be still with this Gospel, and allow words or phrases to sink below the level of your mind and reveal meanings in your heart.

PATRICK WOODHOUSE

Meditation of Thomas

He was just a man, that's what I thought.
A wonderful person,
   fantastic teacher,
   the most caring sort of bloke you could ever hope to meet,
   but just a man.
And nothing wrong with that, of course;
   it's not every day you meet someone as special.
In fact, thank God he was a man,
   as much flesh and blood as we are.

He knew what it was to be human,
    to share our hopes and fears,
    our joys and sorrows,
    our life and death.
He laughed as we do,
    wept as we do,
    suffered as we do.
I know, for I was with him for three years of his life.
But I'd thought that his life was over,
    when they laid him in that tomb and rolled the stone across.
I'd really thought that was it, until something happened,
    something astonishing, marvellous, incredible –
    he appeared to me again,
    just as he'd appeared to the rest of the disciples,
    as large as life,
    and I knew then that he wasn't just a man:
    he was God!
I understood at last what he'd been on about before,
    those words which had never made sense earlier:
    'Whoever has seen me has seen the Father,
    no one has ever seen God, but I have made him known to you.'
'Of course!' I said. 'Of course!'
    and I fell down and worshipped him.
Do you know, God was more real to me then
    than I'd ever dreamed he could be.
So when shortly after he disappeared,
    you can imagine we were gutted.
It felt as though our world had fallen apart,
    as if we'd been cut off from God,
    until all at once we knew he was with us after all,
    nearer than he'd ever been before.
It didn't matter that we couldn't see him.
    it didn't matter that we couldn't touch him.
We felt his presence deep inside,
    guiding us,
    renewing us,
    working through us.
And again I remembered his words,
    'The Holy Spirit, who the Father will send in my name,
    will teach you all things.
    God is Spirit, and those who worship him
    must worship in spirit and in truth.'
He was a man, he really was,
    as human as you and me.

But he was God –
   he showed us the Father;
   I know that sounds incredible but it's true.
Yet he's also Spirit –
   God with us now, deep in our hearts.
You don't need my word for that,
   you don't need anyone's,
   for you can experience it for yourselves.

NICK FAWCETT

Meditation of Isaiah

Could it be true?
Could God, in his mercy, forgive even me?
It seemed incredible,
   too implausible for words,
   for there was so much in my life not as it should be,
   so many ways I daily let him down.
Does that surprise you,
   me being a prophet and all that?
It shouldn't do,
   for I was under no illusions as to my own importance,
   not for a moment.
If God ever wanted to use me
   it would be despite who I was, not because of it,
   that's what I'd always imagined.
My faults were all too apparent to me,
   and all too painful to contemplate.
I wanted to be different, don't get me wrong –
   there was nothing I'd have liked better
   than to offer faithful, unblemished service –
   but there was no escaping reality:
   I was as weak as the next man,
   unable to resist temptation,
   quick to go astray.
What reason was there to think I could change?
So when God appeared to me that day in the temple,
   I hate to say it, but I panicked,
   consumed by a sense of my own unworthiness.
It was only a vision, I know,
   but it brought home the shocking contrast
   between his purity and my sin,
   his strength and my weakness.
How could I ever bridge that gap?

There was no way I could even begin to,
   but the next moment I felt God reach out and touch me,
   summoning me to service,
   taking away my guilt,
   making me whole.
Me, Isaiah, a prophet?
Could it be true?
Could God really make me new?
It seemed beyond belief,
   childish, romantic nonsense!
Yet that's what he promised,
   and that's what he proved,
   not just to me but countless others across the years.
He called me to proclaim forgiveness,
   a new start for all,
   freedom from our sins.
And I've discovered, beyond all doubt,
   the wonderful, astonishing truth of that message –
   the simple, stupendous fact that whoever you are,
   whatever you've done,
   it doesn't matter;
   God is always ready to forgive what *has* been
   and take what is,
   shaping it by his grace to transform what's yet to be.

NICK FAWCETT

All Saints

All Saints' Day

The great company of God's people

A reading from the Gospel of John (11:32-44)

When Jesus got there, he found that Lazarus had already been buried four days.

Many of the city people had come to console Martha and Mary in their bereavement. When Martha heard that Jesus was on his way, she went out to meet him. Mary stayed at home.

'If only you'd been here, sir,' said Martha, 'my brother wouldn't have died. But even now he's dead, God will give you whatever you ask him, I know.'

'Your brother will rise again,' said Jesus.

'I know he'll rise again when everyone rises again at the last day,' she said.

'I am the resurrection,' said Jesus 'and I am the source of life. Whoever trusts me shall come to life again, even though they die; nobody who is alive and trusts in me shall ever die. Do you believe this?'

'Yes I do, sir,' she replied. 'I firmly believe that you are God's Chosen Leader, the Son of God, the Coming One.'*

With these words, she went to call her sister Mary.

'The Master's here and wants you,' she told her in a low voice so that the others shouldn't hear.

As soon as she heard that, Mary got up quickly and went to Jesus.

He was still where Martha had left him, outside the village.

The people in the house who had come to console Mary saw her get up quickly and go out. They followed her, thinking that she was going to the tomb to mourn there.

Mary reached the spot where Jesus was standing, and, as soon as she saw him, she fell down at his feet.

'If you'd only been here, sir,' she said, 'my brother wouldn't have died.'

Jesus saw her crying – and all the people with her crying; he was deeply moved and troubled.

'Where have you buried him?' he asked.

'Come and see, sir,' they said.

Jesus wept.

'He must have been very fond of him,' the visitors said.

'He can make blind people see,' said some. 'Couldn't he have done something to stop this man from dying?'

Jesus was again deeply moved as he reached the tomb. It was a cave with a large stone closing its opening.

* 'The Coming One' was a title for the Deliverer the Jewish people believed God would send to save them from their enemies.

'Move the stone out of the way,' said Jesus.

'The smell must be very bad by now,' said Martha. 'He's been dead four days.'

'Didn't I tell you,' said Jesus, 'that you would see what God can do – if you trust in him?' The stone was moved.

Jesus looked up.

'I thank you, Father, for listening to me. I know that you always listen to me. I say this for the sake of those who are standing round me. I want them to be sure that you have sent me.'

Then he called loudly, 'Lazarus, come out!' and the dead man came out. His hands and feet were bound with bandages, and his face was wrapped in a cloth.

'Undo him,' said Jesus, 'and let him go.'   ALAN DALE

A reading from the Gospel of Matthew (5:1-12)

A crowd of disciples gathered around, and Jesus sat down and began to preach to them:

Happy are the poor in spirit, for the kingdom of heaven is theirs.

Happy are the broken-hearted, for they will be comforted.

Happy are the meek and gentle, for the earth will belong to them.

Happy are those who hunger and thirst for what is right, for justice will be theirs.

Happy are those who show forgiveness, because they will receive forgiveness in return.

Happy are those with a pure heart, for they shall see the face of God.

Happy are the peace-makers; God will call them his children.

Happy are those who suffer because they stand up for what is right; the kingdom of heaven belongs to them.

Be happy when people harass and mistreat you, and tell lies about you because you are my disciples. All this was suffered by the prophets who came before you. Be glad because when the time comes you will be richly rewarded in heaven.

This is the Gospel of the Lord
Praise to you, Lord Jesus Christ   KATIE THOMPSON

Introductory material

All Saints' Tide is traditionally one of the more important seasons of the Christian Year, lasting like Pentecost for eight days. Its significance in times past can be seen in the great number of Anglican churches dedicated to All Saints. Sadly the Christian celebration of the eve of All Saints' Day has become largely squeezed out by the secular festivities of Hallowe'en, with its masks, pumpkins and witches on broomsticks. While this has obvious pagan origins, it now functions mostly as a good excuse for a party, but Churches in many places have recently put on specifically Christian events to provide an alternative to this, and to the increasing interest in witchcraft and the occult. An act of worship on All Saints' Eve aimed at young families and teenagers might also divert some youngsters from the recent trend of 'trick or treat', which at times has become unpleasant and abusive.

However, while this may provide some motivation, the primary objective of worshipping God at All Saints' Tide is not to express opposition to the forces of evil (important though it may be to do so in other contexts). Rather, it provides the occasion for Christians to remind themselves of their hope of eternal life in Jesus Christ, and to give thanks for God's people who have gone before, in every age and place. Throughout our earthly pilgrimage we are inspired and challenged from time to time by a Christian friend or leader whose example has deepened our faith or changed the direction of our life. Those of us who are now more mature in faith might also bear in mind those who take their example from us, often without our realising it. This is an entirely positive message, which should be reflected in a thankful and joyful atmosphere for worship.

Although All Saints' Day itself falls on 1 November, the season lasts for eight days and many Churches may want to focus their celebration of it on the Sunday which falls in this period. Its distinctive themes are especially suitable for ecumenical worship. An alternative to Hallowe'en only makes sense on All Saints' Eve, however, and this in particular has inspired some groups of local Churches to combine forces and organise not only an act of worship, but also a bonfire or firework party with suitable refreshments, something likely to be beyond the resources of a single congregation. STUART THOMAS

Prayers

Praise and confession

Sovereign God,
  Lord of history,
    we come to you in reverent praise.

  We come to praise you
    for the way you have worked across the centuries –
    the way you have moved in so many lives
    to make known your purpose,
    offer your guidance
    and express your love.
  Great is your faithfulness:
    forgive the feebleness of our response.

We praise you for the way you have spoken throughout history –
  to your people, Israel,
  to your Church,
  to countless generations of believers.
Great is your faithfulness:
  forgive the feebleness of our response.

We praise you for the great cloud of witnesses that surround us –
  our fellowship here,
  your Church across the world,
  and all those who have kept the faith
  and run the race before us.
Great is your faithfulness:
  forgive the feebleness of our response.

We praise you for the example we have been given to follow –
  through the disciples and Apostles,
  through the early Church and its life beyond,
  and through the saints of old.
Great is your faithfulness:
  forgive the feebleness of our response.

Forgive us that we sometimes forget all you have done,
  losing sight of the breadth of your purpose
  and the extent of your love.
Great is your faithfulness:
  forgive the feebleness of our response.

Forgive us that we fail to honour the heritage in which we stand,
  our love for you weak,
  our trust hesitant
  and our commitment poor.
Great is your faithfulness:
  forgive the feebleness of our response.

Forgive us that we walk half-heartedly,
  casual in our discipleship,
  careless in our devotion,
  our hearts concerned with what is trivial and unimportant,
  rather than focused single-mindedly
  on the work of your kingdom.
Great is your faithfulness:
  forgive the feebleness of our response.

Sovereign God,
  as we remind ourselves together
    of your activity throughout history,
    as we reflect on your work through your people,

speak now to our lives,
that our love may grow,
our faith be deepened,
and our resolve to serve you be strengthened.
So may we live always to your praise and glory.
Great is your faithfulness:
forgive the feebleness of our response.

Through Jesus Christ our Lord.
Amen.

NICK FAWCETT

The God of history

Lord of all,
God of space and time,
Ruler of history,
Sovereign over all that is and has been and shall be,
we acknowledge your greatness.
O give thanks to the Lord, for he is good;
his steadfast love endures for ever!

We gather before you,
the God of Abraham, Isaac and Jacob,
the God who led your people across the Red Sea
and through the wilderness,
who guided your chosen nation into the Promised Land,
who spoke your word through the prophets,
who led your people out of exile back to Jerusalem,
and above all who lived and moved and breathed
in the person of your Son, Jesus Christ our Lord.
O give thanks to the Lord, for he is good;
his steadfast love endures for ever!

In his name we come,
with confidence, faith, joy and thanksgiving,
knowing that as you have guided your people across the years
so you will continue to guide us today,
and knowing also that in life or in death,
wherever we walk and whatever we experience,
you will be there alongside us –
a rock and a refuge,
a constant source of strength,
an unfailing giver of hope,
an unquenchable fountain of life and love.
O give thanks to the Lord, for he is good;
his steadfast love endures for ever!

Lord of all,
> for all who have gone before us,
>> and for calling us in turn
>> to be part of that great company of saints,
>> we thank you and praise you.
> O give thanks to the Lord, for he is good;
>> **his steadfast love endures for ever!**
> **Thanks be to God.**
> **Amen.**

NICK FAWCETT

Intercession

Sovereign God,
> we have thought of the wider fellowship that we share in Christ,
>> the great company of your people in heaven and on earth
>> to which we are privileged to belong,
>> and so now we pray for those
>> who seek, in turn, to follow you today.
> Rock of ages,
>> **hear our prayer.**

We pray for those for whom commitment is costly –
> those who face hostility, discrimination,
> repression and persecution
> for the cause of the Gospel.
Give them strength and courage,
> so that they may keep the faith.
Rock of ages,
> **hear our prayer.**

We pray for those who are finding the journey of discipleship difficult –
> troubled by doubts,
> plagued by temptation,
> or simply slipping back into old ways.
Give them support and reassurance,
> so that they may walk with new confidence.
Rock of ages,
> **hear our prayer.**

We pray for those expressing their faith in action –
> individuals through personal acts of kindness,
> and agencies like Christian Aid, CAFOD, Tearfund and Shelter,
> together with so many others,
> working, often against the odds,
> to give expression to the love of Christ.

Give them love and compassion,
  so that they may make Christ real for others.
Rock of ages,
  hear our prayer.

We pray for all seeking to communicate their faith –
  ministers, evangelists, missionaries, chaplains,
  but also ordinary, everyday believers like us –
  each telling in their own way what Jesus means to them.
Give them wisdom and inspiration,
  so that they may speak your word with power.
Rock of ages,
  hear our prayer.

Sovereign God,
  we pray for Christians everywhere striving to live out their faith
    in the world of today,
    with all the pressures, challenges and demands
    that confront them.
Give them guidance and encouragement,
  so that they may grow in grace.
  Grant them humility to learn more of you each day
  and the ability to share their experience
  simply and effectively with others,
    making Christ known through word and deed.
Rock of ages,
  hear our prayer.

All this we ask, through Jesus Christ our Lord.
Amen.

NICK FAWCETT

All-age-talk material

Our heavenly home

First show some colourful travel brochures, reading out snippets from them, and then talk about how nice it is to go home after a holiday, because home, for most people, is very special.

Ask everyone to think of the first home they remember. Imagine walking up to the front door, and looking in the rooms that they may not have visited in their imagination for a long time, or they may have left that same home this morning. Take them through various rooms, drawing their attention to things like the furniture, the kitchen window and so on, which will help bring their memories flooding back. That was the home they started out from on a journey which has brought them to Sunday morning, and the particular pew they are sitting in. Heaven is our spiritual home, and although we don't know any details, like the furniture and the windows of our earthly homes, we do know that it is a place of deep happiness and fulfilment, free from all tears and anxieties, lit with love and contentment. (Sounds good, doesn't it?)

If this was on the holiday programme, they may well be waiting now to hear the bad news of how expensive it is to go there, and how little chance ordinary people have of getting in. The wonderful news is that Jesus has already paid for us to go, and the fare was death by crucifixion, with the sins of the world heavy on his shoulders. What is more, we are not counted as tourists, but citizens of heaven. If we choose to walk with Jesus, he will bring us safely through our own death journeys to live in heaven. If we want, heaven can be our home for the whole of eternity.

SUSAN SAYERS

Solve the clues below to find his name.
The first letter of each word will spell out the answer

1. **Opposite of EARLY**
2. **The fruit eaten by Adam and Eve**
3. **An African horse with black and white stripes**
4. **The eighth month of the year**
5. **A red-breasted bird**
6. **A device used to keep the rain off**
7. **A creature which carries it's home on it's back**

KATIE THOMPSON

Jesus was deeply moved when he saw Mary's tears

Write the next letter of the alphabet on the lines above to read what he said to her

'
— — —   —   — — —   — — — —
C H C   H   M N S   S D K K

— — —   — — — —   — — —
X N T   S G Z S   X N T

— — — — —   — — —   — — — —
V N T K C   R D D   F N C R

— — — — —   — —   — — —
F K N Q X   H E   X N T

— — — — — — — — !'
A D K H D U D C

ABCDEFGHIJKLMNOPQRSTUVWXYZ

KATIE THOMPSON

Jesus prayed
to his heavenly Father
before calling . . .

Add or subtract letters to see what he said!

A B C D E F G H I J K L M N O P Q R S T U V W X Y Z

'
$\overline{\text{D+8}}$ $\overline{\text{P–15}}$ $\overline{\text{V+4}}$ $\overline{\text{B–1}}$ $\overline{\text{J+8}}$ $\overline{\text{R+3}}$ $\overline{\text{Z–7}}$

$\overline{\text{A+2}}$ $\overline{\text{X–9}}$ $\overline{\text{L+1}}$ $\overline{\text{I–4}}$

$\overline{\text{F+9}}$ $\overline{\text{K+10}}$ $\overline{\text{V–2}}$!'

Jesus is
the Resurrection
and the life

John 11:43

Katie Thompson

The Glory of God!

Match up the scrambled words to read what she said to him

Jesus went to the village called Bethany, where a woman called Mary ran to meet him

KATIE THOMPSON

God's glory!

Jesus went to a village called Bethany, near Jerusalem

Can you find BETHANY hidden in this puzzle? Circle it

KATIE THOMPSON

Read Psalm 24:1-6

You will have been aware, through the media, that around this time the festival we know as 'Halloween' is often celebrated. The origin of 'Halloween' is in the Celtic festival of Samhain, which celebrated the first day of winter on 1 November. It was thought that supernatural creatures, the spirits of the dead, witches and hobgoblins were most active at this time, which made it a convenient time to tell fortunes. During this time, it was common for people to burn peat on bonfires to 'scare away the witches'. Later the Roman worship of Pomona, a goddess of the harvest, was celebrated around the same time. From these two festivals came the tradition of using fire (a candle) and a pumpkin, which is still practised today.

Throughout the Bible you can read accounts of people worshipping idols or celebrating a festival in honour of some mystical being (see 1 Kings 18:1-40 or Acts 17:16-24). In Psalm 24, David is reminding us about the one and only true God. David is declaring God's credentials (much as Paul does in the rest of Acts 17).

The number of beliefs and superstitions to which we are exposed not only divert our attention away from a relationship with God, but also attempt to persuade us that he is just one of a number of supernatural beings who can be worshipped. This is precisely what the devil would like us all to think, that you can 'pick and mix' who or what you believe in. We constantly need to remind ourselves and each other that God is Lord of all. It is only through a faith and trust in Jesus Christ that we can have a relationship with God. There is no other way to God and there is no set of superstitions or rituals which can allow us to have a relationship with God. There are plenty of things which want to take our focus off God. But God has given us the Holy Spirit to guide us and give us encouragement in every situation. Our decision to follow God is never easy and there are plenty of distractions. The Psalmist sets us a great example of focusing on God and putting our trust in him as we try to follow his ways.

PETE TOWNSEND

Reflective material
(sketches, meditations and poems)

John 13:1-7; 14:1-3; Luke 12:37; Matthew 26:26-29

There is a famous hostel,
    where pilgrims reach their goal,
    and standing there to greet them
    with towel and with bowl
    is Christ the mighty traveller,
    the saviour of their race,
    who pioneered their pathway
    and prepared for them a place.

He kneels and pours the water
  on those weary pilgrims' feet,
  to cleanse the dust of ages
  and to cool the angry heat
  of the bruises and the bleeding,
  and to wash away the grime
  that they've picked up on their journey
  through the world of space and time.

So he welcomes them to heaven,
  as he welcomed them on earth,
  with the gift of living water,
  holy sign of their new birth.
And he brings them to the table
  where the heavenly feast is spread,
  and he pours out wine for gladness
  and for love he breaks the bread.
They no longer need the miracle
  of body and of blood,
  for their Host is ever present
  and their souls' sufficient food.

And they do not talk of trial
  or betrayal or arrest;
  there's no mention of denial,
  even by the meanest guest.
For their sins are all forgiven,
  none goes out into the night,
  as they make a full communion
  in the Lord's eternal light.

So he feeds them in the heavens,
  as he fed them on the earth,
  with the holy bread of mercy
  and the wine of holy mirth.

PETER DAINTY

Order of service

The following service outline provides material which can be used in either context, but assumes that there will be some orientation towards families and children.

Opening praise response

Day and night the vaults of heaven
resound to the praise of God:
Holy, holy, holy is the Lord God Almighty.

All heaven falls down and worships you,
declaring:
**You are worthy, our Lord God,
to receive glory and honour and power.**

Saints and angels in heaven
stand around the throne singing your praise:
**To him who sits on the throne
and to the Lamb
be praise and honour, glory and power
for ever.**

Hymn
Holy, holy, holy is the Lord (HON 211)

Prayer of thanksgiving

For apostles and evangelists,
who taught the way of truth,
we give you thanks and praise.

For saints and martyrs,
who followed you without counting the cost,
we give you thanks and praise.

For leaders in the Early Church,
who strove to establish the truth,
we give you thanks and praise.

For monks, nuns and those whose devotion
shows us the path of prayer,
we give you thanks and praise.

For musicians, artists and poets,
whose skills beautify worship
and reveal your love,
we give you thanks and praise.

For teachers and pastors,
who by their faithful ministry
enable Christians to grow in faith and love,
we give you thanks and praise.

For evangelists and missionaries,
who by responding to the call of Christ
have brought others to know and love him,
we give you thanks and praise.

For all who by their example
have led us in the way of Christ
which leads to eternal life, especially . . .
we give you thanks and praise,
and seek your strength to follow in their footsteps
until we join them in praising you
throughout eternity.
Amen.

Hymn

For all the saints (HON 134) or Ye holy angels bright (HON 564)

Confession and absolution

Our Father God in heaven,
we confess that we have failed
to live in the light of your love.
We have collected wealth and possessions,
instead of storing our treasure in heaven.
We have sought acclaim and status in the eyes of others,
instead of pursuing the vision of your glory.
We have been distracted
by matters of little importance,
instead of upholding your kingdom.
Forgive our failings,
set our minds on things above
and fill our hearts with your everlasting love,
for the sake of Jesus Christ our Lord.
Amen.

Almighty God,
whose mercy endures for ever,
forgive all our sins,
pardon our earthbound ways,
and renew our fresh vision of heaven's glory,
where he lives and reigns for ever.
Amen.

Hymn/song

All heaven declares (HON 14) or City of God, how broad and far (HON 85)

First reading

Ephesians 1:11-23 or Revelation 7:9-17

Song

As we are gathered (HON 40) or Jesus, stand among us (HON 279)

Second reading

Matthew 5:1-12 or Luke 6:20-31

Hymn/song

Let saints on earth in concert sing (HON 297) or Moses, I know you're the man (HON 338)

Address

Response

In an ecumenical setting, it is usually far more difficult to elicit a response from a congregation than in a familiar local environment. One idea is the 'tree of life', which is usually drawn on to several sheets of paper attached to a large corkboard. Each worshipper has a piece of paper on which they can write the name of a Christian who has influenced them in their faith (or a specific occasion or event which proved to be a 'defining moment'). These are then pinned to the tree of life as an act of thanksgiving. An alternative is to write the name of a Christian, or church in another country, for whom the individual has a particular concern, and pin it to the tree as a symbolic prayer.

Intercessions

We join with all of Christ's Church
throughout the world
in praying for its growth,
its unity and its witness, saying
Lord, you call us to be one;
help us to hear and respond.

We pray for the Church in places
where Christians are ill-treated . . .
Give courage to those who serve you
in the face of threats and violence,
and strengthen them in the knowledge
of your eternal presence and our prayers.
Lord, you call us to be one;
help us to hear and respond.

We pray for Christian leaders,
confronted with divisions,
discouragement and apathy . . .
Give patience to those
who feel their ministry has little effect,
and show us how to support and encourage
those you call to lead your people.
Lord, you call us to be one;
help us to hear and respond.

We pray for Christians who work for peace,
justice and reconciliation . . .
Give hope to those who struggle
against the world's prevailing ethos,
and help us to share their burdens and dreams.
Lord, you call us to be one;
help us to hear and respond.

We pray for Christians
who share the good news of Jesus Christ
with those who do not yet know you,
especially among the underprivileged . . .
Give joy to those engaged in mission,
and enable us to be effective witnesses
to your saving love.
Lord, you call us to be one;
help us to hear and respond.

We pray for ourselves,
that in our lives and fellowship
we may demonstrate our unity in Christ . . .
Give us vision to see
beyond present divisions and barriers
to a time when your people will be one,
and the earth be filled with the glory of God,
as the waters cover the sea.
Lord, you call us to be one;
help us to hear and respond,
with actions born of faith,
faith born of love,
and love flowing from hearts
filled with your Spirit,
through Jesus Christ our Lord.
Amen.

Our Father . . .

Hymn/song

Brother, sister, let me serve you (HON 73) or
May the grace of Christ our Saviour (HON 333)

Final prayer

God our Father,
guard us on our journey
through this earthly life.
**May we travel with the hope of heaven
in our hearts.**

Christ our Saviour,
forgive us when we leave the narrow way,
and redirect our feet on to the right path.
**May we travel with the joy of heaven
in our hearts.**

Holy Spirit of God,
guide us when the way is unclear
and keep our eyes fixed
on the prize to which we are called.
**May we travel with the vision of heaven
in our hearts.**

Father, Son and Holy Spirit, blessed Trinity,
bring us in your good time
to the place you have prepared for us,
to sing and praise you with the saints for ever.
**May we travel knowing you are before us,
beside us and within us,
through your Son, Jesus Christ our Lord.
Amen.**

Hymn/song

Thy hand, O God, has guided (HON 518) or From the sun's rising (HON 150)

Blessing

STUART THOMAS

Sources of Material

Bower, Tony: *Buried Treasure*

Butler, Barbara: *Sharing Ways and Wisdoms*

Castle, Tony: *So Much To Celebrate*

Dainty, Peter: *The Electric Gospel*

Dale, Alan: *The Alan Dale Bible*

Fawcett, Nick:
  Getting it Across
  No Ordinary Man
  No Ordinary Man, Book 2
  Prayers for All Seasons
  Prayers for All Seasons, Book 2
  The Unfolding Story
  To Put It Another Way

Forster, Michael:
  Act One
  Three + One – A Book of Beginnings
  Three + One – Festivals One
  Three + One – Great Kings

Forster, Michael and Simon Smith:
  A New Start in All-age Worship

Fuller, Jill: *Looking Beyond*

Hardwick, Susan: *Retreat and Quiet-day Resource*

Hathaway, Mary: *A Word for All Seasons*

Lomax, Tim: *Freedom Within a Framework*

O'Mahony, Gerald: *100 Ways To Hear the Good News*

Richards, H. J: *Plain English Bible*

Rundle, Elizabeth: *You're Never Alone*

Sayers, Susan:
  100 Talks for All-age Worship
  Children Too
  First Fruits
  Including Children
  Including Young People
  Intercessions for the Church Year
  New Intercessions for the Church Year

Thomas, Stuart: *One Lord, One Faith*

Thompson, Katie:
Celebrations for Young People
Footprints in Faith
Hear the Good News
Step by Step

Townsend, Pete:
Café Logos, Year B
Touch Wood

Walker, David: *Sketches for the Church Year*

Woodhouse, Patrick: *Beyond Words*

Indexes

Scriptural Index

Bible texts in **bold** refer to main readings and those in *italic*
to references in photocopiable artwork and quizzes;
texts in roman refer to Bible-based reflections

Index of Principal Subjects

Asterisks* indicate 'Meditations' by principal characters